CENSORSHIP AND PROPAGANDA IN WORLD WAR I

CENSORSHIP AND PROPAGANDA IN WORLD WAR I

A Comprehensive History

Eberhard Demm

BLOOMSBURY ACADEMIC
LONDON • NEW YORK • OXFORD • NEW DELHI • SYDNEY

BLOOMSBURY ACADEMIC
Bloomsbury Publishing Plc
50 Bedford Square, London, WC1B 3DP, UK
1385 Broadway, New York, NY 10018, USA

BLOOMSBURY, I.B. TAURIS and the Diana logo are trademarks of
Bloomsbury Publishing Plc

First published in Great Britain 2019

Cover design: Terry Woodley
Cover image © 'Sus au Monstre', *Le Petit Journal*, 30 September 1914.
Five Allied soldiers are courageously attacking a frightful dragon recognizable
as German and Austrian by the spiked helmet and the Austrian equivalent.
Source: Demm 1988: no. 326
Courtesy of the Bibliothèque de Documentation Internationale
Contemporaine (BDIC) Nanterre, France.

A catalogue record for this book is available from the British Library.

A catalog record for this book is available from the Library of Congress.

ISBN: HB: 978-1-7845-3851-4
ePDF: 978-1-3501-1861-4
eBook: 978-1-3501-1859-1

Series: International Library of Twentieth Century History

Typeset by Newgen Knowledge Works Pvt. Ltd., Chennai, India
Printed and bound in Great Britain

To find out more about our authors and books visit www.bloomsbury.com
and sign up for our newsletters.

CONTENTS

PREFACE AND ACKNOWLEDGEMENTS

The first comprehensive book on World War I Propaganda was published in 1927 by the American political scientist Harold D. Lasswell and re-edited in 1938 and 1971.[1] Since this pioneering work, numerous studies on the propaganda of single countries or on special aspects of this propaganda have appeared, but so far no complete monograph. A book by the German journalist Klaus Jürgen Bremm entitled *Propaganda im Ersten Weltkrieg* (2013) does not present the whole story either, but compares only German propaganda methods with those of Britain, France and the United States.

What are the reasons for this shortcoming?[2] The influential historians around the Historial de la Grande Guerre, the leading school of World War I research, consider the notions of propaganda and its inseparable twin, censorship, as misleading and inconsiderable, and prefer the interpretative paradigm of 'war culture'. Thus, they have omitted these two topics in their authoritative three-volume *Cambridge History of the First World*, with the exception of an excellent chapter on film propaganda.[3] But what is 'war culture'? It is defined as the patriotic sentiment and consent of the population to the war policy of the government which produces a 'whole set of representations of the conflict crystallised into a veritable system [...] which cannot be separated from the spectacular importance of hate towards the enemy.'[4] This definition has encountered several critiques. Elise Julien has pointed out that 'war culture' is being derived from the behaviour of the people which 'war culture' itself tries to explain.[5] Pierre Purseigle contests that a unified 'war culture' can explain the special reactions of the different national societies involved in the war.[6]

The importance of hate has also been largely discarded, especially as far as the soldiers are concerned. Several scholars concur that neither the correspondence of the soldiers nor their trench journals contain hateful invectives or the demonizing of the enemy in the style of atrocity propaganda.[7] British soldiers did not even use the word 'Hun' or 'Boche', but called the Germans affectionately 'Old Fritz' or 'Old Jerry!'[8] Another indication of comradeship rather than hate between the soldiers were the regular tacit or outspoken ceasefires in the well-known 'live and let live' system,[9] the German-Allied truces on Christmas 1914, 1915 and 1917[10] and the fraternizations on the Eastern front.[11] In letters which escaped postal control and in memoirs, one can indeed find hate, but it was directed against the war, the officers and the civilians: 'We have to live in the mud, the blood and the horror so that they [the civilians] can enjoy themselves and pursue their pleasure', said a French captain.[12] Mockery of the enemy as well as humorous cartoons do not correspond to hate either (see pp. 45–7, 77–80).[13] One can also ask why in all countries censorship had to be applied – the most severe being in France – if people were so patriotic and consented to the war. The leading elites knew very well that only permanent brainwashing, rigorous censorship and unrelenting persecution of pacifist initiatives enabled them to continue the war (see motto to Chapter 1).

Opposed to the conception of the 'péronnist consent school' is another group of historians around the 'Collectif de Recherche International et de Débat sur la Guerre de 1914–1918' (CRID). Known as 'coercion school', they argue that the population refused the war and had to be coerced by censorship, state-directed propaganda and brutal discipline at the front.

Although I feel closer to the ideas of the CRID, I cannot entirely accept their conception either. The social responses to the war and to war propaganda were dominated neither by patriotic acceptance nor by violent refusal and dissent. As Purseigle puts it, such a dichotomy 'belies the critical importance of the moral, cultural and political ambivalences that underlie and determine social responses to the First World War'.[14] They depended on several variables: class, gender, religion, social and professional milieu, the political convictions, the military situation and the degree of personal frustration. Last but not least, they varied over time (see pp. 183–5).

In 2014, a group of historians around Oliver Janz launched the www. encyclopedia.1914-1918-online.net, the largest network of World War I researchers. It attributes an appropriate place to propaganda at home and abroad with numerous contributions on the individual states as well as comparative surveys.

I had been invited to write survey articles on 'Censorship', 'Propaganda at home and abroad' and 'Caricatures', and it was the very flattering expertises by the section editors David Welch, University of Kent, and Dominik Geppert, University of Bonn, which have encouraged me to expand my work into this book.

It will thus present a comprehensive history of censorship and propaganda in World War I. It is based on sources and secondary literature from Great Britain, France, Italy, Russia, Belgium, the United States, Germany, Austria and Turkey. I have also benefited from my own pertinent publications on this subject published over the last 35 years. Earlier versions of several chapters of this book originally appeared in abridged form in 2016–17 in the above-mentioned encyclopaedia. The section about children (Chapter 6) is a modified and extended version of an earlier draft of mine, the latter having been translated by Stefan Grüner and Markus Raasch into German and published in 2016 under the title 'Kinder und Propaganda im Ersten Weltkrieg. Eine transnationale Perspektive' in: *Kinder und Krieg,* edited by them and Alexander Denzler as supplement no. 68 of the *Historische Zeitschrift.* Chapter 10 is part of a conference paper read at a conference of the University of Malaysia in August 2014 and published under the title 'Censorship and Propaganda in World War I and Their Impact on Mass Indoctrination until Today' in: *Revisiting World War I. Interpretations and Perspectives of the Great Conflict,* edited by Jarosław Suchoples and Stephanie James in 2016. For the permissions to republish these contributions in revised form, I would like to thank Oliver Janz, Alexander Denzler, Stefan Grüner, Markus Raasch and his Excellency Jarosław Suchoples, now Polish ambassador in Helsinki. I also thank Irène di Jorio,

Kim Oosterlink and Véronique Pouillard for having authorized me to use their unpublished internet article and Martin Schramm for allowing me to copy two organograms from his book.

I was overwhelmed by the wealth of information, a fact which, however, tended to inflate the references necessary for seven countries at the expense of the text. On the other hand, several aspects of this book are underexposed in research, and the consultation of archival sources would have been desirable. Unfortunately two applications for financial support to the historically oriented Foundation Gerda Henkel were turned down. In case supplementary information seemed necessary, I was therefore limited to the archives of Paris and Berlin, easily within my reach. All foreign language quotes have been translated into English. In the instances that I could not get hold of the English translations of foreign monographs, the original editions had to be quoted.

According to the 'iconic turn', I have used many cartoons as sources, an approach I had already applied in 1988 and 1993. However, I could not reproduce all of them here because the number of illustrations was limited. I have therefore applied a 'reverse iconic turn' interpreting certain cartoons without giving the images. Some critics might object to this exuberance of cartoons discussed in the text, but people who enjoy laughing – in Britain certainly a majority – will forgive me. I do consider cartoons as one of the most influential propaganda vehicles, a view I share with the German publicist Maximilian Harden who already before the war wrote that 'no other sort of publication can have such an effect on public opinion as the illustrated satirical magazine'.[15]

I would like to thank Hew Strachan (University of Oxford), Arnd Bauerkämper (Free University of Berlin/London School of Economics), Elise Julien (Université de Lille), Mark Cornwall (University of Southampton), Jürgen von Ungern-Sternberg (University of Basel) and Charles Sorrie (University of Trent/Carnegie Council New York) for having reviewed particular chapters of the book. I am especially grateful to Stefan Goebel (University of Kent) and Adrian Gregory (University of Oxford) who took the great trouble of reading the whole draft and whose valuable commentaries greatly helped me to improve the book. I would also like to thank Lester Crook of the editing house of I.B.Tauris for his helpful counsel and kind support. As usual, my most cordial thanks go to my wife Nathalie Chamba who for more than 20 years has indefatigably supported my research in many ways.

LIST OF ILLUSTRATIONS

I have made every effort to secure the permissions to reproduce the figures. In case of errors or omissions the copyright holders are asked to contact the editor so that appropriate acknowledgements can be included on reprinting.

LIST OF ABBREVIATIONS

Newspapers, magazines and series

BT	*Berliner Tageblatt*
CE	*Canard Enchaîné*
DK	*Deutsche Kriegsnachrichten*
DORA	Defence of the Realm Act
GMCC	*Guerres mondiales et conflits contemporains*
LV	*Leipziger Volkszeitung*
NDAZ	*Norddeutsche Allgemeine Zeitung*
PDHC	Parliamentary Debates of the House of Commons
RTP	Reichstagsprotokolle. Stenographische Berichte der Verhandlungen des Deutschen Reichstags, 13. Legislaturperiode

Organizations

III b	Abteilung III b (German Intelligence and News Service)
AA	Auswärtiges Amt (German Foreign Office)
ALTT	Auksciausia Lietuviu Tautos Taryba (Lithuanian Supreme National Council)
AOK	Armeeoberkommando (Austrian High Command)
BNV	Bund Neues Vaterland (League New Fatherland, Germany)
BP	Bureau de la Presse (French Press Office)
BUFA	Bild- und Filmamt (German Office of Photography and Film)
CDS	Comité de défense sociale (French Social Defence Committee)
CPI	Committee on Public Information (United States)
CRRI	Comité pour la Reprise des Relations Internationales (French Committee for the Resumption of International Relations)
CS	Comando Supremo (Italian High Command)
DG	Deutsche Gesellschaft 1914 (German Society 1914)
FAST	Feindpropaganda-Abwehrstelle (Austrian Enemy Propaganda Defence Agency)
FO	Foreign Office
GQG	Grand Quartier General (French High Command)
ILP	Independent Labour Party
KA	Kriegsarchiv (Austrian War Archives)
KFA	Kriegsfürsorgeamt (Austrian War Welfare Bureau)
KPA	Kriegspresseamt (German War Press Office)
KPQ	Kriegspressequartier (Austrian War Press Office)
KÜA	Kriegsüberwachungsamt (Austrian War Surveillance Office)
LIB	Lithuanian Information Bureau

MAA	Militärische Stelle des Auswärtigen Amtes (Military Section of the German Foreign Office)
MI7	Directorate of Military Intelligence
MdP	Maison de la presse (French Press House)
MP	Member of Parliament
MSPD	Mehrheitssozialdemokratische Partei Deutschlands (Majority Social Democratic Party of Germany)
NAMPI	National Association of the Motion Picture Industry (United States)
NBK	Nachrichtenbureau für die Kriegsanleihe (German News Office for War Bonds)
NCF	No Conscription Fellowship
NO	Nachrichtenstelle für den Orient (German Oriental News Bureau)
NWAC	National War Aims Committee
OHL	Oberste Heeresleitung (German High Command)
OS	Officio Stampa (Italian Censorship Office)
POW	Prisoner of War
PRC	Parliamentary Recruiting Committee
PSI	Partito Socialista Italiano (Italian Socialist Party)
Servizio P	Italian Propaganda Service
SCA	Section cinématographique de l'armée (French Section of Military Cinema)
SPA	Service de propagande aérienne (French Service of Air Propaganda)
Stavka	Russian High Command
TM	Teşkilat-ı Mahsusa (Turkish Special Section)
UDC	Union of Democratic Control
UdN	Union des Nationalités (Union of Nationalities)
UGACPE	Union des grandes associations contre la propagande ennemie (French Union of the Great Associations against Enemy Propaganda)
USPD	Unabhängige Sozialdemokratische Partei Deutschlands (Independent Social Democratic Party of Germany)
VHD	Vaterländisches Hilfsdienstgesetz (German Patriotic Auxiliary Service Law)
WOCC	War Office Cinema Committee
WPB	War Propaganda Bureau at Wellington House
YMCA	Young Men's Christian Association
ZEU	Zentralinstitut für Erziehung und Unterricht (German Central Institute of Education and Teaching)
ZfA	Zentrale für Auslandsdienst (German Central Office for Propaganda Abroad)
ZfV	Zentralstelle für Völkerrecht (German Office for International Law)

GENERAL INTRODUCTION

In 1762, the French philosopher Jean-Jacques Rousseau coined this famous phrase: 'Man is born free, and everywhere he is in chains.' There are many ways to fetter a man, but here I am concerned only with those chains denying him free access to independent information. Who has put him into such chains? The 'extractive elites', as they have been dubbed in a famous book: privileged aristocratic, political, economical or intellectual elites who extract a bigger share from the people's wealth than the amount they contribute to it.[1] From dishonest mandarins to corrupt bureaucrats, from landowners exploiting slaves or serfs to industrialists employing children for salaries below the breadline, from tax exempt nobles to managers with huge bonuses deposited in offshore tax havens – the possibilities are vast and have changed very little over time. These privileges are usually protected by armed men – from medieval warriors to the modern police and security apparatus, but as Nazi Propaganda Minister Josef Goebbels had exclaimed in 1934: 'It may be OK to base one's power on bayonets, but it is better and more rewarding to win the hearts of a people and to keep them.'[2] And how can elites achieve this? Goebbels and Adolf Hitler, both experts in this matter, knew it: by incessant indoctrination of the people. Indoctrination is, like the God Janus, double-faced: as censorship it suppresses all information dangerous to the ruling elites; as propaganda it manipulates public opinion inducing people to accept and to support their aims. In popular language this is also called 'brainwashing', and an anonymous French caricature of 1917–18 illustrates this procedure quite conspicuously: French President Raymond Poincaré, his Prime Minister Georges Clemenceau and Marianne, the symbol of France, are pumping 'lies, optimism and deception' from a huge tank into the brain of a man helplessly sitting on a chair. In front of the tank, several hungry ducks – in French 'canard' meaning canard and duck as well – are eagerly waiting to be let loose.[3]

During World War I, censorship was more indispensable than ever: Officially justified by the protection of military secrets, it was rapidly extended to purely political matters; its task was to keep the people in an atmosphere of utter ignorance and unshaken confidence in the authorities, and to allow their boundless indoctrination so that they would, despite terrible losses and privations, accept the necessity of holding out until the bitter end and the complete 'knock out' (David Lloyd George) of the enemy. Chapter 1 compares the organization of censorship and its limitations in the combatant countries, analyses its methods and cites the principal topics which were usually suppressed, not only in the media, but also in entertainment and in private correspondence. It also investigates the different reactions to censorship: self-censorship, accommodation, criticism and, last but not least, the way in which censorship was manipulated in order to discredit or even ruin political enemies. The first part of Chapter 9 will discuss the numerous manoeuvres to outwit and circumvent it.

The major part of the book deals with propaganda. Chapter 2 compares its organization in the war-faring countries, outlines its fundamental aims and investigates the question of who produced it. Chapter 3 discusses the principal arguments of propaganda in an adaptation of David Monger's categories of patriotism.[4] This author distinguishes between the adversarial type, that is propaganda against the enemies at home and abroad, the duty message fusing civic and sacrificial patriotism with the concrescent community, the proprietal and supranational branch evoking the ideologies of the belligerent nations, and the aspirational type promising future rewards and benefits. Two principal themes recur throughout the argumentation: First that victory will be certain and second that the war is fought in order to defend the fatherland against an unprovoked attack – except in the case of Italy which officially proclaimed a war of conquest and only took up the myth of defence after its defeat at Caporetto.[5] Chapter 4 analyses how propaganda reached the targets and which logistical problems occurred in its distribution abroad. Indoctrination through entertainment is analysed in Chapter 5. As most of its categories such as caricatures, posters and films are also discussed in the other chapters, the emphasis will here be shifted to its specific persuasion techniques. In Chapter 6 selected propaganda targets are analysed: children, soldiers on both sides of the front, enemy minorities, Muslim peoples between both war camps and, finally, the victims of 'financial conscription', that is the buyers of savings certificates and war bonds. Chapter 8 analyses anti-war propaganda which so far has been mentioned only in the context of general studies on peace and revolutionary movements. All these chapters apply the comparative approach and attempt to generalize the resemblances and the differences between the tactics of censorship and propaganda in the belligerent countries. In Chapter 7, eight selected propagandists are presented in order to demonstrate that propaganda cannot be analysed in a Procrustean bed of stereotyped activities, but that it is, like all human behaviour, also shaped by individual attitudes. The second part of Chapter 9 discusses how people reacted to propaganda which leads to the crucial debate surrounding the effectiveness of censorship and propaganda. Chapter 10 presents selected examples for the legacy of war censorship and propaganda until the present. Chapter 11 contains helpful diagrams most of them explaining the organizational structure of censorship and propaganda in the belligerent countries. The iconography section with 38 figures will allow the reader to get a rapid pictorial survey of the subject. The appendix attempts to give a rather approximate comparison between the purchasing power of various currencies in 1915 and 2017 in order to permit the reader to better understand spending figures during the war; in the text all figures of 1915 will be followed in brackets by the corresponding figures of 2017.

Chapter 1

CENSORSHIP

**If people really knew, the war would be stopped tomorrow. But of
course they don't know and can't know. The correspondents don't write
and the censorship would not pass the truth. (David Lloyd George)**[1]

Introduction

Propaganda has a chance only if divergent sources of information can be
suppressed as much as possible. Therefore, the indispensable prerequisite of
successful propaganda is censorship. Thus, in all warring countries, censorship
was established immediately at the outbreak of hostilities.[2] The primary aim of
censorship was to protect military secrets and movements. This could easily be
justified, because during the Franco-German War in 1870 military operation
tactics of the French imperial army were published in the French and the British
press alike to the great profit of the German military command. The same happened
in the Russo-Japanese War of 1904–5 in favour of the Japanese.[3] However, now it
was rapidly extended to political matters as well. Everything which might criticize
the government, distress and trouble the population or weaken its morale was to
be withheld or at least toned down and justified.

How was censorship organized?

While on the continent censorship was justified by the proclamation of the state of
siege, in Britain and later in Italy and in the United States the parliamentary bodies
had to be consulted.[4] Censorship was thus authorized in Britain by the Defence of
the Realm Act (DORA), in Italy by the decree of 23 May 1915, and in the United
States by the Espionage and Sedition Acts.[5] Most urgent was the control of the media,
and also, somewhat later, of correspondence. All countries rapidly organized central
censorship offices: the Chief Censorship Office (Oberzensurstelle) in October 1914
in Berlin, subordinated to the Intelligence and News Service (III b) of the Supreme
High Command (Oberste Heeresleitung, OHL), which did not take up its work until
February 1915; the Press Bureau (Bureau de la Presse, BP) in Paris under the direction

of the Press Commission of the Ministry of War, which also received guidelines from the General Headquarter of the French Army (Grand Quartier Général, GQG); the American Central Censorship Board, established on 12 October 1917, which consisted of representatives of the Secretaries of War and Navy, the Post Master General, the War Trade Board and George Creel, the chairman of the Committee on Public Information (CPI).[6] In London the Official Press Bureau (named after its address Wellington House), jokingly called 'Suppress Bureau', under the direction of the Foreign Office (FO) censored only the newspapers and their telegraph connections and at the same time issued the official information, while private and commercial telegrams and mail were censored by two separate branches under the control of the War Office.[7] In Italy, the Press Office (Officio Stampa, OS) was established in May 1915 under the direction of the Minister of the Interior who was also the prime minister at the time.[8] In Austria-Hungary, censorship was handled in Austria by the War Surveillance Office (Kriegsüberwachungsamt, KÜA) directed by the Austrian War Ministry, and in Hungary it was by the War Surveillance Commission (Krieg süberwachungskommission) directed by the Hungarian Ministry of Defence. Only the KÜA pre-emptively censored newspaper articles until summer 1917. Dissatisfied with the KÜA, the High Command of Austria-Hungary (Armeeoberkommando, AOK) was from October 1915 authorized to give its officials instructions as well. Furthermore, the War Press Office (Kriegspressequartier, KPQ), under the direction of the AOK, took care of the War Area but also intervened in the censorship of the Viennese newspapers, a fact which led to permanent conflicts with the KÜA. The actual censorship with the exception of the press in the capitals and of doubtful cases was handled by the police, by post offices, the public prosecutor and the County Councils (Bezirkshauptmannschaften). Correspondence with foreign countries was regularly controlled, local letters only selectively; phone communications were tapped, interrupted and the lines could be closed.[9] In Russia, on 22 July 1914, rather lax civilian censorship regulations were replaced with military censorship under the Temporary Decree on War Censorship and a supplementary list of military secrets. In Turkey, political censorship, already intensified from January 1913, now passed to military censors, but in a country with over 90 per cent illiteracy it was quite rudimentary.[10]

The organization of censorship was somewhat modified during the course of the war. In some countries the censorship authorities lost their autonomy at a later date. In Germany, in October 1915, they were united with the offices of propaganda at the War Press Office (Kriegspresseamt, KPA), subordinated to III b. In France, the Press House (Maison de la presse, MdP) was created in February 1916; it was subordinated to the French Foreign Office, reorganized the former propaganda office and was supposed to coordinate it with the censorship office. In February 1918, the Italian OS was subordinated to the Undersecretary of Propaganda Abroad (Sotto Secretario della propaganda all'estero).[11] In February 1916, the British War Office expanded a former small office (MO5/MO7) to the huge Directorate of Military Intelligence (MI7) which organized propaganda but also censored military matters. In Germany, the various 'Ministries' of the Reich in the rank of Imperial Offices (*Reichsämter*) and other civilian authorities had their own censorship offices, 22 altogether. Furthermore, the commanders of the POW camps censored prisoners' correspondence and camp papers and prohibited certain books and newspapers.[12]

The central censors in Prussia, Russia and Austria were mostly career officers, and in Britain, Italy, Bavaria and in the occupied territories, mostly civilians. In France, military and civilian censors worked together, but the military were usually in command and could override the civilians. The authorities in France and Germany even hired professional writers such as Guillaume Apollinaire, Marcel Berger, Arnold Zweig and Walter Bloem.[13] The censors received their instructions from the service departments of the military authorities and from various ministries, in some cases also from the prime ministers, and passed them to the press, either directly or through regular press conferences which in Germany were also joined by representatives of the Imperial Offices and the Admiralty.[14] However, sometimes heavy conflicts arose about particular questions. For instance, in Germany the Office of Food Supply advocated an open discussion of the supply problems whereas the Foreign Office (Auswärtiges Amt, AA) wanted to suppress this news in order to avoid the impression abroad that the authorities were not able to feed the people properly. Despite heavy opposition by the German Chancellor, Theobald von Bethmann Hollweg, and the AA, the OHL suppressed the proposal of the Soviet of Petrograd of 23 March 1917 for a peace without annexations and compensations. In France and Britain, there were no conflicts about this question: the authorities suppressed the proposal as well and later also the invitation to the Brest-Litovsk peace conference.[15]

In France and Italy, local authorities had an important part to play, and in Germany, they had a decisive influence. In Italy, censorship was done by the local censorship offices under the authority of the prefects, who received their daily instructions from the OS in Rome.[16] In Paris, the BP, successively organized between August 1914 and January 1915 with 400 censors and subordinated to the Ministry of War, coexisted with the censorship office of the military government of the city.[17] Censorship in the provinces was handled by 385 provincial control commissions with 5,000 censors under the joint authority of the prefects of the 55 departments and the commanders of the 21 military regions, but the role of the prefects was reduced in 1915.[18] These local censorship bodies issued their own instructions which did not always harmonize with the central ones. Censorship in the combat zones was handled by special censors: in France from the War Ministry while in Italy from the High Command (Comando Supremo, CS).[19]

Germany, with the exception of Bavaria, had been placed under 57 military commanders who, only nominally supervised by the Kaiser, assumed the executive power in their districts and were unconstrained 'like rulers of independent satrapies'.[20] Considering the *Instructions for the Press* from the KPA in Berlin as mere guidelines, their local censorship offices arbitrarily decided about censorship measures to be carried out either by subordinate commands, by local police or by public servants. Although from spring 1917 the military commanders had to accept consistent principles transmitted by the OHL via the Prussian Ministry of War, the practical application remained far from uniform.[21] Some military commanders were reputed as being rather tolerant; others were extremely harsh. For instance, the commander in Stettin was completely under the sway of the Pomeranian Junkers and thus in January 1915 suspended the *Greifswalder Tageblatt* for the rest of the war because of its campaign against their exorbitant bread and potato prices. He was also responsible for a part of the province of Posen, where he placed Polish newspapers under preventive censorship and finally prohibited the newspaper *Lech* for the rest of the war. His colleague in Posen, responsible for the other part of the province, even lifted preventive censorship for Polish newspapers in 1916.[22] Bavaria was also governed by six military commanders who were, however, strictly subordinated to the Bavarian Minister of War and had to handle censorship according to his instructions. The Bavarian War Press Office, which was placed under the minister's authority as well, usually enjoyed his support and provoked numerous quarrels not only with the Berlin censors but even with the 3rd OHL, which was established in August 1916 under the generals Paul von Hindenburg and Erich Ludendorff.[23] Censorship in the Dual Monarchy was also differently handled with Slavic and German newspapers being more severely controlled than Hungarian ones.[24] The complicated organization in Austria, Germany and France lead to curious results: articles suppressed in one district or in one newspaper were passed in another; the same happened in Russia, Britain and Italy despite their more centralized systems. In 1915, the French administration introduced the circular 1000, stipulating that censored articles by the provinces had to be sent to Paris for confirmation.[25] In 1914, German local censors were so incompetent that they even suppressed army communiqués and other official statements; in France and in Bavaria, provincial censors were sometimes so negligent that in France the Minister of Defence and in Germany the KPA bitterly complained.[26] Because of frequent accusations against uneven censorship, the KPA organized meetings with the heads of local censorship offices from February 1916, but to no avail.[27]

In Britain, the relations between censors and journalists were much more satisfactory than on the continent. Censors worked more smoothly, because they concentrated more or less on the London press and developed their guidelines in informal discussions and social contacts with the newspaper editors, some of whom were even employed in the administration. Above all, editors, journalists and censors belonged to the same class, whereas the Prussian military censors did not belong to the intellectual elites. Furthermore, the British authorities sometimes ignored infringements on purpose in order to avoid publicity through prosecution.[28]

In the United States, George Creel, leader of the CPI from 13 April 1917, issued one week after his appointment a list of 18 paragraphs with the title *What the Government Asks of the Press*, summing up his regulations for 'voluntary censorship' which concerned only military affairs.[29] In his later 'Regulations for the Periodical Press of the United States during the War', Creel distinguished between dangerous (mostly military or naval), questionable (e.g. disquieting rumours, for instance about an epidemic) and routine categories of information. The first two categories would need explicit approval by the CPI, but in doubt editors could submit their articles to the CPI before publication and obtain approval – a possibility quite often accepted because of the rather vague terms of the rigorous Espionage Act of 15 June 1917, later amended by the even more repressive Sedition Act of May 1918. In both Acts the dangerous or 'seditious' categories were much widened. The Espionage Act announced heavy sanctions – prison for up to 20 years and/or a fine of up to $10,000 ($240,000) – for 'false reports [...] with intent to interfere with the operation or success' of the US military, to 'promote the success of its enemies' or 'to obstruct the recruiting or enlistment service'. Thus it became together with the 'Trading with the Enemy Act' of 6 October 1917 the legal basis for the establishment of the Central Censorship Board which directed the censorship of all communications by cable, wireless and mail. In the Sedition Act, the same sanctions would punish any criticism of the government, the army and the sale of war bonds. One of the few opponents of this law remarked: 'It is not necessary to Prussianise ourselves in order to destroy Prussianism in Europe.'[30]

In Russia, preventive censorship was imposed in Petrograd and in the areas of military operation; elsewhere, censors were expected to suppress only those publications harmful to military interests. This allowed the press to publish highly critical articles on political matters. When the Council of Ministers complained that 'their abuse, their sensational news, their baseless criticism arouses public opinion against the government', the Minister of War Alexei Polivanov pointed out that his military censors were 'not particularly skilled in political nuances', that 'in the law of military censorship no provision was made for political censorship' and the generals could only conform to the decree and the list. Finally, from February 1916, censorship was extended to political articles and later even to speeches in the Duma, but by the end of the year censors could not or would not stem the tide of mounting criticism any more.[31]

In Turkey, newspapers and telegrams were checked, stamped and signed at the censorship room of the Constantinople post office. Newsprint was so scarce that there was hardly space for official communiqués and general war news.[32]

The censors also invited themselves to numerous amusements.[33] Theatre plays, chansons, cabarets and circus performances had, in Britain, Austria and Germany, with the exception of some of the smaller federal states, already been censored before the war, whereas it was only in France that theatre censorship had been practically abolished in 1906 and was then reintroduced immediately.[34] In Germany, this task was assigned to the military commanders, in France to the prefects and the mayors, and in Britain to the censors of the Office of the Lord Chamberlain.[35] In Berlin and Paris, special services stepped in: the Theatre Police (Theaterpolizei), called Office VIII (Abteilung VIII), subordinated to the Chief of Police (Polizeipräsident), and the Special Commission (Commission Spéciale) at the Paris Police Headquarters (Préfecture de Police).[36] These two offices were organized as follows: The Special Commission in Paris consisted of two censors for theatre plays and one for chansons who were detached from another administration but could only make suggestions, the final decisions being taken by the chief of staff of the Police Headquarters.[37] Very rarely, the Minister of the Interior would intervene. In Berlin, the Office VIII was directed by the senior administrative counsellor Kurt von Glasenapp, who in 1914 supervised a staff of 10 police officials and 26 subordinate officials, secretaries and police patrolmen;

this staff was reduced in 1917 to 7 and 16 persons, respectively.[38] Although the jurisdiction of Office VIII was limited to Berlin without the suburbs, from 13 June 1916 on, its decisions were binding for all local authorities in the Prussian provinces.[39] Accordingly the chiefs of police of several cities asked Office VIII for advice.[40] Outside Prussia, however, censorship was not standardized because there was no supreme national authority and Glasenapp was not, as Gary D. Stark puts it, 'the de facto national censor'.[41] Office VIII decided autonomously, but in quite a few cases had to consider interventions from outside: from the chief of police, the military governor of Berlin and Brandenburg, sometimes from the 3rd OHL, the Kaiser and even from the Austrian and Turkish allies.[42]

Censors in Berlin and Paris proceeded quite similarly. The manuscript of a stage play had to be submitted in two copies a fortnight before the first performance. One copy was handed back with modifications and the performances were checked afterwards by a policeman who was 'often the most attentive listener in the hall constantly comparing the spoken words with the manuscript in his hands'.[43] In all three countries the censors were exposed to frequent criticism. Theatre directors argued with them, appealed to higher authorities or stirred up influential personalities, while clerical and other moralistic groups demanded more efficient censorship.[44] In the most spectacular case, Max Reinhardt, director of the Deutsches Theater, invited the chief of police, Traugott von Jagow, to a rehearsal and seated him beside the beautiful actress Tilla Durieux, who successfully diverted his attention from doubtful scenes or phrases of the play. Succumbing to her charms, Jagow indeed overrode the objections of the censors and allowed the performance of the play. But when he later asked the actress for a date, her husband challenged him to a duel and he was obliged to apologize for his faux-pas.[45] Sometimes censors changed their mind. A British censor found the manuscript of a comedy repugnant, but when he saw in the rehearsal that it was not 'of the saucy French kind', he let it pass.[46]

Films in Germany, Britain and France had already been subject to censorship before 1914. During the war, films were centrally censored in Britain by a non-governmental organization, the British Board of Film Censors; in France, this was done locally by the prefects and the mayors, and from 1916 as well by a central commission attached to the Ministry of the Interior. In Germany, the film producer Oskar Messter, who was transferred to the KPA already on 8 October 1914, issued instructions for photographers and filmmakers, but in practice films were censored by the police under the uncoordinated supervision of the military commanders.[47]

How was censorship handled?

Newspapers

All information transmitted by cables and news agencies (Reuters, Havas, Wolff) was censored beforehand, which means that it was completely suppressed, modified or at least delayed.[48] The addressees were not even aware of it unless they received a copy by normal letter.[49] In Britain, a daily average of around 1,000 cables were censored in this way. Wellington House issued censorship notices with letters prefixed according to their importance. Although they had no binding force, offenders could be prosecuted under various DORA regulations, especially those who had received notices with the letter 'D' (Defence).[50] As the regulations of DORA were not always clear, quite a few editors preferred to submit their articles and even books voluntarily to Wellington House in order to avoid problems.[51]

As the British had cut the German sea cables, all news from the European theatre of war to the United States had to pass through British cables and were thus curtailed by British censorship. If a message still appeared dubious, American censors passed it to the press with the request not to publish it. And with notable exceptions (see p. 177), newspapers accepted this, dutifully practising self-censorship. Outgoing cable messages sent by foreign correspondents were filtered by the censors according to the receivers so that, for instance, pro-German newspapers in South America lost 50–80 per cent of their messages. Newspapers leaving the United States were censored as well, in order not to give a wrong impression about their home country or arouse the antagonism of foreign countries.

In Europe, the press received numerous censorship instructions, some of them permanent, others temporary ('until further notice'); in France, a total of 1,100 general and thousands of particular instructions; in Germany at the end of 1916, there were already 2,000.[52] In order to facilitate the journalists' work, the German, British and Austrian censorship authorities summarized the instructions in censorship books which were, of course, secret and not available to the public.[53]

The censors were entitled to send the police to search houses of suspects and to confiscate dangerous material. This happened, for instance, to the French writer Henri Barbusse; to the offices of the Independent Labour Party (ILP) and the No-Conscription Fellowship (NCF) in Britain; to the socialist newspaper *Avanti* in Italy; and to the German pacifist League New Fatherland (Bund Neues Vaterland, BNV).[54]

The most restrictive and arbitrary censorship was practiced in France, Italy and, until summer 1917, also in the Austrian part of the Dual Monarchy. Newspapers, brochures and leaflets (in France all other publications as well) had to be submitted beforehand. The censor marked doubtful lines, often whole passages, and then the printer had to *échopper*, that is, slash from the clichés in printing machines the censored passages which would appear as blank spaces in print; in Italy, in the first months also as interrupted lines, called *zebrata* (like a zebra) (Figure 1).[55] Sometimes articles and also illustrations were so severely censored that nothing remained except the title or the name of the author (Figure 2).[56] Some Austrian newspapers would, as a sign of protest, fill in the word 'censorship' or 'half a page was confiscated' in the blank spaces.[57] In Germany, apart from Bavaria, blank spaces were strictly forbidden because the ordinary people should not be aware that all information was censored.[58] In France and Italy, information from foreign newspapers, even those of Allied countries, was mostly suppressed.[59]

French censors applied an impressive array of graded orders: from 'authorized', 'passed', 'postponed' over 'let not pass', 'halted', 'banned' to 'must not pass at any price', 'will be seized in case of infringement' and 'must be seized'.[60] In important cases, the suspicious censors bought three copies of a newspaper in order to verify if the order had been executed.[61] In doubtful cases, French censors could change opinion and suppress information temporarily until new instructions or consult the ministry.[62] German censors also gave special recommendations: from 'undesirable' (photos of crowds queuing for food) over 'to be avoided' (the escape of prisoners) to 'publish with prudence' (peace possibilities) and 'desirable' (Russian devastations in Poland).[63]

Preventive censorship also existed in Germany and Britain but was limited to special cases only, for instance, in Germany to military articles, to soldiers' letters, to suspect newspapers of national minorities, to extremist political views and, from June 1917, also to private leaflets and pamphlets.[64] As the censors also controlled publications afterwards,[65] it was always safer, at least in delicate matters, to submit an article beforehand. Otherwise, one might face sanctions in varying degrees. A newspaper could be suspended: in France for up to six months; in Britain and Germany usually only for a few days. In some cases, the journalists had to give some sort of a guarantee to be more restrained in the future in order to get the suspension lifted.[66] In 1917, the number of suspensions was 56 in France, and 103 in Italy.[67] In Germany, 21 newspapers were suspended indefinitely; in Russia, radical newspapers such as *Russkoe Bogatsvo* and *Zavety* were suppressed.[68] A very special case occurred in Munich: The *München-Augsburger Abend-Zeitung* was obliged, after heavy criticism of the chancellor, to accept one of the Bavarian censors as director.[69] In the event of repeated offences, 'observations' or 'severe warnings' could be issued, the editors summoned to the censor's office or preventive censorship could be imposed regularly. As a last resort, all copies of a paper could be confiscated and destroyed, the newspaper itself suspended indefinitely and journalists could be forbidden to write or were even prosecuted.[70] In Britain, proceedings could be opened against the author and the printer. Until June 1915, prosecution was carried out by a military court, with punishments of up to life imprisonment, thereafter by the civilian authorities with sanctions of a fine of up to £100 (£4,300) or six months in jail.[71] In Germany, offenders got away more lightly. When the Protestant missionary Johannes Lepsius could not place an article about the Turkish atrocities against the Armenian population in a newspaper, he had a report on the *Situation of the Armenian People* secretly printed in 1916 and sent it to officials and politicians. However, his report was seized and destroyed, but the author was not harmed and could peacefully emigrate to the Netherlands.[72] Worse was the fate of the French newspaper *Le bonnet rouge*: partially financed by the Germans, it was completely suspended on 12 July 1917. Its editor Miguel Almereyda died a month later in prison, 'strangled, it seems, by the police for having threatened to spill the beans'.[73] His collaborator Emile Joseph Duval was executed in July 1918.

Because of increasing tensions in 1917, censorship in the Allied countries was intensified. In Italy, after hunger riots in Turin and the disaster of Caporetto, the

Sacchi decree of 4 October 1917 was passed, which severely sanctioned defeatist propaganda. Members of the Socialist Youth League (Federazione giovanile socialista) were jailed for five to six years for having published an anti-militaristic manifesto, and two Catholic newspapers were put under preventive censorship. On the other hand, the censors also suppressed nationalist hate campaigns against the clergy, enemy aliens and various ministers.[74] In Britain, because of widespread public demand for a negotiated peace with Germany, censorship was tremendously stepped up reaching continental dimensions. At first the censors tried to financially strangle anti-war newspapers such as *The Herald*, the *Labour Leader* and the *Tribunal* by prohibiting the sales overseas; in Germany only one similar case is known. Anti-war activists such as Bertrand Russell and Edmund D. Morel who tried to circumvent this restriction by placing articles abroad were jailed for 'evasion of censorship'. More important was DORA regulation 27 C of 15 November 1917: All articles on the war and the making of peace were to be submitted to preventive censorship, and a witch hunt started, reaching its climax in the 'epidemic of prosecution' of February 1918.[75] When in November 1917 Clemenceau was appointed prime minister of France, he put the head of his civil cabinet, Georges Mandel, in charge of censorship; the guidelines were not only tightened, but censorship was also used in order to prosecute political enemies: journalists, politicians and even ministers[76] (see pp. 24–6).

Postal control

In all armies, sooner or later postal control was introduced.[77] Its aim was to look for disclosure of military secrets, to test the morale of the soldiers and to find out about 'subversive ideas'. At least in the British and the Austrian armies, it was also meant to remedy the problems. British censors for instance even made suggestions of how to improve the training of army cooks – no wonder that the British army was envied by allies and enemies alike for their great comfort in general.[78] Postal controllers in Austria also ascertained the mood of the soldiers and the people, but could only compile reports, not improve the tremendous supply problems.[79] In Russia, postal control had already been introduced in July 1914. It was comprehensive and in some districts also concerned with civilian correspondence. In Italy, only the correspondence between the soldiers and their families in the 'war zones' and areas with strong social agitation was centrally controlled, but by the end of 1917 practically the whole northern part of Italy was included and civilian correspondence was opened as well.[80] In Austria, civilian letters to soldiers mentioning food shortage were confiscated so as not to 'endanger the discipline of front troops and negatively affect their spirits'.[81] In the French army, central postal control started in January 1915, and from July, each army corps had a commission of 20 members who opened the letters. 'Subversive' paragraphs in letters were *caviardés* by the censors – that is, deleted with ink and aniline pencil; only black dots were left – and a significant number was not transmitted at all. The quantity of controlled letters is estimated, for the French army, to be 180,000 out of five to seven million letters per week, as a sample quite superior to most current opinion polls. Nevertheless, as far as efficient control is concerned, Rosie Kennedy's remark about the British army characterizes the situation in the other countries, except Russia and the United States, as well: 'The vast bulk of correspondence meant that censorship was at best patchy.'[82] Quite practical for control were the British preprinted *Field Service Postcards*, where only options could be chosen and no other messages were possible.[83] In the German and British armies, censorship of the soldiers' correspondence was at first handled by their own officers. Even when central censorship was introduced, the secrecy of correspondence was still violated, at least in the German army: 'Even intimate family letters are divulged and turned into a laughing stock', note Bernd Ulrich and Benjamin Ziemann.[84] In Italy, Germany and Austria, soldiers could be punished and even court-martialled for letters criticizing the OHL or containing 'exaggerated and false information'.[85] In France as well, a soldier could be jailed for a 'negative attitude in his correspondence', and many *poilus* were even afraid to be executed for critical remarks.[86] When a Venetian soldier wrote to his family, that 'the soldiers do not fight with pride or enthusiasm, but they go to the slaughterhouse for fear of being executed', he was jailed for four years.[87] The most stringent censorship of soldiers' letters was applied in the US army: All letters were controlled three times – by the company censor, the regimental censor and the base censor who, in this way, controlled each other as well. Family correspondence put into a blue envelope – allowed once a week – and letters in foreign languages were only read by the base censor. Furthermore, the War Department, following the customs of the Catholic Church, established an index of roughly 100 forbidden books including even classics like *Can Such Things Be* by Ambrose Bierce. In order to escape control, soldiers in all armies preferred to be cautious and avoided compromising utterances of criticism and defeatism in their correspondence or asked comrades on leave to post their letters at home; however, in the German army, such voluntary 'postmen' were sometimes controlled in the trains and severely punished.[88] When in France in 1916 three socialist deputies voted against the war credits, one of them, Pierre Brizon, received 154 enthusiastic letters, 84 of them from the front, but mostly forwarded outside the postal system of the army; even so, quite a few were anonymous in order to avoid the risk of sanctions.[89]

Postal control was also extended to civilian correspondence. In Britain, all mail was controlled in special censorship offices either in London or in Liverpool, and in 1918 around 5,000 persons took care of this. As the blockade authorities controlled all ships, censors opened all letters and parcels between neutral countries as well. As a result, they closely surveyed the correspondence of German agents and even replaced German propaganda with their own.[90] In the United States, all mail was controlled in selected postal offices according to the instructions of the Central Censorship Board. However, censors would only open mail relating to Spain, Latin America and the Orient because their British colleagues already took care of the other foreign countries. Following the British example, the American navy also stopped neutral ships in order to control their mail and even performed personal searches of the passengers and crew. Censorship was rather complete. According to the reports by the San Antonio post office for the week ending

25 October 1918, 180 censors had controlled 77 per cent of the mail and held 20 per cent for the next week. A total number of 75,908 letters were controlled, 179 suppressed and 36 suspended. All intercepted communications were sent to military intelligence in Washington.[91] In comparison, French and German postal censorship appear rather modest: In France from September 1915 only the correspondence of 'suspect' civilians – pacifists, trade unionists and other anti-war activists – was controlled and copied by police, but not intercepted. In Germany, letters of pacifists and of members or sympathizers of the war–hostile Independent Social Democratic Party of Germany (Unabhängige Sozialdemokratische Partei Deutschlands, USPD) – were controlled and their correspondence with foreign countries could be confiscated; in addition, family letters to German POWs were partly blackened.[92] In occupied Serbia all correspondence was so severely censored by the Austrian General Government of Serbia that the people had letters passed by messengers (Briefvermittler), either travelling Serbs or Austrian Slavic soldiers. Other methods consisted in using exchange words, for instance, Ljubica for Serbia, writing underneath the postal stamp or sending letters by pigeon carriers.[93]

Oral censorship

Worse than postal control was oral censorship. In Germany, speeches had to be submitted in writing to the censors several days before and could be prohibited or restricted to a certain audience only. In any case, policemen were present, recorded all 'subversive' remarks, denounced speakers to the authorities or even broke up meetings. They sometimes also burst into a conference and arrested the speakers.[94] In Britain, a special approach was quite frequent: big thugs and hooligans, often colonial soldiers, stirred up or even paid by 'patriotic' organizations stormed pacifist meetings and disrupted them with police calmly looking on (see p. 171).

Private remarks could also be sanctioned by the authorities, a procedure which in three countries lead to a wave of denunciations, a terrible 'witch hunt' and severe sanctions for trivialities. In Italy, the 'men of confidence' of the Italian Propaganda Service (Servizio P, see pp. 61, 111), forerunners of the Soviet commissars, spied on soldiers and workers expressing 'defeatist' ideas and had them punished by the authorities.[95] In Britain, the so-called domestic counter-espionage, organized by the 'Special Branch' under Sir Basil Thomson, under the joint supervision of the Ministries of Labour and of Munitions, from the end of 1917 also handled by the army, closely observed suspect soldiers and civilians, especially in areas of industrial unrest and among home-based troops. Plain-clothed security agents reinforced by a volunteer corps of 'competent observers' constituted 'an extensive network of spies' ready to arrest without warrant any person uttering a critical remark. When, for instance, a foolish dockyard worker infuriated by the overcrowding of a dining hall said, 'I hope the German army will win the war and the Kaiser will rule England,' he was condemned to six months of hard labour.[96] In the United States, the situation was much worse. Self-styled detectives, among them 250,000 volunteers of the American Protective League, roamed the country looking for potentially dangerous people such as pacifists, socialists and especially the 'German spy'. There were around 500,000 enemy aliens from Germany and between three and four million from Austria-Hungary, and, as Creel remembered, 'every accident on land or sea, was straightway credited to the spy system'. As it was strictly forbidden to speak German even at home and in some federal states all other foreign languages were forbidden as well, the activists did not hesitate to control people's homes. In one case, a dictograph was secretly installed in the shop of a German immigrant in order to control his critical discussions with friends and denounce them to the authorities. Another 'detective' overheard the talk of a German with his parrot, broke into his flat, had him jailed and the bird removed to a loyal animal store. Some people were tarred and feathered or humiliated in a different way because of critical remarks. However, only two German-Americans were lynched – a rather small number compared to the 39 African Americans lynched on 2 July 1917 in the East St. Louis race riots. It is also quite surprising that during the whole war only approximately 2,000 people were legally prosecuted.[97]

What was censored?

The following categories concern delicate topics which were, in all countries, usually suppressed either explicitly or through preventive censorship:

1) Criticism of the army and unauthorized news about its operations, especially about military failures, mutinies and war crimes. This sometimes led to strange results. When the Germans conquered Fort Douaumont in the Battle of Verdun, French censorship suppressed this information. When the French took it back, this success was proudly announced by the official communiqué, but the population was quite surprised to learn that it had been in German hands.[98] British troops as well were often reported having 'retaken' places which were not known to have been lost.[99] The Russians did not even mention the German advance when the inhabitants of Warsaw could already hear the thundering of the German artillery.[100] Likewise, when the German invasion of France was stopped at the Marne on 8 September 1914 and the army had to retreat hastily, leaving 50,000 prisoners and 30 cannons behind, the German war communiqué spoke of a strategic reshuffle on the right wing and of the capture of 50 cannons and several thousand French prisoners.[101] In Italy, the loss of Libya to the Senussi and the disaster at Caporetto were completely suppressed.[102] Defeats were passed over in silence or minimized, and even the most brilliant victories of the enemy, like the famous Battle of Tannenberg, were either not passed, or were toned down as 'a simple local setback'.[103] It goes without saying that the war crimes of the Germans in Belgium and Northern France were suppressed by German censorship, but Allied censorship followed suite: The first *Baralong* crime was suppressed, but without success, because American sailors reported it in the United States (see p. 42). When an American soldier raped and killed a French woman and was executed, the whole incident was suppressed.[104]

2) The terrible number of casualties at the front. On the German side alone an average of 1,158 soldiers fell per day.[105] Short casualty lists could be published with 'reserve and moderation': for instance, those concerning regional areas or 'Rolls of Honour' about selected fallen officers.[106] The number of victims of epidemics – 20,000 mortal cases of cholera in the Italian army in 1915, and more than 600,000 of the 'Spanish flu' in 1918–19 – were either completely suppressed, or the scale was minimized.[107] However, the authorities could quite convincingly justify their decision: When on 14 November 1916 the deputy Emile Constant asked the Minister of War in the French National Assembly why no complete casualty lists were published, an answer was refused and given one week later in a confidential note: This would allow the enemy to calculate the losses of the French army.[108] Fallen soldiers were usually glorified in the heroic way with the famous verse by Horace, 'dulce et decorum est pro patria mori', but the grief of the family was taboo. Thus French censors suppressed a chanson about the great despair of a family when a letter announced the death of their son.[109]

3) Unauthorized letters of soldiers.

4) Information about espionage and counter-espionage.[110]

5) Pacifist publications and activities.[111]

There were many other thorny subjects as well, but censorship was not handled equally in all belligerent countries, and the instructions could vary from time to time. As a general rule, all events which could alarm the population were suppressed, toned down or put under preventive censorship: strikes and other labour disturbances, demonstrations, mutinies, confiscations of newspapers, peace efforts, food riots and doubts about victory.[112] Press coverage of strikes and other labour disturbances were rigorously regulated by numerous D-notes in Britain and censorship guidelines in France.[113] Under Clemenceau, a complete news blackout about strikes was ordered and all letters from strike areas were confiscated so that information about the violent strikes in the Loire and Paris areas and their repression by police in May 1918 reached neither the rest of France nor the front.[114] Strikes were not mentioned in the German censorship book but journalists were told to condemn them and formally forbidden to advocate them.[115] When on 29 January 1918 the newspapers *Vorwärts* and *B.Z. am Mittag* published appeals for a strike, the reprint, discussion and exportation of these articles were forbidden and the newspapers suspended until further notice.[116] In Britain, which initially had no conscription, 'statements to prejudice recruiting of persons' were forbidden, but most newspapers supported enlistment anyway. More difficult was the interdiction of false reports which were difficult to define.[117]

Any doubts about victory were completely suppressed. When the Austrian author Stefan Zweig wrote a rather critical article against the hate hysteria in 1914, he was rather surprised to see it published by the *Berliner Tageblatt* – only one sentence was cut: 'whoever might win the war'.[118] When Richard von Kühlmann, the German State Secretary of the AA, explained on 24 June 1918 in the Reichstag that the army did not believe in a military victory any more, the OHL issued a formal denial and Kühlmann was sacked.[119]

The terrible food shortages in Austria and Germany culminating in the 'turnip winter' of 1916–17 could not really be passed over in silence but had to be excused and minimized. In November 1916, the KPA issued four instructions to the press: Journalists were asked to avoid sensational presentations of high food prices and attacks on traders and shopkeepers, reports about food riots and even jokes about food shortages.[120] The Chief Censorship Office on 10 March 1917 and the Censorship Book of 1917 permitted information about food problems only on a local level and prohibited criticism of the general supply situation and reports about conflicts between rural and urban populations.[121]

Even advertisements were controlled. In Germany, a newspaper was blamed for an advertisement with the revealing title: 'Fat dogs wanted'.[122] In Italy, the exportation of newspapers carrying advertisements was forbidden because they might contain codified messages destined for enemy espionage – a ruse used indeed elsewhere, for instance, by the Czech revolutionaries in Prague's daily papers and probably in Vienna, too.[123] The CPI as usual found the most efficient solution: It enrolled all advertising men in its organization and obliged them to follow its guidelines.[124]

Jokes and information about the infidelity of wives, nicknamed in France 'the devil in the body' (*le diable au corps*), were a thorny problem because many soldiers, absent from home for a long time, did not trust their spouses.[125] Classical adultery comedies by Eugène Labiche and Georges Feydeau and frivolous medieval chansons by François Villon were therefore either suppressed or at least modified.[126] In Austria, a postcard with the picture of a soldier on leave surprising his spouse arm in arm with a Russian POW was forbidden.[127]

Shirkers were another thorny problem for the censors. On the one hand, the censors had to pass propaganda cartoons criticizing the different ways to escape military service by pretending to be sick, nearly blind or mad,[128] while on the other, they had to suppress information about the real trick to avoid the trenches – the right connections. Influential friends helped shirkers to stay at home or found them at least a quiet place as 'base wallahs' in the communications zone.[129] Their number increased in the French army between January 1916 and January 1918 from 19.7 to 28 per cent.[130] It was the people's counter-propaganda which in Germany interpreted the abbreviation *k.v.* (*kriegsverwendungsfähig*) meaning 'fit for military service' as *keine Verbindungen* (no connections). The following French chanson explaining how to shirk was immediately refused by the censors:

In order to shirk you must have:
A private income;
A graceful mum who is not shy;
A sister or a cousin of exciting manner
Who speaks in your favour on the edge of a couch;
A daddy considered a VIP
Whose wallet is not too tight;

A stiff neck or a little cold.
That's all you need to become a shirker.[131]

Another popular trick with the censors was to delay information. When the Bolshevik government announced that it would not honour tsarist bonds, this information was delayed for 10 days so that well-informed VIPs could dispose of their assets.[132] Some news was not disclosed until the end of the war, like the sinking of the dreadnought HMS *Audacious* in October 1914.[133] A more famous case is that of the British passenger ship *Lusitania*. Sunk on 7 May 1915 by a German submarine, it had also carried ammunition and soldiers, a fact that was not admitted by the British government until 1982 (see p. 39).

Each country had special restrictions: In France, articles about peace (and even the word itself) were, for a long time, forbidden as well as reports about the possible devaluation of the French franc.[134] In Germany, speculation about the future constitution of Alsace-Lorraine, news about deportations from occupied territories, articles about the Kaiser, information about Turkish atrocities and until November 1916 discussions about war aims. Besides, all illustrations had to be submitted to preventive censorship.[135] The Italian censors greatly distrusted the foreign press. Not only newspapers of the enemy, but 50 newspapers from neutral countries were prohibited and, until May 1916, even the Allied press was not admitted.[136] The United States invented a very special variety of censorship: American films conveying a negative image of the country, for instance, about slavery or the Civil War, were not authorized to be exported.[137]

The censors produced so many regulations that they sometimes contradicted themselves. According to the German censorship book of 1917, reports about bad treatment of German prisoners or atrocities against German wounded soldiers should either be accepted with prudence or submitted to preventive censorship;[138] jokes about the scarcity of food should either be made with prudence or were forbidden, while in reality such jokes and cartoons were abundant.[139]

There were also official exceptions to censorship. In Britain, censorship was, so to speak, 'geographically' limited: It suppressed a few left-wing newspapers such as *Forward* and *Worker* but otherwise concentrated on the London press and left the provincial papers alone.[140] In Italy as well, local newspapers were sometimes overlooked, which meant that subversive news, for instance, even the pacifist manifestoes of the socialist conferences of Zimmerwald and Kienthal, could be placed in a regional edition of the otherwise severely censored socialist newspaper *Avanti*.[141] In France, newspapers from neutral countries were not forbidden, only confiscated at the border if they contained articles which did not please the censors. For the importation of newspapers of enemy countries, a special authorization was necessary.[142] In Germany, censorship was even less complete. Although it is widely held today that papers from enemy countries were prohibited, the censoring guidelines of the KPA permitted all foreign newspapers except those of an inflammatory character. They were indeed available: Czech political activists regularly crossed the frontier to Germany in order to purchase

The Times – a fact that was bitterly resented by the Austrian authorities. In a small town like Sigmaringen one could buy the *Corriere della Sera* in 1916, the anti-war activist Kurt Eisner could read *Le Temps* in a Munich jail, and in a caricature a German defeatist says: 'This [some bad news] is also reported in *The Times*.' From the end of 1914, even enemy army communiqués could be published, which seemed to pose only a problem when in summer of 1918 the German armies were defeated.[143] Whereas parliamentary debates in Austria, Britain and Germany were not censored, although German censors sometimes tried to intervene, in Italy and France speeches by opposition groups and discussions in the commissions were suppressed or at least curtailed.[144] Despite close surveillance, some pacifists like Ludwig Quidde and Friedrich Wilhelm Foerster could secretly or openly distribute their propaganda. In Austria, censorship became more relaxed under Emperor Karl I because in April 1917 he reconvened the Austrian parliament, the *Reichsrat*, with the alarming effect that highly critical statements and speeches by Slavic deputies could not be suppressed.[145]

What was censored in the artistic scene?[146] There was no need to intervene against anti-war or defeatist plays because nobody dared to propose them. Censors did not give formal instructions, except sometimes in Britain, but the theatre directors – authors of plays were not even consulted – rapidly understood which aspects had to be avoided. First of all, films, operettas and stage plays by contemporary authors and composers from enemy nations were forbidden, and even classical plays such as Molière's play *Don Juan* 'because of its specifically French character […] and its moral and religious contents' led to controversies in Germany between censors and theatre directors who successfully argued that Goethe's *Faust* was morally worse.[147]

Most interventions in all countries concerned moral questions such as vulgar language, immoral scenes or allusions to sex: even a chamber-pot or a bed had to be suppressed, and criminals and prostitutes were completely banned from the scenes.[148] Officers and people in other ranks, as well as police officers in Berlin and Paris, could not be shown in an adverse or ridiculous light. A play like *Der Leutnant in Unterhosen* (The Lieutenant in Under-pants) was considered as 'not appropriate for the war period', *Le commissaire bon enfant* (The Naïve Police Inspector) was 'not to be authorised in this moment'.[149] The same happened to plays about officers involved in adultery or amusing themselves with cocottes instead of doing their duty.[150] In pre-war Paris, the funny soldier, always ready for a laugh, was quite popular in the music hall. Now he had to be replaced by the *poilu* – serious, happy and heroic – who became until 1916 the principal figure of many music hall shows.[151] Deserters and shirkers were not welcome on stage at all. The trenches were sanitized; there was no place either for the injured or for the dead.[152] In Berlin and Paris, criticism or denigration of royals or of politicians, even if directed against the enemy countries, was suppressed. In Berlin, the censors repeatedly informed the chief constables of the Berlin suburbs, which were not under their jurisdiction, that plays with the tendency to stir up the population against the enemy were not authorized in order to avoid pogroms against foreigners living in Germany.[153] Britain was different. Here, ridicule of the Kaiser was finally permitted in August 1915, showing German atrocities was encouraged and even pogroms against the Germans were re-enacted on stage.[154]

It is difficult to compare the frequency and the severity of theatre censorship in the three countries because figures are available only for Paris whereas for Berlin one has to resort to some fortuitous statistics, and I have not found any British figures so far. In Paris, a total number of 4,583 stage plays were controlled during the war, and in 1915, 17 per cent of them were suppressed; in later years, the percentage of plays suppressed was much less so that sometimes plays refused in 1915 could successfully be presented in 1917. In Berlin in 1916, 65 dramas were suppressed; in Paris, according to Odile Krakovitch, 25 per cent were passed with modifications; in Berlin, according to my estimates, 80 per cent.[155] This higher percentage is perhaps due to the fact that the Berlin censors had to prove how useful they were because between 1914 and 1917 their number was reduced from 37 to 23. It seems that in Berlin theatres often ignored censorship instructions. In 1915, the theatre police controlled 1,321 performances and found 773 infractions: 58.5 per cent. In such cases theatres had to pay fines or were closed for periods between a few days and a month.[156]

Censorship of chansons was much more tolerant. Thirty per cent of French chansons were full of the most ignoble invectives against the Germans and their atrocities, especially against the Kaiser and the crown prince, and contrary to the stage plays, they were free to criticize the abominable life in the trenches, the defeatists and even censorship itself. However pre-war anti-militarist chansons had to be adapted, frivolous strophes were cancelled.[157] In Berlin in 1914, chansons could denigrate the enemy as well, but in the later years this was usually suppressed. Even dances did not escape the attention of the censors: In France, tango was forbidden because in Argentina it was prohibited for its 'subversive' character, and Argentina was an important supplier of commodities for France.[158]

Film censorship was harsh: In France in 1916, 145 films were suppressed, and in 1917, 198 were suppressed or curtailed.[159] In Germany, even if a film was passed by the censors, it might later be refused.[160] A good example is the German movie *The Iron Cross* which has the following storyline: a German and a Belgian family were friends before the war and now their sons had to fight against each other. The film concludes with the commentary: Where will all this suffering end? The film was banned, and all copies were seized and destroyed.[161] Violent scenes, crimes and atrocities, even those perpetrated by the enemy, were suppressed in France and Germany and toned down in Britain. Scenes with injured or dead soldiers were usually suppressed, except in the famous British film *Battle of the Somme* (1916), which remained an exception. In the United States, formal film and theatre censorship did not exist, and the CPI intervened only very rarely and left the censoring to local censors.[162] However, film producers could be sanctioned for violation of the Sedition or Espionage Acts. Thus, a film about the War of Independence showing historically confirmed atrocities committed by British soldiers was locally forbidden after the first showing and later confiscated in another federal state. The producer, Robert Goldstein, was jailed for 10 years. In 1920, his appeal was refused.[163]

Compared to other forms of censorship, like that of newspapers, chansons and cartoons, theatre censorship was, in general, much stricter. Stark has proposed a convincing explanation: The censors were afraid of the crowds. They all had read Gustave Le Bon's bestseller *Psychology of the Crowd* (1895), in which the crowds were considered as stupid, excitable and prone to irrational actions. The dramatic acting in theatrical performances, more impressive than the reading of an article, could stir emotions and easily provoke unrest and disturbances. The censor's main task was to prevent this by all means.[164]

A good example of the censorship of *belles-lettres* is the novel *Sous Verdun* by Maurice Genevoix. The blank spaces in the edition of 1916 compared with the complete edition of 1925 show which topics censors did not like: when *poilus* fled from the enemy, the censor substituted the words 'runaway' and 'coward' by 'straying' and cut out the main scene completely. Other suppressed parts were about badly fed soldiers having to steal their food, officers treating the soldiers like slaves and giving senseless orders, and a dying *poilu* saying: 'What have I done, that I must get killed in the war?'[165] In a comparison between the censored lines in this novel and those in the German war novel *Der Hauptmann* by Friedrich Loofs, Nicolas Beaupré found that similar scenes and topics were cut out but that on the whole French censorship was far more severe and unjust, even deleting expressions of patriotism and approval of war.[166]

Censorship had and still has a very bad reputation. In France, it was personified by 'Anastasia', an ugly old woman with spectacles and enormous scissors (Figure 3). However, censors were not all the same. Some were surprisingly lenient while others demanded stupid and useless suppressions.[167] Besides, one must not forget that they too were under permanent surveillance. If they passed a dangerous article, in France at least, they could be fired or even sent to the front.[168] In some cases, censors would cautiously examine the pros and cons of an intervention. In a chanson submitted to the censor, a mother tries to prevent her son from going to the front, but he replies:

> I can only live as a poilu.
> If I die here I die without glory.
> My country first! – My dear child!
> You are only mamma. My mother is France!

The censor hesitated and preferred to consult the prefect. And then despite its heroic ending the chanson was suppressed with the remark: 'Unbearable appreciation of a mother's feelings.'[169]

Censors in all countries sometimes stopped or attenuated exaggerated hate propaganda and appeals to the worst instincts because they were worried about the emotional effects on the population. Thus German censors suppressed postcards with the aggressive slogan '*Jeder Stoß ein Franzos*' (Every Hit a Frenchman), a sketch in a circus about Belgian francs-tireurs and German reprisals, and the shameful stripping of a French governess in a stage play. In France and Germany, it happened that stories about German and Russian atrocities were suppressed because they might spread panic and lead to an exodus of the population from threatened areas. The British censors cut the execution of women in a film, as well as the whipping of a naked mother superior, and obliged a newspaper to revoke false information about 250,000 armed Germans in London.[170]

What was the role of self-censorship?

Self-censorship either for patriotic reasons or for fear of sanctions was widespread. It was facilitated by the attitude of most journalists willingly cooperating in order to support the fatherland in danger.

In France, journalists, editors and authors avoided thorny subjects in order to secure publication or performance. For instance, the socialist newspaper *L'Humanité* did not dare to publish the reports of either the assembly of the Socialist Party of July 1915 or the congress of the primary schoolteachers' union of August 1915 because in both cases resolutions against the war had been passed.[171] When an editor wanted to publish a famous anti-war tract by the French writer Romain Rolland, he suppressed the critical passages and changed the original title from *Au dessus de la mêlée* (Above the Battle) to *Au dessus de la haine* (Above the Hatred).[172]

All war correspondents were 'embedded' by officers and were severely censored by the military and sometimes a second time by the national press bureaus.[173] The United States applied an even more stringent measure: All journalists accompanying the American forces to Europe had to swear not to publish any information helpful to the enemy, and their newspapers had to deposit a $10,000 ($240,000) bond as a guarantee, which was retained in cases of infringement. For instance, when in December 1917 the war correspondent Heywood Broun wrote a series of articles about American supply blunders, the War Department cancelled his accreditation and cashed the deposit.[174]

In the United States, pre-war books and films, for instance, the movie *War Brides*, were recalled by the editors and revised in order to give them a more pro-Allied slant or to modify pacifist messages which could hamper recruiting – forerunners of the methods of Joseph Stalin in the Soviet Union.[175] In Britain as well, stage scripts with anti-American tendencies were rapidly rewritten after the American declaration of war.[176]

How was censorship criticized?

Censorship was detested and frequently criticized, especially by deputies and journalists. Lieutenant-Colonel Charles Repington, military correspondent of *The Times*, considered censorship 'as a cloak to cover all political, naval and military mistakes'.[177] British newspapers repeatedly demanded: 'Abolish the Press Bureau' and 'Tell the Truth'.[178] When, in November 1917, through DORA regulation 27 C, preventive censorship on leaflets and articles on war and the making of peace was introduced, this was considered as the 'assassination of opinion' (*The Nation*).[179]

The harshest critic of censorship in France was Clemenceau, before he became prime minister. When his newspaper *L'homme libre* (The Free Man) was suspended after severe criticism of the lack of hygiene in a military train, he replaced it with *L'homme enchaîné* (The Man in Chains), only to see it immediately suspended as well. On 24 September 1914, he said: 'Everybody with common sense will understand that censorship can only be applied to military matters. Otherwise it is nothing but an abuse of power.' However, when he became prime minister in November 1917, he told the censors: 'To suppress censorship – never! I am not a complete idiot. You are my best policemen.'[180] In Germany, press and Reichstag alike bitterly attacked the military control of public opinion. However, the military insisted on their censoring activities, with the argument that journalists could not distinguish between suspicious and harmless news.[181] In the Italian parliament, like in Britain, critical deputies explained that censorship only occults the mistakes and abuses of the government, or mocked it like Giacomo Barcelotti, who said: 'Censorship wants to suppress what everybody knows.'[182] On the other hand, censorship was also criticized for censoring too little, especially by ministers, army commands and right-wing politicians and journalists.

A special form of criticism was ridicule. In a French chanson, a group of people try to explain the meaning of the blank spaces in the newspapers. The first says, it is 'in order to save ink', the second thinks that it is destined to 'those people who cannot read', and the third maintains that it is more hygienic than the printed parts and should thus be used for a special need (as toilet paper). But the author concludes:

> The blank space is produced by the censors
> Who suppress the articles.
> But these gentlemen, dear me,
> Do not always know why.

Another chanson with the title *Down with Censorship* demands the abolishment of censorship, 'this outdated institution which reminds of the time of the inquisition'. Surprisingly both chansons were passed.[183] A British caricature mocks at the delaying of information by censorship: A gentleman is shocked by the frightening news about a terrible defeat which was finally 'passed by the censor': 'Battle of Hastings A.D. 1066' (Figure 4).

How was censorship used for political intrigues?

Normally, censors protected leading statesmen from criticism and suppressed any information which could harm them. When, for instance, 2,000 kilos of coal were delivered to the French Minister of Supply during a terrible shortage in frozen Paris, the government asked the censors 'not to let this pass under any circumstances'.[184] However, in the event of dissension among the political and military elites, censors were supposed to suppress articles favourable to certain politicians or, worse, to pass defamatory articles against them. Most victims were supporters of a negotiated peace, while the people behind the censors insisted on a victorious peace and mostly belonged to the military.

In France, the Minister of the Interior Louis Malvy was subjected to a calumnious campaign by Léon Daudet, editor of the right-wing daily *L'Action française*, 'with the complicity of censorship', as was commented in the Chamber of Deputies.[185] Already on 30 July 1914 Daudet had started a hysterical campaign against German spies in Paris, which was partially responsible for the devastation and pillage of the shops of Swiss and German firms. When in spring 1915 Malvy prohibited a renewal of this campaign, Daudet attacked him as the protector of the German spies, with the tacit approval of the censors. Another pretext to attack Malvy was his close relationship with the socialist newspaper *Le Bonnet Rouge* which had been bribed by the Germans. In 1917, Daudet explained that the numerous French defeats, mutinies and strikes were caused by a conspiracy under the direction of Malvy, who allegedly had betrayed the plans of General Robert Nivelle's offensive to the Germans – an accusation gladly supported by Nivelle who was overjoyed of having found a scapegoat for his disastrous military failure. Although the censors suspended *L'Action française* for one week, they allowed the other papers to reprint this accusation. From July 1917, Clemenceau started to exploit Daudet's campaign and on 31 August brought about Malvy's resignation. The MdP hardly censored Daudet's newspaper but heavily censored newspapers defending Malvy, and Daudet was not even molested when a collection of weapons was found in his office. When Clemenceau came to power in November 1917, he used censorship ruthlessly not only against Malvy but also against his political foes such as Aristide Briand and Joseph Caillaux who sought peace understanding with Germany.[186] A series of trials began, and Malvy was sentenced to exile for five years for not having opposed enemy propaganda. In the case of Caillaux, the PB on 15 and 16 December gave the censors strict guidelines of how to have him appear guilty: all articles from Germany favourable to Caillaux should be mentioned, and all articles doubting his guilt should be suppressed. The censors even had to pass reports about fake documents which lead to his inculpation. He was jailed without verdict among common criminals until 1920 when he was finally sentenced to three years in prison for having threatened the security of the country. The French High Commission in the United States even tried to suppress *The Caillaux Case*, an objective American film about the affair, but could not prevent its release on 15 October 1918.[187] Thus censorship was not an independent institution but completely under the sway of influential persons in the ministry of war, in the army, in the army commission of the Senate, in the police and, last but not least, in the office of the prime minister, and they all used censorship for their own interests.

When in Britain the conservative elder statesman Henry Petty-Fitzmaurice, Marquess of Lansdowne, former Viceroy of India and Governor-General of Canada, submitted to *The Times* in November 1917 an article indirectly recommending peace negotiations with Germany, this newspaper did not dare to publish it. It finally appeared in the *Daily Telegraph*, but a further edition as leaflet was forbidden by censorship[188] (see pp. 67–9).

In 1916, Chancellor Bethmann Hollweg was more and more under the political pressure of annexationist military, industrial, conservative and Pan-German circles because he refused to launch the unrestricted submarine warfare which in their view was the only way to enforce a victorious peace with huge conquests. In order to bring about the dismissal of the chancellor, a denigrating campaign against him broke loose: his enemies intrigued, organized public rallies against him and published numerous insulting pamphlets. How did the censors react?

In Bavaria, the Minister of War, more often than not at odds with the Prussian authorities, urged the military commanders in Bavaria to crack down on all agitation against the chancellor. Indeed the censors prohibited rallies, confiscated pamphlets and controlled the correspondence of leading agitators.[189] However, outside Bavaria, the illegal brochures culminating in a hateful leaflet of the Pan-German League with the slogan '*Fort mit diesem Kanzler*' (Away with This Chancellor) were even advertised and freely distributed because the military commanders, completely in line with the OHL, held the ferocious dog of censorship in leash.[190] Even the KPA complained on 23 January 1917 that the local censors had not done their duty.[191] When Bethmann's proposal of peace negotiations of 12 December 1916 was refused by the Allies, he had to yield to the pressure. On 1 February 1917, he agreed to unrestricted submarine warfare, and on 13 July 1917, incidentally at the same time when the complete failure of this measure had become obvious, he was forced to resign.[192]

In Russia, at the end of 1916, the censors did not suppress serious allegations from the leading Kadets politician Pavel Milyukov, who asked in the Duma if the regime's failure was due to 'stupidity or treason'. Images ridiculing the family of Nicholas II, Emperor of Russia; accusations about the alleged treason of the German-born tsarina; and semi-pornographic caricatures about her alleged liaison with the sinister monk Grigori Rasputin circulated freely all over the country.[193] In this case, the censors even helped to prepare for the revolution.

Chapter 2

PROPAGANDA – AIMS AND ORGANIZATION

The ultimate purpose of this war is propaganda, the destruction of certain beliefs and the creation of others. (Herbert G. Wells)[1]

What were the aims of propaganda?

The different tasks of propaganda can be categorized by their four principal targets: the home front, the military front, neutrals and enemies. At home, propaganda must mobilize a nation, maintain its morale and induce its soldiers to fight until the very end. It has to arouse hatred against the enemy, idealize the own war aims, warn of the consequences of defeat, confirm belief in the superiority of the fatherland and make clear that the final victory will be certain. Moreover, it must explain setbacks by blaming scapegoats from strikers to war profiteers, so that the people will not question the war itself or even the social and political system. Propaganda should also win over the neutrals by encouraging friendly elements and local warmongers or, if this is not possible, by keeping the neutrals out of the war through the support of non-interventionist or pacifist views. Propaganda against the enemy should demoralize his soldiers, encourage them to desert and stir up its civilians. Its favourite objects are dissatisfied elements such as underprivileged classes, revolutionary movements and national minorities.[2]

At home, propaganda was sustained by censorship (see pp. 5–26, 177–9). In neutral countries, one could only try to delay, impede or destroy unfriendly and inimical information, and against the enemy one had to concentrate on evident weaknesses and promise a golden future in case of defection.

Who produced the propaganda?

At the outbreak of the war, all governments had succeeded in bringing home to their respective civil societies that the fatherland had been unjustly attacked, and the result was overwhelming. With the exception of a small minority of pacifists and left-wing socialists, they forgot their quarrels and were ready to rush to its defence. According to the words of Kaiser Wilhelm, 'I do not know parties any more, I know only Germans', the 'Burgfrieden', that is the 'peace inside a beleaguered fortress', was proclaimed in Germany. The same happened in the other countries: in France with the 'Union sacrée', in Russia with the 'Union of Tsar and People', and in Britain with the appeal 'to close ranks'. Nevertheless, despite the thousands of bad poems sent to newspapers – in August 1914 alone *The Times* received 100 of them every day and the *Berliner Tageszeitung* 500[3] – the general exaltation in August 1914 was nothing more than the 'coffeehouse enthusiasm of a minority', as Thomas Raithel puts it.[4] It was limited to the students and the bourgeoisie in the big cities, whereas the workers, the peasants and the inhabitants of the towns and of the rural districts reacted with dismay, sadness or at best dutiful resignation.[5] In Tannenlohe in Württemberg, a bitterly weeping woman said to her children: 'We'll see, our father will not come back.'[6] And the exuberant soldiers' writing on their trains 'Rail excursion for Berlin' or 'Auf Wiedersehen in Paris' soon replaced these slogans by 'Slaughter stock for Flanders'.[7] In Italy, the situation was worse: When it joined the Allies in May 1915, its decision was backed by a minority of warmongers of whom only 8,000 finally volunteered. According to the reports of the prefects one month before, the overwhelming majority of the Italians refused an offensive against Austria-Hungary and denounced it as the 'war of the signori'. Most soldiers were impoverished peasants who did not care about Italy, even less about the Irredenta, and had only one desire: to emigrate. Influential political groups were opposed to the war as well: the socialists denounced it as an imperialist war, the followers of the neutralist politician Giovanni Giolitti criticized it as a war of revolutionaries, and for many Catholics it was, in the later words of Pope Benedict XV, 'a useless carnage'.[8]

For these reasons, propaganda played an important role from the very beginning of the war. Initially it was not so much the state but civil society which took the lead. Unleashing an unprecedented indoctrination campaign with the intention to increase nationalist engagement in the people, journalists, writers, professors, teachers and artists enlisted in an 'intellectual military service', as Thomas Mann put it.[9] Journalists and writers were, of course, the most important fighters on the propaganda front, but some other categories were also more active than ever before. University professors glad to reinforce their role as the spiritual leaders of the nation were especially committed to the war cause. They gave lectures to the public and even on the front, in neutral countries and in occupied territories, published numerous propaganda brochures and signed appeals and counter-appeals.[10] The backbone of local propaganda on the home front were schoolteachers and clerics. The clerics supported the war in their homilies, and the teachers brainwashed children in their lessons; both organized patriotic meetings and campaigns for war bonds (on individual propagandists, see Chapter 7). Various businessmen also joined the propaganda effort: from producers of armaments, munitions and military toys over editors of war books to enterprises sending specialized hold-out papers to their work force at the front – they were all busy taking their advantage of the war.

Especially remarkable was the engagement of the caricaturists. The term 'caricature' is derived from the Old Italian word 'caricare' which means 'to exaggerate' and 'to attack vehemently'.[11] Thus, the normal task of a caricaturist was to attack and to ridicule society and government, usually in an exaggerated or distorted way.[12] The most influential of the cartoon magazines in Germany was the *Simplicissimus*, which permanently criticized the Junkers, the Catholic Church and the military. Between 1903 and 1907 alone, the paper was confiscated 27 times. The cartoonists frequently had to appear in court, and at least one of them, Ludwig Thoma, spent six weeks in the Stadelheim prison on the charge of lese-majesty.[13] When war broke out, the cartoonists faced a dilemma. Should they continue to antagonize society and criticize the government? At a meeting with his colleagues, Ludwig Thoma, at that time the editor-in-chief of *Simplicissimus*, proposed that the paper should cease publication, because all satirical opposition to the government should stop while Germany was fighting for its existence. But Thomas Theodor Heine refused and said that satirists now had a new task: to behave as good patriots and to support Germany's war policy at home and abroad.[14] His point of view was accepted, and the other cartoon magazines took the same decision. On 8 August 1914, Paul Warncke, the editor-in-chief of *Kladderadatsch*, explained to the readers that his magazine would also renounce all political satire and would instead fight against the enemies, the 'disturbers of peace'.[15]

Similar developments took place in other countries. Owen Seaman, editor-in-chief of the leading British humour magazine *Punch*, also wondered if he should discontinue publishing, but finally decided to mobilize the *Punch* for the national cause.[16] In France, in August 1914, the cartoon magazines halted publishing. *La Vie Parisienne* explained to its readers that its collaborators were at the front and the Germans at the doors of Paris.[17] When they resumed publishing in November 1914,[18] some of them like *Le Rire*, renamed *Le Rire Rouge*, felt obliged to justify their decision:

> In these horrible and tragic, but highly glorious hours [...] the Rire [literally 'laughter'] is by no means inappropriate, but on the contrary necessary. [...] How many heroic deeds must be vaunted by the masters of satire and drawing? And is it not also necessary to mark the contemptuous and grotesque William II with the red iron of the caricature?[19]

Thus, in all countries the cartoonists joined the propaganda war, transforming the cartoon into a 'weapon of combat' as the French cartoonist John Grand-Carteret put it.[20]

Quite a few of these *Heimkrieger* (home warriors), as some people called them,[21] joined numerous official and private propaganda associations not only in order to be involved in propaganda production but also to avoid being sent to the front. This fact is well known for Austria and France. In Austria, the War Welfare Bureau (Kriegsfürsorgeamt, KFA) and the War Archives (Kriegsarchiv, KA) housed many shirker-propagandists such as Hugo von Hofmannsthal and Stefan Zweig (see pp. 153–6). In France, journalists campaigned against shirkers in the MdP. In Germany, home warriors joined the Bureau for the Dissemination of German News Abroad (Bureau zur Verbreitung von deutschen Nachrichten im Ausland)

and the Cultural League of German Scholars and Artists (Kulturbund deutscher Gelehrter und Künstler).[22] In Britain, the Central Committee for National Patriotic Organization published pamphlets such as *Why We Are at War* or *Great Britain's Case*, but later its hate propaganda irritated the British authorities so much that in 1917 it was incorporated in the National War Aims Committee (NWAC).[23] In France, numerous private associations such as the Committee of Socialist Propaganda for the National Defence (Comité de propagande socialiste pour la défense nationale) were unified in 1917 with the creation of the Union of the Great Associations against Enemy Propaganda (Union des grandes associations contre la propagande ennemie, UGACPE) with 11 million members. The most important semi-official organization was the Alliance Française which was engaged in cultural propaganda abroad from 1883 and now created specialized war branches for Women, Catholics, Protestants and Jews.[24] The associations 'Trento e Trieste' and 'Dante Alighieri' agitated in Italy, while the semi-official 'Skobelev Committee' and numerous patriotic associations did so in Russia.[25] Four different Anti-German Leagues, two in Britain, one in France and one in Italy, fulminated against the 'Huns'.

How was propaganda organized?

According to Olivier Forcade, the propaganda institutions developed 'in a certain symmetry'.[26] Propaganda in neutral countries initially played a predominant role.[27] In Britain, three different offices were established, among them was the secret War Propaganda Bureau (WPB) of Charles Masterman at Wellington House; in Germany, 27 different offices were finally united in October 1914 in the Central Office for Propaganda Abroad (Zentralstelle für Auslandsdienst, ZfA) at the AA, later transferred to its News Office; in France, a Press Office (Bureau de la Presse, not to be mistaken for the BP) was organized by the Foreign Ministry; in Austria-Hungary, the Department 5 of the Austrian Ministry of Foreign Affairs indoctrinated Germany and neutral countries, while the KPQ organized and directed the war correspondents and the war painters (see pp. 63, 75). In Russia, three ministries – War, Internal Affairs and Foreign Affairs – had Press Bureaus, and the High Command (Stavka) created an intelligence and propaganda unit. However, propaganda was poorly coordinated and passive, and no state propaganda office existed, because as Richard Stites puts it: 'The Russian monarchy was uncomfortable with mobilising mass opinion and sentiment.'[28]

The home front was not neglected but at the outset propaganda was limited to press conferences, organized in Britain by the News Department of the FO, jokingly called 'Fiction Department'; in Germany by III b; in Austria-Hungary by the Department 5, KÜA and its Hungarian equivalent, whereas in France and Russia various ministries would supply information to the journalists. Otherwise, no propaganda at home was organized, except by III b in Germany and by the Parliamentary Recruiting Committee (PRC) in Britain which tried to enlist volunteers for army and navy, as no conscription existed in this country.

Furthermore, in all countries with the exception of the Ottoman Empire, various ministries and other state organizations had their own press and propaganda offices, for instance, in Germany the ministries of the federal states and in Austria-Hungary the provincial governments and imperial governors (Statthalter). For this reason duplication of work and conflicts were inevitable. In 1915, more propaganda offices were founded and several reorganizations took place. In Germany, censorship and propaganda offices were united in the KPA; in France they were coordinated by the 5th Bureau of the GQG called 'Information and Propaganda'. In February 1916, the latter was transferred to the MdP now attached to the Foreign Ministry, and propaganda was extended to the home front and to the enemy as well. Furthermore, the Alsatian Johann J. Waltz (Hansi) created a small Office for Propaganda against the Enemy (Bureau de propagande contre l'ennemi), incorporated in August into the newly founded Service of Air Propaganda (Service de propagande aérienne, SPA) attached to the General Staff.[29]

As in the years 1916 and 1917 people became more and more war-weary, a 'second mobilization' took place with a reorganization and an enormous increase of propaganda, which was hampered, however, by permanent quarrels between the various administrative and private bodies, especially between civilian and military authorities.

In Germany in March 1916, the Field Press Office (Feldpressestelle) under the writer Bloem, and in October, the Office IV for Troop Information, were added to the KPA. In July 1916, the OHL established the Military Section at the AA (Militärische Stelle des Auswärtigen Amtes, MAA), answerable to III b and later directly to the OHL and responsible for propaganda at home, abroad and at the front. The 3rd OHL and the government – the chancellor and the AA – had different ideas about war aims and propaganda, and each tried to win the upper hand by creating new bureaucratic structures or reorganizing them. In July 1917, the OHL enlarged the KPA into the huge propaganda machine of Patriotic Instruction (Vaterländischer Unterricht), and now mass propaganda started at the front and at home but had to rely on the 57 military commanders, who established local offices and engaged the support of local propagandists such as teachers and priests.[30]

In Britain, the PRC was dissolved after the introduction of conscription in May 1916 and replaced in August 1917 by the NWAC which stepped up propaganda for the hitherto neglected home front. In the beginning of 1917, most former propaganda offices were merged into the Central Department of Information under John Buchan at the FO, but it was responsible to the prime minister. The War Office, at odds with Buchan, created the huge MI7 which was very successful in front propaganda.

In Italy from November 1916, Ubaldo Comandini, minister without portfolio and without funds, was supposed to organize propaganda, and in August 1917 he united several private propaganda organizations, but an efficient propaganda campaign was not realized.

In Austria, not only the KPQ but also several other organizations such as the KFA and the KA dabbled in propaganda. However, none of them developed an aim-oriented approach, except for some campaigns for war bonds and a few isolated initiatives. Although from November 1916 the KPQ stepped up its personnel to nearly 900 people, this haphazard approach did not change under the new Emperor Karl I, 'certainly the gravest sin of omission' during his reign.[31] On 15 March 1917, the Austrian Foreign Ministry set up a section for propaganda abroad in the KPQ, and the AOK, following the German example, established efficient propaganda units at the Russian and the Italian fronts, but little happened at home.

By the end of 1917, the situation of the Allies had greatly deteriorated. The French offensive of General Nivelle had ended in a blood bath, the Italians had been routed at Caporetto, Soviet Russia was making a separate peace, the Germans were preparing a mighty offensive with 50 supplementary divisions and the American intervention was slow.

In order to counter the resulting crisis of home front morale, the British undertook a tremendous reorganization of propaganda. In February 1918, they created the Department of Propaganda in Enemy Countries under Lord Northcliffe (Alfred Harmsworth), named after its locality as Crewe House, and in March 1918, they established the Ministry of Information under Lord Beaverbrook (Max Aitken) for all other domains of propaganda; both institutions were responsible to the prime minister. However, several propaganda offices refused to be attached to the new ministry and conflicts also arose with the FO.

In France, Clemenceau started a slow administrative reorganization but left the bulk of propaganda to private organizations, for example, the UGACPE and the smaller organization Propaganda and Education by Word and Theatre (La propagande et l'enseignement par la parole et le théâtre). In May 1918, the MdP was not dissolved but practically replaced by the General Commission of Propaganda and Information (Commissariat général à l'information et à la propagande) for neutral and Allied countries, first responsible to the prime minister, after protests to the Foreign Ministry. Like in Britain, a separate Centre of Propaganda Action against the Enemy (Centre d'action de propagande contre l'ennemi) was set up which incorporated Hansi's office and was also supposed to combat mounting pacifist propaganda.

In Germany, the authorities wasted their time with administrative quarrels. In 1918, Ludendorff referring to the British example repeatedly demanded the establishment of a Ministry of Propaganda based on his MAA. The new Chancellor Georg Michaelis refused and tried to strengthen his influence by creating a Central Press Office at the chancellery in September 1917. His successor George Count Hertling united it in February 1918 with the News Office of the AA to the United Press Office of the Imperial Government (Vereinigte Presseabteilung der Reichsregierung); on 2 April 1918 he created another Central Office for Propaganda at Home (Zentralstelle für Heimataufklärung), both with the intention to reduce the influence of the KPA and the MAA. However, his new offices did not stand a chance against Ludendorff's powerful machine of Patriotic Instruction. Another useless office was created in September 1918, and the MAA was transferred from the OHL back to the AA. Finally on 29 October 1918, a few days before the end of the war, all civil propaganda services were united in the new Central Office for Home Propaganda (Zentrale für Heimatdienst) directed by State Secretary Matthias Erzberger and responsible to the last imperial Chancellor Prince Max von Baden.

In Italy, the catastrophic defeat at Caporetto in October 1917 brought home to the authorities that the war could not go on without propaganda. On 1 November, an Under-Secretariat for Propaganda Abroad (Sotto Secretario per la Propaganda all'estero) was created, and in February 1918, Comandini took over the General Commissariat for Civil Assistance and Domestic Propaganda (Commissario Generale per l'Assistenza Civile e la Propaganda Interna). However, it was the new CS under General Armando Diaz which in January 1918 created the first efficient and properly financed propaganda organization, the Servizio P, responsible for both home and military fronts. In spring 1918, the so-called Padua Commission for propaganda against the Austrian front at the Piave was created, which consisted of Italians and representatives of the alien peoples of Austria-Hungary.

In March 1918, perhaps inspired by the German Patriotic Instruction or the Servizio P, the Austrian army created an Enemy Propaganda Defence Agency (Feindpropaganda-Abwehrstelle, FAST) with the task of stabilizing the morale at the military front and at the rear.

Belgian propaganda was at first directed by several embassies and later centralized in the Belgian Documentary Office (Bureau documentaire belge). The Flemish separatists founded the Central Flemish Propaganda Office (Centraal Vlaams Propagandabureau) financed by the Germans.

Only two belligerent countries and three national liberation movements escaped administrative quarrels to a certain extent because they established centralized offices from the very beginning: The Turkish Minister of War Ismail Enver Pasha employed his secret Special Section (Teşkilat-ı Mahsusa, TM), founded already in 1908, for propaganda, espionage and sabotage abroad and also for propaganda at home; he was only sometimes annoyed by the overactive propagandists of his German ally. In the United States, Creel organized the almighty CPI with a domestic and a larger foreign section which established offices in over 30 countries; but even he encountered problems with the Congress and various administrations while the Departments of Treasure and Food made some propaganda on their own (see pp. 141–3).[32] The Lithuanian politician Juozas Gabrys had already created in Paris the Lithuanian Information Bureau (LIB) and the Office of Nationalities in 1911 and 1912, respectively, and moved them in August 1915 to Lausanne (see pp. 148–50); the Czechoslovak National Council and the Polish National Committee also established Press Offices in London and Paris (see pp. 124–6).

Chapter 3

WHAT WERE THE PRINCIPAL ARGUMENTS OF PROPAGANDA?

A fight between good and evil? – the Manichean approach

The war between the Allies and the Central Powers was represented as a struggle between the forces of good and evil – a dualistic approach heavily influenced by Manichean tendencies inherent in the Christian belief since St. Augustine. In all countries, the Church identified with the State, and the clergymen – in Germany and Russia even instructed by official guidelines or parish bulletins – claimed that their nation was chosen and supported by God in order to wage a 'Holy War' against 'His enemies' and the champion of the Antichrist. In Russia, 'holy' had the specific meaning of 'getting rid of the German spirit in life'.[1] Consequently, victory was absolutely certain because it was God's will, and the churches thus referring to Jesus' words, 'I did not come to bring peace but the sword', propagated a victorious war till the very end.[2] A German Protestant parson explained: 'Whatever might happen, we are certain that our cause will win, it must win because it is the great holy cause of our God.' 'Our God' refers to the national God of the Germans, while the French also evoked their God and the national saint Joan of Arc – anachronistic ideas typical for gentile-religious communities of forlorn times.[3] In such an apocalyptic fight against the evil, killing the enemy was justified. The Anglican Bishop of London, Arthur Winnington-Ingram, one of the most bellicose churchmen of Britain, exhorted his flock in a sermon: 'Kill Germans, kill them! [...] not for the sake of killing but to save the world.'[4] A few more peaceful clerics considered the war as a divine project destined to punish the people for their sins and to purge and purify them.[5]

Although not all the people were still faithful believers, most of them were under the spell of values deeply rooted in Christian tradition and thus they readily accepted the Manichean background of propaganda.[6] As in fairy tales, novels and films, where the forces of good after going through a lot of trouble usually triumph over their malicious enemies, a war waged against sinister powers would as well require great sacrifices but was supposed to end happily, and propaganda only needed to reinforce this conviction.

The easiest way to bring home the evil character of the enemy nations was to choose one of their conspicuous representatives. Kings, political leaders or generals were associated with negative or fear-inspiring symbols, and the resulting emotion was transferred to the people as such.[7] Between 1888 and 1914, for 24 years, the number of Kaiser cartoons in Britain amounted to 600, and during the war it swelled to 900 in four years.[8] Allied propaganda portrayed the Kaiser as a devil or his associate – in Britain alone 24 times – and held him personally 'responsible for all the crimes perpetrated by individuals', as *La Dépêche de Toulouse* affirmed (Figure 5).[9] Another target was Field-Marshal Paul von Hindenburg who was depicted as a Moloch pushing the soldiers into the fire of the trenches.[10] The German and Austrian propagandists never went to such extremes, but used the hate transfer method as well. According to Werner Sombart's despicable connotation of the British as 'haberdashers', they depicted Foreign Minister Sir Edward Grey as a shopkeeper explaining coldly, 'War is a business like any other', while presenting two piles of skulls on his counter.[11] Grand Duke Nicholas Nikolaevich, the Supreme Commander of the Russian Armies, wades in blood like Macbeth. John Bull, symbol of Britain, ruthlessly oppresses small nations and violates international law by his total blockade of the Central Powers.[12]

Propagandists also reinforced negative stereotypes from pre-war culture in order to vilify the enemy, such as the spike-helmeted German glutton with sausages and beer, the frivolous and vainglorious Frenchman, the perfidious and comfort-loving Englishman, the cowardly, malicious and treacherous Italian and finally the drunken, dirty and superstitious Russian.[13] The declaration of war by the former ally Italy was answered by denigrating the Italians as traitors and comparing them with Judas.[14] Sometimes older stereotypes had to be changed. While before the war in Germany the French were attacked as the hereditary enemy, now they were considered victims of the British, who had dragged them into the war and wanted to fight 'till the last French soldier'.[15] Some propagandists, for instance, Alfred Weber, even suggested a reconciliation with France. A cartoon shows a German soldier seducing French Marianne by *fensterln* according to the Bavarian custom, that is climbing on a ladder to her window and whispering her endearments while his comrades are holding back jealous Russian and British soldiers.[16] Other German cartoons of France depicting men in a correct and even distinguished way and women as exquisite and seductive beauties were so positive that 'one could wonder if between 1914 and 1918 Germany was at war with France'.[17] However, the French were too exasperated by the German invasion and did not return this sympathy. German women in Allied cartoons, chansons and stage plays were presented as ugly, fat, fade, badly dressed and without grace.[18] In a series of drawings, called *Deutschland über alles* (Germany Above All), the French cartoonist Fernand Fau contrasted pejorative drawings with an ironical praise of the German 'superiority in matters of sausage and sauerkraut, of elegance and culture'.[19] And not only journals like *Le Figaro* and the *Chronique médicale*, but even serious scholars claimed that the Germans stink.[20]

In August 1914, Russia was considered the most important foe of the Central Powers, but in October 'perfidious Albion' took its place.[21] In an enumeration of propaganda invectives in *Simplicissimus* and *Lustige Blätter*, Britain figures at the first, France at the last place and Russia was not considered at all.[22] The entry of the

British into the war was unexpected, and they were hated for starving the Germans by the blockade. *Gott strafe England* (God Punish England) replaced 'Good day' as a greeting and was also printed on postcards, wedding rings, handkerchiefs, brooches, household items and even on coal (Figure 6).[23] This hate was also directed against British POWs: They were more brutally treated than were the French, and when they died and were buried in a public cemetery, it could happen that the inhabitants greeted the coffins with jeers.[24] A German-Jewish poet, Ernst Lissauer, wrote the ill-famed *Haßgesang gegen England* (Hymn of Hate against England). This is the first stanza:

> French and Russians, they matter not.
> A blow for a blow, and a shot for a shot.
> We love them not, we hate them not.
> We hold the Vistula and the Vosges-gate.
> We have but one and only hate,
> We love as one, we hate as one,
> We have one foe and one alone.
> England.[25]

This poem became extremely popular. Stefan Zweig remembered:

> The poem fell like a bomb into a munitions depot. [...] The Kaiser was enthusiastic and awarded Lissauer the order of the Red Eagle, the poem was reprinted in all the newspapers, the teachers read it aloud in front of the pupils, the officers recited it in front of the soldiers until everybody knew the hate song by heart [...] soon the whole world knew it, though with less enthusiasm.[26]

A German poster listed various deprivations like rationing cards accompanied by an Englishman and the comment 'It is his fault.'[27] According to one of the principal German propagandists, the economist Alfred Weber (see pp. 150–3), the British had started the entire war in order to destroy German trade, and many German writers like Thomas Mann shared his view.[28] His colleague Werner Sombart, drawing his arguments from the anti-capitalist arsenal of the socialists and the German cultural pessimists, had denounced in his book *Die Zukunft der Juden* (1912) (The Future of the Jews) the Jews as representatives of liberalism, commercialism and capitalism, and could now easily transfer the same accusations to the British. By contrasting Britons and Germans in his war pamphlet as *Händler und Helden* (Merchants vs. Heroes), he denigrated the British as a petty nation of treacherous shopkeepers.[29]

The most important argument of the Manichean campaign was the atrocity issue, which triggered a furious war of propaganda between the Allies and Germany. During their invasion of neutral Belgium and North Eastern France in August and September 1914, the German army had butchered 6,427 innocent men, women and small children: It either shot them in formal executions, or bayoneted and killed them with axes in a blind rage.[30] Although German censorship suppressed most information, Belgian refugees reported the atrocities in France and Britain. Public opinion in Allied and in neutral countries as well was shocked by the brutality of German militarism. Even friends of Germany, for instance, Rolland, were perplexed: 'I am more struck', he wrote, 'by the incredible clumsiness of the Germans than by their brutal force. They are themselves their worst enemies; they do everything to be hated and afterwards they are surprised.' The historian Jay Winter recently commented: 'The *Kaiserreich* dug its own grave.'[31]

The Germans tried to deny everything. In their appeal *An die Kulturwelt* (To the Civilized World) of 4 October 1914, 93 distinguished German professors and writers vigorously affirmed 'It is not true' and defended and justified German militarism as a part of their *Kultur*. Similar other appeals and public declarations followed, passionately refuted by British, French and even Russian professors.[32] Finally the British commissioned a thorough investigation by the Committee on Alleged German Outrages. Its chairman James Bryce was a very distinguished scholar who held several honorary doctorates of German universities and the *Ordre pour le Mérite*, the most distinguished German scholarly distinction.[33] The commission based its report on 12,000 depositions of Belgian and French refugees which were confirmed by diaries of fallen German soldiers, 'translated with great care'.[34] The diaries indeed contained accounts of executions but not of sadistic outrages against women and children. Above all, the depositions were only indirectly taken by barristers and over the objections of one member of the commission never verified by personal examination of the witnesses, an important blunder confirmed since by historical research.[35]

Nevertheless, during the war the *Bryce Report*, 600 pages long and translated into 30 languages, was, as David Welch puts it, 'a severe blow to Germany's international reputation'.[36] It was rapidly followed by similar propaganda pamphlets: *Crimes of Germany* by Theodore Cook, *The Horrors of Wittenberg* accusing the Germans of mistreating their POWs, the *Reiss Report* about the Austrian atrocities, several French publications including an official *Red Book* and *Les crimes allemands d'après des témoignages allemands* (The German Crimes according to German Testimony) by Joseph Bédier. Even the atrocities of the Turks, analysed in the Blue Book *The Treatment of Armenians in the Ottoman Empire* by Bryce and Arnold Toynbee, were ascribed to German pressure.[37] Combined with exaggerated Allied army communiqués reprinted by official government reports, this huge propaganda campaign heated up anti-German hysteria around the world. Some topics became real classics repeated and amplified time and again, such as the cutting of small children's hands by German soldiers as a war souvenir or the crucifying of a Canadian soldier. The latter story was so impressive that it was gloomily reproduced 99 years later, on 12 July 2014, by Russian television: This time the Germans were replaced by the Ukrainians, and the crucified person was a three-year-old boy.[38]

The Germans reacted with refutations and counter-attacks claiming for instance that propagandists had misunderstood the soldiers' diaries because of their insufficient knowledge of German. The AA in its White Book *Die völkerrechtswidrige Führung des belgischen Volkskriegs* (How the Belgians Waged a People's War in Contravention of International Law) accused the Belgians of atrocities as well. They were supposed to have gouged out the eyes of German prisoners, but despite frantic searches in hospitals not a single case was found. Above all, it claimed that the German soldiers had only fought back against attacks by francs-tireurs – an argument partly revived by various scholars who recently brought to light sporadic acts of irregular francs-tireurs' resistance.[39] However, in 1914 this argument was not accepted by public opinion in most countries.

During the whole war, German atrocities continued. On 7 May 1915, a German submarine sank the British passenger ship *Lusitania* with 1,198 passengers on board, among them 128 Americans, and on 15 October 1915 a German firing squad executed the British nurse Edith Cavell – events which led to another 'outbreak of worldwide moral indignation more disastrous for Germany than a lost battle.[40] Of course, facts excusing or even justifying the German actions were either denied or offhand repudiated by the Allies. On 22 April, the German embassy in Washington had published notices in 50 American newspapers explicitly warning people to book passages on British ships; on 1 May, it renewed this warning with special reference to the *Lusitania*. This ship did not carry only passengers, but also 50 tons of ammunitions and 67 Canadian soldiers – a fact that had been confirmed one day after the sinking by an American inquiry kept secret on explicit order of President Thomas Woodrow Wilson. British and American authorities did not admit the *Lusitania* stratagem until 1982, when several diving expeditions discovered the remains of the war materials.[41]

Miss Cavell worked in Brussels and had helped approximately 200 Allied soldiers trapped in Belgium escape to the Netherlands. She was court-martialled and as the historian Isabel Hull recently confirmed, rightly condemned according to § 90 of the German Penal Code of 'Conducting soldiers to the Enemy'. However, § 90 did not stipulate the death sentence, but only lifelong imprisonment, and demands for clemency by the Pope and two ambassadors were to no avail.[42]

The Allies skilfully exploited both events. According to them, Miss Cavell was shot 'for taking pity on and showing mercy to the helpless'. A medal in memory of the sinking of the ship by a German sculptor was reproduced, claiming that the erroneous date on the medal (5 May instead of 7 May) would prove that the attack was premeditated by the 'Huns'.[43] The results of the propaganda campaign were overwhelming: *Lusitania* propaganda triggered the worst pogroms against Germans in Britain,[44] and both cases immediately lead to a dramatic upsurge of British enlistment (see p. 183 and organogram on p. 212).

During the occupation of Belgium, North Eastern France and Lithuania, the Germans continued living up to their reputation: heavy requisitions and contributions, arbitrary executions for trivialities, forced labour and deportations to Germany created absolute hell for the populations and were thus easily exploited by Allied propaganda.[45] Whereas the situation in Lithuania was not much noticed, the Belgian deportations lead to an outcry in the world with protests by the Vatican and neutral countries so that finally the Germans were obliged to repatriate at least a part of the Belgians. Atrocity propaganda continued till the end of the war, though in somewhat reduced intensity.[46]

A special branch of atrocity was 'cultural atrocity'. The Germans freely admitted that they had burnt the library of Louvain, but their bombardment of the cathedral of Reims on 9 September 1914 aroused a heated propaganda controversy with the French. Both sides lied about the event. The Germans pretended that they had seen a French observer on the cathedral signalling the position of German troops to French artillery and that they had only fired a single shot at him which misfired. French General Ferdinand Foch denied the use of the cathedral for military purposes. Both sides agreed that a fire ensued. The Germans produced authentic photos of wounded German soldiers who tried to leave the burning cathedral but were driven back by shooting French guards. Some died; others were saved by clerics. A French witness called the photos a falsification and in 1919 excused his statement with the words: 'I thought of the honour of my country'. The propaganda battle was, of course, won by the French, and the cathedral, soon object of pilgrimages and other propaganda visits, became the symbol of German atrocities.[47]

More impressive than words were posters and cartoons. Here as well the German was depicted as a barbarian brute, for instance, in an Italian poster as a primitive Ostrogoth with a long scrubby beard, a torch and a medieval club (Figure 7), and in an American poster, as a soldier wading in blood over corpses of children.[48] Normally one expects cartoons to be funny, and the majority of them are, but in the overheated atmosphere of the war, Allied and also neutral cartoonists depicted the German soldier as a violent monster burning houses, raping women and mutilating children.[49] On the other hand, at least 78 caricatures contradicted this image, showing him as a coward always ready to surrender, even to children.[50] Certain cartoonists, for instance, the Dutchman Louis Raemaekers and the Frenchman Henri Zislin, were masters of atrocity and hate cartoons, and they succeeded in arousing fanatic hostility against the Germans all over the world[51] (see pp. 156–7). The technique of these cartoons was quite simple: They depicted real or invented atrocities of German soldiers or showed ugly Germans in disgusting postures, both in a very expressive style. A typical example by Raemaekers is a scene in a French or Belgian village where an obviously insane woman bemoans her dead baby while in the background two old men lie slain on the ground. No text was necessary, because the message was clear: They were killed by the German 'Huns' (Figure 8). While British cartoonists depicted atrocities very rarely, their Italian and French colleagues enjoyed them, especially in the first two years of the war. In its Christmas edition of 1915, the Italian cartoon magazine *Asino* depicted the Nativity attacked by German soldiers who were spearing Jesus, murdering Mary, strangling Joseph and robbing their belongings.[52] Even more repulsive than the well-known propaganda lie about the corpse-conversion-factory – where the Germans allegedly transformed human corpses into soap – was a cartoon by Zislin with the title 'The Imperial Shambles': It showed a cruel-looking German butcher selling corpses, hands, feet and heads of German soldiers 'directly imported from Verdun' and was cynically commented, 'No more meat shortage in Germany'.[53] When at the end of the war Germany was definitely beaten, the French cartoonists demanded severe punishment in a peace treaty which, in the words of the British general staff officer Archibald Wavell, would 'end all peace': The Germans would have to bring back all their booty, repair the destroyed houses and reimburse all the war expenses. The empress would work under the whip, Hindenburg and Ludendorff would be kept in the trenches, and the hands of the crown prince's children would be cut.[54]

The Kaiser, already considered the symbol of evil, became the personification of German barbarism as well. In Allied novels, films, stage plays, songs and even children books he appeared as a monster, as the 'Beast of Berlin', as one American filmmaker named him.[55] He is presented as a pirate with dagger and pistol and a black bandage over one of his eyes, as a vampire living off the blood of people who perished in the destroyed towns of Louvain and Reims. A Russian cartoon shows the 'stair case of civilization': on the higher stairs sits the Turk, then come the Eskimo, the African and the Indian. The very last stair is occupied by a cannibal with the leftovers of his dinner and the Kaiser with the wreck of the *Lusitania*, the ruin of the cathedral of Reims and the corpse of a baby.[56] Another extremely hateful cartoon shows the Kaiser naked in a cage with a sign asking visitors to beat him with umbrellas and walking sticks.[57]

Formerly, the atrocity caricatures were qualified as the principal theme of Allied cartoon propaganda, but according to recent research they constituted less than 5 per cent.[58] The heyday of the atrocity cartoons was 1914–15, for instance, *La Baïonnette* published nine special atrocity editions in 1915 but dropped the topic after 7 September 1916.[59] Atrocity cartoons were not an invention of the Great War but had been drawn before.[60] Especially the story about cutting hands of children was not a product of this war but can be traced back to well-documented and photographed crimes committed in the Belgian Congo colony.[61] Although neither a photo nor a single eye witness could be presented during the war, such cartoons proliferated from modest beginnings of a child praying at the tomb of its hand to Kaiser Wilhelm cutting personally the hands of numerous children with an axe.[62] It must be emphasized, however, that the Allied trench journals did not report such stories and even mocked at such lies (see p. 107).

A particular feature of Allied propaganda, especially in British cartoons and in Russian *lubki* (broadsides), was the animalization of the Germans. According to the appropriation technique, the literary figures of Dr. Jekyll and the man-animal Mr. Hyde invented by Robert Louis Stevenson were now set in the context of the war. British propaganda claimed that the 'studious race of Jekyll Germans' had been transmuted into 'a horde of bloodthirsty, murdering Hydes'.[63] In other cartoons, the German completely lost his human form and became an ape, a swine, an octopus, a vulture or a dragon, recognizable only by the spike-helmet.[64] Allied politicians, newspaper headlines and posters called the Germans 'wild beasts', 'Germ-Huns' and 'mad dogs'.[65] The Central Powers rarely adopted the animalization topic – I could find only two caricatures of Sir Grey as a harpy and an owl – and were in general much less aggressive as shown in the comparison between the frightening German-Austrian dragon wading in a bloody sea of murder and destruction (see cover illustration) with a rather timidly acting French dragon in an Austrian cartoon.[66]

It is peculiar that hate propaganda and hate cartoons concerned only German atrocities and only those at the Western front. That the Austro-Hungarian army executed around 30,000 innocent civilians in Serbia and in Galicia, roughly five times more than the Germans had in Belgium and France, was rarely mentioned and represented, although these atrocities were well documented. Turkish atrocities against the Armenians also played only a very minor role despite a detailed documentation in the Bryce-Toynbee report of 1916. Bulgarian atrocities in Macedonia were reported, but not represented.[67]

As there were no French and British soldiers on German soil, apart from a small area in Alsace, it was difficult for the Germans to retaliate in the same way.[68] But they widely exploited two war crimes on sea, the *Baralong* cases and the *King Stephen* affair, where British captains had surviving German crews shot or let them drown in the sea, in the latter case heartily congratulated by the notorious Bishop of London.[69] They also accused the French of having bombarded German hospitals – a particular ill-grace because the same charges were made time and again against the Germans.[70] Otherwise in cartoons and also in films like *Das Tagebuch des Dr. Hart* (The Diary of Dr. Hart), they pointed out to the crimes of the Cossacks in Galicia and East Prussia, but more popular were caricatures about their dirtiness and stupidity.[71] The official report of the AA on *Greueltaten russischer Truppen gegen deutsche Zivilpersonen und deutsche Kriegsgefangene* (Atrocities of Russian Troops against German Civilians and German Prisoners of War) of March 1915 failed to give sufficient evidence, omitted most of the atrocities compiled by the local administrations of East Prussia and could not compete in propaganda value with the sufferings of the Belgians.[72] An especially popular topic of German propaganda was the mobilization of coloured troops from the Allied colonies, 'half animal like peoples', who were accused to cut the throats of German soldiers and drank their blood.[73] Cartoonists depicted black soldiers as cannibals – or even monkeys – fighting for Western civilization, and showed French women pregnant with black children.[74] The French very skilfully responded with a cartoon about a German POW trembling with fear when his black guardian takes out his knife. But the black says: 'Don't worry, Mohammed never eats pigs' – a play upon words, because in French 'cochon' means both 'pig' and 'filthy wretch'.[75]

German propaganda also missed several chances: Already the German ambassador to the United States, Johann Heinrich Graf Bernstorff, had criticized that they never exploited the worst war crime of the Allies: the illegal sea blockade of the Central Powers which caused undernourishment, starvation and the death of numerous civilians, later estimated in Germany at about 700,000. This was partially due to British propaganda which skilfully explained that in their blockade operations 'the utmost precautions were taken to respect legal rights and the sanctity of human life' while the German submarines did not recognize 'neither the mandates of international law nor the dictates of humanity'.[76] More important was that the Germans tried to conceal their supply problems for fear that the Allies would count on their economic breakdown and not be ready to make peace. Thus they even sabotaged a 'milk-for-German-babies' campaign in the United States by affirming that their babies were healthy and got enough milk.[77] Another wasted chance of propaganda was the shooting by the French of two German nurses and eight other alleged spies, among them the harmless Mata Hari.[78] While Allied propaganda heavily exploited the Cavell case, a German propaganda officer according to Harold Lasswell said: 'What? Protest? The French had the perfect right to shoot them.' Although German newspapers did blame the French for these executions, for instance, the *Norddeutsche Allgemeine Zeitung* (*NDAZ*) of 7 October 1917, it is true that they did not really succeed in mobilizing public opinion abroad.[79] Equally insufficient was the attempt to counter the accusations against the German 'barbarians' with the aid of films, photos and cartoons in which paternal soldiers were shown sharing their food with elderly women, playing with children or saving historic relics from destruction.[80] One wonders who would believe that outside Germany – except some of the children in the occupied territories themselves. Based on autobiographical testimony, Manon Pignot has convincingly demonstrated that German privates often had affectionate relations with children, gave them chocolates, cakes and gifts, whereas British and American soldiers entering these territories in 1918 were remembered as much less friendly.[81] A French cartoonist very skilfully counteracted German propaganda by showing a photographer who takes a picture of a German soldier with a baby on his knees, and the soldier says: 'One would not believe that I killed the mother' (Figure 9).

It seems that finally the OHL realized this deficiency in the field of cartoon propaganda. In September 1917, the German news agency Wolff sent a circular to German newspapers and magazines asking them to counter the atrocity propaganda against Germany by publishing cartoons about similar events on the Allies' side.[82] In fact, as Anne Schmidt explains, in the second half of the war German propaganda partially adopted the Allied approach trying to stir up the emotions of the masses through hate and fear propaganda[83] (see pp. 86–7).

There is a deeper reason for the difference between Allied atrocity propaganda and the rather weak responses of the Central Powers. The Germans offered peace negotiations several times, hoping to achieve a compromise peace, but it is questionable if in this case government and Reichstag were prepared to accept a status quo ante. The French and British authorities refuted or ignored them and succeeded in prevailing over their own partisans of a compromise peace.[84] Already in 1977 Mario Isnenghi pointed out that the hate and atrocity campaign against the leaders of the enemy had the purpose 'to convince the reader that there is no room for peace negotiations but only for a fight until the last drop of blood'.[85] Gerhard Ritter made a similar remark in 1968, and Holger Afflerbach and Roger Chickering have recently confirmed this interpretation[86] (see also p. 67).

An aspect overlooked by most historians is that the atrocities themselves explicitly served propaganda purposes. Already in 1915, the French psychologist Le Bon explained: 'The German General Staff justified the killings and fires by the necessity to frighten the populations so that they would ask for peace – such terrorism was employed at all times.'[87] Spreading fear in order to keep people quiet was indeed one of the motives of the German mass executions in Belgium and France which were in some cases ordered in cold blood some time after an incident.[88] In Poland, too, the Germans hanged alleged spies at street corners in order to warn against betrayals[89] – an anachronistic recurrence to the practices of absolutistic times where after the public beheading of a criminal his head was put on display in order to intimidate the population. When the Austrian army summarily executed tens of thousands of alleged spies and traitors in Galician, Italian and Serbian areas, they even took photos and had them widely distributed in order to spread fear among the population.[90] While the *Bryce Report* could not produce a single photo – Lord Northcliffe once offered £200 for this and never got one – the *Reiss Report* presented many photos relating to Austrian atrocities which Allied propaganda rarely reprinted.[91] On a much smaller scale in British army schools, the main propaganda maxim was 'to instil fear into the opponent'.[92]

In contrast to the evil qualities of the enemy, it was important to depict the own political and military leaders 'as faithful, resolute and reliable servants of the nation'[93] who would guarantee the final victory. While the Allies were at a loss to find such heroes until summer 1918 and could only feed their peoples on 'the paper victories of the press bureau' and *Nelson's History of the War*,[94] the Germans very early presented Hindenburg, the famous victor of the Battle of Tannenberg, as a confidence-inspiring father figure.[95] In fact Hindenburg organized the propaganda campaign himself. He gained the support of journalists, war correspondents and politicians, apologetic writers, among them even Sven Hedin and Ludwig Ganghofer, hundreds of painters and famous sculptors, and saw to a huge sale of reproductions and postcards. Clever businessmen joined his campaign and produced herrings, cigars and gingerbread, porcelain plates, cups and other household items, all of them with Hindenburg's image. This stuff soon embellished nearly every German home, and the general became the charismatic symbol of victory, completely ousting the Kaiser in this aspect.[96] No wonder that he was finally used as a 'marketing icon' for war bonds propaganda and other means of collecting money[97] (see pp. 94–5). In France, General Joseph Joffre, commander-in-chief of the French army, was glorified after his victory on the Marne, but not in such an exaggerated way and not for a long time.[98] Golo Mann remembered: 'One needed names for hate as well as for admiration.'[99]

Second to the leaders came the soldiers appearing in articles, cartoons and films of the field grey genre 'as paragons of military virtue and human mercy'.[100] Austrians and Italians alike enjoyed presenting the athletic *Alpino* (mountain soldier), who heroically defied the challenges of an inhospitable nature.[101] In French drawings and in a film, a lieutenant, the only survivor in a trench, cried: 'Get up, all the dead!' and the German assailants miraculously understanding his words panicked and ran away.[102] It goes without saying that the brutal reality was usually left out and front descriptions by writers and journalists presented the war in an idealized and sanitized way – an approach which was somewhat corrected by Barbusse in 1916[103] (see pp. 143–6). As George F. Kennan has already remarked in 1964, this hero cult of the soldier 'exaggerated the role of personal bravery and determination in a war fought with modern weapons'.[104]

Women could also be presented as heroes, for instance, Cavell or the wife and mother of two fallen officers in the French film *Les mères françaises* (The French Mothers), played by the famous actress Sarah Bernhardt.[105] In some countries, children were also elevated as heroes and admired as splendid examples of bravery (see pp. 103–4).

How was the enemy ridiculed?

Ridiculing was a very popular and frequent means of propaganda, as Winter puts it: 'In the Great War, the enemy was mocked as much as he was hated.'[106] In this context, the work of cartoonists was of primary importance. Their principal techniques will be analysed in an adaptation of Nicholas Roukes's categories of humour in art.[107]

One of the simplest techniques was punning, that is producing a comical effect by misspelling words or using homophones and homonyms. Examples are the transformation of the German 'crown prince' into 'clown prince'[108] or representing Sir Edward Grey as Dorian Gray from the eponymous novel by Oscar Wilde: Grey's immoral war policy does not leave any visible marks on his face while his hidden portrait reveals his real nature: a depraved face and bloody hands, like the fictional Gray.[109]

The most common technique was exaggeration and distortion. Less important features were reduced and a characteristic trait was magnified in order to produce a humorous effect.[110] An example widely used by German propaganda was the small stature of Victor Emmanuel III, King of Italy. In one cartoon he was even reduced to the size of a baby sitting helplessly on the knees of his wife who consoles him after the defeat at Caporetto with the words: 'Hushaby, what shall we do? We shall join grandpa Nikita.'[111] Her father Nicholas I, King of Montenegro, had already capitulated and lived in exile in Lyon. The small king was the symbol of a country which was hopelessly overstrained by the war.

Transposition, alienation and disguise transfer persons into a new context, another social or historical setting. Examples are Austrian, German and British cartoons presenting the enemy leaders as a circus variety troupe – a very appropriate picture because they had to perform ingenious tricks in order to have their peoples accept more and more privations and sacrifices. In an Austrian caricature of 1914, King Peter I of Serbia and Nicholas of Montenegro are playing tragicomic clowns; Albert I, King of the Belgians, is falling from a ladder; and the Parisians afraid of the German invasion invent the shaking dance.[112] One year later, the German *Lustige Blätter* followed with the 'Anglo-French gang of illusionists': The Minister of War Lord Herbert Kitchener playing a propaganda-drum desperately tries to recruit soldiers; the First Lord of the Admiralty Winston Churchill balances Britain's rule of the seas on a shaky water column; Grey as a hypnotist keeps French Foreign Minister Théophile Delcassé floating in a magical ring; and newspaper tycoon Northcliffe has his parrots *Daily Mail* and *The Times* screech filthy lies (Figure 10).[113] In 1917, the *Punch*, probably inspired by the Austrian and German models, showed Kaiser Wilhelm dancing on a revolving globe, his chancellor manipulating rationing cards, General Hindenburg swallowing nails and the Austrian Emperor Franz Josef singing the *Hungarian Rhapsody* (Figure 11).[114]

In order to denounce the soldiers of the Allies, the German cartoonists presented them as incompetent or ridiculous. That was relatively easy when it came to the Italians who lost one battle after the other and to the Russians who were portrayed as illiterate drunkards.[115] It was more difficult in the case of the French and the British soldiers who were as good as the Germans. But as several Allied offensives failed and brought at best very small territorial gains, one could mock the inefficiency of their strategy. In a German caricature with the title *Gloire,* a French soldier enthusiastically reports to his superiors that the victory at 'Nullepart' (Nowhere) is much greater than has been assumed: Their army has advanced 2.53 meters instead of only 2.50 meters.[116]

The recruitment problems of Britain were another rewarding subject. This country had no conscription and depended on volunteers. Initially there were enough of them, but after the heavy casualties, enthusiasm was very much on the wane. A German cartoon shows a British recruiting office with a poster promising volunteers a wonderful life: They will eat enormous slices of ham, obtain a huge sack of money, will be promoted to general in six months and meet *Gretchen* waiting for them in the future British garrison at Cologne. Despite all these promises, the only person who turned up in the week was the charwoman (Figure 12). Before general conscription was introduced in May 1916, it was imposed for a short time to bachelors only, and according to German propaganda everybody was going to marry. A caricature shows the British bachelor desperately navigating on a river: on the left hand side a grumpy colonel calls him to the trenches, and on the right an ugly old spinster invites him to the registry office.[117] But when enlistment became compulsory for everybody in May 1916, they feigned illness in order to avoid being enlisted. Other countries encountered similar problems.[118] But there was still one alternative: Women to the front! According to the German cartoonists, that was the last chance for Britain and Russia.[119] In reality, it was only in Russia that individual commanders or even the tsar himself had exceptionally authorized approximately 1,000 women to join the colours, but only after the February Revolution female troops numbering 5,000 soldiers were officially raised, for instance, the famous 'Battalion of Death' under Major Maria Bochkareva.[120] In the British forces, the Women's Army Auxiliary Corps employed approximately 40,000 women, but only as telephone operators, typists and orderlies. When in view of the heavy casualties the Allies enlisted older men of up to 55 years and even freed criminal prisoners, the cartoonists illustrated these desperate measures in typical exaggeration: prisoners in cages, old men with crutches and babies with their nannies are sent to the trenches as the last reserves. The Allies were good at repartee: *Big and Little Willies' Reinforcements* show Kaiser and crown prince leading invalids in wheelchairs and babies in prams to the front.[121]

One example of very subtle manipulation is the German cartoon *Vierbund-Vierverband* (Figure 13): the Central Powers (Germany, Austria, Turkey and Bulgaria) are contrasted with the most important Allies (Britain, France, Russia and Italy). The representatives of the Central Powers – the chiefs of staff of the German and Austrian armies, Erich von Falkenhayn and Franz Conrad von

Hötzendorf, Tsar Ferdinand of Bulgaria, and the Turkish Minister of War Enver are depicted very positively: calmly and confidently, they sit around a table, obviously in complete harmony, whereas their counterparts on the Allied side are quarrelling violently. The Russian and French commanders-in-chief, Grand Duke Nicholas and Joffre, reproach Grey, while the small King of Italy tries to climb on a table and shouts as well. A critical reader might consider this comparison as rather biased, but he still runs the risk of being massively manipulated, since this caricature can be viewed from another angle. By using the number 'four' – four Allies, four Central Powers – the cartoonist is attempting to convince the reader that both coalitions are of 'equal' value. Yet this was obviously not the case – the Allies were by far superior – numerically, financially and economically. In a French cartoon, the coalition of the Central Powers is depicted in a more realistic way: Austria as a sick old man; Turkey as an invalid.[122]

In Russia and Italy with their numerous illiterates, traditional entertainments enjoyed a comeback. In Russia, millions of cheap war *lubki* (broadsides) were sold or shown in a *raek* (peep show), a box with magnifying glasses and a commentary. In puppet theatres, the traditional German doctor was replaced by Kaiser Wilhelm who was beaten to death by Petrushka, the Russian Punch. In circus pantomimes, dressed pigs looked like Hindenburg, wrestlers with Kaiser Wilhelm whiskers were hissed and invariably lost their fight. In circuses, Wilhelm, Francis Joseph and Sultan Mehmed V turned around in wheel barrows and were tormented by dancing devils. The style of the *lubki* also influenced movies with satirical episodes about Kaiser or Sultan. A typical *lubok*-war movie was *Off with the German Yoke* released in September 1914: The Kaiser and his generals with huge beer bellies gallop on hobby horses. After his smashing victory, the Kaiser distributes the European countries to his generals. All of them are quite content with one exception: the one who got Luxembourg. However, as the tsar was annoyed about the ridiculing of crowned heads, in summer 1915 this sort of amusement was forbidden.[123] In Italy, the puppet theatre (*teatro dei burattini*) was revived: When Giuppino and Pulcinella clad as soldiers beat Kaiser Wilhelm, the soldiers laughed and asked the marionettes to beat more strongly. Instead of talking about the fatherland to the illiterates, it was easier to show them the pleasure of combat and victory in entertainment.[124]

Speaking of humour, Charlie Chaplin's famous film *Shoulder Arms* must not be forgotten. He uses a gas mask against the odour of Limburger cheese, captures a whole troop of Germans and finally even the Kaiser – funny entertainment but not devoid of a propaganda message: Life in the trenches is after all quite amusing, and the Germans are stupid and will thus lose the war.[125]

Cartoons are characterized by a 'double-edged character' which Sigmund Freud had analysed in his famous book *Der Witz und seine Beziehung zum Unbewussten* (The Joke and Its Relation to the Unconscious): By attacking the enemy and showing him 'small, low, despicable, comic, ridiculous, we give ourselves the enjoyment of a victory', and at the same time our laughter gives us a certain release from constraint and fear – an analysis also pertinent to other humorous entertainment and corroborated by modern research.[126]

Which scapegoats were accused?

In the most famous French war cartoon, one soldier says to another: 'Let's hope they will hold out. – Who? – The civilians.'[127] Morale at the home front was indeed one of the major challenges, especially the inadequate supply of food, coal and other commodities. The priorities of war production, bureaucratic control of the economy, naval blockade and submarine warfare led to inflation and supply shortages in all belligerent countries – problems which could not be solved by propaganda exhortations like 'eat less bread, meat and sugar'.[128] The Central Powers and Italy were hardest hit, so that in Germany already in 1915 local functionaries had to calm protests against the rising food crisis.[129] Profiteering and speculation aggravated these problems. Here the propagandists had an important function. It was their job to shift the responsibility from the real culprits – government and bureaucracy – to various scapegoats such as war profiteers and hoarders, but also to defeatists, socialists, spies, shirkers, strikers and enemy aliens.

At the beginning of the war, irresponsible propaganda produced a real spy and saboteur fever. In Germany, at the beginning of August, the Press Bureau of III b proclaimed: 'We are surrounded by spies! Everybody is called upon to undo their machinations.'[130] The Wolff news agency announced that 80 French officers were crossing Germany with cars full of gold destined to Russia. According to other official and semi-official reports, French doctors were poisoning wells in Germany.[131] In Britain, too, newspapers and hysterical VIPs warned against a network of spies and disguised German soldiers. Lord Frederick Roberts, the former commander-in-chief of the British army, and *The Globe* even had exact figures: 80,000 in Britain and 250,000 in London alone.[132] In France, Daudet launched a relentless campaign against German spies (see p. 25). In both countries, German grocers were accused of poisoning their customers and barbers of cutting their throats.[133] In Russia, the 'Society of 1914', strongly supported by the tsarist regime, fulminated against the 'internal German threat'.[134] In order to jump upon the bandwagon, filmmakers and theatre authors rapidly launched numerous movies and stage plays where the 'Kaiser's spies' and saboteurs poisoned wells and blew up munitions factories or even the London water system.[135] The French film *The Traitor* aptly combines propaganda against spies and enemy aliens: a German is married to a French woman. His wife opens one of his letters, finds a communiqué from the German secret service and shoots him with a revolver. A similar story is presented in the Italian film *My Country Is Always in My Heart*.[136] When the United States joined the Allies in 1917, German immigrants were accused of spying and sabotage, which was not totally unfounded, because the German embassy had indeed organized acts of sabotage in order to hamper production and shipment of war material to Britain (see p. 66). Here as well films played an important role: In *The Huns Within* and *The Secret Game* valiant American citizen revealed the machinations of German spies.[137]

These propaganda campaigns lead to a terrible witch-hunt. In Germany, barricades were erected in order to stop the cars loaded with gold, and numerous persons, most of them senior German reserve officers or noble ladies, were attacked and 28 of them lynched.[138] Youth bands were roaming the street and dragging 'the most harmless individuals' to police stations, in one case 64 'spies' during one single day.[139] A woman was taken for a Russian spy because she ran quickly down a street and was only saved by a policeman from being beaten by a crowd; when she later spoke English with friends in a beer garden, they were all arrested as Russian saboteurs planning to blow up a nearby bridge.[140] In a small town in Silesia, three foreigners were condemned to death by a military tribunal for having allegedly planned to poison water with cholera microbes or to blow up a plane factory.[141] In France as well, suspect people were hunted in the streets, officers were taken for spies and shot, the German director of a hotel was accused of picking up wireless spy instructions at a special installation on the hotel's roof, and a poor deaf-mute who could not explain his behaviour was beaten up. Near the front the situation was worse: In the village of Rosigny, 20 persons being accused of having betrayed the exact location of the GHQ to German artillery were summarily executed by order of the General Staff.[142]

The most tragic victims of the spy mania were the enemy aliens in the Allied countries. Thousands of people were falsely inculpated, interned and their apartments and shops were looted.[143] In Britain, the pogroms were spread over the whole war: from August and October 1914 over May 1915 and June 1916 until July 1917,[144] in France and Russia limited to August 1914 and May 1915, respectively. However, in Russia the pogroms were only the first act in a joint propaganda crusade of the administration and private associations against the 'German stranglehold' which finally lead to the expropriation of hundreds of thousands of German settlers and businessmen and their deportation to Siberia and Central Asia.[145] In the United States, self-appointed detectives surveyed German immigrants, denounced them to the authorities and humiliated them in various ways (see pp. 15–16).

Propaganda against spies led to so many errors that German censorship finally stopped it. In France and Britain, cartoonists tried to calm it down by ridiculing it.[146] In Britain, Alfred Lette created 'Schmidt the Spy', a ridiculous figure who misunderstands everything. When he sees women fighting each other during the sales, he reports to Berlin that a revolution has broken out. In a French cartoon, a wife says to her husband: 'Can you imagine, our German nanny – that was General von Kluck!' And he replies: 'Shocking! Imagine that I have deceived you with her!'[147]

The war profiteers were especially hated by the people because they contributed to the soaring cost of living. As an English saying put it so well, 'they were bleeding the country contrary to those who were bleeding for the country'.[148] Propaganda ridiculed their pretentiousness, vulgarity and bad taste, and accused them of supporting the enemy and jeopardizing the victory.[149] In an Italian cartoon, a woman dining with her lover in a posh restaurant asks him: 'What have you done for the fatherland?' And he answers: 'I have supplied the army with shoes.' On top of the drawing, one sees the soldiers' feet either with completely rotten shoes or with no shoes at all (Figure 14). In another cartoon, Emperor Franz Josef congratulates the Italian profiteer with the words: 'Bravo, you are working for the

Austrian victory.'[150] However, as anti-profiteer propaganda did not convince people that the authorities were really doing enough, in France, Britain and Austria people reported war profiteers and speculators to the authorities, and in order to appease the disgruntled population some of them were indeed prosecuted.[151] In Austria, the population was so much exasperated that it demanded to hang them, flog them or place them in cages. Finally from January 1917 onwards the authorities published pillory lists with the names of convicted profiteers in newspapers and on notice boards. However, mostly only petty crimes were indicated, and the people were convinced that the 'big fish' were not convicted.[152]

The strikers were accused of aiding and abetting the enemy and thus prolonging the war. 'To go on strike now helps the enemy' said a German poster, and in the German film *Unsühnbar* the agitation of strikers was heavily criticized.[153] In British cartoons, a striker tries to stab a soldier in the back; another obtains the German iron cross.[154] In British stage plays, nationalists discussing with strikers convince them to stop striking and to enlist.[155] One can, however, wonder if the workers on strike in the Clyde area had enough time and money to see such plays in London theatres.

Pacifists and socialists like the Independent Social Democrats in Germany (USPD), the Italian Socialists (PSI) and members of the British Union of Democratic Control (UDC) were accused of high treason and collaboration with the enemy.[156] The German socialist Karl Liebknecht, an uncompromising enemy of the war (see pp. 159–60, 163–5), is shown in a *Simplicissimus* cartoon comforting the beaten Russian General Nicholas: 'Don't despair, Nicholas, you can still count on me' – a masterpiece of brainwashing: the revolutionary Liebknecht portrayed as an ally of hated tsarism.[157] In the United States and Italy, pacifists were naturally very active before these countries joined the war and were thus particularly attacked by the warmongers. Nevertheless the danger of organized pacifism was rather exaggerated by official propaganda, 'it had little impact on the war itself'.[158]

In a war that never seemed to end, there were more and more defeatists and yellow-bellies, and propaganda had a difficult task to fight them. In France, it even invented a town called Trouilleville – where the *trouillards* (yellow-bellies) were supposed to take refuge and treat their fear.[159]

From 1917, not only in Germany and Austria, but also in England, France and Italy the food situation worsened: rationing cards had to be introduced, and more and more people demanded negotiations about armistice and peace; in France, thousands of women went on strike claiming 'We want our husbands back', while in Italy riots broke out[160] (see pp. 166–9). Government propaganda reacted swiftly and efficiently. In Britain, the German atrocities were warmed up and Arthur Conan Doyle revived Sherlock Holmes who put an end to the activities of a German top agent. Furthermore, rumours were launched about the 'Hidden Hand', an alleged group of bankers, judges and civil servants inside Britain working with 'super-Satanic skill' for the German victory. Such agitation made especially by the Anti-German League, combined with the re-enacting of pogrom scenes in stage plays, led to new riots against German and Jewish establishments.[161] In

France, Clemenceau could stop the strikes by producing falsified documents about their connections with the German secret service (see pp. 166–9).

How was the clash of civilizations proclaimed?

The war was conceived not only as a battle of arms, but like the medieval crusades or the wars of the Reformation, it was also considered as a conflict of ideologies, a 'religious war' (Sombart) or a '*Kulturkrieg*' (clash of civilizations).[162] It was fought out in particular between Germany and the Western powers. According to the Manichean argumentation, the propagandists affirmed that their country was fighting against a bunch of barbarians. For instance, the French philosopher Henri Bergson declared on 8 August 1914: 'The combat against Germany is the combat of civilisation against barbarity', and he accused the Germans 'of having regressed to a wild state.'[163] Barbarity was considered as the logical result of the authoritarian character of German society and constitution. Thus the Western Allies proclaimed the war as a crusade for freedom and democracy against *Kaiserism* and militarism manifest in the German war crimes, and in 1917 the United States joined them with the slogan 'To make the world safe for democracy'.[164] Such arguments found their way as well into popular propaganda. For instance, in the French song *Les aigles noirs* the author reminds of the German massacres and insists on continuing the war in the name of freedom:

> Frenchmen, get up! At the vile horde!
> Englishmen, Flemings, Serbs, Russians, get up!
> In order to assure the freedom of the world,
> We shall fight the black eagle until the end.[165]

Furthermore, the Allied countries had their own particular missions: The Russians wished to unite all Slavic peoples under the banner of Panslavism and *Dushba* (the Slavic Soul).[166] The French were fighting for the principles of 1789 – liberty, equality, brotherhood – and the English claimed to defend the freedom of the small nations, and both promised that, according to the famous formula of H.G. Wells, this would be 'the war that will end war'[167]. As initially the Germans could not present any political ideas of their own, they developed the following strategy: They tried to justify their political system by affirming the unity of militarism and *Kultur* (p. 38) and, as Thomas Mann showed it in an exemplary way, heaped calumny on Western democracy as the outdated 'parliamentarism of the lawyers' and as a 'plutocracy' which only led to useless quarrels and falsified the genuine will of the people.[168] Thereafter, with the support of sympathetic neutrals such as the Swedes Rudolf Kjellén and Gustav Steffen and the germanized English writer Houston Stewart Chamberlain, they forged a specific German conception of democracy, the Ideas of 1914, as the political economist Johann Plenge had dubbed them. They were supposed to substitute the time-worn notions of the French Revolution: Liberty was to be replaced by 'German freedom', defined as 'authority and obedience'; equality by 'solidarity and discipline'; fraternity by 'the service to the community', 'discipline' and 'duty' (see pp. 2, 54). Plenge defined as follows: 'Cooperate, that is the liberty to act; adapt yourself, that is the equality of the service; live in the community, this is the fraternity of the veritable socialism.'[169] In this way the so-called *Volksgemeinschaft* (national community) representing the unified people would reconcile the antagonistic social and political groups.[170] The practical realization of these new ideas in the social and economic sphere would assure the superiority of the 'young German people' and relegate France and Great Britain as declining nations to a second place. This organicist theory considering nations as organisms which are born, mature, age and die was happily applied by the German cartoonists depicting Britain and France as sick, senile and doomed.[171]

Another propaganda topic was the contrast between Western *Zivilisation* and German *Kultur*. In the German parlance, *Zivilisation* had a decidedly negative connotation. It stood for 'mechanical' industrialization, urbanization and capitalism – while German *Kultur*, comprising not only aesthetic values, but also higher education, literacy and social welfare, was creative and spiritual. The widespread poster *Sind wir die Barbaren?* (Are we the barbarians?) contrasted in exact figures the German cultural achievements such as the number of Nobel Prizes, patents and published books, the percentage of illiteracy and the social security benefits with the rather modest figures of the British and the French (Figure 15).

The combination of *Kultur* and German freedom permitted to proclaim a moral task for Germany: to liberate the oppressed nationalities and to raise them to a higher cultural stage. While referring to slogans by the philosopher Johann Gottlieb Fichte such as 'The world mission of German freedom', this conception was also inspired by British and French colonial propaganda which affirmed to act in the service of justice by liberating and civilizing the underdeveloped peoples. Several German propagandists, among them Chamberlain, Paul Rohrbach, Weber and Kurt Hahn, specialist for British affairs at the ZFA and the News Office of the AA, respectively, asked the government to base its imperialistic aims as well on ethical principles: the idea of the self-determination of the peoples and the spread of *Kultur*. Explaining that Britain's moral pretensions had been discredited during the war, it was now Germany's turn to take up the role as the world's moral leader.[172] However, as the practical elaboration of German imperialism in Brest-Litovsk completely thwarted all these idealistic principles (see pp. 69, 123), it was rather the 'great generalissimo on the propaganda front, President Wilson', who with his 14 points took the sting out of the secret treaties of his Allies and established the position of the United States as the world's moral leader.[173]

The dichotomy of *Kultur* and Civilization became a forceful weapon in the hands of the propagandists of both camps. In German cartoons, the Allies perpetrated their war crimes in the name of civilization.[174] They also mocked at the fact that the Western crusaders for democracy were allied with the most reactionary power on the continent, tsarist Russia, which threatened European *Kultur* and chased its peasants with the knout into the fight for 'civilization'.[175] The Allies answered by comparing German *Kultur* with the war crimes of the German army. In a French caricature, a *Herr Professor* walks on corpses and announces: 'What do you want?

This is for *Kultur.*' In another cartoon, the Germans posing as the new Salvation Army proclaim '*Kultur* or Death' and explain: 'If we shoot you, it's only for your good' (Figure 16).

However, such high-brow discussions about the ideas of 1914 were more directed to the elites. In a more popular form of the polarization between Germany and the Allied powers, all foreign influences in language, fashion and culture were to be stamped out. Contemporary and sometimes even classical enemy authors were banished from theatres and opera houses (see pp. 20, 82), unless one could change the name of the composer: in Russia, Franz von Suppé became 'Zupeiskij', in Italy, Franz Lehár became Léon Bard, and Emmerich Kálmán's war operetta *Gold gab ich für Eisen* (I Have Exchanged Gold for Iron) with the new title *Her Soldier Boy* and modifications of music and text had more success in New York and London than in Vienna and Berlin. While contrary to London in New York his name was kept, the enemy composer never received any royalties.[176] In Germany and Austria, men and women were exhorted to abandon London and Parisian fashion and to adopt *Deutsche Mode* instead, preferably made of paper fabric, as cotton and wool were scarce – a laughing stock for Allied propaganda. On 2 August 1915, the French cartoon magazine *La Baïonette* published a special issue on the new fashion in Berlin, and the British cartoonist Frank Reynolds drew some plump and overweight Germans accompanied by an alleged quotation from a German feature: 'Remember that our [the Germans'] physical form is not that of the English and French. German fashion after the War must be modelled on some particular national costume', which referred to Bavarian leather shorts and dirndls.[177]

Cities, villages and streets as well as places of entertainment and dishes had to be renamed. In Russia, St. Petersburg became Petrograd, the Berlinskaya Street became Londonskaya Street. In France, the 'Rue d'Allemagne' in Paris and half a dozen villages with the names 'd'Allemagne' or 'des Allemands' were rebaptized. In Berlin, the Café Windsor and the cabaret *Chat noir* were renamed Kaffee Winzer and *Schwarzer Kater*; military commanders even threatened to close establishments which would not comply, and youth bands smashed their windows. The Americans preferred to eat liberty cabbage instead of *Sauerkraut*. In Britain, German names became a liability: On 27 October 1914, Prince Louis of Battenberg had to resign as First Sea Lord. Finally thousands of naturalized Germans preferred to adopt English names, followed in July 1917 by the English Royal Family who were obliged to change their name from Saxe-Coburg-Gotha to Windsor.[178] Two other incidents sound like jokes: German school children had to pay five pfennig if they used a word of foreign origin like *interessant*, and the Académie française received a proposal to eliminate the 'German' letter 'K' from the French alphabet.[179]

What was the role of duty and sacrifice?

With the exception of Italy, all governments claimed that they went to war only in order to defend the fatherland. But even the Italians tried to justify their intervention by maintaining that they were waging war only to prevent a future aggression by Austria, and after the defeat at Caporetto and the occupation of Venetia by the Austrians, propaganda evoked the defence myth as well.[180] The defensive argument was evident in the case of the Belgians and the French,[181] less so for the British whose 'single biggest propaganda message' (Adrian Gregory) was that they were not responsible for the war and only intervened in order to defend 'poor little Belgium'.[182] But it worked. A British labourer later remembered: 'During these first months [of the war] I had no doubt that our country was in the right.'[183] The Austrians invented a Serbian attack at Temes Kubin in order to fit the pattern,[184] and even the Germans pretended to have been attacked by Russians and French alike. Chancellor von Bethmann Hollweg blamed the Russians through skilful diplomatic manoeuvres[185] and on 3 August 1914 falsely accused the French of having started the war by bombarding Nuremberg and Karlsruhe and invading some German districts – the biggest propaganda lie of the whole war. Even the invasion of Belgium was sometimes justified by the alleged presence of French troops in Namur and Liège (see p. 66). Of course, the ruling elites were well aware of these falsifications. On 1 August 1914, on the very day when Kaiser Wilhelm publicly announced: 'In the middle of peace the enemy attacks us', Admiral Georg A. von Müller commented in his diary: 'The government has been fortunate enough to make us appear as being attacked.'[186] Thus a defence myth was created, which in propaganda was cleverly boiled down to the emotional protection of home and family.[187] It permitted to apply the concept of civic patriotism or dynastic loyalty with its emphasis on duty and holding out – values which became so important for soldiers and civilians alike that, according to Winter, the whole war can be described as the history of holding out.[188] As publicity often referred to war vocabulary – for instance, the scouring powder 'vim' became a 'gun which smashes dirt' and the fashion magazine '*Vogue* dropped bombs of fashion'[189] – the slogan 'Holding out' was adapted correspondingly: 'We must hold out, we will hold out, we shall hold out with our leather soles if they are equipped with the covers "Hold out".'[190]

The idea of duty was sometimes even proclaimed as the highest religious aim, for instance, in the German Lutheran Church.[191] French soldiers' letters as well reveal the efficiency of the ideology of duty: they evoke obedience, authority and following orders.[192] The most important duty of the civilians was to contribute to the war expenses, 'financial conscription' as the German State Secretary of the Treasury, later of the Interior, Karl Helfferich, called it (see p. 91). Intrinsically intertwined with duty was sacrifice. The soldier had to be prepared to contribute the 'blood tax', that is to accept death as the ultimate sacrifice for his fatherland, a conception well prepared by pre-war youth literature and accepted by some soldiers until the end of the war.[193] Some clergymen, for instance, the notorious Bishop Winnington-Ingram and the German Jesuit Christian Pesch, even announced that a glorious death in war was equal to the expiatory death of Jesus and would bring soldiers the crown of martyrdom.[194] In Turkey as well, Islamic propaganda glorified the soldier-martyr offering his life as the supreme sacrifice for religion, fatherland and family.[195] Italian and French propaganda put the concept of 'martyrdom' in the service of the nation's revival: In France, the soldier-martyr 'had given his life so that France may live', in Italy, he will continue his life in the resurrection of a greater and purified fatherland.[196]

The civilian was exhorted to accept food restrictions, longer working hours and financial losses.[197] In an 'Open Letter to the Women of the Nation', Handley C.G. Moule, the Bishop of Durham, wrote endless paragraphs about sacrifice and concluded: 'Sacrifice yourself, give yourself up, to be "something of God", and something for others.'[198] The religious background with its conception of martyrdom is recognizable also for the civilians.[199]

Which rewards were promised?

An Allied caricature of July 1918 compares the German situation in the years 1914 and 1918. In 1914, it shows the German people as a donkey drawing a chariot with Germania, a prince and a general on it and following a carrot called 'Victory'. In 1918 Germania, the donkey and the chariot are completely worn out, the prince and the general are replaced by two fat war profiteers, and the carrot is called 'Ersatz Victory' (Figure 17). Whatever the situation was, a victorious peace was promulgated as the great reward for all the sacrifices and sufferings during the war.[200] A song in the German stage play *1914* hammered into the audience: 'We can win, we will win, we must win, we shall win.'[201] Thus, propagandists of both camps often supported by posters always affirmed that their troops were on the road to victory.[202] This topic was usually accompanied by allegations that the enemy was nearly finished, for instance, when French newspapers affirmed: 'The enemy has lost five million men' or 'Half the German shells are made of cardboard, they don't even burst.'[203] Initially most people believed such news. When in September 1914 Allied newspapers reported that Berlin was in a state of famine, an American visitor brought provisions for three weeks including two huge sacks of flour.[204]

It was equally important to deny any defeats and drawbacks or at least play them down with comforting interpretations such as 'Russia's Traditional Tactics: "Reculer pour mieux sauter" '.[205] Examples on the German side were the defeat at the Marne (see p. 16) or the declaration of war by Romania on 27 August 1916. The political and military elites considered the latter as a heavy blow because of the significance of the Romanian oil fields. Ludendorff had a nervous breakdown and did not know where to find troops against this new enemy. The German people, of course, should by no means be alarmed by this difficult situation. A caricature of the *Simplicissimus* tried to reassure public opinion by a very clever trick: It shows the sinking ship of the Entente, full of ugly rats, with Romania as another rat climbing on board. The commentary says: 'The last rat is jumping on the sinking ship of the Entente' (Figure 18). Normally if a ship sinks, the rats are leaving, and this classical metaphor had been used already in another caricature, when Montenegro capitulated in January 1916.[206] In the Romanian case, a ship sinks and the rats climb on it against all logic. With the help of a downright paradox, a great disadvantage of the Central Powers is being transformed into a triumph – a masterful example of psychological brainwashing. As the human subconscious does not think logically and works with transferences, such an image can have a deep influence once it has passed the sphere of reason and establishes itself in the mind.

Prophecies about the bad fate of the enemy leaders could also reassure people that their country would certainly win. In Allied cartoons, the Kaiser shudders because he sees the gallows awaiting him, and he worries about the climate of St. Helena where he will be sent after his defeat like Napoleon – a theme also used in a British war comedy where he sits on a stone with the inscription St. Helena.[207] The Germans depict the guillotine waiting for French President Poincaré.[208] They also show Tsar Nicholas II melting lead and throwing it into cold water in order to see the future: the lead turns into a skull; at the same time in the underground, revolutionaries are melting lead as well for the production of bullets (Figure 19).

Despite all propaganda efforts, from 1917 onwards, soldiers and civilians in both camps had enough of a war which did not seem to end and, as Gregory has pointed out, the promise of the inevitable victory contrasted with the increasing demand for more sacrifices.[209] As a consequence, quite a few people openly declared that they had no hope for victory anymore and demanded peace by negotiation.[210] Propaganda, however, insisted on a victorious peace: Charismatic personalities such as Clemenceau, Lloyd George and Hindenburg successfully stemmed the tide by proclaiming to fight 'up to the very end', 'until the knock out', and 'victory is certain' – slogans which represented not only the unfailing confidence in final victory but also a typically military point of view refusing any peace settlement.[211] Several specific arguments can be discerned:

First of all, people should not accept the '*morte per niente*' (to die for nothing), as it was called in Italy, that they had suffered all those years and even died for nothing.[212] In a French caricature, a man advocates peace on the basis of the status quo ante, but an invalid replies: 'OK, but in this case give me back my lost leg.'[213] In Britain, some people said: 'We want to take revenge for the death of our sons!', and French and British generals tried to hammer such messages into their soldiers' heads.[214] In their manifesto of September 1917, the delegates of the socialist conference at Stockholm explained why rewards were necessary: 'All the capitalist governments are afraid to return from the battlefield without spoils, burdened only with debts [...] and the curse of millions of widows and orphans'.[215]

In France and Britain, people were made believe that after the victory over Prussian militarism eternal peace would reign on earth[216] (see also pp. 51, 146). In Germany, people were told that only a smashing victory with territorial conquests would guarantee the geopolitical safety of the country. For the masses, victory and peace were convincingly blended together in pictures with catchy slogans: for instance, on German match boxes a soldier and a worker shake hands and pronounce, 'Through labour to victory, through victory to peace.'[217]

In Germany, the impressive number of victories produced the following argument expressed in Ludendorff's *Guidelines for the Patriotic Instruction* of July 1917: 'The result of the war is already in our favour, we only have to safeguard this' – an argument literally repeated as late as 19 July 1918 when the war was definitely lost.[218]

Another argument was the appeal to fear. After a 'bad peace', that is a 'German peace' after a defeat, Britain would be at the mercy of the Kaiser.[219] Conversely, if Britain were victorious, the Germans, crushed under enormous war indemnities, loss of territories, high food prices and the ruin of their economy, would be slaving along for the Allies in Europe and even in the Sahara (Figure 20).[220] Hunger was an additional argument: Already in Ireland and during the Boer War in South Africa, the British had caused famine and transformed these blooming countries into 'hunger states', and after their victory they would continue the blockade and starve out the Germans. A poster of 1918 cleverly resumed: 'If, with his army and his hate, the enemy wins, the workshops will be empty. The doors will be closed, and you will hungrily have to go away.'[221] Leaflets reinforced this argument with hateful quotations from the Allied press like 'The only good German I know is a dead one'.[222] The sole alternative was: 'We must hold out and win at any cost.'[223] Even when in September 1918 the Germans had definitely lost the war, the Prussian Minister of War still argued in the same way: 'As the enemy insists on a peace paid with our enslavement, we have to continue fighting.'[224]

Rewards to combatants also served propaganda purposes: medals, decorations, promotions and other distinctions had a 'stimulation effect' arousing the feelings of pride and happiness.[225] Thus, the military elites were quite generous with them: The Germans awarded the Iron Cross first class 218,000 times, second class 5.2 million times; the French the Military Medal 230,000 times and the War Cross, not introduced until April 1915, 1.2 million times; and the Austrians the Medal for Bravery in gold 4,661 times, in silver first class 175,000 times, second class 360,000 times, in bronze 1.2 million times. Their medals also carried additional benefits: allowances of 30, 15 and 7.50 kronen per month for golden and silver medals, respectively. Higher medals such as the Military Order of Maria Theresa and the French Légion d'honneur were usually reserved for officers, while the British Victoria Cross was also bestowed on quite a few privates. In Britain and France, the 'Rolls of Honour' containing the mentions in dispatch, the military medals and the nominations in the Légion d'honneur were regularly published and, just like in the German *Deutsche Kriegsnachrichten* (*DK*), the corresponding heroic deeds were reported in a detailed way, in the French *Bulletin des armées de la République* and in *The Times History of the War*. Typical is the following story of a 'successful onslaught': two British lieutenants with 10 soldiers attacked a German machine gun brigade of c. 100 men, killed or wounded 30 and took 50 prisoners.[226] In France, however, so many shirkers got the war cross and also false chevrons indicating the length of service and the number of wounds that angry *poilus* saying 'chevron does not mean risk' did not wear them anymore.[227] In Italy, most war medals were awarded only after the war and therefore could not stimulate soldiers to a better performance. Courageous soldiers would get other benefits, for instance, additional leave and more assistance to their families.[228] Some army chaplains and religious broadsides promised a more obscure reward: When the soldier fell on the battlefield, all his sins would be forgiven and he would go straight to heaven or at least spend less time in purgatory – a rather heretical view.[229]

Civilians got no immediate rewards except war bonds because the interest rate of 5 per cent was quite good compared to the usual rate of 3 to 3.5 per cent, and few people expected that the money would not be paid back. Furthermore, they were promised a golden age after the war. In Britain, cheap housing under the slogan 'Homes fit for heroes' was announced, but the low-rent housing construction scheme starting in 1919 was already abolished two years later.[230] In Italy, land was promised to peasant soldiers but after the war nothing came out of it. In all countries, class distinctions were supposed to disappear and a *Volksgemeinschaft* (egalitarian community), an *égalisation sociale* (social equalization), a 'more equitable society' would emerge with equal votes and social reform[231] – unbelievable visions which were pulled over people's eyes in touching novels, films and stage plays (see pp. 52, 80).

Some measures were indeed adopted, such as more adequate war pensions, better allowances for soldiers' families and protection against eviction. The French government even introduced a rent moratorium for families of soldiers and low rents which in Paris represented 88 per cent of the bails. Furthermore, various economists and socialist party functionaries elaborated more or less detailed plans about future social welfare policies, about 'Christian' or 'German' socialism and the participation of workers in corporate direction, called in Germany *Mitbestimmung*, and in Britain 'a fuller share in the gains of industry'.[232] However, the political leaders preferred to leave everything vague. For instance, in a speech in the Reichstag, Bethmann Hollweg only vaguely mentioned the 'enormous political, intellectual, economical and social tasks which were supposed to be solved after the war', but refused explicitly 'to reward the people for what it had done [during the war]'.[233] In his 'Easter message' on 7 April 1917, the Kaiser promised a reform of the infamous Prussian suffrage system after the war but omitted to include equality of vote – a crucial point. Two months later this was announced but the final decision was left to the discretion of the Prussian Lower Chamber which could not be expected to accept this.[234]

In Italy, the chimera of a more just and egalitarian future society was inspired by the 'Wilsonian myth' promising exactly this to all Italians.[235] When in 1918 the YMCA and the American Red Cross joined the Italian propagandists, they distributed immediate rewards: refugee camps, orphanages, food and clothing, cookers, money for poor families, hundreds of thousands of propaganda booklets and pamphlets, not to speak of innumerable souvenirs such as American flags, ribbons, posters and postcards.[236]

Let us not forget the rewards promised to neutral countries if they entered the war: The Allies offered Italy Trent and Trieste plus vast Slavonic and German speaking territories, but kept their word only partly after the war. In vain Germany offered Spain Gibraltar; Italy, Savoy, Nice, Corsica and Tunis; and Mexico, Texas and California.[237] Both camps also promised independence to the oppressed nationalities in the colonies and supranational empires, though only to those, of course, who lived under the rule of the enemy (see pp. 118–37).

Chapter 4

HOW DID THE TECHNIQUES AND THE
DISTRIBUTION OF PROPAGANDA FUNCTION?

In a world without radio, television and internet 'our only means of getting news was through the papers and by word of mouth' remembers a British shop assistant in her autobiography.[1] These two essential media will be presented in the following two sections, while the supplementary but equally important indoctrination through the channels of entertainment will be analysed in Chapter 5.

How were people orally indoctrinated?

The most elementary medium to brainwash people was still oral indoctrination.[2] Politicians, mayors, teachers, clergymen and trade union leaders organized numerous meetings with patriotic songs, recitals and speeches. Teachers brainwashed children, clergymen their flocks, trade unionists their workers, and last but not least, officers their soldiers. University professors gave lectures everywhere (see pp. 28, 109), but addressed only educated people, not simple folks. In Austria, 'information workers' travelled round the country indoctrinating soldiers and civilians alike with lectures and slide shows.[3] In Turkey, writers and poets occasionally read poems and stories to the soldiers.[4]

In Britain, the only country without compulsory military service, the PRC organized 800 mass rallies throughout the country. In a quasi-religious atmosphere, military and chapel bands played patriotic songs, and proficient speakers including ecclesiastic dignitaries warned against the hellish consequences of the invasion by the Kaiser and urged all able-bodied men to take up arms.[5] Even those unwilling to become cannon fodder were frequently pushed to enlist on the spot by the cheering crowds, especially by women of the Order of the White Feather who insulted procrastinators at the meetings and in the streets and decorated them with white feathers, in Britain a symbol of cowardice. Allegedly somebody got so many feathers that he made a fan of it.[6] In France as well, women started a witch hunt against alleged shirkers, harassing young men in the streets and even sending tens of thousands of denunciation letters to the authorities.[7] In Austria, women were less aggressive, but their disdainful looks were meaningful enough.[8]

The undisputed masters of oral indoctrination in World War I were the so-called Four Minute Men of the American CPI. They spoke in public buildings such as theatres, clubs, churches and especially in cinemas during the usual four minutes intermission between movies. This method was not new; it had been used already by army recruiters in Canada from 1915.[9] They were local men – with a few women and even school children as well – addressing the crowds in familiar language, sometimes also in the languages of the immigrants, but the topics of the campaigns were developed centrally in weekly changing bulletins with model speeches and detailed instructions of how to present them. Topics were for instance 'Danger to America', 'Unmasking German propaganda' or 'Liberty Loan'. Starting in July 1917 with 2,500 speakers, they finally numbered 75,000 speakers at the end of the war, and held a total number of 7,555,190 speeches to 400 million people even in the most remote towns and villages and in colonies like the Philippines.[10] In addition, the CPI organized a speaking division which coordinated several national speakers' offices, organized conferences with war veterans and established a list of 10,000 speakers.[11]

Oral propaganda extended also to neutral and even Allied countries. Embassies and cultural institutes organized lectures of intellectuals; for instance in spring 1916, Alfred Baudrillart, professor at the Catholic Institute of Paris and president of the Committee for Propaganda in Neutral Countries, toured Spain for five weeks.[12] Politicians were also very active: In Italy, Belgian deputies propagated war against Austria, the German social democratic deputy Philipp Scheidemann travelled to the Netherlands, and in Italy his colleague Albert Südekum so actively advocated the neutrality that his interlocutors were called *sudekumizzati*.[13] In the United States, British and German propagandists competed for winning public opinion, often with the help of locals, but those in the German service were either brought over from Germany or were of German origin and not familiar with the American way of thinking. As Horace Peterson points out, they were 'constantly preaching, intemperately and pugnaciously, without moderation nor tact and finesse'.[14] In the Ottoman Empire with its numerous illiterates, oral indoctrination was even more important; hence traditional story tellers and soothsayers were employed, and the Germans organized pro-German rallies with Turkish and Arab speakers.[15] The CPI was especially active in France and Italy. In France, it organized lectures in universities and armament factories in order to prevent labour disturbances and 'to put the story of America's greatness [...] into the minds of the local leaders of thought, as well as into the minds of the people'. In Italy, the CPI sent public speakers with lantern slides to 13,000 cities and towns who were enthusiastically received by a population under the spell of the 'Wilsonian Myth'.[16] The CPI had also found an ingenious method to influence public opinion in Germany: It placed appropriate news in neutral newspapers, especially in the Netherlands, which were then picked up by German journalists.[17]

In summer 1917, oral indoctrination in the European countries reached new dimensions in order to boost the morale of war-weary soldiers and civilians alike. In Britain and Germany, workers were so fed up with propaganda that they would not come to propaganda rallies and had to be indoctrinated in the factories.[18] In Britain, the successor of the PRC, the NWAC, founded in July 1917, even surpassed the activities of its predecessor and held a total number of 100,000 meetings, all of them with well-paid and carefully briefed speakers, some even with professionals, and like in Germany with soldiers on leave.[19] The campaigns were very well prepared. From Monday to Saturday, two meetings took place in different locations of a town or in different villages, local dignitaries and distinguished guest speakers implied public approval, and a ritual with songs and the national anthem produced some sort of 'participatory patriotism'.[20] The speakers recalled the German atrocities, warned against the dishonesty of the German diplomats, the betrayal of the British pacifists and above all the disastrous consequences of a 'German Peace' and admonished the people: 'Should civilians fail to accept necessary sacrifices now, [...] future generations would suffer'.[21] In summer 1918, ritualized 'War Anniversaries' were celebrated with open air religious services, processions to commemorative shrines and the attendance of numerous dignitaries from the mayor and the bishop over distinguished war veterans to members of the fire brigade and the Sunday School Union.[22]

In Germany, Patriotic Instruction employed special 'instruction officers', mostly reserve officers with appropriate professions such as teachers, lawyers or clergymen who after intensive training organized compulsory lectures for the soldiers on a weekly basis. At the home front, the usual propagandists – clerics, professors, teachers, trade union leaders – were now joined by these officers and 'reliable' soldiers, who helped them organize patriotic assemblies and gave speeches admonishing desperate civilians to hold out.[23] As schoolchildren, soldiers' wives and workers were important targets, each school inspector was to be advised by an instruction officer, and members of women's organizations and trade unions were solicited as speakers. In April 1918, the military commander in Württemberg even organized a propaganda conference with 25 instruction officers and numerous representatives of trade unions of Christian and liberal leanings.[24] Great emphasis was placed on personal discussions, because 'many people either do not read or do not believe what they are reading'.[25] In a private talk, propaganda would be less invasive and rather low key. For instance, a teacher in the small town of Schopfheim in the Duchy of Baden in autumn 1916 reported to the School Board how he had consoled a war widow in a bar and cautiously refuted the anti-war arguments of soldiers on leave.[26] Especially in smaller towns and at the countryside, 'the teacher worked, in practice, as a propaganda agent of the state'.[27] In France, oral propaganda remained in the hands of the teachers and private organizations like the UGACPE.[28] In Italy, the Servizio P employed specialized officers for oral indoctrination of soldiers and civilians alike, who used prefabricated forms of conversation with simple and convincing arguments adapted to the intellectual capacities of the people.[29]

Oral propaganda in enemy countries was more difficult to organize, and only the French and to a lesser extent the British succeeded: The French smuggled approximately 400 propaganda agents with passports of German POWs from Switzerland to Germany where they could rely on a network of members of the war-hostile USPD ready to propagate their messages. In the Netherlands, the

British employed 300 agents, some of them Dutch war correspondents who could freely travel to Germany and even inspect the frontlines. Besides, 50,000–60,000 Dutch cross-border workers did not only smuggle propaganda material and were paid fl. 30 (€202) per kilo but also indoctrinated their German colleagues in the factories.[30]

A special variety of oral indoctrination were international conferences with their messages being multiplied by press covering. The greatest German success was the Third Nationalities Congress in Lausanne in June 1916, presided by the Belgian archivist Paul Otlet. More than 400 delegates from Ireland, Egypt and from the alien peoples of the Tsarist Empire denounced British colonial rule and Russian oppression, and completely discredited the Allied claim to fight for the freedom of the small peoples. It was so cleverly organized by two German undercover agents (see pp. 122, 148–53), that nobody imagined that the AA was pulling the strings.[31] In April 1918, the Allies organized a similar congress with delegates of the minorities of Austria-Hungary in Rome where Italians and Yugoslavs pretended to agree about their territorial quarrels.[32]

How were people indoctrinated by the media?

After oral indoctrination, the most common instrument of propaganda was printed matter: newspapers, leaflets, brochures and books, except in Russia, Italy and Turkey where the illiteracy rate was high. Such propaganda at home was relatively easy because it was efficiently supported by censorship. Propaganda material was lavishly distributed and press conferences were convened. Their main task was not to convey information but to spread propaganda and downright lies. A well-informed witness, Hellmut von Gerlach, editor-in-chief of the German left-liberal weekly *Welt am Montag*, later reported how the Press Office of III b, later the KPA, proceeded in Germany. The conferences were held by officers according to military principles. Questions were allowed but not necessarily answered. Journalists known for their critical attitudes like, for instance, Rudolf Breitscheid of the social democratic *Leipziger Volkszeitung* (*LV*), were not admitted. At the first press conference on 10 August 1914, the reporting colonel imposed patriotic lies: 'Even if half of the soldiers have fallen you should still write that the success has been met with fabulously few victims.'[33] When journalists had doubts about the official information, the army representatives insisted that the foreign newspapers were lying. Losses were minimized: for instance, on 15 November 1914 it was announced that a few hundred soldiers were missing, although the official lists of losses contained already the names of 55,000 soldiers. In the same way, the defeats of July and August 1918 were explained by strategic reshuffles.[34] In Britain as well, optimistic articles were de rigueur not only for the home front, but also for neutral countries. Already in September 1914, Masterman had recruited 25 leading writers and journalists, among them Doyle, Wells and John Galsworthy, to produce propaganda pamphlets.[35] As in Germany more and more people preferred to read socialist and pacifist leaflets instead of newspapers, the KPA and the military commanders proceeded to print and distribute leaflets as well.[36] In the United States, press conferences were not necessary: The Printed Word Division of the CPI had the monopoly on information. It mobilized the leading writers of the country who produced syndicate features for the press without payment.[37]

War correspondents and cameramen played an important role in reporting from the front. Already from August 1914, the German OHL admitted them while the British and French High Commands hesitated for fear that they might divulge military secrets. Hence at the outset of the war, the market of newsreels in neutral countries was dominated by German propaganda.[38] Some British and French correspondents with fake passports and laissez-passers tried to get around the restrictions but met with mixed success.[39] The only person authorized by the British headquarters to make reports was Lieutenant-Colonel Ernest Swinton, but his work was censored by no less than six different officials including Kitchener in person. Swinton soon suffered from 'censoritis', that is he was always afraid to say too much and thus practiced rigorous self-censorship. Finally in July 1915 he was relieved from his task because from May 1915 the authorities had admitted British journalists to the front, in autumn 1916 also their French colleagues, overseen by MI7 and Wellington House.[40] In France, it functioned the other way round: From 1915 to 1916, British and American war correspondents were accepted whereas their French colleagues had to wait until June 1917.[41] As a result, French newspapers published detailed articles about the British troops but very little about their own soldiers. It goes without saying that the correspondents were always 'embedded' by officers, had to travel and even to write in pool with colleagues and were heavily censored, so that they finally resigned themselves to group self-censorship.[42] From September 1917, the war correspondents at the German front were replaced by special officers.[43] The more than 100 Austrian correspondents under the control of the KPQ – among them famous writers like Rainer M. Rilke, Alexander Roda Roda and Alfred Polgar – got an exceptional treatment: They were lavishly housed, wined and dined in a splendid Hungarian chateau, but could visit the front only after one of the rare victories and otherwise had to rely on the succinct information of the AOK, copy their reports from newspapers or write fake stories.[44] On the Russian front, neutral war correspondents could visit some rear lines in Galicia and were afterwards restricted to Warsaw and soon further back.[45] In August and September 1915, the Italian army organized a *gita*, a sort of sightseeing tour for 50 Italian and foreign journalists. They were accompanied by military censors imposing explanations for the military failure such as the numeric superiority of the Austrians and the incompetence of certain generals. Thereafter no more visits were allowed until the creation of a special press bureau which admitted nine Italian and three foreign correspondents writing heavily censored reports on a regular basis.[46] In America, against the desperate resistance of General John J. Pershing, the CPI organized the sending of war correspondents to Europe who under severe censorship conditions (see p. 23) 'produced the finest propaganda that ever appeared in any country', as Creel later remembered with pride.[47]

Propaganda material to neutral countries had to be prepared very well. The most important targets were Spain, the United States before their declaration of war, and Italy before and after its declaration of war. Backward states like Russia, Italy and Austria-Hungary did very little, whereas Britain, France, Germany and later the United States heavily invested in propaganda abroad. Their offices functioned along similar lines and were divided into various sections:[48]

- Translating and analysing the foreign press, collecting cuts and writing reports. In France, 50 persons analysed 400 journals; in Germany initially only 13.
- Writing propaganda articles and submitting them to foreign newspapers. Preparing brochures, leaflets, posters and special newspapers such as the *Continental Times, Die Wahrheit ins Ausland, El Heraldo* (German), *Die freie Zeitung* and *Feldpost* (French), and sending them abroad (see pp. 112–14).
- Collecting the addresses of foreign institutions and individuals as receivers and multipliers of propaganda – the British extracted from the *Who Is Who* and other sources 260,000 addresses in the United States while the Germans collected only 5,000 there and 21,000 from other neutral countries.
- Receiving foreign journalists and organizing conferences and tours for them.
- Establishing missions abroad, recruiting agents and selecting speakers.
- Coordinating private propaganda organizations.
- Later adding sections for photography, film and newsreels in cooperation with independent firms or attached to them.

Newspaper propaganda in neutral countries was much easier than one might expect. Already before the war, articles in foreign newspapers were easily placed against appropriate payment. These activities not only continued but reached unprecedented heights.[49] Newspapers were regularly bribed, subsidized, completely bought or even founded. Agents bought the complete circulation of an enemy-friendly newspaper early in the morning and destroyed it, acquired distribution firms and made sure that at their newsstands only friendly newspapers were sold. They denounced enemy-bribing cases to the local police and had editors and enemy agents arrested. They also published lists of enemy-bribed newspapers and indicated the amounts of money used. Bribing was even necessary in some Allied countries, as the British came to know when they wanted to insert articles in French newspapers.[50] Sometimes Germans and French would try to bribe the same journalist, and this man would simply tailor his articles in favour of the highest bidder.[51] Eduardo Scarfoglio, the editor of the Italian newspaper *Matino*, received from the Germans 25,000 lire per month (€69,000) and from the Austrians 1,000 lire (€2,750). When the French banker Louis Dreyfus asked him to work for the Allies, he demanded 500,000 francs (€1.35 million). Dreyfus would not or could not pay this sum, and Scarfoglio continued to support the Central Powers and advocate Italian neutrality. Even when Italy joined the Allies, some bribed newspapers like *Vittoria* continued to print German propaganda, but were promptly censored or suspended for several weeks. When the Germans stopped paying, the editor went bankrupt.[52] Clever people such as Salvador Cánovas Cervantes, the editor of the Spanish newspaper *La Tribuna*, and Gabrys, the editor of the *Annales des Nationalités*, *Pro Lithuania* (in French) and *Litauen* (in German), received money from both sides.[53] Very efficient was also the corruption of news agencies because in this way propaganda would reach several newspapers at the same time. The Spanish news agency *Fabra* became a branch of the official French news agency *Havas* and inundated Spanish newspapers with French propaganda.[54]

The sums used for corruption fluctuated between £100 and £1,000 per month, depending on the importance of the newspaper. To buy or to found a newspaper cost £8,000 (£344,000); to bribe a foreign news agency could cost up to 600,000 French francs (€1.6 million) per year.[55] Throughout the war, the French spent for newspaper corruption 20 million French francs (€54 million) from the secret funds of the French Ministry of Foreign Affairs. The Germans spent for propaganda abroad, from August 1914 till 31 January 1918, a sum of 382 million mark (€1.45 billion). However, there was no guarantee that such substantial expenses led to noticeable results.[56]

The CPI did not bribe foreign newspapers but flooded neutral and some Allied countries like France and Italy with American feature articles, illustrations and other information by mail, cable and wireless; it distributed pamphlets upwards of 100,000 copies to schoolteachers and other multipliers and daily news bulletins to journalistic, military and political circles; it also opened reading rooms and brought neutral journalists to France.[57]

The system of bribing newspapers functioned even in enemy countries: The Germans bribed *Le Journal*, *Le Bonnet rouge* and *La Tranchée républicaine* with limited success because their machinations were finally discovered. *Le Journal* did not change its patriotic tendency, while the two latter journals were suspended and the involved journalists executed (see p. 12). The French intention to bribe the *Kölnische Volkszeitung* failed completely; the money was transferred through an unreliable middleman, and the political course of the newspaper remained staunchly Pan-German and anti-Allies.[58]

Italy was a special case. During its neutrality, it was flooded with propaganda by both camps. But after the country had joined the Allies in May 1915, it was considered the weakest member of the coalition, and the Germans even stepped up their propaganda. They obliged 60,000 Italian workers in Germany who were organized in the League of the Emigrants (Lega degli emigranti) to forward their German-controlled newspaper *Il lavoro* to families and friends in Italy. They established a network of socialist and pacifist agitators, funded them generously – 200,000 Swiss francs (CHF 1.8 million) in 1918 alone – and tried to send them weapons and ammunition via Switzerland, but this was prevented by Swiss police. They attempted to organize hunger demonstrations, strikes, acts of sabotage and mutinies, and they allegedly even tried to win the support of the Sicilian Mafia and to proclaim a separatist republic in Southern Italy and Sicily. However, it is questionable if their activities were successful. In case they really had a hand in the pie during the Turin riots in May 1917, they were unable to transform them into organized revolutionary action.[59]

The United States was the most contested target in the propaganda war between Britain and Germany.[60] While the British tried to win them as an ally, the Germans were content to keep them neutral. The British had by far the better chances. All news from Europe had to pass through British censorship and postal control (see pp. 12, 14) and thus American journalists were only exposed to the British version of the war. Soon the American authorities also monitored the coded messages transmitted by wireless from Germany and imposed a decoded English translation. Furthermore, the British propaganda approach was much better than the German one. While the Germans established an official press office in New York under the former State Secretary of Colonial Affairs, Bernhard Dernburg, and a bit later two other information offices which forwarded German propaganda brochures and news sheets to the press, Wellington House sent Gilbert Parker, a Canadian novelist settled down in Britain and married to a rich American heiress, to the United States. However, he did not open an official office but forwarded all his material discreetly and unmarked as a 'concerned citizen' under his name or under the names of the authors.[61] He always accompanied his deliveries with a cautiously phrased personal letter to 13,000 and in 1916 to 260,000 multipliers. Partly due to his wife's widespread social network, he also contacted numerous people privately and enlisted quite a few politicians, journalists and teachers as propagandists for the British cause. Parker's material was partly written by well-known British writers and well adapted to the American mentality and the American way of thinking and reasoning.

The Germans disposed of only 5,000 addresses and their propaganda was pompous and legalistic without taking into consideration sentiment and emotion. For instance, in his pamphlet *Germany and the War* published in *Fatherland*, an American weekly subsidized by the Germans, Dernburg found no word of regret for the civilian victims in Belgium but insisted that this country had already stationed French troops in Namur and Liège in July 1914.[62] When he legitimized the sinking of the *Lusitania* (see p. 39) in the same way, he offended American public opinion so much that he had to return to Germany. German propaganda was also hampered by the sabotage actions against the American armament factories organized by the German military and naval attachés, and by the foundation of a fictitious armament factory. It ordered important quantities of war resources, later delayed and finally cancelled the orders, but in this manner prevented the British to purchase urgently needed supplies for a certain time. When the American Secret Service found about these activities, it was widely reported in the press and the Germans never got rid of the indelible mark of spies and saboteurs.

On the other hand, the Central Powers could count on the numerous German immigrants and their descendants, organized in various associations, the most important being the National German-American Alliance and the newly created American Independence Union. Their main propaganda action was in favour of an embargo on arms and munitions shipments to the Allies as a retaliatory measure against the British blockade interfering with American trade. Numerous mass meetings and petitions with millions of signatures supported the Vollmer and Barthold resolution in Congress, which demanded to completely prohibit

American military exports. Quite a few politicians, even members of the president's cabinet, approved of it. However, the resolution found no majority in Congress, and President Wilson, entirely under the sway of the Allied animalization propaganda, defended the exports in private with the words: 'Gentlemen, the Allies are standing with their backs to the wall, fighting wild beasts.'[63]

A special variety of propaganda were official peace proposals of the Central Powers and the Allied replies. These were widely published and tried to elicit a favourable reaction not only in the neutral countries, especially in the United States, but also in the war-weary populations of both belligerent camps. Bethmann Hollweg's note of 12 December 1916 inviting the Allies to peace negotiations was welcomed by a great part of the German people, especially the followers of the liberal and social democratic parties and also distributed as a leaflet among Russian and French troops.[64] In their answer on 29 December, the Entente denounced the Germans as aggressors, warmed up their war crimes and pointed out that their note eluded 'penalties, reparations and guarantees'. In France, newspapers and politicians like Briand condemned the note with the same words as 'a German trap' aimed at dividing the Allies.[65] These arguments were, of course, only propaganda pretexts. Britain and France refused or ignored the chancellor's note and also the following peace resolution of the Reichstag of July 1917 because they could only realize their principal war aim – 'to sustainably weaken Germany politically, militarily and economically', as the French historian Georges-Henri Soutou puts it – by a war *à outrance*.[66] However, in Germany the Annexationists (see p. 119), with General Ludendorff at their head, welcomed the Allied attitude because they in turn wanted to completely crush the Entente in order to realize a 'German peace' with huge conquests.[67] In 1919, the former Austrian Minister of Foreign Affairs, Ottokar Count Czernin, wrote in his memoirs: 'Neither the Entente nor the ruling, all-powerful military party [in Germany] wished for a peace of understanding. They both wished to be victorious and to enforce a peace of violence on the defeated adversary.'[68] For this reason, in both camps all demands of the opposition for peace negotiations were refuted by blaming the intransigence of the enemy. As Afflerbach rightly observes, the hard liners on both sides 'needed each other, both to pursue their external goals and to keep the opposition in check at home'.[69] One could even add that they appreciated each other. In his war memoirs, Ludendorff condemned the conciliatory course of the German government and wrote: 'In this war Clemenceau and Lloyd George with a strong force of will put their peoples in the service of victory'.[70] In Germany, the refusal of the Entente strengthened official propaganda to continue the combat by all means.[71] Four weeks later the unrestricted submarine warfare was declared.

In February 1918, Ludendorff had the opportunity to return the favours of the Allied warmongers.[72] On 29 November 1917, Lord Lansdowne had published in the *Daily Telegraph* a dramatic appeal against the prolongation of the war, warned that this would 'spell the ruin for the civilized world', and asked the government to encourage the German peace party by promising that it did not desire the annihilation of Germany as a great power or to change its constitution. At the same time, he considered the evacuation and compensation of Belgium as an important

British war aim.[73] This letter triggered a whole propaganda war in Britain and Germany alike which is worthwhile analysing. In Germany, a fortnight later Prince Max von Baden in a speech at the First Badenian Chamber replied to Lansdowne. He did not mention him directly but spoke of forces in Britain and France who 'do not want a peace of violence, but a peace compatible with the honour and the security of their countries'. However, he did not dare to propose the independence and compensation of Belgium stubbornly refused by the Annexationists.[74] In Germany, the liberal press positively reacted to this speech while in Britain only two newspapers took notice of it: *The Morning Post*, depending on the heavily curtailed and censored version of the news agency Reuter, published a few one-sided extracts, and the pacifist journal *The Nation*, having secretly procured the complete text with a delay of four weeks, considered it as 'an answer to Lansdowne and Hugh Cecil' and printed extensive quotes in its edition of 12 January 1918.[75] In Britain, Prime Minister Lloyd George rejected Lansdowne's initiative in public, but behind the scenes he was busy opening peace negotiations himself. Already in September he was ready to accept separate peace negotiations proposed by the German State Secretary of the AA, Kühlmann. However, when on 24 and 27 September he submitted the question to his War Cabinet, all members were opposed and insisted on consulting the Allies first. In November, it was the turn of Czernin to propose peace negotiations. This time Lloyd George sent the South African General Jan Christian Smuts, member of his War Cabinet, twice to discuss this matter with an Austrian representative in Geneva. When on 25 December Czernin invited the Western Allies to join the peace conference at Brest-Litovsk, Lloyd George tried to rally support for his project of a compromise peace in the War Cabinet and in the army. He even cautiously tried to mobilize public opinion by telling the editors of the *Manchester Guardian* who supported Lansdowne: 'I can't go on with this bloody business [of war]: I'd rather resign.'[76] During the decisive meeting of the War Cabinet on 28 December, he argued again in favour of a compromise peace and was even prepared to offer Courland and Lithuania to the Germans in exchange for their colonies and Alsace-Lorraine. However, he again encountered fierce opposition, especially from Foreign Secretary Lord Arthur J. Balfour and Minister of Blockade Lord Robert Cecil, and was obliged to give up his conciliatory attitude. In his speech of 5 January 1918, he closed the door to any negotiations by demanding the dismemberment of Turkey, the cession of Alsace-Lorraine and the African colonies from Germany and the 'genuine self-government on democratic principles' for the peoples of Austria-Hungary which would result in the disintegration of the Danubian Monarchy. His vacillations on this point, which rather modify his traditional image as the 'knock out' blower of the Allies, were unfortunately overlooked by recent research.[77]

Despite Lloyd George's speech of 5 January, neither British nor German political circles gave up their propaganda for peace negotiations. In Britain, a special Lansdowne committee under the liberal politician William Lygon Earl Beauchamp and the journalist Francis W. Hirst of the pacifist journal *Common Sense* was founded, and in a speech on 31 January, Lansdowne demanded a revision of the British war aims and announced the possibility of a 'clean peace in good time'. During a stormy debate in Parliament on 11 and 12 February 1918, several deputies insisted on a change of government, on 12 February 1918 the liberal pacifist MP Robert Outhwaite demanded a cabinet Lansdowne, and next day he was supported by the liberal MP Charles Trevelyan with the words 'that a Lansdowne government would respond to the real will of the moderate British people'.[78] Somewhat later, Walter Runciman, former Minister of Trade in the cabinet of Herbert H. Asquith and prominent adversary of Lloyd George, launched an appeal for 'an intimate meeting' of responsible representatives of the belligerent powers in order to bring things out into the open and to get closer to peace. On 25 February, Chancellor Hertling felt obliged to intervene as well. He welcomed Runciman's proposal and even suggested that general peace could be discussed on the basis of the 'Four Principles' just proclaimed by President Wilson on 11 February. He also disclaimed any project to annex Belgium and had indeed never acknowledged neither the independence (*onafhankelijkheid*) of Flanders proclaimed by the separatist Flemish Council on 22 December 1917 nor its light version of political autonomy (*zelfstandigheid*), imposed on 19 January 1918 by the appropriate administration in Berlin. On the other hand, he indirectly warmed up the classical German propaganda argument that before the War French troops had been stationed in Belgium (see pp. 54, 66) and insisted on preventing this country to become 'a deployment zone of enemy machinations' – a clause which would clearly limit Belgium's sovereignty after the war.[79] On 5 March, Lansdowne answered the chancellor in a second letter to the *Daily Telegraph*. Although he asked the British government to accept Hertling's suggestion of peace talks, he demanded a clear announcement from the chancellor about the evacuation of Belgium with the guarantee of its complete independence after the war.[80] However, in his next speech in the Reichstag, Hertling did not mention Belgium at all but accused the Allies of being solely responsible for the continuation of the fighting.[81] Nevertheless, Hirst continued organizing a Lansdowne/Labour propaganda campaign in favour of peace negotiations with several conferences until July.[82]

In Germany, a group of liberal publicists around Prince Max von Baden attempted to win the public, as well as political and military leaders, for peace negotiations with Britain, but met with stubborn resistance by Hertling and Ludendorff (see pp. 152–3). Two months later, the peace diktat of Brest-Litovsk was an excellent occasion for Allied propaganda to warn against a 'German Peace', and the Austrian peace feelers of 16 July and 16 September 1918 were, in view of the military situation, either not answered or flatly refused by the Allies, and finally served as Austrian propaganda leaflets on the Western front.[83]

How was propaganda material distributed?

At the home front, private propaganda organizations, central and regional propaganda offices of the civilian and military authorities, policemen, postmen and even educational institutions distributed propaganda material to trade unions and women's organizations, to newspaper offices, schools, parsonages, townhouses and parliaments, and put it on display in popular kitchens, railway stations, waiting rooms, ticket offices, tramways and shop windows.[84] In Germany, private editors offered subscriptions of special war brochures with most of them being cancelled as early as 1915.[85]

Propaganda to neutral countries was usually transmitted by ship or train and once arrived, transferred to embassies where numerous propaganda agents – the German embassy in Bern alone employed 500–600 people – would forward them to editors' offices, libraries, hotels, barber shops, public reading rooms, doctors' waiting rooms, social clubs and thousands of private addresses. In some countries, locals were hired as propagandists, often expatriates who in some cases even founded propaganda organizations, news agencies and wireless radio stations.[86] Two original propaganda displays are worth noting: At Piccadilly in Central London, the Czechoslovak National Council rented a shop and exhibited there the most recent news, pamphlets, maps and other propaganda items. In Barcelona, the Germans set up propaganda boards with blinking headlines of German victories.[87]

Propaganda abroad was especially difficult for the Germans, because at the outset of the war the British had cut the sea cables. At first it was possible to transmit the material via neutral countries like Sweden, Switzerland and Italy, but soon the Germans faced major problems when the sea blockade was tightened and even shipping between neutral countries was controlled. Finally, the Germans had to resort to special techniques such as reducing newspapers and leaflets to the size of four times a postal stamp, smuggling them to a neutral country and having them aggrandized there again.[88] Other papers and leaflets were printed on tissue paper, wrapped in a harmless envelope with a falsified private address in Switzerland and forwarded by the German embassy in Bern to Spain or other neutral countries. An alternative method for transmitting propaganda news was thrice-a-day wireless via the transmitter in Nauen, and the Overseas Transocean Company (Überseedienst Transozean) took care of this.[89] The so-called 1000 words service comprised in reality 8,000–9,000 words, but the British intercepted and deciphered it and could rapidly prepare counter-material.[90]

In order to pass propaganda to enemy countries, more sophisticated methods were necessary. Switzerland was the European centre of spies and propaganda agents, and it was also the transit country for smuggle.[91] The French and the British smuggled propaganda to Germany, the Czechs smuggled it to France, and the Germans smuggled it to Italy.[92] Books and brochures were sent with camouflage covers like *Lexikon deutscher Zitate* (Dictionary of German Quotations); leaflets were hidden in leather sacks and bottles and floated down the Rhine, across the Lake Constance or the Lake Lugano, tied underneath of boats, hidden in chests with a double floor, in handles of bags, in milk churns and coffee sacks, in books, pencils and keys carried by school children, thrown over a frontier fence, or sent by post with wrong wrappers or jackets from falsified official addresses, even with well imitated seals from the Bavarian legation and the Austrian consulate.[93] French agents frequently crossed the frontier (see p. 61) and distributed propaganda material in mailboxes, railway carriages and restaurants. A special trick was to give returning soldiers on leave small gifts wrapped in leaflets.[94] The French could also benefit from the support of numerous German émigrés in Switzerland whose newspapers like *Die freie Zeitung* and pamphlets like *J'accuse* by Richard Grelling permanently arrived in Nuremberg households, were also sold from under the counter in certain book stores and even found their way to the pacifist BNV in Berlin.[95] In the Near East, propaganda was also smuggled in flatbread and inside shoe leather.[96] A very special tactic was employed one day by a German-born American captain in a Scandinavian country: Looking and speaking like a Prussian, he approached the courier of the German Legation, handed him over a bundle of American pamphlets asking him to deliver it to newspapers and Socialist groups in Hamburg by order of the German Minister. The courier obeyed and the pamphlets safely reached their destination.[97]

Propaganda abroad was usually seconded by the secret services. For instance, Emile Haguenin, director of the French Secret Service in Bern, closely cooperated with Hansi's propaganda organization (see pp. 31–2), and in Spain it was even the British Secret Service itself, which established two special offices for propaganda and for counter-propaganda against the Germans.[98] Of course, propaganda activities could also be hampered by the secret services of the neutral country or of the enemy camp. For instance, the American Secret Service tapped the telephone wires of the German and Austrian embassies in Washington, and Czech undercover agents copied compromising photos and sabotage plans (see pp. 46, 68). The rather complicated distribution of propaganda material to the enemy troops at the front will be discussed on p. 113.

Chapter 5

HOW WERE ENTERTAINMENT AND THE VISUAL ARTS TRANSFORMED BY PROPAGANDA?

Propaganda penetrated the whole cultural fabric. Films, stage plays, operettas, songs, concerts, staged pageants, *tableaux vivants*, novels, toys, children books, photos, posters, cartoons, gramophone records, exhibitions – everything was related to the war. Newspapers published war poems, phonograph cylinders re-enacted the conquest of a fortress, millions of patriotic postcards circulated, statuettes, ceramics such as ash trays and plates (Figure 21), matchboxes, vivat ribbons, medals and tear-off calendars – for instance, the *German Crimes Calendar* with an atrocity for each month and the *British Victories Calendar* – all carried propaganda messages.[1] Some of these propaganda instruments – postcards and posters, for instance – continued until the end of the war. Others like stage plays and films reverted to escapist entertainment as early as 1915 because people wanted to forget the terrible war for a few hours. As the particular support provided by entertainment towards the various propaganda strategies is being discussed in other chapters, here the emphasis will be shifted to its specific persuasion techniques.

Photos, drawings, paintings and postcards[2]

In view of their large number in the illustrated magazines photos were one of the most convincing vehicles of propaganda, even defined as 'true combat weapons'.[3] During the war, photos were still considered as objective witnesses, although at that time it was already possible to alter or rearrange them, to cut out elements or to combine them with other photos. For instance, the cathedral of Reims which had been very lightly touched would appear on a photo as partly destroyed.[4] Another propaganda method was to give older photos a new title. For instance, atrocity photos about a Russian pogrom of 1905 were redated 1915 and renamed *Crimes of the German Hordes in Poland*. A photo of 9 June 1914 showing three German cavalry officers with silver hunting prices in their hands was republished in Russian and British newspapers of 1915 with the title *Three German officers with Their Booty*. One Austrian firm was specialized in nameless atrocity photos which could be titled according to the propaganda purpose.[5] The illustrated edition of the

Gazette des Ardennes (see pp. 112–13) relying on the books of Ferdinand Avenarius revealed numerous Allied falsifications.[6] Otherwise, devastated landscapes were perhaps the most frequent motive – of course they had always been destroyed by the enemy.[7] Soldiers were presented in a rather familiar atmosphere, far from any danger: doing shopping in a local market, singing or dining with comrades and even bowling in a trench. The home front as well was shown like in peace times with smiling locals and no trace of a food polonaise. It goes without saying that military successes were lavishly illustrated while photos of defeats were made but not published.[8]

In France, official photos, distributed mostly abroad by the Army Photographic Section (Section photographique de l'armée), were sanitized or even purged. However, from 1915 on, the magazines *L'Illustration* and *Le Miroir* launched appeals to submit striking photos of the war and paid between 250 and 30,000 francs (€675–80,000) for the best ones. *L'Illustration* published all of them, that is 2.06 per cent of all photos, and they showed a fairly realistic image of the war and of the soldier's life. The magazine did not even hesitate to publish photos of corpses of French civilians and soldiers 'in grisly details […] with all the degradations of the bodies caused by death'.[9]

In Britain and Germany, photos of dead soldiers were problematic. Although censorship did not prohibit their publishing, as Kai Artinger has shown, one can find only a few photos of dead soldiers in illustrated magazines, for instance two in the autumn issues of 1915 of *The Graphic*, four in the *Illustrirte Zeitung* (0.07 per cent) and two in the autumn and winter issues of 1916 of the *Weltspiegel*, but they show only corpses of enemies.[10] In Germany, photos of dead Germans were only allowed in order to help clearing up who they were.[11] Generally, though, Death was glorified by propaganda in the form of portraits, 'rolls of honour' or as a grave in romantic surroundings.[12]

As it was quite difficult and even dangerous to take photos of fighting scenes at the front, drawings, somewhat neglected in magazines from around 1900, made a comeback. Their dramatic arrangements were quite superior to the rather static approach of the photos.[13]

In France, Britain, Germany and Austria, painters and illustrators were allowed to accompany the troops. As they received no official guidelines from the authorities, their production varied greatly and the propaganda value was not always evident. The Russian landscapes of the German Art Nouveau artist Heinrich Vogeler and pictures of empty roads, craters or a battlefield without fighting of Muirhead Bone, Britain's first official war artist, might be of interest for the connoisseurs, but could they stimulate war enthusiasm?[14] It is true that Paul Nash's famous painting of the destroyed landscape of Passchendaele with the distorted image of burnt trunks has a much stronger effect than the boring photo of the same object, but how could such 'an anti-war image' also be considered as 'official propaganda', as Sue Malvern would have it?[15] Horror paintings of objects such as devastations and wounded soldiers slogging along from the battlefield could indeed produce propaganda effects, as the examples of the German artists Ludwig Dettmann and Ernst Vollbehr have demonstrated. Vollbehr explicitly showed the horrors of war 'when they illustrated the strength of the Germans' (Artinger), and Dettmann, accredited war painter of the OHL, stressed the heroic element so much that his paintings were again exhibited in World War II and the painter was personally honoured by Hitler. Hugo Vogel with his official portraits of Hindenburg and finally the whole OHL made propaganda for the great military leaders assuring the final victory.[16]

Especially popular with artists of the Allies were illustrations of the German atrocities: women and children fleeing from the Huns, brutal German soldiers executing hostages or pushing them to nowhere, and Russian POWs starving in German camps. In vogue were also supernatural visions and allegorical apparitions of the goddess Victoria, St. George, French Marianne or even Jesus bringing freedom to oppressed people or putting the crown of victory on the head of a dying soldier. In his painting *Blood and Iron*, Charles Butler succeeded in merging both tendencies: Jesus consoling a dying woman with her child on a mountain of corpses.[17]

In Austria and Britain, the authorities mobilized painters for propaganda and commemorative record on a large scale. Maximilian Ritter von Hoen, the director of the KPQ, created a group of 150 artists who were authorized to paint at the front. Until May 1917, they achieved nearly 7,500 paintings, drawings and sculptures which were presented by the KA in numerous exhibitions and later conserved in the Museum of Military History. In April 1916, Masterman created a picture section in Wellington House, employed 90 official painters and founded the magazine *War Pictorial* with a circulation of 50,000 copies and art series such as *The Western Front*.[18] A special case was Christopher R. W. Nevinson. In March 1918, he exhibited 60 paintings in a London Gallery under the high patronage of the recently appointed Minister of Propaganda Lord Beaverbrook. One of the paintings, *Paths of Glory*, showed three dead British soldiers and had not been admitted by the censors, but Nevinson, covering the corpses with a large paper stripe and the notice 'Censored', simply kept it in his exhibition. This was a clever marketing trick which attracted numerous spectators and enormously increased the propaganda impact of the exhibition. Although Nevinson was summoned to the War Office and finally had to withdraw his painting from the gallery, he remained an official war painter and continued enjoying the protection of Beaverbrook.[19] In Germany, on the contrary, painters showing the dark side of the war such as Max Beckmann, Otto Dix and Armin Reumann could not exhibit their paintings until the 1920s or even the 1950s.[20] In 1918, the British War Memorial Committee gave painters the same task as the KPQ in Austria: to create pictures for posterity.[21]

The production of postcards increased immensely during the war due to the frequent postal exchange between soldiers and their families.[22] Their motives resembled those of paintings, drawings and photos: destructions and heroic cavalry attacks, soldiers in peaceful activities at the base or in occupied areas. Heavy howitzers like the *Big Berta*, British tanks and modern airplanes were supposed to reinforce the confidence in the strength of the army. Death was not concealed but embellished; the dying soldier was never alone but was either comforted by a comrade or rewarded by an angel or an allegorical figure. Women were shown in relation to their husbands or fiancés, writing letters or packing parcels for them, swearing fidelity and embracing them in a kitschy way. In an exceptional Art Nouveau series, the Italian artist Umberto Brunelleschi depicted women successfully doing men's jobs, for instance, as tram conductors or as barbers sharpening a razor while a male customer is frightfully observing them.[23] Funny motives such as women and children in uniform or ridiculous images of the enemy popular in 1914 disappeared rather quickly. While the official propaganda institutions in Germany did not use postcards, in Austria the Red Cross, the KFA, the War Aid Office (Kriegshilfsbureau) and later the Photo Department (Lichtbildstelle) of the KPQ turned out millions of them.[24] Vivat ribbons were produced only in Germany and Austria. They consisted of silk mixed with cotton and commemorated victories and the generals who had achieved them.[25]

Posters

Posters were an important instrument of communication conveying their message to a very large number of people: orders of mobilization and calling up, appeals to come to patriotic rallies or to grow vegetables in front of the house, publicities for theatre performances and ersatz-products or information about the passing of high dignitaries – posters accompanied the whole life of the people. Even people who were indifferent to propaganda could not avoid the view of them. They were omnipresent, plastered on every wall, waved in rallies and parades, displayed in public buildings and church entrances, in train stations, buses and trams.[26] In this field as well, the United States surpassed the European nations. While the poster campaign of the PRC with six million full-size posters and one million smaller posters for trams and shops 'represented less than 1 per cent of the commercial poster advertising budget of a normal year', the Americans with 20 million posters displayed more than all other war-faring nations together and produced the greatest daub of the war: 25 feet high and 90 feet long (3.27 times the length of a London bus).[27]

Poster propaganda had two principal tasks: to collect money for war loans (see pp. 94–5) and in Britain and in the United States until May 1916 and May 1917, respectively, to enlist recruits.[28] One of the most popular posters of British conscription propaganda was not, as is usually held today, 'Your Country needs YOU', with Kitchener pointing severely his finger at the viewer – later copied by the Americans – but a less aggressive poster with an older photo of Kitchener, a longer text and the threat of conscription.[29]

Women also played an important role in recruitment posters: Two women with a child observe departing soldiers and exclaim: 'Women of Britain say – Go'. This was a clever appeal to the protective instinct of men ready to defend vulnerable women and children turned into symbols for the home and the homeland. Another propaganda stratagem was the mobilization by shame: An aggressive Irish girl armed with a rifle and pointing at burning Belgium asks her indifferent looking boyfriend: 'Will you go or must I?'[30] The shame motive, in Britain abused by the

White Feather movement (see p. 59), also played a role in the voluntary enlistment of other countries. When a young man in August 1914 met a young woman in Leipzig, he was 'nearly ashamed to be seen in civilian dress'.[31] Such social pressure did not only affect students but a broad section of the urban population.[32]

Caricatures

Caricatures were quite popular in the first half of the twentieth century. Newspapers not only contained caricatures but occasionally published weekly cartoon supplements; furthermore in all major countries, between five and 10 cartoon and humour magazines competed for the favour of the public. As many people, exhausted by the sufferings of the war, were longing for some distraction, the sale of humour and caricatures exploded, especially in the first two years of the war.[33] For instance, the percentage of cartoons in the French daily *Le Journal* increased from 0.3 per cent in 1913 to 18.6 per cent in 1914 and to 22.6 per cent in 1916–17; its circulation rose from 700,000 in 1913 to 1.4 million in 1915.[34] In Britain, the caricatures by William Kerridge Haselden helped to boost the circulation of the *Daily Mirror* from 630,000 in 1910 to 1.5 million in 1915.[35] Cartoon magazines sold much better as well: In Germany, the eight cartoon magazines had a total circulation of 986,000 copies, just a little less than the *Berliner Illustrirte Zeitung* (1,000,000) and could thus rightly be considered a mass medium.[36] *Punch* increased its number of issues per week from 120,000 in 1913 to 150,000 in January 1915, *Lustige Blätter* from 60,000 to 125,000 and *Der Wahre Jacob* from 286,000 to 380,000. Only magazines such as *Meggendorfer Blätter* and *Fliegende Blätter* which somewhat neglected the war declined a bit.[37] In view of this boom, new cartoon magazines were founded in 1914–15: in Germany *Der Brummer*; in France *L'Europe anti-prussienne*, *L'Anti-Boche*, *La Baïonnette* and, last but not least, the anti-war cartoon magazine *Le canard enchaîné* (see pp. 174–5).[38] Famous cartoons were not only published in newspapers and magazines but also could multiply their propaganda effects due to different visual aids: They were shown in cinemas, printed on cigarette packets and reproduced on shooting targets at schützenfests.[39] In the second half of the war, circulation fell owing to the shortage of paper and the price increases, but also because some people had enough of war propaganda. The authorities tried to stem the tide by organizing cartoon exhibitions at home and abroad, showing not only actual popular caricatures but also pre-war cartoons and even selected enemy ones.[40]

As the cartoonists put their pens and brushes at the service of their country and readily based their caricatures on the most unbelievable stories and wildest calumnies (see pp. 40–2), the authorities were quite content with their propaganda. Indeed, in 1916 Poincaré congratulated the cartoonists 'for their pro-French propaganda produced from the beginning of the war', and even the censors mostly spared them. In France, which practiced the most severe censorship of all belligerent countries, only 1 per cent of caricatures in the newspapers were suppressed.[41] When in Germany the KPA prohibited jokes about food shortages, the cartoonists published even more caricatures of this type and got away with it.[42]

Very soon the official propaganda bureaus in some war-faring states used cartoonists for their own ends. In Germany, the News Office of the AA tried to give them instructions; although they did not always comply, they happily accepted well-paid propaganda assignments. Thus, Heine and his colleague Olaf Gulbransson of the *Simplicissimus* as well as Walter Trier of the *Lustige Blätter* contributed to cartoon albums in foreign languages for the ZfA, which had 12,000 copies per week distributed abroad.[43] A similar album with topics selected by the News Office was realized in summer 1917.[44]

In Britain, Masterman published albums of Raemaekers and also launched them abroad (see p. 157). Among the artists of his picture section were also quite a few cartoonists.[45] The MI7 also recruited writers and artists, among them the famous caricaturist Bruce Bairnsfather who drew caricatures at the front.[46]

In the United States, Creel also appreciated the work of cartoonists: 'The world is much too busy to stop and listen to the orators, or even read all the story of the war [...] but your appeal is irresistible.' He eventually set up a Cartoons Office, which forwarded to 750 caricaturists a weekly bulletin containing instructions on the basis of topics desired by the administration.[47]

French propaganda offices were less active in this aspect than their British, American and German counterparts. However, one of their diplomats, Henri Allizé, an envoy in The Hague, stood out. He regularly phoned Jaap Goedemans, chief editor of the *Telegraaf*, and instructed him about what to write on the war. In a Dutch cartoon, Goedemans is depicted as a dog listening to the voice of his master, the Entente. Upon Allizé's instructions, he did not only write pro-Allied articles but also inspired Raemaekers's atrocity caricatures who at that time worked for this newspaper.[48]

The different types of caricatures between hate and laughter have already been discussed in the pertaining parts of other chapters (see pp. 40–2, 45–7), and two caricature magazines with anti-war propaganda will be analysed on pp. 174–5.

Perhaps inspired by the 'clash of civilizations' between Germany and the Western Allies, some scholars claim that cartoonists were also separated by cultural or national barriers. In their view, British cartoonists were less combative and more humorous that their German and French colleagues, and the German humorists were extolling the superiority of their nation.[49] As far as the latter point is concerned, I rather have the impression that they felt inferior to the refined culture of the French and sought to shake off their overwhelming influence in elegant fashion, exquisite cuisine and high-brow parlance (see pp. 53, 82–3). On the other hand, the exceptional quality of British humour has been confirmed by a contemporary German author, the philosopher Max Scheler. In his book *Der Genius des Krieges und der deutsche Krieg* (1917) (The Genius of the War and the German War), he wrote: 'Is there any humour outside Britain which has not been copied from the British? [...] Be that as it may, British humour is the most humorous humour in the world.'[50] It speaks volumes that this was the only compliment in a most hateful diatribe against Britain so typical for German war propaganda. It seems that even German soldiers appreciated British cartoons, because at the front they have allegedly asked their British counterparts for copies of Haselden's Cartoons. British cartoonists even went so far in their humorous attitude that despite the horrors of German warfare in Belgium and Northern France they managed to ridicule a future German invasion of Britain. In a cartoon book called *The Hun's Handbook for the Invasion of England,* they depicted the German soldiers as hopelessly incapable of accomplishing their tasks while the British were not impressed at all and calmly continued their usual life.[51]

There are very few other differences. While the French and Italians published the most outrageous atrocity caricatures (see pp. 40–2), they are hard to find in British and German magazines.[52] Most Englishmen refused Raemaekers's hate cartoons as un-British and only Edmund J. Sullivan followed his example.[53] A few Russian cartoonists applied a particular technique: The funny effect is provoked by the contradiction between image and text. For example, in a narrative cartoon German women demonstrating for bread and peace are dispersed by police, beaten up and put in jail. In the text, the women explain that their patriotic demonstration was welcomed by the Kaiser and that they are living very comfortably now.[54]

Apart from these examples, it seems that the resemblances outweigh the differences. All cartoonists used the same topics and in some cases even copied from each other. One example has already been discussed (see p. 45), but there are many more, the most convincing being three caricatures of war toys with partly the same design.[55] Other examples for the easy acceptance of foreign cartoons were the so-called *propagande à rebours* in France (see p. 114) and the French magazine *L'Europe anti-prussienne* which published only cartoons from abroad and had no problem of tying them in with the French mentality.[56]

The cartoonists, all of them men, had another point in common. They felt uneasy about more and more women taking the place of men in professional life. Maybe afraid of these first signs of women's emancipation, they reacted by ridiculing working women. In *Passing Show* and *Punch,* embarrassed-looking women drive cars, do construction work awkwardly or try to empty a postal box against the fierce protest of an aggressive dog.[57] In *La Baïonnette,* a man is mending socks while his wife is going to her office and says: 'Once you have finished, go to the department store, to-day they have fabric remnants.' Another wife reproaches her husband for the expensive tailor's bill, and he gives the classical woman's answer: 'I hadn't got a thing to wear any more.'[58] The *Canard enchaîné* mocks at the future political rights of women: A woman tells her husband, 'If you are kind and buy me this hat I shall vote for your candidate.'[59] I could not find any German caricatures of this tendency, but in a theatre play *Muttchen hat's Wort* (Let Mummy Speak) the authors, the famous German cabaret singer Otto Reutter and Max Reichardt, also ridicule the new woman power: Women in men's professions from mason to physician march in ridiculous outfit over the scene, in a chanson about the future a woman gives speeches in the Reichstag while her husband takes care of the children, and one year after a wedding a frustrated wife will have the right to choose another man – the latter topic being suppressed by the censors.[60]

Differences between cartoon magazines did not depend on the nation but more on the audience. The style of *Simplicissimus* which addressed the higher echelons of society had more in common with *Punch* than with *Der wahre Jacob*, the organ of the socialist workers, or with the *Meggendorfer Blätter* which appealed to children and to the lower middle class.[61]

Theatre

Theatre[62] in wartime also had a propaganda task, but the German approach was somewhat different from the methods of the French and the British. British plays, especially in the first two years, had to increase recruitment through hatred. For this direct purpose, 25 new plays were written and recruiting officers were waiting in the lobby trying to enlist young men enthused by the shows.[63] More than 100 plays were written about 'German-spy-villains' and an indefinite number about German atrocities. *The Graphic* of 17 July 1915 commented about one of them: 'Without doubt this popular melodrama has been responsible for a number of recruits'.[64] The atrocity scenes were so realistically presented that sometimes it took three attendants to restrain a furious spectator 'from rushing up on the stage and assaulting the villains'.[65] In France as well, the usual atrocities were denounced and German *Kultur*, transcribed as 'Koultoure', was ridiculed[66] (see also pp. 36, 52–3). Kaiser and crown prince were also denigrated as well, but very offending attributes such as 'imbecile', 'completely moron' or 'of impure race' for the Kaiser and 'burglar' for the crown prince were usually suppressed by the censors.[67] In Austria, much emphasis was put on characters representing the various nationalities swearing without hesitation their fidelity to the Hapsburg Monarchy.[68] In Germany at the beginning of the war, many plays showed the splendid exploits of the German soldiers but soon had to consider the increasing problems of the home front and engaged in propaganda for the abolition of class barriers. In French plays as well, radicals, socialists and royalists forgot class distinctions and party quarrels at the front. In one play, a soldier saves the life of his director in the trenches and afterwards marries his daughter.[69]

Alsace-Lorraine was a tricky subject for the stage in France and Germany. Some plays reinforced the national claim to these provinces by demonstrating the loyalty of the people to one of these countries. For instance, in a French play a young Alsatian informs a French outpost about German movements at the front and dies heroically. René Schickele's play *Hans im Schnakenloch* about the dilemma of a family in Alsace, where one son fights on the German and his brother on the French side, even lead to a long controversy between the censors in Berlin and General Ludendorff, who finally forced them to drop the play – after 99 performances.[70]

In all countries, theatres tried a 'cultural mobilization for war'.[71] Popular theatres and music halls applied some sort of a 'national liturgy', as Martin Baumeister puts it: Speeches, recitations of war poems, announcements or at least promises of victory alternated with dancing, common patriotic singing, including the national anthem and sometimes the hymns of the allied nations, and so-called *tableaux vivants* with several girls representing all the allies.[72] Some elements of this propaganda entertainment also preceded or terminated the performance of classical plays which, of course, were chosen accordingly to their jingoist and militaristic aspects. Most popular in Berlin and Vienna were dramas by Heinrich von Kleist such as *Die Hermannschlacht* featuring the victory of Germanic tribes over the Roman troops in 9 AC, and *Prinz Friedrich von Homburg oder die Schlacht bei Fehrbellin* about the victory of Friedrich II von Hessen-Homburg over the Swedes, written in 1810 as an appeal against Napoleon's oppressive rule in Germany. When the famous phrase '*In den Staub mit allen Feinden Brandenburgs*' (To ashes with all the enemies of Brandenburg) was pronounced, the spectators rose rejoicing and frenetically applauding. The most popular opera was *Lohengrin* by Richard Wagner in which the German King Heinrich I warns the public against the permanent danger from the East and summons the warriors of Brabant to the coming battle against the Hungarians – an opera underlining the German desire to reunite Belgium with the German fatherland like in the Middle Ages.[73] In Paris they played *Horace* by Pierre Corneille – a drama about the war between Rome and the neighbouring city Alba Longa in which the hero kills his sister and his brother-in-law – the play being interpreted as a symbol for the sacrifice of the French nation.[74]

Another propaganda coup of the war theatre was the glorious representation of the respective allied countries. In Germany, Turkish and Bulgarian folklore troops performed shows; the premiere of *Die Rose von Stambul* took place in Vienna in 1916, an operetta showing the modernization of Turkish society. In Paris, Russian ballets under the famous dancer Serge Diaghilev entered the stage, and in the drama *Michel Strogoff*, after Jules Verne, an adventurer travels from Moscow to Irkutsk in order to warn the tsar's brother against the invasion of the cruel Tatars, a clear allusion to the German 'Huns'.[75]

On the stage, the trenches were shown as a pleasant place. In France, the funny soldier with his jokes of pre-war times was now replaced by the 'heroic *poilu*, delighted with his fate and certain of victory'. He happily leaves for the front, enjoys the trenches with their amazing attractions such as 'concerts, parties, dances, and fire works' and when he returns wounded he either wants to go back at once or at least convinces a shirker to enlist.[76] Criticism of shirkers and defeatists was sometimes allowed, sometimes suppressed, even in the same play.[77] From October 1916 on, however, 'the *poilu* deserts the stage', as Mathilde Joseph puts it.[78] In Germany, *Immer feste druff* (Always Thrash Strongly), according to a parole allegedly used by the crown prince, showed valiant German soldiers marching over the scene and thrashing the fleeing British and French troops; one German is wounded, another rides on an Englishman, a village is set on fire, and the whole war is presented as a rather cheerful enterprise. More important than the very loosely knit plot were the chansons. Mostly in the rhythm of marches, they stress the superiority of German courage and German arms – *Deutscher Mut und deutsche Waffen siegen stets* – remind of the victories of 1813–15 and 1870, praise the Prussian generals Gebhard L. Blücher and Helmuth Moltke the Elder, and underline the principal aim as it was seen in autumn 1914: to cross the Rhine and conquer Paris. This play was performed in the Berlin suburb of Schöneberg from 1914 until the end of the war 800 times. The success was probably due above all to the composer Walter Kollo whose amusing Berlin chansons are still enjoyed today, and to Claire Waldoff, one of the most popular chanson singers of Berlin.[79] Now a few war plays from Britain, France and Germany will be presented in order to demonstrate the different propaganda techniques.

One of the most hateful plays in Britain was G. Henderson's *Beast of Berlin* which denounced Kaiser Wilhelm and the treacherous Germans, and recreated the anti-alien Deptford riots of October 1914 so well that it triggered new riots. Gordon Williams concludes that 'its inflammatory role was not unwelcome'.[80] In the play *In the Hands of the Huns* (1915), Count Otto, a German officer, wants to burn down a nunnery and then let the nuns fall prey to his men. In *Armageddon* (1915), prisoners were shot, women insulted and so on.[81]

In France, Georges G. Thénon, under the pseudonym Rip, wrote two revues where sketches alternate with songs, ballets and pantomime. In his first revue, *1915*, he praises the militarized fashion, approves that Wagner's operas and the Vienna operettas are banned from Paris, shows how a pacifist becomes a happy recruit and mocks at the German navy which never leaves its harbour and the bombs of the zeppelins which can destroy only a small kiosk. A large part of the sketches is directed against the German soldiers qualified as Huns, war microbes and scorpions, against the military incompetence of Kaiser and crown prince, and against the German K-bread, called KK-bread which sounds like 'poop' bread and is made of horse manure.[82] In his next revue, *L'école des civils* (School for the Civilians), performed from 25 November 1915, hate propaganda is more specified: The Germans march from victory to victory, but their bank notes, called by Bethmann Hollweg 'scraps of paper', are more and more devaluated. A Professor Kuatsche ('*quatschen*' in German means 'talking rubbish') claims that Adam was the first German Kaiser and that all great generals such as Alexander, Cesar and Napoleon were Germans. This time the German atrocities are presented as well, from the corpse of a baby victim of a German naval attack to the execution of Miss Cavell. Some defeatist Frenchmen are also criticized: Mr. and Mrs. Trouille (= anxiety) flee to Switzerland and a shirker is employed by the censorship office – the latter topic being suppressed by the censors.[83]

In Germany, Reutter captivated his audience with amusing songs and stage plays until 1917.[84] In his first comedy, *1914*, co-authored with Max Reichardt, he demonstrated the positive consequences of the war. The principal character, who runs the restaurant 'Bellevue' with a menu in French and English in the posh suburb Grunewald of Berlin, is an effeminate henpecked husband, but he escapes from his humiliating life to the front and rediscovers his male dignity. His wife is an elegant nouvelle riche who wears expensive jewels, always uses some French words and even wants to marry her younger daughter to a miserable Frenchman. During the war she becomes a convinced German nationalist, donates her jewels to the Red Cross, bans all foreign words and marries her daughter to a German worker. The menu becomes German, even Russian caviar disappears for patriotic reasons, and the restaurant is now called 'Zur schönen Aussicht'. A noble civil servant with monocle is engaged to the couple's elder daughter but insists that class barriers separate him from his future parents-in-law. When he fights together with her father at the front, he loses his noble allure and apologizes to his fiancée. Thus the war has created the *Volksgemeinschaft* (national community) and liberated the people from the cultural domination by the French, two of the main promises of German war propaganda.

In their last play *Gehn Sie blos nicht nach Berlin* (Don't Dare to Come to Berlin), performed from October 1917, Reutter and his co-author Hugo Hirsch present several negative characters such as an arrogant saleswoman, who because of the scarcity of food can choose customers at her ease, a war profiteer who hoards sausages and produces food-ersatz pills, a nouvelle riche who speculates and an elderly bon vivant posing as an ersatz-lover because most young men are at the front. All these 'bad Germans' come from the provinces and are contrasted with the only Berliner in the play, a Herr Lustig, who demonstrates the unbroken morale in the city by dutifully obeying all regulations: He never buys anything on the black market, loves to eat turnip, the only food available in winter 1916–17, and when he is still hungry, his wife hypnotizes him so that he eats a sole of a shoe as calf's liver and an old false plait as eel – several years before Chaplin did it. He even resists various temptations by a devil who tries to find a sinner in Berlin. The comical effects are intensified by all sorts of jokes and funny situations: The devils in hell are freezing because they cannot obtain coal any more, and various items of ersatz are presented – for instance, ersatz-clothes made from paper disintegrating in the rain and an ersatz-newspaper, which because of the lack of paper is as small as a tram ticket but big enough for the stereotype local news, which reads 'coal is scarce, there is no gas, vegetables disappeared, fruit not found, no butter, no lard, everything gone'. The tendency is the same as in many cartoons. By using the techniques of 'comic relief' and 'burlesque exaggeration' as Baumeister and Jan Rüger dub it, the authors successfully mitigated the increasing privations and thus strengthened the propaganda of holding out at any price.[85]

Circus enterprises were a special hit in Germany. Still in 1918 they successfully performed military exploits with a spectacular machinery and up to 500 actors showing the conquest of Liège, the sinking of a British dreadnought by a submarine and the bombarding of London by zeppelins.[86] A special task was entrusted to German theatres in the occupied areas and in neutral countries. They were supposed to convince the inhabitants of the superiority of German Kultur by presenting famous classical stage plays and concerts. However, at least in Brussels, the locals boycotted them, and a well-known Flemish university professor who had attended them was obliged to leave the place after the war.[87]

By 1915 most people wanted to forget the terrible presence of the war for a few hours. Therefore theatres were obliged to revive pre-war comedies, shows, operettas and farces.[88] Already on 9 December 1914 the Herzfeldtheater in Berlin had to withdraw its war play *How We Live* because of its tragic tendency and replaced it by a light comedy.[89] In Britain, the most popular show of the war with 2,000 performances was *Choo chin chow*, an oriental fantasy with harem girls.[90]

According to Eva Krivanec's theatre statistics, in October 1915 only 4 per cent of the stage plays and 9 per cent of the performances in Berlin dealt with the war, in Vienna 3 and 4 per cent, respectively, while in Paris war revues and war plays combined arrived at 6 and 13 per cent.[91]

Films and newsreels

Quite early in the war the authorities recognized the propaganda value of films and newsreels. 'I hate to confess it', stated the newspaper tycoon Lord Northcliffe, 'the motion picture is doing more for the Allied cause than any other means of thought transmission'.[92] Films could indeed reach the masses better than any written material; they were not only, as Trevor Wilson puts it, 'the Bible of the working class', but were also more and more enjoyed by the bourgeoisie.[93] While in the first months of the war private films companies turned out enough war and propaganda films, with the decreasing interest of the war-weary population from 1915–16 on, official and semi-official agencies had to step in.[94]

In France in 1915, the Minister of War established the Section of Army Cinema (Section cinématographique de l'armée, SCA), which later produced all footage about the war.[95] In Britain in August 1915, Masterman founded the Cinema Committee for Film Propaganda Abroad, which later was absorbed by Buchan's Department of Information, in October 1916 extended to the War Office Cinematograph Committee (WOCC) under the chairmanship of Lord Beaverbrook and in March 1918 integrated into his Ministry of Information. It controlled all films and newsreels shot at the front.[96]

In November 1916, the OHL founded the Military Section for Film and Photographs (Militärische Film- und Photostelle) attached to the MAA, transformed in January 1917 to the Department of Photography and Film (Bild- und Filmamt, BUFA) and in December 1917 at the initiative of Ludendorff extended to the famous Universum Film Company (UFA) which, however, came too late to produce meaningful propaganda films.

In Austria in 1917, the KPQ established a Cinematographic Office as well, but left most activity to the private Sascha Company. In Italy, only the catastrophe of Caporetto lead in November 1917 to the establishment of a film section by the army. In Russia, film production remained in private hands or was organized by the semi-official Skobelev-Committee.

At the outset of the war, heroic films in the 'field-grey' genre were most popular. However, as actual filming at the front was not yet allowed, fighting scenes had to be recreated and some scenarios were highly improbable: How could a single hero put dozens of enemy soldiers to flight, capture or kill them? When these films such as the German *Wie Max sich das eiserne Kreuz erwarb* (How Max Won the Iron Cross) and *Der zwölfjährige Kriegsheld* (The 12-Year-Old War Hero) or the French *Les héros de l'Yser* (The Heroes of the Yser) and *Debout les morts* (Get Up, All the Dead) were shown to the public, soldiers 'howled with laughter or with rage', and the propaganda effect was nil.[97] An Italian journalist wrote in 1915: 'The real war is diametrically different from that one portrayed by the un-warlike fantasies of some of these masters of mise-en-scene who know nothing of war, only of parades.'[98]

In Italy following the path-breaking film *Sempre nel Cor la Patria* (My Country Is Always in My Heart), approximately 130 films of this type were produced in 1915–16 with titles and slogans such as *Viva la Patria* (Hurrah for the Fatherland), *Vittoria* (Victory), *A Trieste – vincere o morire* (To Trieste – Win or Die), but it is doubtful if they could really change the war-hostile attitudes of most Italians.[99] More popular was Maciste, a very Italian hero who in two films, *Maciste bersagliere* (Maciste Sharp Shooter) and *Maciste alpino* (Maciste Mountain Soldier), could single-handedly ward off hundreds of Austrian soldiers and punch down his main enemy, the Austrian Fritz. Thus, the war was reduced to a private affair between two men.[100] Russian films were even worse: staged battle scenes, old footage from the Balkan wars, newsreels from the Franco-German front, and films like *The Storming and Capture of Erzerum* which 'showed everything except the capture of Erzerum'[101].

By far the best film of this genre was *Battle of the Somme*, launched by the British in 1916. This film had an immense success because it was realistic instead of chauvinist, did not glorify the war as a heroic adventure, but showed the common experience of both sides with horrors and sufferings including even images of dying British soldiers.[102] It is true that it used some faked attack scenes, but like in photography fakes in movies were quite normal. When the Italians produced a film in the Abruzzo mountains, they pretended to show destructions by Austrian bombardments, but in reality the destructions had been caused by an earthquake.[103]

Germans, French and Italians tried to imitate the British success with *Bei unseren Helden an der Somme* (With Our Heroes at the Somme), *L'Offensive française sur la Somme* (The French Offensive at the Somme), and *Guerra sull' Adamello* (War on the Mountain of Adamello), but with little success, because they showed no credible scenes from the front and applied a 'sanitised approach', purging all scenes of violence and suffering. Probably because of military censorship, later British films such as *Battle of the Ancre* were also sanitized.[104]

Some films showed no battle, but presented the fine equipment of the army and the exemplary training of the soldiers. The private British Topical Committee for War Films in 1915 turned out the documentary *Britain Prepared*, the French *La puissance militaire de la France* (The Military Power of France) and the Italians films on the industrial preparation for war.[105] In addition, the CPI produced films about the military preparations such as *Pershing's Crusaders* and *America's Answer* based on the newsreels of the US Army Signal Corps. Some other films, produced through cooperation with commercial filmmakers, showed the treatment of wounded soldiers or women's war work.[106] As the Allies had not gained a single victory so far, these films demonstrated neutrals the power of the Allied war machines and sustained the morale at the home front.[107]

Atrocities played an important role as well. The French newsreel *Annales de guerre* (War Annals) showed the well-known results of the Huns' warfare: burnt landscapes, destroyed towns and dead bodies. The editor of a film revue explained that this was important in order to 'sustain within us the healthy hatred of the barbarian and the assassin'. The Italians made a film about the inevitable Miss Cavell: *Come mori Miss Cavell* (How Miss Cavell Died). A French film like *L'impossible pardon* (Impossible to Forgive) of 1918 showing German soldiers violating women and pillaging houses anticipated the spirit of the Treaty of Versailles in its title.[108] With the film *Once a Hun, Always a Hun*, British propaganda as well drew far-reaching consequences from German atrocities: Two German soldiers strike a woman with a baby to the ground, after the war they become commercial travellers trying to sell German goods in Britain, but when the badge 'Made in Germany' is discovered, their merchandise is bluntly refused. The message is clear: 'There can be no trading with these people after the war'[109] – a propaganda application of the Paris Economic Conference of June 1916 which had decided to continue the blockade of the Central Powers in revised form after the war.

In Russia films like *The Belgian Lily* or *The German Barbarians in Belgium* showed German atrocities as well; *The Breath of Antichrist* depicted the Kaiser as the Satan. The biggest Russian hit was *Under the Thunder of Canons: Prussian Rapists*, which aptly combined atrocity propaganda with the hate of the enemy alien: Fritz Müller, the son of a German factory owner in Russia, woos a Russian girl who repels his advances because she loves the Russian Soruk. Her lover joins the army and is taken prisoner by Müller's soldiers. Müller threatens to kill him unless the girl gives herself up to the German. Already in Müller's bedroom, she is rescued by Soruk who kills Müller. Soruk is saved from execution by the arrival of the Cossacks.[110]

In the United States, already before the declaration of war, preparedness propaganda began in the film industry. In *The Battle Cry of Peace* (1915), a foreign country resembling Germany invades America and destroys New York and Washington. Carmaker Henry Ford, a convinced pacifist, denounced in 250 full-page advertisements the film as 'a disguised attempt to bring the United States into the war'.[111] After the American declaration of war, films with a pacifist message had to be withdrawn and rewritten with an anti-German tendency. As quite a few Americans did not believe that their country was really threatened by the Germans, atrocity films had to arouse unbound hate against them. Typical were *The Kaiser – the Beast of Berlin*, *The Unbeliever* and *Heart of Humanity* where Erich von Stroheim playing a German officer rapes women, murders civilians and throws a baby out of the window (Figure 22). *Hearts of the World* shows German brutes terrorizing a peaceful village until it is liberated by Allied troops. This film ends with the message: 'America – returning home after freeing the world from autocracy and the horrors of war for ever and ever.'[112]

Only very rarely did German films show atrocities of the enemy, for example, about the Cossacks and the *King Stephen* incident (see pp. 42, 95). In 1917, the BUFA exasperated by the never ending reproaches of atrocities, made a film *Wie Frankreich das Elsass befreit* (How France Liberates Alsace) showing destructions by the French which could only have happened in September 1914 and were probably supplemented by later fake shootings. In the same year, upon explicit order of the BUFA, a private company produced *Die Schuldigen des Weltkrieges* (The Culprits of the World War) which vilified politicians of the Allies: Former British Prime Minister Herbert H. Asquith bent on starving German mothers and children by the blockade and former French Minister of Foreign Affairs, Delcassé, personally ordering to torture, amputate and murder German doctors, officers and soldiers. However, this film was not appreciated by the public.[113] Usually German films preferred a reconciliatory attitude. For instance in the film *Wenn Völker streiten* (As Long as People Quarrel) a Frenchman and a German are good friends. During the war, the Frenchman is taken prisoner by his German friend, meets his sister, falls in love and both decide to marry after the war. Finally all three youngsters swear each other eternal love and fidelity.[114]

Following the example of stage plays and novels, some films also proclaimed the future *Volksgemeinschaft* (national community) showing an alleged 'camaraderie of the trenches' between noble men, bourgeois and workers which culminated in unbelievable marriages and blood brotherhood between the different social classes.[115] For instance, in a German film with the title *Weihnachtsglocken 1914* (Christmas Bells 1914) the daughter of a Junker marries an agricultural worker who had saved the life of her severely wounded brother.[116] However, in Russia this topic was not accepted but replaced by the image of family bonds with paternal officers commanding filial respect from their soldiers.[117]

From spring 1915 onwards – in Italy from the end of 1916 onwards – the interest in war films decreased. People in all countries wanted to forget about the war and preferred to see traditional comedies, Hollywood films, detective stories or adventure films such as *The Count of Monte Christo* or *Vendémiaire*.[118] A list of the most popular German films in 1918 included only two films about the actual war.[119] In Austria the percentage of war films decreased from 26 per cent in 1915 over 17 per cent in 1916 to 9 per cent in 1917 and 1918;[120] in Russia it fell from nearly 50 per cent in 1914 to 3 per cent in 1916;[121] and in Britain the war and propaganda films combined decreased from 13 per cent in 1914 and January 1915 over 4–5 per cent in 1916 and 2–3 per cent 1917 to 4–7 per cent in 1918.[122]

Newsreels about the front were either produced by newsreel offices of the army like the SCA, or by private companies, in Germany the Messter and Eico Movie Societies (Messter Film Gesellschaft and Eico-Film G.m.b.H.), in Austria the Vienna Movie Producing Society (Wiener Kunstfilm-Industrie-Gesellschaft) and somewhat later the Sascha Movie Enterprise (Sascha-Film-Fabrik), in Britain the Topical Budget Company.[123] It goes without saying that journalists and operators were 'embedded' by officers who selected the appropriate scenes to shoot and censored them before release.[124] In Britain in 1917, the WOCC bought Topical Budget, rebaptized it Pictorial News and supplied it with film material from the front. From March 1918, the WOCC was controlled by the Ministry of Information.[125] The *Sascha-Kriegswochenbericht* (Weekly War Report) was the principal newsreel of Austria. A typical program of 8 November 1914 showed the following scenes: An infantry unit and a machine gun division advance under the protection of fog; Austrian troops fire 15 cm howitzers; a pilot prepares a reconnaissance flight; soldiers demolish a house.[126] The most patriotic and active of all newsreel producers was Messter who not only elaborated in 1914 detailed instructions for film censorship (see p. 10), but somewhat later also for propaganda films. Messter's newsreels were not only shown in Austria, Turkey and Bulgaria, but also in many neutral countries including the United States where he reached, in 1916, an audience of 1.5 million spectators and his international earnings amounted to 4,800,000 mark (€18.2 million).[127]

All war-faring states except Russia made huge efforts to show films at the front and in remote towns and villages. They used 'cine-motors', that is lorries equipped with a projector, a generator and a screen. Germany and France also disposed of several hundreds of mobile army cinemas; in Austria, the Sascha company maintained a private network.[128] In Britain, throughout 1918, a special campaign with patriotic films was organized with war veterans and local notables explaining the pictures.[129] After the United States had entered the war, they supported Italy with cine-motors, projectors for movies and organized 22,000 movie-shows.[130]

Exhibitions

After modest displays of war artefacts in 1915, the Germans and the Austrians one year later organized huge exhibitions with photos, books, medals, flags, uniforms and above all authentic paraphernalia such as helmets, rifles, mortars, gasmasks, planes and full-scale model trenches.[131] They also exposed civilian donations: golden rings and gift parcels with woollen socks and other warm clothing for the soldiers. These exhibitions were multimedia events with films, stage plays, concerts, culinary offers and sales of war souvenirs. In Austria, it occupied 50,000 m² in the Vienna public park Prater; in Germany, it was the Red Cross which started the German War Exhibitions (Deutsche Kriegsausstellungen) as a travelling display in five cities, later shown in 30 smaller cities and towns. The ZfA also organized exhibitions abroad, for instance in Switzerland.[132] They were quite lucrative: In Berlin, the gross profits in 1916 amounted to 235,000 mark, and in Stuttgart to 276,000 mark (€900,000 and €1.05 million).

These exhibitions perfectly combined entertainment and propaganda. By juxtaposing their splendid equipment with damaged enemy trophies, the Germans demonstrated their military strength and the effectiveness of their guns. Most impressive were also the ugly puppets of enemy soldiers: mischievous Belgian francs-tireurs with their rifles, British soldiers with dum-dum cartridges and repugnant colonial cannibals with knives between their teeth showed the unfair practices and the inferiority of the enemy soldiers. One journalist commented: 'Every piece of this war exhibition [in Frankenthal] informs us about the German superiority in military and economical affairs. And from this joy and confidence arises the permanent determination: *To hold out* until victory'.[133] The problem of the war invalids was reduced to purely technical aspects, 'to the wonders of military medicine' which would allegedly heal them all.[134]

War exhibitions in France, Britain and Russia were much more modest. In Paris, the French organized a permanent display at the War Museum, an inter-Allied exhibition with 50,000 visitors at the turn of the year 1916–17, a few private exhibitions with German atrocity scenes, captured guns or war memorials and, at the very last moment in October 1918, the *Panthéon de la Guerre*, a gigantic panorama of the war, painted by 128 artists.[135] In London, the Imperial War Museum, founded in March 1917, organized an exhibition in January 1918 and had an enormous impact during the inter-war period and beyond. Furthermore, war paintings were exposed in galleries, not always with great success.[136] In Russia, in summer 1915, a private association, the Imperial Society of History Devotees, organized an exhibition of war trophies and, one year later, also set up a Museum of the Great War.[137]

In the last year of the war, some exhibitions referred to the degenerating supply situation. In Austria, they presented all sorts of ersatz such as egg powder or clothes made from paper fabrics while the British limited themselves to instructing housewives about how to make food last longer.[138]

Some exhibitions targeted special groups, for instance the permanent display on 'School and War' inaugurated in 1915 by the Central Institute of Education and Teaching (Zentralinstitut für Erziehung und Unterricht, ZEU) in Berlin. Its catalogue describes artefacts such as drawings, poems, songs, journals of pupils, letters of soldiers and various teaching aids. The institute also organized propaganda courses (see p. 98), presented the model of a school museum which inspired the creation of numerous school museums all over Germany with war memorabilia collected by the children or their fathers at the front: for example, war trophies, food-ration coupons and emergency banknotes.[139] The approach of the French was more modest: In Paris, classrooms were transformed into sites of memory with photographs and commemorative catalogues of the fallen teachers.[140]

All these laudable actions in Europe were by far surpassed in quantity and amusement value by the exhibitions in the United States.[141] They were held in 21 cities, were seen by more than 10 million people, and earned a total income of $1,438,004 ($34.5 million). In Chicago alone two million people attended in two weeks. They exposed more or less the same trophies like in Europe, but the amusement effect was higher. While in Europe trenches were dug and could be visited, the Americans did much more: At the Chicago Exposition, every afternoon the visitors could observe a remarkable sham battle with the rattle of rifles and machine guns and real soldiers going over the top.

Chapter 6

WHICH GROUPS WERE ESPECIALLY TARGETED AND HOW DID THEY REACT?

Victims of financial conscription

'The idea of financial conscription', remembered Helfferich in 1919, 'had to be drummed into the heads a hundred thousand times.'[1] Indeed, the official German propaganda newspaper *DK* and French propaganda speeches propagated in unison: 'As the soldiers are giving their blood, the civilians should give their money.'[2] A German war bonds poster underlined this demand visually by showing a wounded soldier with the title 'And your duty?'[3] In order to meet the enormous costs of the war all governments had to raise money through various means: collections in the streets for all sorts of charities, sale of war savings stamps and war savings certificates, loans from the Allies and above all war bonds or similar domestic loans such as treasury bonds. Gold and valuables were also desperately sought for. People were exhorted to exchange gold coins into paper money or to donate golden rings, watch chains and other precious possessions and replace them with iron items bearing the inscription *Gold für Wehr, Eisen für Ehr* (Gold for the Defence – iron for the Honour, Figure 23). In Germany, the directory of the Imperial Bank financed propaganda trips of the Lutheran clergy for such gold collections, and the BUFA produced films like *Gold gab ich dahin* (I Donated Gold).[4] In France, revues in music halls included songs such as 'Apportez tous votre or, la patrie en réclame chaque jour' (Bring All Your Gold, the Fatherland Requires It All the Time).[5] In Britain, people were asked to donate valuable objects, and artists were encouraged to contribute their works so that they could be sold for charities at auction houses.[6]

Germany and Austria-Hungary were especially hardpressed because President Wilson in his faithful support of the Allies had already in 1915 excluded them from Wall Street, and they could only raise some money in neutral European countries such as Sweden, Switzerland and the Netherlands.[7] All war-faring countries organized enormous propaganda campaigns with public speeches and appeals, posters, advertisements, cartoons, circulars, raffles, collection days, special propaganda events and, later, films.[8] In France, this was organized by the Committee of the National Loan (Commissariat à l'emprunt national); in Britain, by the National War Savings Committee (NWSC); and in Germany, from November 1916, by the

News Bureau for War Loans (Nachrichtenbüro für die Kriegsanleihe, NBK) of the German Imperial Bank. The German soldiers were indoctrinated by the KPA. Despite their 'blood tax' and their meagre pay – 53 pfennig per day (€2.01) – they were flooded with propaganda in the army newspapers and solicited personally by the instruction officers of the Patriotic Instruction.[9] In Austria as well, special war bond officers made propaganda inside the army. The success could not have been overwhelming because in both countries many soldiers on leave openly expressed defeatist opinions in the trains and warned their families that signing war bonds would prolong the war. In order to survey and curb defeatism finally, secret railway controllers had to be employed.[10] In France and Germany, the principal agents of financial conscription for the civilians were more or less in the same professional categories as those who played a key role in general war propaganda: teachers and their school kids, clergymen, public servants, professors, and in Germany supported by the officers of the Patriotic Instruction. In their Sunday sermons, the German pastors asked their flock to subscribe war bonds, and at the door of the church they were supposed to sign at once. In France, teachers received booklets with detailed guidance and readymade packages with appeals, posters, images and lists of appropriate exercises in mathematics and grammar, for instance about how to conjugate the verb 'to subscribe'. They were even rewarded with a commission of six centimes for each franc of a bond subscribed. Furthermore, successful subscribers of war bonds were admonished to convince others to do the same and thus became 'workers of propaganda'.[11] In Britain, the writers of war plays asked people either to enlist or to buy war bonds. In British schools, students read on the blackboards: 'War Loan: 100 pennies earns 4 ½ a year and means Victory', and for subscribing special machines were put at their disposition.[12] However, at the outset, not all teachers were so cooperative and some of them even regarded the campaigns of the NWSC as an 'intolerable interference in school affairs'. But in 1917, propaganda was stepped up, 746 new local War Savings Committees and 20,989 War Savings Associations were founded, and 'War Bond Weeks' were instituted. Thus by autumn 1917 the London Teachers' Association too began to organize 400 local offices, and finally the elementary and secondary schools of London raised £500,000 (£21.5 million) of war savings.[13] From May until August 1918, the NWSC organized 12 'War Weapons Weeks' all over the country, the most effective savings campaign ever seen in Britain which raised nearly £50 million (£2.1 billion). The strategy was very clever: not individual donors were asked but whole communities which after having spent a certain sum were entitled to name a weapon. Weekly bulletins indicating the results of the collections honoured winning communities and stigmatized less successful ones. In order to ensure the reputation of their villages or towns, many people went out of their way in giving money for the war machine.[14]

Propaganda for war bonds was threefold: by word of mouth, printed matter and films. In France, model speeches were handed out to speakers. They stressed three principal arguments: 'The loan is necessary to win, it will shorten the length of the war, and it is both a civic duty and a good investment'.[15] Together with the carrot came the stick: If the bonds could not be sold in sufficient number, the state would be obliged to increase taxes. Additional arguments were addressed to specific groups: Workers were told that after a German victory the French industry would be ruined and they would lose their jobs or have to work for lower wages. Townspeople were lured with the promise that the successful sale of the bonds would halt price rises. In Germany, 'men of confidence', for instance, the local mayor or a teacher, were instructed and trained in special seminars and received brochures with models of speeches and a carefully planned campaign program.[16] They would form a 'commission of confidence' for the organization of conferences and meetings. They would hire the speakers and also prepare the discussions after the speeches: selected persons would ask helpful prefabricated questions, while others would sign bonds immediately in order to set a good example. Sometimes such speeches were combined with popular events or rallies, march songs like 'Help Us Win' and free film performances.[17]

In both countries the direct contact with customers, 'man-to-man talk', was considered as the most efficient means of propaganda.[18] In a brochure, the NBK outlined a model discussion with a distrustful woman customer.[19] All sorts of arguments possibly raised against the purchase of war bonds are referred to along with instructions on how to refute them. When, for instance, she evokes the problem of tax progression, the propaganda agent should assure her that the tax office will not be informed about her bonds. He also has to refute the rumour that private banking accounts will soon be confiscated by the state. It is also explained what will be bought with the money: Weapons for the trenches, for instance, 80 machine guns which could ward off 1,000 enemy soldiers – so that Germany would be better protected against a foreign invasion. Here as well the stick was not lacking either: If not enough war bonds are signed, the Germans risk defeat and a cruel treatment by the Allies.

Children were victims and at the same time agents of propaganda. They were exhorted or even forced to donate their pocket money for the war effort, either to buy thrift or savings stamps (United States), to contribute to a 'penny collection' (France) or even to buy small war bonds with bank loans (Austria).[20] Penniless children were ridiculed, reprimanded by the teachers or excluded from class excursions.[21] As agents of propaganda, children roamed the streets, collecting money, selling badges and little pictures of charitable organizations and marching with placards such as 'Whoever Signs War Bonds Shortens the War' (Figure 24).[22] They were also expected to convince their parents and relatives to curtail expenses and to buy war savings certificates, sign war bonds or donate gold to the Central Banks. Propaganda asked them to put the utmost pressure on their parents or even to steal the money from them. In the *Corriere del Piccoli*, the children's supplement of the *Corriere della Sera,* supposed to mobilize the *'popolo bambino',* a small boy pesters his father so much that in order to calm him he invests his entire savings in war bonds.[23] In a French film, a schoolboy breaks open his father's savings box and buys war bonds with the money.[24] The reality was sometimes worse: In the context of the German campaign to exchange gold for iron, children harassed their father to donate his golden watch chain by quoting their teacher: 'Whoever still wears a golden watch chain is a traitor to his fatherland.' In the United States, some children went on hunger strike to force their less patriotic immigrant parents to buy war bonds.[25]

In the United States and in Germany, children were instructed on propaganda tactics by their teachers and were told to besiege local residents with requests for buying war bonds. The success depended on the area. The campaign of a secondary school in a bourgeois quarter of Berlin in 1916 raised a sum of 186,600 mark (€709,000), whereas vocational schools in working districts had poorer results or raised no money at all. In successful cases, the propaganda children were rewarded with medals, special 'certificates of honour' or with a day off at school.[26] In some parts of the United States, children did not only sell war bonds but, armed with a formal questionnaire, also had to test the loyalty of unwilling or critical people and denounce them to the authorities.[27]

War bonds propaganda by printed matter was at first limited to advertisements and editorials in newspapers, to leaflets, brochures and prospectuses.[28] From 1916, posters became more and more important, although the traditional means of propaganda continued. For the campaign of the 6th German war loan in March 1917, 24 million leaflets were produced, compared to 65 big posters (96x144 cm), 634,000 medium ones (44x58 cm) und 655,000 smaller ones (24x34 cm).[29]

Allied and German/Austrian posters had certain similarities, but also differences: They all displayed suggestive figures of women, children, soldiers and generals, but the style was quite different.[30] In German and Austrian posters, women are calm, serene and smiling, while in French and American counterparts, they are aggressive – either shouting or swinging a sword. The Italian posters are somewhere in between: the women may use a sword, but look calm and restrained, with the exception of a panicking mother with a child harried by Austrian soldiers.[31] These differences are even more pronounced in the images of soldiers. German, Austrian and Hungarian soldiers look strong and determined, but they are rather static and usually presented in a defence position. Nevertheless, they demonstrate force and the will to hold out, sometimes with a large golden coin as a protection shield.[32] Two posters even present a soldier with the peace dove and the slogan 'It moves us closer to peace'.[33] Golden coin and dove, of course, refer to the war bonds. Three posters present a classical topic: St. George fighting the dragon, Siegfried drawing a sword against the British lion and, even more restrained, a medieval knight riding slowly away from the spectator – 'idylls of a harmless world of legends and fairy-tales', as Bernhard Denscher puts it.[34] Even Hindenburg, besides the soldier the most important figurehead of German propaganda posters, is posing for the 7th war loan in September 1917 solid as a rock, accompanied by the text 'Times are hard, but victory is certain' (Figure 25).[35] The Allied soldiers, on the contrary, are always on the move, shouting and storming aggressively as cavalrymen with daggers or as infantrymen with drawn bayonets. A well-known example is the French poster '*On les aura*' (We Shall Get Them).[36] Two posters even show the actual killing: a British soldier is stabbing a German with his bayonet; an American one has already killed a German who lies at his feet, and with a grim expression in his face he says: 'Come on! Buy more liberty bonds.'[37] Italian posters are again in between, showing the soldier in a static pose but pointing with his finger at the observer, and in one rare case he is mutilated but swinging one of his crutches.[38]

The US bonds were named liberty bonds, and the frequent argument 'For Liberty' was exclusively reserved to the Allies including the Russians,[39] while 'For Victory' was used by both sides.[40] Furthermore, certain posters reveal ideological positions: in a French poster 'Victory' is related to 'Liberty'; in a German one to 'Peace'.[41] The French accusing the Germans of hypocrisy refuse their 'cunning offensive of a compromise peace', and the Italians do not conceal the imperialistic character of their war with the argument: 'And what was ours will be ours again'.[42]

All the states used also films as means of war bonds propaganda. The French film *Pour la victoire* (For Victory) cleverly mixes authentic war scenes and propaganda speeches with fiction, comics and posters. It also demonstrates how important the war bonds were in order to finance the armament industry.[43] In the German film *Rentier Kulickes Flug zur Front* (Prosperous Mr Kulicke Flies to the Front), produced at the instigation of the NBK, a well-to-do man does not want to buy war bonds. One night he dreams that he flies to the front. When he sees how terribly destroyed and ruined the enemy land is, he understands that only war bonds can spare the Germans such damage. After the dream, he invests all his money in war bonds. In another film, *Das Kriegssofa* (The War Sofa), a woman finds money hidden in her father's sofa and spends it on war bonds. When house and sofa are burnt down by the Cossacks, the father is glad that the money had been saved.[44] In the Italian Film *Mariute,* a peasant woman is raped by Austrian soldiers, her father-in-law shoots them and at the end the actress asks the spectators to buy war bonds.[45]

In the United States, William Brady, the president of the National Association of the Motion Picture Industry (NAMPI), created in May 1917 a Joined Industry Government Committee which, in cooperation with the CPI, made propaganda films for war bonds. During the campaign for the 4th Liberty loan in September 1918, it produced 38 short films with famous actors such as Chaplin, Douglas Fairbanks and Mary Pickford. Some of these films successfully employed the slapstick techniques. For instance, in the film *The Bond*, Chaplin beats the Kaiser senseless with a huge mallet entitled 'Liberty Bond'.[46]

A special way to extract money in Germany and Austria were nail statues, a propaganda technique of a specific national tradition.[47] In cities, towns and even villages, enormous wooden crosses, doors, animals, weapons, statues of generals, saints and even of a Madonna were erected (Figure 26), into which the people would hammer iron, silver or golden nails in exchange for donations between 1 and 100 mark or kronen. The first nailing occurred in Vienna on 6 March 1915. The biggest statue was the 'Iron Hindenburg' erected on 4 September 1915 in Berlin, which weighed 26 tons and was 14 meters high. There were around 700 nailing statues in Austria and several thousands in Germany. The advantage for the authorities was evident: They did not need to pay the nail money back. When the sale of nails slackened, they organized special nailing weeks and forced children to buy nails at school.[48] This fad reached its peak in 1915–16, after which people were fed up with it.

The Allies mocked at this nailing business, interpreted it as another case of German barbarism and compared it to 'Negro fetishes'.[49] However, from autumn 1917, the NWSC started raising money in a similar way with the 'tank banks'. Visitors could inspect the inside of tanks against the purchase of a war savings certificate. As such tanks were displayed in more than 150 towns and cities, the campaign raised millions of pounds, in Glasgow a record of £14.5 million (£623.5 million). When in autumn 1918 people had enough of it, a new campaign called 'Feed the Guns' was started with howitzers into which visitors could put coins.[50] Like the iron statues in Germany and Austria, the British tank banks and cannon banks were meant, as Stefan Goebel puts it, 'to symbolise the civilian's iron will to see the military campaign through'.[51]

It has been asserted that the amount of money invested in war bonds was an indicator for the will of the population to hold out.[52] This depended, however, on how much people still believed in a positive outcome of the war. In Germany, the most successful sale of war bonds – 15 billion mark (€57 billion) – occurred in March–April 1918 after the peace of Brest-Litovsk and during the great German victories at the Western front, but after the defeats of August and September the last war loan amounted to only 10.4 billion mark (€39.5 billion).[53] On the other hand, the degree of pressure exerted on people also played a role. Germans were not formally obliged to sign, but especially in smaller towns social constraints played a great role and people could be denounced to the authorities for negative attitudes.[54] In Italy, a worker who refused to buy war bonds with the argument 'It was not me who wanted the war', was condemned to 40 days arrest and a fine of 100 lire (€275), a week's wage.[55] In the United States, self-appointed financial controllers intruded the homes of the poorer classes and the immigrants, demanded detailed information about their financial situation and obliged them to sign war bonds by threatening to have them jailed or even expulsed from the community. It happened that people had to borrow money at 10 per cent in order to buy imposed liberty bonds at 4 per cent.[56] In Britain, a 'conscription of securities' took place. Regulations were made under DORA either to borrow them for a certain time from the holders or to requisition especially foreign securities against compensation and to sell them with a profit abroad.[57] The worst cases happened in Austria: Soldiers were practically forced by their officers to buy bonds in order 'to be left in peace again'; public servants received part of their salary in war bonds, and some companies were paid by the state in the same way.[58]

Children

Victims

The situation before the war: War Propaganda for children[59] did not start in 1914. Even before the war, Germany was considered a militarist country par excellence. In her famous book *The Century of the Child,* the Swedish writer Ellen Key wrote: 'Already in the kindergarten the souls of the Germans are drilled for the uniform.'[60] Marieluise Christadler has analysed a large collection of books inspiring hate and self-sacrifice in children and youth.[61] Highlights of nationalist agitation in children and youth literature were the victory of Arminius over the Romans and the wars of liberation against Napoleon I. A striking example for exalted militarism was the popular book *Wie erziehen wir unsern Sohn Benjamin?* (How Do We Educate Our Son Benjamin?) by the school headmaster Adolf Matthias who propagated as the aim of education that 'the juvenile should from early age consider [...] death in a battle as the most sublime aim of patriotic action'.[62] Furthermore, the paramilitary drill in organizations like the Boy Scouts (Pfadfinder) and the Young Germany League (Jungdeutschland-Bund) as well as the numerous military events of the Veterans' Associations (Kriegervereine) led to a 'social militarisation' of the uncritical juveniles.[63] On the other hand, school curricula were not militarized and books glorifying war amounted to only 12 per cent of the juvenile book production. Only a small minority of young boys joined the militaristic youth associations, and pacifist teachers were quite active in the elementary schools.[64]

The situation in France and Britain was quite similar. In both countries pedagogues oscillated between bellicose and pacifist tendencies. In France, partisans of patriotic and militaristic education like Ernest Lavisse fought downright battles with militants of pacifism such as Gustave Hervé and Félix Pécaut. But in view of increasing tensions in Europe since 1905 and peace seemingly threatened by Germany, patriotic messages like 'to die for the fatherland is the most beautiful and the most enviable fate' finally carried the day.[65]

In Britain, due to George Alfred Henty and his successors, a more aggressive message was propagated since the 1880s: As the Germans intended to make war in Europe, the British Empire had to be defended through unceasing warfare. Translations of militaristic German youth books such as *Der Weltkrieg – Deutsche Träume* (The Coming Conquest of England) both of 1904, and anti-German propaganda novels like *The Enemy in Our Midst: The Story of a German Invasion* (1906/1914) added fuel to the jingoist fire.[66] However, a leading magazine like *The Boy's Own Annual* limited itself to adventure stories and in 1912–13 barely mentioned the Balkan Wars.[67] In both countries also some sort of military training was introduced: in France in school battalions, and in Britain in organizations like the Boys' Brigade and the Church Lads' Brigade, which, however, between 1885/1891 and 1915 did not train more than 650,000 and 450,000 boys, respectively.[68]

In Austria, 'an alliance between military and school' was made with the introduction of *Bürgerkunde*, which combined political instruction, sports and from 1910 also shooting and drill exercises. School books emphasized patriotism, heroism and allegiance to the Hapsburg dynasty with slogans like 'Vanquish or die for Kaiser and Empire'.[69] It seems that only in Italy bellicose propaganda played no role in pre-war education.[70]

Indoctrination at school during the war: When war broke out, in Germany, Austria and Italy the ministries of education limited themselves to general patriotic appeals; in Britain, the National Board of Education suggested special courses and recommended text books; and only in France were the schools showered with many circulars, but initiatives were left to the local authorities.[71]

In 1915–16, the German education authorities stepped up their propaganda efforts. From March 1915, the ZEU in Berlin organized exhibitions and courses for teachers like 'The military training of our school children' or 'War compositions in secondary schools' and distributed various teaching materials like soldiers' letters, albums and postcards.[72] In 1916, the ministries of the federal states reacted as well. For instance, on 10 June 1916, the Ministry of Education and Cult in Baden asked the teachers to combat discontent and pusillanimity so that the people 'in fervent patriotic enthusiasm would hold fast to their determination to vanquish and refuse any idea of a humiliating peace'.[73] From July 1917, Ludendorff's Patriotic Instruction mobilized school inspectors and teachers more and more and even obliged some of them to attend propaganda courses[74] (see pp. 31, 56–7, 61, 92). In the United States, education was decentralized. Thus it was a branch of the CPI which issued various newsletters, pamphlets and a bi-monthly school bulletin called *National School Service*, informing the teachers about German atrocities and proposing teaching subjects like 'Why the US entered the war' or 'How children can help'.[75]

A greater activity was displayed by local authorities: in France, Britain and the United States by the school inspectors or local boards; in Germany by the school councillors and sometimes the district youth workers; and in Italy by the teachers' unions and private organizations – all of them giving practical advices and distributing teaching material.[76] For instance, in France an inspector imposed the following procedure: 'The lesson will explain the reasons for the war and the unprovoked attack which unleashed it. It will furthermore explain that France, the eternal fighter for right and progress, will rise again and together with her valiant allies repudiate the attack of the barbarians.'[77]

The main bulk of propaganda, however, was shouldered by the individual teachers, especially in the small towns and at the countryside.[78] Under their supervision, the students wrote war-related compositions, songs and poems, made drawings, interpreted exciting stories, pictures and posters of heroic battles, engaged in singing and role-playing in the school yard or even in public places; in Italy they even staged the conquest of an Austrian fortress.[79] Although at least in Germany and Britain child-centred teaching methods emphasizing the autonomous activity of the students had already been introduced before the war,[80] the compositions and drawings usually mirrored the lessons and propaganda texts of the teachers.[81] A six-year-old German boy noted in his copybook: 'The Englishmen are our enemies', 'The German and the Turk are allied brothers.' A 14-year-old girl wrote in a school composition: 'The German woman fights in the same manner for home and stove as the men on the battlefield', and the teacher gave her the best grade.[82] Of the German school compositions, 17 per cent concerned victory celebrations and the new national spirit of the population and 29 per cent described the war as an exciting adventure with heroic soldiers storming the trenches and taking tens of thousands of prisoners.[83] Girls painted trenches as comfortable places.[84] In Britain, children wrote compositions about rather complicated subjects like war taxes and war loans and, like in the United States, exercised their facilities by writing numerous letters to soldiers or to children's magazines.[85] In France, dictations and compositions were full of revenge and hatred of the enemy.[86] In one such dictation for younger students, the German Kaiser was described as 'a monster, an abominable cannibal', while the composition topic provided to older students had been: 'Give some examples of the atrocities committed by the Germans during this war. Imagine you were a soldier and would invade Germany with your troop, what would you do? And why?'[87]

In some countries, the school lessons began with some war-related ceremony: in the United States, with a salute to the flag, the singing of the national anthem and in some places a pledge of allegiance; in Germany, with the salutation 'God punish England'; and in France, with a minute's silence for the fathers and brothers in the trenches.[88] Then in all countries teachers usually read and explained the war communiqué.[89] In history class, students would discuss actual or historical victories, admire the bravery of their military heroes or learn about the boundless atrocities of the enemy.[90] In geography class, they learnt about the conquered territories, and in natural science, they were informed about arms, munitions, suffocating gas, trenches, aeroplanes and submarines.[91] In religion class, German students were told that they could not be starved by the Allied blockade because Jesus had nourished thousands of people with a few fishes and loaves of bread.[92] Most convincing was the following math problem: In the Battle of Neuve Chapelle, the British conquered a strip of land 3 km long and 950 meters broad. This 'success' cost them 25,000 dead. How many soldiers do they have to sacrifice in order to liberate the entire occupied French territory of 22,300 km^2? When the students performed their calculations they arrived at a total of 195,600,000 dead soldiers. 'This is impossible' ", said one student. 'Yes', the teacher confirmed, 'that's why they can't win the war – don't forget to tell this to your parents.'[93]

The school principals also celebrated many patriotic days – in France the Serbian Day or the Day of the War Bond and in Germany the numerous victories – with jingoist songs, edifying poems, heroic tales and enthusiastic speeches.[94] One German student wrote in her diary: 'Every day a battle, and we do not need to go to school any more.'[95] Paramilitary activities and drill in France, Germany and Britain, partly at school as well, had little military value, but should enhance enthusiasm for the war.[96] On 16 March 1916, the socialist leader Liebknecht resumed the situation at German schools in the Prussian Lower Chamber: They have become 'centres of indoctrination and [...] training institutions for the war'[97].

Abusing children's leisure time: According to contemporary authors, children were fascinated by the war and enjoyed playing mock battles and war games, reading war books and painting ruins and fighting scenes, at least in 1914–15.[98] A German girl explained in her war diary: 'We could not play anything but war, because there was no peace.'[99] The battles in the streets started with toy guns and wooden rifles, but soon degenerated into bloody fighting between gangs of boys equipped with knives, catapults, air pistols and detonating toy hand grenades. This could lead to serious injury and sometimes even to death when children were killed by a collapsing trench.[100] Although such war plays imbued children with militaristic norms of behaviour,[101] it must be emphasized that the authorities were somewhat frightened and did not press for war-related games and books. Propaganda through toys, games and books was more an affair of businessmen who reacted to popular demand.[102] However, at least in Britain, a few authors of juvenile literature were associated with the WPB, and in Austria, a special office in the Ministry of the Interior invented games of dice like 'Who will win' and 'We must win'.[103]

Beginning in autumn 1914, war games were much in demand.[104] In Britain, the young people played board games such as 'Trench football', 'Dash to Berlin' or 'Can Great Britain be invaded?' and in Germany and France, strategic games, for instance, about the passage of the Dardanelles, or the 'Victoria war game'.[105] Other games were inspired by well-known victories like the German 'Encirclement of Russian armies and their defeat' or the British 'New game of Jutland'.[106]

Singing in a group was also an important instrument of mobilization. It was supposed to bring about the 'integration of the individual into the whole people' and reinforce hate, discipline and the spirit of sacrifice under the slogan 'Whoever sings, will also vanquish'. Brutal war songs were composed and traditional songs militaristically rewritten.[107] In England, children would march like soldiers and sing:

This is the house that Jack built.
This is the bomb that fell on the house that Jack built.
This is the Hun that dropped the bomb that fell on the house that Jack built.
This is the gun that killed the Hun that dropped the bomb that fell on the house that Jack built.[108]

In Germany, children sang 'Hail Hindenburg', walking around in a circle and accompanying the song with violent movements. At the words 'punch him well' or 'shoot him dead', they punched one another; the refrain was 'Hail Hindenburg, shoot all the Russians dead'.[109] In France, adults and children alike enjoyed singing songs about German atrocities and heroic French children.[110] Children were also obliged to pray for the success of their country's soldiers and to recite prayers of hatred toward the enemy.[111] In 1915, Catholic priests in France, Germany and Austria organized the 'children's crusades', whose members engaged in permanent prayers for the victory of their respective countries.[112] 'Praying thus became', as Bérénice Zunino puts it, 'children's patriotic duty'.[113]

Magazines and books: While traditional children's magazines such as *Herzblättchens Zeitvertreib* or *Auerbachs Kinderkalender* in Germany and *Child's Companion* or *Child's Own Magazine* in Britain hesitated to confront the children with too many war-related subjects, French magazines immediately concentrated on them.[114] American counterparts conveyed a pacific message until February 1917, but after the American declaration of war, they abruptly changed the cap and flooded their readers with war propaganda usually received from the CPI.[115] *Saint Nicholas* and *The Rally* summed up children's duties and sacrifices like knitting sweaters for the soldiers or donating gifts to the Red Cross, and Theodore Roosevelt declared in the *Child Welfare Magazine*: 'Only those are fit to live who do not fear to die.'[116]

In Italy, each Sunday the *Corriere dei Piccoli* presented different heroes as models for children, one of them, Tofoletto, was the hero of the home front – a poor boy, ready to sacrifice everything, even his life, for the fatherland.[117] In Russia, simple popular entertainment was not only addressed to children but also to millions of illiterates (see p. 47).

Books for younger children in Britain and Germany, for instance, picture, war colouring and ABC books, usually played down war as a sort of thrashing or ridiculed the enemy with techniques copied from caricatures,[118] whereas in France they confronted the little ones with most cruel details about German atrocities and the terrible revenge of French troops with the purpose of promoting hate in children – one of the main aims of French war pedagogy.[119] Pictures of the war rarely showed the monotony of the trenches but preferred at first anachronistic cavalry attacks and later heroic aerial and naval battles with a rhetoric as well being copied from feudal times.[120] Such books were usually bought and read by the parents who explained them to their children and were thus exposed to the same message.[121] An excellent example of such propaganda for adults and children alike are the war versions of the famous German children book *Struwwelpeter*. In the German wartime version he was now called *Bombenpeter*, King Peter I of Serbia, depicted as a conspirator and violent murderer. All authority figures in the story are meant to represent Germany and Austria, whereas the naughty children stand for the wicked and inferior enemy nations which would clearly lose the war. In Britain, *Struwwelpeter* became *Swollen-headed William* 'with the blood upon his hands' (Figures 27 and 28). One of the stories is worth retelling here: In the original, a girl plays with a matchbox and ultimately burns to ashes despite the friendly warnings of two cats. In the German wartime version, she is called Marianne, the symbol of France. The matchbox bears the inscription 'Ideas of Revenge', and the two cats wear German and Austrian helmets. In the British version, it is the Kaiser who plays with the matchbox referred to as 'world politics', while the two cats are his grandfather Wilhelm I and Bismarck (Figures 29 and 30).

In 1914–15, the production of war books for older children and juveniles became a great commercial success.[122] Such books praised the great merits of young volunteers and inculcated in children how 'wonderful it is to have fallen on the battlefield'.[123] Presenting the war as a great adventure, some stories were totally absurd: A young German boy takes 126 prisoners and receives a medal directly from the Kaiser.[124] A British juvenile flies several dangerous missions, fights together with Belgian infantry, takes part in a successful cavalry charge and a naval action, is captured and escapes, tracks down and kills an enemy master spy – all this within a few months.[125] In Britain, throughout the war, stories propagated the danger of German spies and saboteurs who were hunted down and caught by courageous boys and girls.[126] In a serial published in *The Boy's Own Paper* in 1914, an English schoolboy on holiday in Belgium finds out that the teacher of German in his secondary school was a German spy and had invented poisonous gas. And the boy wonders if 'the seemingly innocent and industrious Germans scattered throughout England, were for the most part, secret service agents'.[127] *The Girl's Own Annual* was addressed to girls and women alike. In the first years, references to the war were rare. Later in Britain as well as in Germany and France, women and girls were presented in novels and posters as war nurses, spy catchers, army drivers and factory workers like, for instance, in the famous novel *Munitions Mary* by Brenda Grivin.[128] Ideological propaganda for democracy and against German militarism and the 'Huns' played a certain role in Allied books, while the 'Ideas of 1914' were seemingly absent from German juvenile literature.[129] In view of the deteriorating supply situation in the second half of the war, exhortations to save food, renounce luxuries like cookies or sweets and advices about the raising of small animals at home became more important.[130]

Duty, sacrifice and labour for the fatherland: Children were deeply affected by the war situation. As resources were limited, special virtues such as renunciation, abnegation, thriftiness and a sense of duty were inculcated in children.[131] This 'ideology of parsimony and sacrifice', as Antonio Gibelli puts it, was an economic necessity to the power of all war-faring states, in starving Germany, Austria and Italy even essential for national survival.[132] Children were regarded as home front fighters subject to the same discipline and frugality as the armed forces.[133] An American slogan ran: 'Our army is at the front. We must be its soldiers behind the lines.'[134] A French teacher's journal put it this way: 'Juveniles, to work! Or rather, to arms, because you too are in the fight.'[135] In Germany children were told: 'We are not in this world to be happy, but in order to do our duty.'[136] Such massive indoctrination in favour of 'domestic heroism', as Bérénice Zunino calls it, prepared them for what was typically unpaid labour in the service of the fatherland.[137] Children cultivated vegetables in parks and school gardens and raised small animals there, shredded linen for sharpie (in France and Austria even small children between two and five years were put to this work), knitted woollens for soldiers, sent parcels to the front, worked in farms and factories, collected waste paper and scrap metal and looked after siblings.[138] In 1917 due to the voluntary service of the children the crop yield in France increased by 4.7 million francs (€12.7 million).[139]

In Britain and in some cases also in Italy, children guarded bridges, coastal points and telegraph poles; they worked as messengers, as orderlies, in hospitals and for ambulance troops. In Britain, 600,000 of them were encouraged by the British Board of Education to leave school prematurely at the age of 11 in order to work in the fields, in munitions factories and even in mines.[140] In starving Germany and Austria, additional tasks were imposed: procuring food by queuing all night at food stores, begging for it at farmsteads or even stealing it somewhere. Lead by their teachers and permanently exhorted by propaganda posters, they were also made to gather wild fruits like acorns and beechnuts, fruit kernels for oil making, and plants such as stinging nettles which were used as ersatz cotton for making pullovers.[141] The results were quite impressive: In 1917, the schoolchildren of the Prussian province of Schleswig-Holstein collected 37,546 kg of wild fruits, 41,380 kg of rowanberries, 46,486 kg of hawthorn fruits, 13,658 kg of fruit kernels, 62,201 kg of acorns and beechnuts, 211,425 kg of chestnuts, 30,692 kg of nettles,

804,505 kg of stalks and cuttings, and 64,950 kg of scrap.[142] A very special case of child activity was invented in France – acting as 'godmother' or 'godfather' of a soldier: Such children, individually or as a group, sent letters and parcels to soldiers and cared for them when they were on leave.[143]

However, the most varied and widespread mobilization of child engagement took place in the United States, according to the blackmailing slogans 'Prove your Americanism by eating less' and 'If you are willing to work and sacrifice to bring victory to her [US] in this just cause, then you are an American. If you are not, you are a traitor.' Apart from the usual collecting, gardening and picking activities, American children had to earn money by raising livestock, washing windows, selling cakes and other items at bazaars, even organizing a circus or an afternoon matinee and donate not only all the profits to the Junior Red Cross but also their beloved dogs and pigeons to the army.[144]

Propagandists

Multipliers: The children were not only objects but also subjects of propaganda with the task to reinforce the patriotic sentiments of the public in general and of their parents in particular – called in Italy 'war didactics'.[145] In the first place, children were used as figureheads in propaganda posters for savings certificates, war bonds, orphans' relief, in Italy even for grenades and in Britain for recruitment campaigns before the introduction of conscription in 1916.[146] In the United States, copying the 'Four Minute Men' program of the CPI, teachers organized the writing of propaganda speeches, and the best texts were delivered by the children at special school events. Children also paraded with placards like 'Wake up America' or 'Dad's at the front'.[147] In the mobilization of children, teachers played a preponderant role. They often explicitly asked them to indoctrinate their parents. Harmless were advices not to waste food, to manage things more economically or to bottle and dry fruit.[148] More pestering were children who reprimanded their parents for lavish expenses and insisted on thriftiness and sacrifice. When a well-to-do German lady in Munich wanted to buy an expensive hat for 25 mark (€90), her 14-year-old son vigorously protested and made such a fuss that she did not dare to enter the store.[149] The extensive propaganda activity of children for war loans is discussed on pp. 93–4.

Martyrs and heroes: Children were presented as splendid examples of suffering or bravery. In stories, drawings and films, they figured either as victims of German, Austrian or Russian atrocities[150] or as war heroes. In films like *Der zwölfjährige Kriegsheld* (The 12-Year-Old War Hero), the boys ran away and joined the troops or demanded to be enlisted despite their young age.[151] Inspired by such propaganda, quite a few boys, and in Russia and Italy even girls in boy's garment, tried to turn fiction into reality and some of them were successful: 12 Russian school girls, aged between 12 and 14 fought indeed for one year at the Austrian front.[152] However, such absconders became a nuisance at the front, and were, except in Russia, normally returned to their parents. While at least in Britain such stories were even warmed up in 1917 because of the desperate need for more recruits, in Germany the whole topic was finally either dropped or even criticized in children fiction, and the above-mentioned film was prohibited for youth by censorship.[153] However, recruiting offices usually accepted children and juveniles between 12 and 17 years. As Rob Ruggenberg has convincingly demonstrated, 'all armies in the Great War used kid soldiers'. Some of them were decorated and became propaganda idols, while others died without glory or were even ruthlessly executed for desertion when their nerves broke down and they ran away from the trenches.[154]

More spectacular was the cult of allegedly over hundred 'child heroes' in France. The most famous case was Emile Després alias Victor Dujardin, 13-year-old, who during the German invasion gave water to a wounded French sergeant who had just killed a German soldier in order to prevent a rape. When the Prussian officer demanded him to shoot the sergeant in order to save his own life, he shot the Prussian and was in turn executed himself. Propaganda exaggerated the story; in reality Després, like most other 'child heroes', was already 18 years old.[155] A similar cult figure emerged in Britain. Jack Cornwell, 17-year-old, was the last surviving member of a gun crew on a cruiser and, although seriously wounded, remained passively (!) at his post. This 'heroic' deed was heavily exploited. Children all over the empire collected £18,000 (£ 775,000), and the boy was posthumously awarded the Victoria Cross and commemorated with portraits, plaques, and monuments.[156] In Russia, the greatest schoolboy hero, Orlov, fought in 11 battles and was finally decorated by the tsar with the Order of St. George.[157] In Austria, the Polish girl Rosa Zenoch was presented as an example of dynastic patriotism. During a battle against the Russians, she gave wounded Austrian soldiers water and was wounded herself. When her leg had to be amputated in a Viennese hospital, Emperor Franz Josef and other members of the Hapsburg family visited her, showered her with gifts and agreed to pay for a prosthesis.[158]

In Germany and Italy, children played a more modest role. In Italy, war orphans assisted as guards of honour at the patriotic funerals of fallen soldiers.[159] In Germany, a few stories circulated about children who helped the soldiers in the trenches and sometimes performed heroic deeds, but weird enough, all of them were of foreign origin, mostly Slavic.[160]

Soldiers

Normally it was the officers' task to instruct the soldiers and to sustain their morale – an exercise usually called 'brainwashing' by the soldiers.[161] All armies also employed chaplains for the same purpose; in the British and American armies even after a special training.[162] Their numbers varied between two and three to four chaplains per division in Prussia and Bavaria, 12–16 in Austria-Hungary, and from 1,550 for the whole French army to 2,700 of them plus 24,000 other clerics in the Italian forces. In the British troops, the number increased from 117 in 1914 to 3,475 in 1918, with 878 of them being Anglicans; the US army in November

1918 had 2,300 chaplains. The Russians employed 2,000 in addition to 3,000 other Orthodox priests and also Catholic, Jewish and Muslim clergymen who preached 'devotion to the point of self-sacrifice for the Tsar' and admonished the soldiers 'to meet suffering calmly and to be always ready to die'.[163] The Austrian chaplains received readymade propaganda sermons from the commander of the Apostolic Field Vicariate, but only some of them would give 'fire-breathing, unquestioned-obedience-to-authority discourses'. A chaplain in a famous Tyrolean battalion successfully combined fighting with sermons raising the spirit of the soldiers.[164] In the British army, according to several memoirs, especially the Anglican chaplains met with resent and contempt because they got on the soldiers' nerves with 'bloodthirsty' propaganda, had to do menial work and other odd jobs and were at the beginning of the war not allowed in the frontline trenches. However, Edward Madigan by analysing the Anglican War Record has proved that according to their decorations, including even two Victoria Crosses, and the satisfaction of their superiors the chaplains had after all exercised a rather positive effect on troop morale.[165] General Douglas Haig even went so far as to ascribe to them the role of political commissars mixing spiritual guidance with patriotic propaganda for the Allied cause. In the German army, the chaplains were advised to make propaganda discreetly and not too often. Besides, the Bavarian Archbishop Michael von Faulhaber supplied them with readymade field sermons which did not stress the chauvinist interpretation of the war but emphasized the mysterious character of divine providence.[166] France was a special case: The clergy were conscripted, thus 'their first task was to kill and not to take care of the soldiers' souls or to make propaganda'; only the titular and a few older voluntary chaplains were exempted from fighting. In the British dominions and colonies, some clergymen also joined the combatant forces.[167]

As in Italy, official propaganda did not start until November 1917, and the chaplains and a few selected speakers sometimes addressed the soldiers. An eyewitness gives a sarcastic account of such an exercise: 'After eight hours of tiresome activity the soldiers had to renounce one hour of liberty, stand in a yard and listen to the chatter of an advocate who was not used to the tiring of the war.' Despite the condemnation of the war by the papacy, the whole army was consecrated to the *Sacro cuore di Gesù* (Sacred Heart of Jesus) with two million soldiers practising this devotion.[168] But on the whole the commanding general, Luigi Cadorna, relied less on propaganda but on severe military justice. A total of 262,481 soldiers passed before the military tribunals; 4,028 were condemned to death, and 750 were executed. The comparative figures for the other countries were: in France 650, in Britain 346 and in 'militaristic' Germany less than 50. On top of that, at least further 350 Italian soldiers were summarily shot by 'decimation' – a procedure which did not exist in the other armies. For smaller disciplinary errors, Cadorna had soldiers bound for several hours to the stakes of the barbed wire in front of the trenches. Finally in the Battle of Caporetto in October 1917, the soldiers retaliated by a 'military strike': 300,000 soldiers surrendered, and around 70,000 deserted. Only after the dismissal of Cadorna this 'discipline of coercion' was replaced by the 'discipline of persuasion'.[169]

In this long war of attrition, specialized propaganda was necessary. In order to indoctrinate the soldiers and to boost their morale the armies, except in Russia, published special newspapers usually written by reserve officers. From August 1914 until November 1917, the French army distributed the *Bulletin des armées de la République* which reported the usual atrocities of the Germans and their supply problems and nourished the soldiers on the great battles of the past as long as there were no victories. The Belgians issued two journals, in French the *Courrier de l'Armée* and in Flemish *De Legerbode*. [170] In Turkey from November 1915 until June 1918, the Ministry of War published the monthly *Harb Mecmuası* (War Periodical) which extolled the greatness of the Ottoman Empire and its army. In view of the high rate of illiteracy, the periodical especially used illustrations accompanied by short explanations.[171]

The German army opted for a decentralized approach. The military commands of the various armies, corps and divisions edited 50 different field newspapers, and from 1916 the KPA published the thrice-weekly *DK* and the *Deutsche Kriegswochenschau* for the front and the home front alike.[172] Furthermore, approximately 100 private firms also issued war newspapers to their workers at the front in order to intensify patriotic 'corporate identity'.[173] In Austria-Hungary, the KPQ published a weekly as well, called *Heimat* in German and *Uzenet* in Hungarian. There was also a bad Czech translation, but none in the languages of the other nationalities. Furthermore, some army commands insisted on having their own newspapers, for instance, the Supreme command of Carinthia edited the *Karnisch-Julische Kriegszeitung*.[174] In Britain, MI7(b)1 published the *Weekly Letter for Soldiers*; the War Office and the Admiralty from 1916 distributed *Blighty*, a humorous weekly; and the NWAC from March 1918 *Welcome*, some sort of an addition to *Blighty*, destined to soldiers on leave, with practical information about accommodation, amusements and sports.[175] In the United States, the national headquarters and the CPI distributed bulletins and pamphlets for the officers of the home cantonments which were identical or similar to the regular Four Minute Bulletins and were intended to prepare the soldiers not only at the military, but also at the propaganda level for their combat in Europe.[176]

The German official field newspapers and the *DK* emphasized the superior strength of the German armies and reported time and again in the rubric 'Table of honour' heroic deeds of their units. For instance, the *DK* compared 'the holding out beyond praise of our troops, [...] their better formation and their exemplary discipline' with the 'weakened fighting spirit of the French' and the 'end of British optimism' – quite a successful device to strengthen the morale of the German combatants.[177] Correcting 'lies' of the enemy press was also a popular topic. A great problem, however, were family letters complaining that they were starving at home. The army newspaper *Die Somme-Wacht* asked the soldiers to destroy such letters, because if they were found by the enemy they would reinforce his resistance and prolong the war. The *DK* confirmed this argument by quoting an article of the *Daily Chronicle* referring to such letters found in the pockets of German prisoners.[178] Finally bourgeois women of the National Women's Service drafted propagandistic model letters for soldiers' wives.[179] The greatest problem, however, was the massive arrival of American troops in 1918 and the pertaining information in numerous British leaflets dropped over the German lines. German propaganda falsified arrival figures and did its utmost to ridicule the American soldier (see p. 181). The defeats in July and August 1918 were equally toned down in German army communiqués, and people who believed them were completely shocked when Prince Max von Baden had to ask for an armistice.[180] The Carinthian army journal in 1917 mocked at the permanent failures of the Italian army and as late as 14 August 1918 maintained that the desperate Allies were hoping in vain for American troops.[181]

The soldiers in all armies were usually annoyed by this official indoctrination which was too far from their concern. When for instance the *DK* was delivered in the trenches, a German soldier remarked: 'There he is again with his central swindle'.[182] Thus low-ranking reserve officers and soldiers of journalistic or artistic background – in Germany 34 soldiers out of 180 were even editors-in-chief – published at the level of a company, a battalion or a regiment and in some cases a division their own trench newspapers which must not be lumped together with the official army and corps newspapers as Robert Nelson would have it.[183] They wrote with humour and irony about everyday life in the trenches, but also about more serious problems like their fear of death, and they even dared to parody the atrocity propaganda of the civilian newspapers. For instance, in December 1915, *Rigolboche*, the French trench journal with the largest circulation, depicts a German soldier sitting in a well; when the lieutenant asks him: 'Are you mad to take a bath in this season?' the soldier replies: 'I have been instructed to poison the sources.'[184] Typical for British trench papers was the humorous and ironical approach, for instance service jokes and parodies, a 'happy blend of the *Sporting Life* and *Punch*' so that censors rarely had to intervene.[185] With the exception of Anne Lipp, historians claim that these trench journals were devoid of propaganda,[186] but they seem to overlook that propaganda is not only an affair of bellicose brainwashing, but also the art of concealing undesired or even subversive news from the soldier and lulling his mind with idle gossip in order to prevent any critical reflection about his awful situation. Furthermore, this press was, of course, subjected to military censorship and to self-censorship. 'All too often', was explained in a French journal, 'the editorial staff was forced to reject as inappropriate certain articles'. And it is not fortuitous that in French journals *gloire* and *grandeur*, patriotism, national sentiment and the conviction to win played a greater role than in their German and British counterparts.[187] After all General Joffre had ordered in March 1916 that trench journals should not only amuse the fighting men 'but demonstrate that they are all full of confidence, of courage and have excellent morale'.[188] In German and especially in Italian trench newspapers, propaganda is even more evident. In Germany, from spring 1916, the authors of trench journals were obliged to insert some propaganda articles explicitly prepared for them by the Field Press Office under the professional writer Bloem.[189] Italy was the worst case: In the first two years, life in the trenches was trivialized with silly and lascivious jokes, student-type amusements and escapist remarks, while problems were not to be discussed and criticism not allowed. The task of propaganda was openly admitted: In a programmatic article in the first issue of the trench journal *L'elmetto*, the editors wrote: 'We intend to popularise as far as possible the voice of our leaders and to bring them to the ear and the mind of all the soldiers, encouraging, comforting and inciting them at the same time' – an approach called by Gibelli 'mass pedagogy' (*pedagogia di massa*).[190] After the defeat at Caporetto a new generation of trench journals was produced by bourgeois writers and official propagandists of the Servizio P, sitting in the offices of the rear and completely separated from the ordinary front soldiers.[191] Their messages contained hate caricatures and referred to the usual stereotypes: 'the aggressive spirit of the Central Powers bent on subjugating the whole world', 'the lineage of the ancient Italic Roman Empire', 'the 200 years' tradition of the House of Savoy' and 'the radiant day of the final victory'.[192]

In order to make soldiers more receptive to propaganda, the armies tried to mix it with entertainment. They organized theatre and film performances, songs and musical sketches, free beer, dances, acrobatic shows and collective singing.[193] In 1918, nearly all military units had established cinemas; a typical movie show would present a drama (one hour), comedies (one hour) and propaganda (half an hour).[194] In 1917, the French and the Germans created professional mobile front theatres, often with professional actors in uniform, such as the Frontbrettl (Little Front Stage) and the Dachauer Bauernkapelle im Felde (Peasants' Field Orchestra of Dachau) while all British divisions had permanent theatrical troops such as The Follies and The Fancies, which in 1918 also toured the front. Ludendorff's Patriotic Instruction considered front theatres as particularly useful for keeping up morale. The rare statistics tell us that 34 German divisions had their own theatres and that a total number of 760 mobile theatres were available while the French organized nearly 6,000 performances. Patriotic stage plays or conferences were rare, but by dealing with grievances in a humorous way and presenting performances in a music hall style, the performances helped the soldiers to forget their depressing lives in the trenches. One British program in September 1917 announced 'a trick cyclist', a Chaplin mimic, a 'girl' vocalist, a 'Zummerzet yokel' describing his love affairs, and a 'tall droll-faced Jock' playing a simpleton.[195] On the Italian front, the CS had asked the Authors' Association (Società degli Autori) to organize a 'Theatre at the front'. Here as well declamations of patriotic verses had to give way to funny comedies, farces, songs and plays with the traditional Pulcinella.[196] In Austria, the KPQ organized civilian theatres in Vienna which toured the various fronts.[197]

In the spring of 1917, soldiers on all sides 'were losing the will to do it anymore',[198] and the High Commands had to react. In tsarist Russia where official home propaganda was practically non-existent, immediately after the February Revolution a Central Committee for Socio-political Enlightenment was set up in order to organize war propaganda in the army, but not much is known about its activities.[199] The first to step up propaganda for the armed forces was Ludendorff with his Patriotic Instruction (see pp. 31, 61, 98) in July 1917, which recommended to mix conferences for the soldiers with theatre and film entertainment, but the authoritarian military approach was retained: 'In the sessions of the patriotic instruction discussions are not allowed.'[200] From autumn 1917, prestigious university professors gave lectures in order to strengthen the morale of the soldiers.[201] One of them, Edgar Jaffé, explained that in September and October 1917 he was deeply impressed by the fighting spirit and the high morale of the army, but when he came back in September 1918 he was shocked by the run down organization and the complete resignation of the troops.[202]

It seems that the Germans never set up special propaganda programs for their minority soldiers, the Poles, Danes and Alsatians. On the contrary, 1,900 Alsatian civilians deemed to be anti-German were placed under Protective Custody (Schutzhaft), and Alsatian soldiers were distrusted, discriminated and finally, according to a secret order of the Prussian Ministry of War of March 1915, partly shifted to the Eastern Front.[203] The 850,000 Polish soldiers were considered as more reliable by the OHL and therefore not exposed to the same humiliating treatment. Nevertheless because of increasing group desertions, especially of Poles from Posen in 1915, they were more widely dispersed from November 1915 and integrated in ethnical German units.[204]

In the Austrian army in March 1918, much later than in Germany, the FAST was created which trained special propaganda officers according to the following guidelines: They should encourage the sense of duty, discipline and order, avoid discussions about nationality problems, promise to take care of the war invalids and bring home to the soldiers that only Austria-Hungary could guarantee freedom and equality for all citizen.[205] However, it came too late and did not consider the rear and the home front where the people, among them many roaming deserters, were either indifferent or in open revolt.[206] In any case propaganda could do nothing against the desperate supply situation. As starving people started hunger riots and lootings of bread transports, food shops and farmsteads, the police forces could not keep order anymore, and in 1918 nearly half the Austrian army instead of fighting at the front was busy at home suppressing riots and mutinies, forcing farmers and producers to deliver badly needed goods and chasing deserters in the hinterland.[207]

In Italy in 1918, the Servizio P organized patriotic lectures by intellectuals, politicians and officers, but in view of the high rate of illiteracy preferred personal indoctrination by his 'men of confidence'[208] (see p. 15). The director of the Servizio P was Giuseppe Lombardo Radicea, a university professor of pedagogy, who tried to apply the concept of an activating non-authoritarian education to the soldiers.[209]

In the British army from 1915 officers gave lectures about war aims, and 20 professional lecturers spoke to the troops behind the lines. When in spring 1918 Britain was faced with the Wilsonian and Bolshevik slogans of peace without victory, the number of chaplains was considerably increased, more additional education officers were appointed and a formal of Political Education was envisaged. However, it was finally not needed because the success of the Allied offensive in summer improved the fighting morale considerably.[210] In France, propaganda was greatly strengthened by the famous war novel *Le Feu* published in 1916 by Barbusse, long time misunderstood as a pacifist work (see pp. 143–6).

Enemy troops

The first sporadic propaganda appeals were made at the Eastern Front. On 14 August 1914, Grand Duke Nicholas issued a proclamation to the Poles: 'Poles! Let the boundary lines which have cut the Polish nation asunder be obliterated. Let the Poles be reunited under the sceptre of the Russian Tsar.'[211] In another manifesto, he promised to liberate all Slavic peoples of Austria-Hungary and had 100,000 copies distributed, not only at the front but also in Bohemia.[212] Furthermore, the Russians dropped some leaflets over the German front and organized a special propaganda unit to win over the Czech soldiers. In 1916 and 1917, they distributed, probably in cooperation with the French Secret Service, leaflets in French and German asking soldiers from Alsace and Lorraine to desert and promising to take them to France.[213]

Local German and Austrian commanders also published manifestos promising the Polish soldiers liberation and independence, but they carried no weight because their appeals were not confirmed by the OHL or the AOK.[214] Somewhat later the Germans distributed a propaganda newspaper and letters of Russian prisoners, and in 1916 the Austrians dropped leaflets from balloons with the peace offer of the Central Powers and the promise to create an independent Poland.[215] Although on 1 June 1917 the French president had authorized the creation of an autonomous Polish army, mostly recruited from the Polish communities in America, French propaganda leaflets of September 1917 did not mention it yet and asked Polish soldiers in the German army to desert in order to escape the oppressive Prussian occupation system. It was only after a joint declaration of the Allies in June 1918 had promised Polish independence that French propaganda leaflets in August and September 1918 asked the Poles to join the Polish army in France and to fight there for Poland.[216]

The first vast propaganda campaign in the East was made by the OHL and the AOK after the Russian February Revolution.[217] Germans and Austrians dropped leaflets and newspapers over the Russian front and put up wooden propaganda placards. As from April an unofficial ceasefire existed; German and Austrian intelligence officers met with Russians and treated them with vodka and tobacco. In March, the German propagandists still counted on sympathies for the tsar and denounced the British to have cast him from the throne 'because he has realised and made public the cunning and treacherous English schemes'. They explained to the soldiers that they shed their blood only for England and that their families 'lived in hunger and destitution' because the 'profiteers, allied with England, were holding back all foodstuffs'.[218] 'Don't you really see', read a proclamation, 'that the English are leading Russia to the verge of ruin?'[219] When the Russian Provisional Government rejected armistice talks and in June even started a new offensive, German, Austrian and even 'Turkish' leaflets, produced by the German Oriental News Bureau, denounced it as a tool of the imperialist Entente, printed parts of Bethmann Hollweg's peace talks and offered the Russians an honourable peace.[220] When in September 1917 French units bloodily clamped down on mutinying Russian troops in France, German propaganda happily claimed that thousands of Russians had been slaughtered.[221] It also diffused Bolshevik demands for land reform and their protests against the offensive over the Russian front. When after his takeover on 22 November 1917 Vladimir I. Lenin ordered armistice negotiations and the Stavka refused to let this message pass, the Germans informed the Russian soldiers so that armistice negotiations could start (see pp. 170–1).

In autumn 1917, the Central Powers also turned to the Southern fronts and launched two successful propaganda campaigns against the Romanians and the Italians, as well as another one with mitigated success against the Serbian front in Thessaloniki.[222] The decisive Austrian-German victory at Caporetto in October 1917 was not really prepared by propaganda apart from a few scattered initiatives.[223] Propaganda practically started during the battle. Austrian planes showered the fleeing Italian troops with leaflets informing them that revolution had broken out in their country and that a peace could be concluded without annexations or indemnities. At the same time the Austrian navy distributed propaganda in the Italian hinterland and the KPQ smuggled pacifist tracts via Switzerland. The main propaganda campaign started in December 1917: Special officers organized the composition of propaganda leaflets and newspapers; they also trained and supervised patrols (Nachrichtentruppen) who either threw or shot propaganda material in the usual way to the enemy trenches or deposited it at certain localities where it could be collected by the Italian soldiers. In some places even fraternization happened for a certain time. Austrian propaganda tried to bring home to the Italian soldiers that the Entente had lost any chances to win this war while misery and famine ravaged the countryside, and that they should better overthrow their government like in Russia instead of sacrificing themselves for British interests. From February 1918, the campaign became more and more difficult: British planes dominated the air, the establishment of Servizio P tightened up the supervision of the soldiers, effective Italian counter-propaganda started, and soon Austrian leaflets did not reach the Italian lines any more.

In spring 1918, it was the turn of the Italians to make propaganda.[224] They had created the so-called Padua Commission consisting of Italians and representatives of the Slavic and Romanian peoples of Austria-Hungary and were now going to launch a multi-lingual propaganda campaign at the Piave front. Although this was stimulated and supported at the outset by British agents of MI7 and Crewe House, it was largely an Italian enterprise and, as Mark Cornwall emphasizes, 'the most extensive and sophisticated of its kind during the whole war'. From May until November 1918, the Italians distributed three times more propaganda material than the British at the Western Front. Their planes dropped 60 million leaflets and two million news sheets with nationalist and defeatist propaganda often based on correct information from the Austro-Hungarian press smuggled to Italy via Switzerland – information about the desperate situation in the empire which the authorities tried to conceal from the soldiers. Furthermore, they recruited volunteers for propaganda units in the prisoner camps, especially among the Czechs while the other nationalities were reluctant or even hostile to their action. Finally a whole trench propaganda network was created with patrols feeding Slavic soldiers horror stories about the situation in their homelands and appealing to national memories like the death of Jan Hus at the stakes in 1415. As the Austrians, by now in the grip of a most severe economic crisis, could not produce enough counter-propaganda, the AOK because of increasing desertions was compelled to replace some regiments with other troops. The morale of the Austrian soldiers never recovered from this blow.

While the Germans were very active in the East, they took a rather hesitant approach in the West because Ludendorff considered the French too nationalist and propaganda resistant, and even refused the proposition of French socialist prisoners to write propaganda texts.[225] At least he did not stop the dropping of the *Gazette des Ardennes* and the *War Chronicle* over the French and British fronts[226] (see below p. 113). From 1918, German propaganda was very active on the Belgian front at the Yser.[227] A Flemish activist movement in the Belgian army protested against the threats of the Belgian government to punish all Flemish collaborators of the Germans after the war. It demanded complete equality for the Flemings and announced that it would defend, guns in the hands, the Flemish University of Gent and other forms of Flemish self-government introduced under the occupation. From January 1918, the Germans launched propaganda leaflets and newspaper articles over to the Belgian trenches, asking the Flemish soldiers to desert. Until May 1918, 3,727 of them deserted indeed, but not all of them made it to the German trenches. In May 1918, eight leading activists, later called the 'sublime deserters', went over to the occupied area and four of them appealed to all Flemish soldiers at the Yser to follow their example. Their support of German propaganda was quite important: They fabricated letters of Flemish POWs about the wonderful life in the German camps, asked family members to write them letters of longing and announced very seducing news – Flanders has now become autonomous and is just about to conclude a separate peace with Germany and thus, the soldiers should fight no more for Britain and France, but come over and support the new Flemish state. The deserters also supported the activist Council of Flanders in its propaganda at home (see p. 124).

When Ludendorff's offensive in spring 1918 failed, he asked Hans von Haeften, at that time director of the MAA, to prepare a propaganda strategy in France and Britain with the aim 'to bring about a "peace crisis" in the enemy home front and to obtain a negotiated peace', a strategy which Haeften had already proposed on 15 January 1918, but it is not clear what Haeften exactly did in spring.[228] Only when in late summer 1918, the situation of the German army became desperate, Ludendorff on 28 August 1918 lifted the ban on dropping leaflets by plane and at last a frenetic propaganda campaign against the Allied soldiers began.[229] In September, even a propaganda camp was created with POWs ready to draft propaganda brochures.[230]

Otherwise it was Allied propaganda which dominated the Western Front. The SPA was already very active from August 1915, with its propaganda newspapers *Die Feldpost*, *Kriegsblätter für das deutsche Volk* and *Das freie deutsche Wort*.[231] On the British side, it was MI7(b)4 under George K. Cockerill, called 'Propaganda Library and Aerial Propaganda over Enemy Lines', which produced and distributed propaganda against the Germans from June 1916 on. Crewe House did not produce leaflets for the German front until 4 September 1918 when the fate of

Ludendorff's army was already sealed, and even then their leaflets were distributed by Cockerill's service till the end of the war.[232] The Americans did not send their first leaflet to the German lines until 29 August 1918.[233]

For transmitting propaganda on the front, an immense panoply of measures was developed: information boards, megaphones, gramophone recordings, in appropriate cases boats, bottles and buoys via waterways. Leaflets were thrown directly by hand or in cans, fixed to the enemy's barbed wire, shot over the front by bow and arrow, later with 'propaganda grenades' and rockets fired by mortars or special guns. The mortars gradually improved their range from 200 m to 5 km; the guns had a range of 15 km.[234] In some cases also contact patrols of deserters distributed propaganda material and invited their former comrades to join them.[235]

It was much easier to distribute propaganda by planes or balloons. While the first single leaflets had already been dropped on 9 and 30 August 1914, each of them by a French and a German aviator, promising the liberation of Alsace-Lorraine and demanding the surrender of Paris respectively, it was Swinton who with the financial help of Lord Northcliffe produced 25,000 leaflets and had them dropped over the German front in October. Further actions were soon stopped by the respective Army Commands.[236] Regular distribution of propaganda by planes did not start until spring 1915: The Germans dropped the *Russkaia Izvestia* and *Russki Westnik* over the Russian front; the Austrians after their occupation of Venetia in autumn 1917 the *Gazzetta del Veneto* over the Italian front and the occupied area. The *Gazette des Ardennes* under the responsibility of III b was very early distributed in the occupied areas and dropped over the front, from August 1917 even in English translation. It was widely read – the circulation rose from 4,000 issues in 1914 to 180,000 issues in January 1918 – because it was rather credible and accurate and contained information about French prisoners.[237] In order to counter the influence of this newspaper, MI7(b) dropped *Le courrier de l'air*, the SPA *La voix du pays*, several falsified editions of the *Gazette*, and also hundreds of thousands of French and British newspapers over the occupied area as well.[238]

Similar initiatives on the Eastern front were stopped in April 1915 because of limited success and legal protest by the Stavka followed by the court-martialling of two captured German aviators. The Germans accepted the Russian argument that this activity was a violation of International Law and in January 1918, in turn, court-martialled two British aviators. While the French continued to launch propaganda from planes, the British switched for a while to another technique: dropping leaflets from balloons.[239] The leaflets were attached to woven tinder which was fixed to the balloon. When the balloon was released, the tinder was lit and after 40 minutes the balloon was driven by the western winds between 20 and 100 km, sometimes more, into the German lines where the tinder burned out and the leaflets fell to the ground. Each balloon could transport two kilos of paper. Until November 1918, 30,000 balloons dropped 60,000 tons of paper, that is 18–19 million leaflets (Figures 31 and 32).[240]

The principal aim of the front propaganda was to convince enemy soldiers to give up the fight and to desert. Accordingly it tried to destroy their conviction that the war was defensive and that they would certainly win. The French bombarded the Germans with lengthy brochures about German war guilt, written by German emigrants.[241] They also evoked the Battle of Jutland and some isolated Russian victories and affirmed that the new Allies Italy, Romania and later the United States would guarantee their victory.[242] From September 1916 until May 1917, they dropped copies of authentic letters of complaint – which had been found in the pockets of German prisoners – written by German families about the catastrophic situation at home.[243] Excellent was also their mockery of one of the key words of German propaganda: *Durchhalten* (Hold Out). They invented three other slogans which characterized the situation much better: '*Durchleiden, Durchhungern, Durchmorden*' (Continue to suffer, continue to starve, continue to kill).[244] Remarkable was also a special technique called *propagande à rebours*: They reprinted German cartoons with slight but important modifications:[245] A German cartoon in *Ulk* shows the so-called Food-Dictator Adolf T. von Batocki-Friebe sitting on an eagle and throwing baskets with food on a happy family below. In the French counter-cartoon in *Kriegsblätter,* the man and his food baskets are replaced by rationing cards raining down on an unhappy family which comments: 'Decrees and butter cards, if only we could eat them.' The same technique was applied to pre-war caricatures. A *Simplicissimus* cartoon of March 1910 showing heavily armed police clamping down on a demonstration against the Prussian suffrage was reproduced in *Die Feldpost* under the title 'Demonstrations against the Bad Food Supply and for Peace.'[246] A somewhat related technique was to reproduce a German leaflet with a slight change: *Auf zum Endkampf* (Ready for the Final Fight) shows three figures pushing a huge rock from a mountain on the head of John Bull, the French simply exchanged John Bull with the Kaiser.[247]

From March 1918 the style of French propaganda became much more aggressive. It blamed the bloodthirsty Kaiser, Prussian Junkers and militarists, war profiteers and speculators for 'duping and sacrificing the soldiers' and appealed to mass strikes, the shooting of the officers, desertion and revolution. 'Surrender', demanded one leaflet and continued: 'if you want it, you can do it. Remove the princes who lead you to the slaughterhouse. They and they alone are your enemies. Three days of mass strike, and you will win.'[248]

The British knew how to call the attention of the Germans to their propaganda: As the OHL never informed the soldiers about their transfers and imminent battles, let alone the military situation in general,[249] the British distributed so-called priority leaflets with maps about the changing frontlines and actual statistics about the German losses, thus demonstrating in a seemingly objective way the 'futility of making further sacrifices in a lost cause.'[250] They did not refute German propaganda, but limited themselves to juxtaposing contradictory arguments of the Germans themselves and cleverly left the decision to the reader: Under the heading 'Who Caused the War?' they compared a speech of the Kaiser with quotes from the memorandum of the former German ambassador in London, Karl

Prince Lichnowsky.[251] Under the heading 'Where Is the Truth?' they contrasted two speeches in the Reichstag:[252]

Paul von Hintze, State Secretary of the AA:	Friedrich Geyer, deputy of the USPD on 13 July 1918:
'We are fighting for the fatherland and nothing else. Not for conquests and not for the subjection of other peoples.'	'This war was never a war of defence; it is a war of conquest with imperialistic aims [...] the masses of the people are starving [...] Down with the War'.

Striking were also the British caricatures. One of them distributed in June 1918 showed the Kaiser and his six sons on a parade, a copy from a well-known photograph, and contrasted it with hundreds of dark skeletons clenching their fists in rage and despair. The commentary said: 'One family which has not lost a single member.'[253] However, the most convincing British argument was the numeric superiority of the Americans. An impressive caricature showed a long line of American soldiers arriving in Europe with the text: 'The first million' (Figure 33). This confirmed the view of most soldiers and civilians that the German cause had become hopeless. A porter in Berlin said in September 1918: 'Even if we hold out until spring, they will get us – there are more and more coming.'[254]

German propaganda had a difficult task. As it was too evident that the French soldiers defended themselves against an unprovoked German invasion, it was impossible to affirm the opposite. It was a bit easier to accuse the British of having committed a blunder in supporting Belgium by alleging that this country had concluded secret military arrangements with France and Britain.[255] The argument against the Russians was that their government had been bribed by the British in order to make war against the Central Powers and that Britain was Russia's gravedigger and would ruin it.[256] The greatest propaganda lie of the Austrians and the Germans in this context was a falsified appeal by the tsar informing the soldiers that they had been forced by his uncle Nicholas to declare the war and asking them not to obey the unfaithful generals and to fight against all those who menace the life and the freedom of the tsar.[257] In view of the numerous victories of their armies, Germans and Austrians could easily tell the Allied soldiers that they had no chance to win, and even in August 1918 they insisted that despite the tanks the Americans would lose the battles like the British at the Dardanelles.[258] They also told Russians, French and Italians that they were sacrificed for British interests, quoted from anglophobic French writers such as Bertrand Barère and Emile Driant and pointed at British atrocities against France from Joan of Arc being burnt at the stake via Napoleon being banished to St. Helena to the French victims of British bombs in the occupied areas – after all 1,365 dead and 2,628 wounded. Well known was a slogan which nearly became proverbial during the war: 'While the Germans will fight until the last German soldier, the British will fight until the last French (or Russian/Italian) soldier.'²⁵⁹ Propaganda also showed the Irish their freedom fighter 'Sir Roger Casement hung by the thugs' and promised the Black American soldiers a nice life in Germany without Ku Klux Clan and lynch justice.²⁶⁰

The appeal to desert combined with the reward topic played an important role. Numerous Allied leaflets, most of them with facsimile letters from prisoners and impressive photos distributed from September 1916, promised a wonderful life in the prisoner camps: POWs were wined and dined in elegant halls and enjoyed beautiful gardens, football fields and swimming pools (Figure 34).²⁶¹ In August 1918, a German soldier wrote in a letter: 'The British treated us like their own children. [...] Food was like in a fairy-tale. White bread always with butter and sausages. At lunch more meat than anything else.'²⁶²

Many German soldiers, however, deeply distrusted such promises because of gruesome stories about Allied prisoner camps.²⁶³ For instance, in an alleged letter a German POW complained that he had to eat 'dog food', that in one week 46 persons died from various diseases, and he concluded: 'It is thousand times better to die amongst the comrades on the battlefield.'²⁶⁴ It is quite inconceivable that British censorship would have passed such a letter, but there were indeed confirmed reports about bad treatment, mostly by the French. 'Better dead than a prisoner of the French' read a headline in a German army journal. In April 1915 and still in 1916, they had obliged German prisoners to work in African desert zones where many of them died, and the OHL had retaliated by sending French prisoners and deportees to work in ice-cold areas of occupied Russia.²⁶⁵ Similar reprisal measures affected German and British POWs alike who were forced to work in the trenches under enemy shell fire.²⁶⁶ The cruel treatment of wounded German prisoners found even its way into German children's books,²⁶⁷ and the fury of the German people was so great that claims for revenge had to be put under preventive censorship.²⁶⁸ Allied propaganda did its utmost to refute such accusations, even dropping leaflets with the formal statement '*Die Engländer töten keinen Gefangenen*' (The British do not kill any prisoners).²⁶⁹ However, the German authorities had compiled reliable eyewitness testimonies about German prisoners being killed immediately after having surrendered which was confirmed during and after the war in personal letters, reports and various autobiographical testimonies, sometimes even with pride.²⁷⁰ And despite all Allied propaganda, a German soldier wrote still in October 1918 that he and his comrades preferred not to surrender but to go back, 'for all are frightened of being caught by the Americans [in whose hands] prisoners do very badly and are mostly beaten to death or shot'.²⁷¹

The Germans as well had to refute accusations that they killed all prisoners, tortured them or at least gouged out their eyes – accusations based on the notorious case of Major-General Karl Stenger who in August 1914 had explicitly ordered to shoot all French prisoners.²⁷² French propaganda also blamed the bad and cruel treatment of the POWs in German camps which allegedly were divided into three sections: camps of parade shown to neutral commissions, camps of reprisals and camps of hard labour. French and British reports alike denounced the systematic torturing of POWs who, for instance, were tied for hours to trees or stakes.[273] Usually prisoners were bullied by NCOs who were accustomed to treating their own recruits in such a humiliating and sadistic way that some of them even committed suicide in order to escape this hell – a fact well understood by a British author who concluded: 'The German non-commissioned officer [...] did not see why he should not do the same with mere prisoners of war.'[274] However, the main problems in the German and also in the Austrian camps were lack of food and inadequate health care which even lead to cholera and typhus epidemics, for instance, in the notorious camps of Wittenberg, Knittelfeld and Mauthausen.[275] After some ameliorations in 1916 owing to the interventions of the American ambassador James W. Gerard, a new phase began in 1917: Regardless of the Hague regulations, POWs were forced to work in munitions factories and mines – denounced by British propaganda as modern slavery.[276]

German propaganda had not much to promise to would-be prisoners: Russian deserters would get 7 roubles or 14 mark (€53.2) and vodka if they brought over their guns. Pallid photos of German prisoner camps matched the misery of Russian POWs, many of whom were starving or dying from tuberculosis.[277] Probably some information about this situation had filtered through to the Russians, so that in 1917 some leaflets promised them to be sent to villages where they could live in liberty and even earn money.[278] Indeed, Russians lived much better on farms, sometimes even harmoniously with the owner's family.[279] After all German propaganda was not so ineffective because throughout the war 22 per cent of the Russian soldiers were captured of which a number of them had voluntarily surrendered.[280]

As Allied front propaganda was considered a severe threat to the morale of the soldiers, the OHL reacted rapidly. From mid-1917 it asked the soldiers to collect the leaflets and hand them over against payment of 30 pfennig (€1.14) for one leaflet and 2 mark (€7.6) for a new tract. Considering that a simple soldier was paid only 53 pfennig (€2.01) per day, this sum was quite attractive.[281] The instruction officers also fabricated fake Allied leaflets in which enemy propaganda was either ridiculed or repudiated. As they resembled Allied leaflets so much, soldiers sometimes obtained 30 pfennig for them as well.[282] When more and more soldiers deserted, the authorities announced severe sanctions. In a circular of 25 June 1918, Ludendorff announced:

> 1. Every defector to the enemy will be punished with a death penalty when returning to Germany. 2. All his domestic assets will be confiscated. 3. He will lose his citizenship. 4. His relatives will lose their entitlement to receive benefits.[283]

A *Manifesto to the German People* by Hindenburg on 2 September 1918 warned against the 'drum-fire of printed paper' intended to 'kill the soul' and exhorted them not to be fooled by the propaganda of the Allies who want to 'annihilate us'.[284]

Allies and Germans also tried to enlist POWs for their own armies, setting up propaganda newspapers for them and even encouraging and supporting 'camp newspapers' published by the prisoners themselves.[285] The Russians after some hesitation organized the Czechoslovak Legion of 80,000 men – of whom only a few fought twice against the Austrian army and who later roamed Siberia and were finally shipped to France.[286] The Russians also recruited 30,000–40,000 Austrian Serbs and used them against Bulgaria and at the Salonica front.[287] Russians and French asked Alsatians to fight on the French side, but only 8 per cent of 20,580 prisoners in France were prepared to accept this kind offer despite heavy pressure by the French GQG.[288] Equally disappointing was the creation of a Polish army in France because not many Polish POWs were ready to enlist and the French officers did not trust them anyway. Finally only one regiment consisting of Polish volunteers from the United States saw action at the Western front.[289] The British had some limited success in recruiting Arab POWs from the Ottoman army to serve in Sharif Hussein's rebel forces.[290]

The Germans established comfortable camps, called 'Information-Camps', for Flemings, Ukrainians, Balts, Irish and Muslims, and installed there special 'men of confidence' who tried to win them over. They had some limited success at the Crescent Moon Camp (Halbmondlager) for Muslims (see p. 134), but most other efforts failed completely. For instance, 2,500 Irish POWs were concentrated in a special camp at Limburg, but when the Irish independence fighter Sir Roger Casement, distributing various pamphlets, the German propaganda newspaper *Continental Times* and Irish-American newspapers, invited them to form an Irish Brigade and to 'fight against England and free Ireland', only 52 soldiers accepted. However, when on Easter 1916 a submarine brought him to Ireland, only two volunteers accompanied him, and the small group was arrested at once.[291]

The most successful were the Italians. They had carefully placed the POWs of the various nationalities of Austria-Hungary in special camps and succeeded in mobilizing them for battle in their army. From March 1918 Czech legionaries did intelligence and propaganda work at the Piave, and in October 1918 a company of Romanian volunteers was engaged in the trenches and a Polish legion was raised but did not see action.[292]

National minorities

One of the most important propaganda slogans of the war was the right of self-determination for all nationalities.[293] However, on both sides there were supranational states menaced to fall apart once this principle would be put into practice: namely Austria-Hungary, Russia and the Ottoman Empire. Furthermore, Britain, France, Belgium, Italy and Germany had colonies, Britain oppressed the Irish, Germany the Poles, the Alsatians and the Danes. Finally the Central Powers and, rather belatedly, the Allies as well, promised self-determination – but only to those nationalities living under the enemy's yoke. The Germans were the most active in this aspect, but even they hesitated in case a more rewarding alternative was possible, for instance, a separate peace with Russia. The Allies were even more cautious vis-à-vis the nationalities of Austria-Hungary and left most of the propaganda to the representatives of the nationalities themselves, because for a long time it seemed to them that the balance of power in Europe would be better realized by preserving the Dual Monarchy. Only in the Near East, British and Germans alike went to great lengths to stir up the nationalities against the Ottoman Empire and the colonial rulers, respectively.

Alien peoples of the Allies

From the outset of the war the Germans defined their war aims.[294] Although Bethmann Hollweg's famous program of September 1914 was only a 'dilatory compromise of formula', as Wolfgang J. Mommsen put it, German imperialist circles were busy discussing how to expand the Reich after the war and trying to bring government and public opinion over to their side. According to the German-American scholar Hans W. Gatzke, one can distinguish between two imperialist movements: The Conservative Imperialists – I prefer to call them Annexationists – supported by the 3rd OHL under the generals Ludendorff and Hindenburg, conservative and national-liberal politicians, the Pan-German League and representatives of the heavy industry, demanded direct annexations of vast Allied territories in Russia, France, Belgium and Africa. Their opponents were the Liberal Imperialists – I prefer to call them "Reluctant Imperialists" after the classical book by Cedric J. Lowe about the reluctant foreign policy of Britain from 1878 until 1902[295] – supported by left liberal and social democratic politicians, representatives of the consumer industry, the 2nd OHL under Erich von Falkenhayn, the AA and, after his negotiations about a separate peace with Russia had failed, also by the chancellor. Their aim was 'Mitteleuropa', a federation of semi-independent states in Central and Eastern Europe, popularized through the bestseller *Mitteleuropa* by the liberal politician Friedrich Naumann. These states would enjoy freedom and political autonomy at home, yet would be bound to the German superpower in military, political and economic affairs. Thus, the imperialistic aims of Germany and the aspirations of modern economy for large territories without tariff barriers would be reconciled with the desires of the peoples for self-determination. However, the dividing line between the two movements was somewhat blurred, and the exact scope of Mitteleuropa was controversial. Some propagandists contented themselves with the adjunction of the Western provinces of Russia, others wanted to reduce also Austria-Hungary to the status of a German satellite state, and a third fraction insisted on including the Balkans or even the Ottoman Empire under the slogan 'Axis Berlin-Baghdad'. Both imperialistic camps hotly disputed other basic questions: While the Reluctant Imperialists strived for a negotiated peace, opposed unrestricted submarine warfare and demanded to guarantee the full independence of Belgium, the Annexationists insisted on fighting until victory, resuming the unrestricted submarine warfare and controlling Belgium in one way or another. During the war, they built specific propaganda organizations: The Reluctant Imperialists in February 1915 created the Free Patriotic Association (Freie Vaterländische Vereinigung), in November 1915 the German Society 1914 (Deutsche Gesellschaft 1914), in July 1916 the

National Committee for an Honourable Peace (Deutscher Nationalausschuß für einen ehrenvollen Frieden) and in December 1917 the Popular League for Freedom and Fatherland (Volksbund für Freiheit und Vaterland). The Annexationists in July 1916 founded the Independent Committee for a German Peace (Unabhängiger Ausschuß für einen Deutschen Frieden) and in July 1917 the German Fatherland Party (Deutsche Vaterlandspartei). These organizations submitted petitions and counter-petitions to Reichstag and government, organized numerous meetings and rallies and published a flood of articles and brochures in order to mobilize public opinion in favour of their aims. The annexationist platform was much better financed and had more supporters. For instance their first petition of 20 June 1915 was signed by 1,347 personalities, the counter-petition of 9 July only by 141. The small Popular League had no chance against the Fatherland Party which numbered 1.5 million members. Furthermore, the slogan 'German peace' with huge conquests allegedly indispensable for the military protection and the economic future of Germany was clear and easy to understand. Mitteleuropa was a more ambiguous notion. Vis-à-vis the concerned nationalities, the propagandists had to promise that Germany would respect their liberty and refrain from annexations. At home they could not say the contrary and had to hide their conception of an indirect hegemony behind vague formulations unsuitable for propaganda purposes.

How could these war aims be realized? At least towards Russia the methods were clear: By supporting revolutionaries and stirring up the alien peoples. From January 1915 on, the Germans allegedly financed revolutionary agitation and sabotage like the blowing up of railway lines in Russia, but their agents and intermediaries never produced any receipts or detailed proofs for successful action.[296]

The first target of German propaganda was Finland. Already on 8 August 1914 German diplomats in Stockholm discussed the question of how to foment an uprising there.[297] Three months later, the Finn Herman Gummerus agitated in Finland as a German agent and informed the AA that his compatriots wanted to become independent and asked for German help.[298] Soon adventurous young Finns enlisted as volunteers and were secretly trained in Lockstedt, a small town in Schleswig-Holstein. At the same time, weapons and munitions were bought in Sweden and stored near the Finnish border.[299] However, this troop of 2,000 men was finally deployed at the Baltic front near Riga and did not see action in Finland until February 1918 when they intervened in the Finnish civil war.[300]

The most spectacular German measure against Russia was, of course, in April and May 1917 the famous transport of Lenin and 310 of his followers in two trains (not sealed) from Switzerland to Finland from where they gained access to Russia and managed to seize power in a few months.[301] The Russians insisted on paying their third-class fare themselves because they would be completely discredited in Russia if it came out that the Germans had financed them.[302] When in the beginning of July the Provisional Government indeed affirmed this, the Bolsheviks immediately issued a rigorous denial.[303] Of course, the Germans secretly financed them through intermediaries, but the sum of 50 million gold mark (€400 million), invented by the social democratic politician Eduard Bernstein in the *Vorwärts* of 14 January 1921 and still retained by the last publication on the subject, belongs to the war myths.[304] At the outset of the war, all belligerent countries had given up the gold standard and paid in paper money except under very special circumstances such as the transfer of one million mark in gold bars from Germany to Turkey in August 1914. The AA had indeed set aside 40 million paper (!) mark (€152 million) for propaganda in Russia, but already on 2 March 1916 the paper mark compared to the gold mark of 5 March 1914 had lost 30 per cent of its value vis-à-vis the Swiss franc and 39 per cent vis-à-vis the Swedish krona; on 1 March 1917, the corresponding devaluations amounted to 45 and 54 per cent. The loss compared to the US dollar was 28 and 31 per cent, respectively.[305] Besides, the AA did not only finance the Bolsheviks but also other groups as well because it was not sure who would finally carry the day. Even after the October Revolution, the Germans continued paying various Russian activists including even monarchist circles, because there were rumours that either the Soviet government would resume fighting or be overthrown by counter-revolutionaries in the pay of the Entente.[306] According to the German documents mentioned in 1961 by Fritz Fischer and quoted since time and again, on 31 January 1918, 14.5 million of the available money of 40 million paper mark were not yet spent but would be distributed until June in allotments of three million per month and another 10 million mark until the end of the war. How much of it went to the Soviets is not clear, but it appears rather modest compared to the six billion mark they had to pay to Germany according to the financial agreement of 27 August 1918.[307] After Brest-Litovsk, the Germans did not only continue paying, but also resumed propaganda: In a series of pictures for the illiterates, they praised the German-Russian cooperation; liberated from the fetters of the Entente, the Russians would now peacefully trade with the Germans like before the war. If, however, the Allies (depicted as vampires) had their way, they would suck Russia's blood, plunder its economy and carry away all its money in huge sacks (Figure 35).[308]

The Austrians were especially interested in the Polish territories under Russian domination and wanted to create a reunited Poland tied to Austria. Unfortunately an appropriate proclamation of Emperor Franz Josef was prevented by the Hungarian Prime Minister István Count Tisza. It was Józef Piłsudsky, the leader of the Polish Socialist Party in exile in Galicia, who started the first action of Austrian propaganda. Already before the war he had organized Polish Rifle Men's Associations in Galicia with the support of the Austrian army, and on 6 August 1914 his company of 163 riflemen invaded Russian Poland and, with the support of Austro-Hungarian intelligence, tried to stir up the population against the Russians. However, as their revolutionary propaganda met with widespread incomprehension and even enmity, Piłsudsky's troops concentrated on combat within the Austrian army and even succeeded in growing up to 30,000 men.[309]

When in summer 1915 the armies of the Central Powers rapidly occupied the Russian provinces of Poland and Lithuania, Poland was divided into two administration zones. The Governor General Hans von Beseler, head of the German zone in Northern Poland, advocated the creation of a Polish state with close ties to

Germany and tried to win the favours of the population by his cultural policy: On 15 November 1915, he reopened the two Russianized universities of Warsaw as Polish institutions and allowed the Polish School Association to reorganize public education. On 5 November 1916, the Central Powers proclaimed the Kingdom of Poland as an autonomous state under their control. Unfortunately, Poland's borders were not specified and the Provisional Council of State, appointed on 6 December as the new Polish government, had no political authority at all. Nevertheless the fiction of an independent Polish kingdom was well exploited by propaganda. The Germans proudly announced the 'liberation of Poland associated with the victory of the Central Powers' and the 'triumph of the national idea'. A caricature depicts Poland as a happy young woman showing her broken chains to an enthusiastic crowd while a German woman is holding her hand, protecting her with a drawn sword and trampling on the knout, the symbol of Russia.[310] Allied propaganda, however, denounced the 'so-called autonomy of Poland [as a] gesture of supreme hypocrisies' with the only purpose of enlisting the Poles in the German army. A French cartoon depicts Poland as a woman as well, but bound, gagged and guarded by a German soldier who offers her a crown with the words: 'Take it because you are free.' The *Punch* depicts a German as a half naked, fell-clad savage with a sword and a whip who is chasing a long line of Poles to a barn with the inscription 'Cannon-Fodder Department'.[311] This corresponded exactly to the aims of the OHL, but its recruiting campaign had practically no results because the Poles were not permitted to set up an independent Polish army.[312]

The next target of German war aims were the Baltic countries with their influential German minority of large landowners and wealthy bourgeois, in addition to the Ukraine and other Russian territories.[313] In March 1916, the German-Lithuanian landowner Friedrich von der Ropp, supported by the AA and numerous deputies of the Reichstag, founded the League of the Alien Peoples of Russia (Liga der Fremdvölker Rußlands). Its aim was to win public opinion in Germany, Russia and abroad for the 'liberation and independence' of the oppressed nationalities of the Tsarist Empire. Ropp's achievements were quite impressive:

- A telegraphic appeal of 1,700 words to the American President Wilson complaining about the awful situation of the alien peoples in Russia.
- An International Congress of Nationalities oppressed by the Allies which Ropp organized in June 1916 together with another German agent, the Lithuanian politician Juozas Gabrys, in Lausanne (see pp. 62, 149).
- A brochure *Kennen Sie Rußland?* (Do You Know Russia?) published in German, Swedish and French, in which 12 representatives of the alien peoples informed the world about their sufferings under the tsarist regime. It was published in German but had allegedly been translated from the Swedish and the American editions. The reason for this curious manoeuvre was that it should not be considered as an instrument of German propaganda. The only problem was that a Swedish edition, translated from the German one, appeared at the same time, but that an American edition was never ever published.[314]

In the Polish affairs, Ropp also had his hands in the pie. The Polish activist Michał Łempicki was formally the president of his league and directed also the League of the Polish Statehood. On 26 July 1916, he and Ropp submitted to Arthur Zimmermann, Under Secretary of State of the AA, a memorandum recommending the creation of a Polish state politically and economically tied to Germany. During the next weeks Ropp made several propaganda trips to Poland and won numerous conservative Polish politicians for this project, for instance Franz Prince Radziwiłł and Adam Count Ronikier.

Even more important were Ropp's activities for the creation of a Lithuanian state. The situation was favourable. On 7 May 1917, Bethmann Hollweg issued his instruction to 'dress Lithuania as an independent state' but to attach it militarily, politically and economically to Germany. Ropp supported the chancellor by convincing Ludendorff, one of the principal leaders of the annexationists, to allow the establishment of a Lithuanian Council (Taryba) in Vilnius as an embryo of a future government. He also organized a propaganda conference in Berlin where the president of the Taryba, Antanas Smetona, cautiously advocated the establishment of an autonomous Lithuanian state. Ropp's activities were fiercely attacked by the Baltic Council of Confidence (Baltischer Vertrauensrat) which agitated for the annexation and colonization of the Baltic provinces.[315] On 30 November 1917, Ropp founded the newspaper *Das Neue Litauen* and the German-Lithuanian Society (Deutsch-Litauische Gesellschaft), and both propagated the establishment of an autonomous Lithuanian state, defending this project not only against the German Annexationists but also against socialist Lithuanian politicians who demanded real independence for their country.

As it turned out, propaganda was less decisive for the fate of the alien peoples of Russia than the actual power situation. At the conference of Brest-Litovsk in March 1918 and under the subsequent treaties of August 1918, the Germans forced the Soviets to accept the cession not only of Poland and the Baltic provinces, but also of Georgia and the Ukraine which would permit their transformation into German satellite states. On 11 December 1917, the Taryba signed the declaration of independence under the condition of a permanent alliance with Germany to be realized in the military, economical and financial domains. When on 16 February 1918, under the pressure of its left wing, it issued another declaration without these conditions, the new Chancellor Hertling refused it and the Lithuanians had to yield. Finally on 23 March 1918 their country was recognized by the Kaiser as an autonomous state with the aforementioned ties to Germany. However, no governmental activity was possible because the country remained under German occupation and the military tried in this way to realize their own project of transforming Lithuania into a German colony.[316] The Allies were not duped by the German propaganda of the 'liberation' of the alien peoples of Russia and correctly prophesied that they would be enslaved again. An American caricature entitled 'The Liberator' shows Germany as a stork in a pond just swallowing a frog called Lithuania while other frogs with countries' names are waiting their turn.[317]

In Belgium, the Germans attempted to win the favours of the Flemings.[318] They could count on the fact that the Flemish majority felt oppressed by the

Walloons and that two small but active Flemish separatist movements, namely the Association Young Flanders (Jong-Vlaanderen) and the Flemish Committee of Leiden (Vlaams Comité van Leiden), were making propaganda for an integration of Flanders into the German Reich or a greater Germanic State. Such far-reaching projects were enthusiastically supported by the German Annexationists: in Belgium by the German military administration of Eastern and Western Flanders which was not subject to the Governor General Moritz von Bissing, and in Germany by conservative deputies of the Reichstag and the Pan-German League which already before the war propagated an 'independent' Flanders under German protection.[319] Apart from financing the Flemish activists, Bissing himself was more cautious. On 24 October 1916, following the example of Beseler in Poland, he transformed the French-speaking Walloon university of Gent into a Flemish institution. However, the 'von Bissing-University', as it was condescendingly called, was rejected even by 38 Flemish professors and despite intensive German propaganda encountered serious recruiting problems. It had to appoint Dutch and Dutch-speaking German professors and to offer students special privileges such as higher grants and extra meat rations. In February 1917, the Flemish activists founded the Council of Flanders (Raad van Flanderen) and on 22 December 1917, encouraged by the new governor general of Belgium, Ludwig von Falkenhausen, proclaimed the independence of Flanders. However, Chancellor Hertling would only accept autonomy and did not recognize a Flemish state. The new council had no tasks except one: to make Flemish propaganda generously financed by the Germans. Towards this, it distributed 2.5 million pamphlets and brochures, organized rallies and popular festivals, and from July 1918 its local speakers were joined by deserted leaders of the Yser activists (see p. 112). In Flemish newspapers and in 26 speeches held in front of up to 3,000 people, they informed the people about the miserable life of the Flemish soldiers who were badly treated by their Walloon officers and allegedly even sacrificed at the front in order to reduce their number in forthcoming elections.[320]

The German defeat in summer 1918 sounded the death knell of Mitteleuropa. Poland and the Baltic countries became really independent, the other provinces returned under the Russian yoke, and most of the Flemish activists had to emigrate to Germany or to the Netherlands.

Alien peoples of the Central Powers

The Russian authorities, strongly supported by numerous private associations finally regrouped in the Czecho-Slovak People's Council and the Council of Assemblies of Polish Associations, promised to liberate all Slavic peoples of Austria-Hungary and to unify Poland as an autonomous state within the Tsarist Empire.[321] By September 1914, around 170,000 copies of a pertaining pamphlet appeared in Prague, and the Austrian authorities declared their spreading an offence punishable by death.[322] Impressed by Russian propaganda, a Polish National Committee (Komitet Narodowy Polski) was founded in Warsaw which sponsored a small military force of 1,000 Polish volunteers supporting the tsarist army and asked the Poles in Prussian Posen and Austrian Galicia to cooperate with the invading Russian army.[323] In September and November 1915, Polish émigrés in Lausanne founded the pro-Allied propaganda organizations Polish Agency (Agence Polonaise) and Polish Circle (Koło politiczne) fighting bitterly against Polish organizations of pro-Austrian leanings. In a conference in Lausanne in February 1916, Roman Dmowski and the Polish Circle decided to cooperate with the Entente. However, the Western Allies because of their alliance with Russia hesitated to promise anything to the Poles. While public opinion in Britain also remained rather reserved, in Paris numerous left-wing journalists and politicians who never had much sympathy for despotic Russia made propaganda in favour of the Polish cause, founded a French League of the Friends of Poland (Ligue française des amis de la Pologne) and finally in June 1916 issued a declaration demanding to restore the Polish state. Under the pressure of public opinion, in May 1916 a French delegation composed of former Prime Minister René Viviani and Minister of Munitions Albert Thomas went to Petrograd pleading the Polish cause; however, their proposals were brusquely turned down by the Russian Minister of Foreign Affairs Sergei Sazonov. In 1917 the fate of Poland reached a turning point. In January 1917, in a speech President Wilson argued somewhat ambiguously that 'there should be a united, independent and autonomous Poland', and in Russia after the February Revolution, the Petrograd Soviet and the Provisional Government on 28 and on 29 March, respectively, granted the Poles the right to establish an independent state. On 15 August 1917, Dmowski transformed the former Polish Agency in Lausanne into a Polish National Committee (Komitet narodowy polski), but transferred it to Paris. In autumn, the French and the British governments recognized it as an unofficial representation of the Polish nation, but despite all diplomatic and propagandistic efforts of the Committee, they refused to acknowledge Poland's independence because they were negotiating with Austria-Hungary about a separate peace. Even Wilson's promise of an independent Poland in his Fourteen Points of 8 January 1918 did not alter their policy. Only when these expectations had vanished after the definite submission of Emperor Karl to his German ally at the headquarters in Spa on 12 May 1918, the Inter-Allied Conference at Versailles on 3 June 1918 demanded the creation of a united and independent Polish state.

Like in the case of the Poles in Posen and Galicia, direct propaganda to stir up the Czech population against the Austrian authorities was made only once at the outset of the war. In November 1914, four soldiers of the Družyna, a Russian unit of Czech soldiers recruited among emigrants, passed the lines in order to ask the politician Karel Krámář to organize a revolt, but he consented only to passive resistance.[324] Otherwise Czechoslovak propaganda for independence had to struggle with the same problems as its Polish counterpart although their agitation was much better organized. Already in October Tomáš Masaryk, professor at the Czech University of Prague, met his British colleague Robert Seton-Watson in the Netherlands and convinced him of the necessity to propagate Czech independence. Seton-Watson produced a pertaining memorandum, which he passed to *The Times* and to the Foreign Offices of Britain, France and Russia. Later Masaryk went to

Switzerland, and on 5 July 1915 organized there a reception on the fifth centenary of the execution of Jan Hus. His idea was that by talking about Czech history, literature and arts one could arouse interest for his country and so make indirect propaganda for Czech independence.[325] Together with two of his former students, Edvard Beneš and Milan Štefánik, he organized the Czech Committees Abroad, later renamed Czechoslovak National Council (Conseil national tchécoslovaque), and undertook a vast panoply of different propaganda actions: He published the newspaper *Českaslovenskà Samostanost* and had two other magazines, *The New Europe* and *La nation tchèque,* published respectively by Seton-Watson and the French professor Ernest Denis. He elaborated memoranda such as *The Slave among Nations* and *Austrian Terrorism in Bohemia* and had them distributed by Wellington House. When he was appointed as a lecturer at King's College, he held his augural lecture on the fate of the small nations in the presence of Lord Cecil, then Undersecretary of the Foreign Office, and later made many other lectures and speeches at various places. Beneš as well held a lecture with the title 'Destroy Austria-Hungary' at the Sorbonne which was also issued as a pamphlet.[326] Time and again both succeeded in inserting a few propaganda lines in French and British dailies. Masaryk attached great importance to propaganda for a large audience and even rented a shop exhibiting Czech propaganda material at Piccadilly in London. The Czechs were very active in the United States as well, distributing Czech and British propaganda through the Bohemian National Alliance. Above all, they organized an efficient spy network of around 80 people who in the embassies of the Central Powers copied secret documents about their organization of strikes, sabotage, support of Mexican and Hindu revolutionaries and reported them to the American press. Last but not least, they organized fundraising tours and collected millions of dollars for their propaganda activities.[327]

Although the Czechs went to great lengths in mobilizing the Allied governments for Czech independence and were received by important deciders such as Briand, Poincaré or Balfour, they encountered even more opposition than did the Poles. When in December 1916 President Wilson asked the Allies to explain their war aims, the Czechs after much bickering could persuade them to demand the liberation not only of the Slavs in general from foreign rule, but expressis verbis also of the Czechs. However, in his Fourteen Points, President Wilson demanded only autonomy for them. As we have seen, France and Britain still hoped for a separate peace with the Dual Monarchy, and it was not until 29 June 1918 that the French Foreign Minister Stephen Pichon recognized the Czechoslovak National Council as the nucleus of a future government. On 9 August and 2 September, the British and the Americans, respectively, recognized the Czechoslovaks even as an Allied nation.[328] Considering the initial rather lukewarm interest of the Allies for Czechoslovak independence, one can agree with Herbert A. L. Fisher who stated: 'Most states have been fashioned by the sword or have grown out of colonisation. Czechoslovakia is the child of propaganda.'[329]

A terrible blow against Allied liberation propaganda was the publication of the secret treaties of 1916 between the Western Allies and tsarist Russia by the Bolsheviks in November 1917, which blatantly violated the right of self-determination. Russia would get Turkish Armenia and Kurdistan, and Britain and France would divide up among themselves the Arab territories of the Ottoman Empire.[330] A German propaganda cartoon under the title 'Proud Albion' contrasted a veiled figure holding a placard with the inscription 'Protection of the small nations – Self-determination of the peoples' with the same figure, unveiled by Trotsky: a monster standing on skulls and the inscriptions 'Secret Treaties' 'Conquests' 'Violation' and 'Robbery of Territories'.[331]

The French made extensive propaganda by balloons in Alsace-Lorraine, emphasizing the long-standing ties with France and the horrors of Prussian rule. They also seemed to consider the Bavarians and Badenians as alien peoples dominated by the Prussians, tried to stir them up with the argument that Prussian militarism was responsible for the war and even promised to restore the independent Kingdom of Bavaria.[332] Their propaganda leaflets and newspapers were, from February 1915, smuggled over the Swiss frontier and, for instance, landed regularly in the letter boxes of Nuremberg (see p. 71). In Baden, quite a few people were sufficiently mobilized against the *Saupreiß* (Prussian bastards), considered them as worse enemies than the Allies, protested against film footage of Kaiser and crown prince in newsreels, and expressed that they would not mind being governed by the French.[333]

Muslim peoples and jihad

The Middle East was one of the principal targets of the propaganda of both warfaring coalitions. My analysis will proceed in two steps: At first it will discuss how Germans and Turks attempted to spread the jihad in the Muslim colonies of the Allies, and then it will analyse how the British raised the Arabs to revolt against the Sultan.

From the end of the nineteenth century, some German journalists recommended the mobilization of the Muslims against the British in order to win the battle for supremacy in the world. For instance, Naumann, editor of the influential periodical *Die Hilfe*, prophesied in his book *Asia* (1899) Germany's 'World War against Britain' and wrote triumphantly:

Then the Caliph in Constantinople will again raise the flag of the Prophet, this time against Britain which extends over the whole world. The sick man rises again from his bed and calls Egypt, the Sudan, Eastern Africa, Persia, Afghanistan and India: Fight against Great Britain.[334]

In the next decade, rumours about a coming alliance with Turkey were spread time and again;[335] they were closely related to projects about exploiting Turkey economically and even about reducing the country to a German colony, ruled by the Sultan in the same way as the Khedive ruled Egypt for the British.[336] In 1907, Rohrbach, the propagandist of a 'Greater Germany', saw in Syria and Mesopotamia 'a large part of our future world power'.[337] However, in reality German economic penetration of Turkey was rather limited, and at the eve of the war it still lagged behind Britain, France and Austria.[338]

Wilhelm II, like many Germans of his time, had a special liking for the Orient, but an Orient in which exotic images from the *Arabian Nights* were mixed with condescending stereotypes[339]; however, he also overestimated the power of the Muslim princes as pawns in the imperialistic game of German worldwide expansion. During his second visit in the Ottoman Empire, he said in a famous speech in Damascus on 8 November 1898: 'I assure his Majesty, the Sultan, and the 300 Million Muslims – who live dispersed in the world and venerate him as their Caliph – of the everlasting friendship of the German Kaiser.'[340] In 1905, he demanded an alliance with the Sultan and other Arab princes, but Chancellor Bernhard Prince von Bülow refused such projects. When in 1910 after the revolution of the Young Turks Wilhelm consulted several experts about this question, neither Field-Marshal Colmar von der Goltz, long time a military adviser to Sultan Abdul Hamid II, nor the German ambassador in Constantinople, Adolf Baron Marschall von Bieberstein, considered the Ottoman Empire as a useful ally.[341]

Despite its reluctance to conclude a formal alliance, the Prussian and later the German governments were quite active in the military domain. Already from 1840 onwards, German officers modernized the Turkish armed forces – an engagement which in 1913 was enormously stepped up with the establishing of a German military mission of 40 officers under the direction of General Otto Liman von Sanders.[342] However, the German military staff distrusted Turkey's military abilities, and even General Friedrich von Bernhardi who in 1912 in his notorious book *Germany and the Next War* had praised Turkey as a possibly important ally, revised his opinion somewhat in the sixth edition of 1913 and even remarked in a postscript to a popular version of his book that, in a future world war, one could not count on the military support of this country.[343]

The Turks were quite conscious of their military weakness and with a genuine flair for the warmongering in Europe desperately looked for an alliance and a guarantee for their borders. In May 1914 they put out a feeler in Russia and in the middle of July in France, unfortunately without any success. Thus, Germany became their last resort, something like an 'emergency solution' as Hans W. Neulen puts it – an argument lately contested by Mustafa Aksakal. Although he cannot deny that the Turkish Minister of the Interior, Mehmed Talaat Pasha, suggested twice in May an alliance to the Russian Foreign Minister Serge D. Sazonov at Livadia in Crimea where Tsar Nicholas II and his entourage were on vacation, and shortly later to the Russian ambassador in Constantinople, Mikhail N. von Giers, he claims that the Turkish offer was made without clarity and must be considered as a temporary manoeuvre.[344] The second effort to join the Entente took place during a visit of the francophile Turkish Navy Minister Ahmed Djemal Pasha in France. In his memoirs published eight years later, Djemal gives a detailed report about his voyage to Paris and Toulon and his conversations with the prime minister and Foreign Minister René Viviani and especially with his subordinate Pierre de Margerie, director of political and economic affairs.[345] Especially interesting is his final discussion with Margerie, recapitulated on three pages. He asks for French support in a controversy with Greece about two Aegean islands and indicates the interest of Turkey to join the Entente. Unfortunately his interlocutor politely refuses and Djemal is 'terribly disappointed'.[346] Aksakal contests the verity of Djemal's report and claims that 'no evidence of this offer has been found in the French records'.[347] At first glance it is quite irritating that Aksakal did not consult directly either Djemal's memoirs or the French records but quotes only secondary literature.[348] Furthermore, one may ask why Djemal admits a complete failure of his mission – a fact very rare in autobiographies. Above all the conversation between Djemal and Margerie is well documented in the French records: In his report no. 504 of 13 July 1914, Margerie summarizes his conversation with Djemal:

> Djemal Pasha came informing me about the situation of Turkey vis-à-vis the Triple Alliance and the Triple Entente and assured me that his ideas were shared by the whole Ottoman government: From now on Turkey had to turn towards the Triple Entente.

Then Margerie continues to deal with Djemal's arguments in more detail: The Turkish minister blamed rumours about a combined Turkish-Bulgarian attack on Greece as 'purely imaginary', but affirmed that Turkey could only turn to the Entente after a peaceful solution of the controversy with Greece about some islands.[349] Like in the Russian case, there is indeed no formal request for an alliance, but it is clear that such a politically and militarily weak country, which even most Germans considered as a liability in case of war (see p. 128), could only very cautiously ask for an alliance, a demand which after all would more resemble a desperate plea for protection.

On 22 July, Enver, formerly military attaché in Berlin and a fervent admirer of Germany, sounded out the German ambassador Hans von Wangenheim about an alliance. However, the AA as well as the military staff, considering Turkey more as a liability, wanted to decline this offer. At this point the Kaiser, full of enthusiastic hope for the supposed power of the jihad, forcefully intervened and insisted on accepting this offer. On 2 August, the alliance was concluded but kept secret for the moment because several Turkish ministers being partisans of the Entente were not yet informed and the Turks also hoped to bargain for some additional advantages.[350]

Already on 30 July the Kaiser gave propaganda instructions: 'Our consuls in Turkey and India, our agents etc. have to incite the whole Islamic world to a wild revolt against this hateful, hypocritical and unscrupulous people of shopkeepers. If we have to bleed to death, Britain should at least lose India.' Two weeks later he specified his propaganda asking Enver to have 'the sultan appeal to the Muslims in Asia and Africa to wage the holy war for the caliphate'.[351]

On 2 August 1914, exactly on the day of the German-Turkish treaty, the AA reactivated Max von Oppenheim, its best specialist for the Orient, who had worked at the German consulate in Cairo from 1896 until 1909.[352] He had frequented pan-Islamic circles and had already in a memorandum of 5 July 1898 evoked 'the jihad, the holy war against the infidel' and recommended an alliance with the Turkish

Sultan.[353] The Islamic Section which he directed in the AA from August 1914 was at first only some sort of a translation bureau. On 18 August 1914, he proposed to the chancellor the creation of a special propaganda bureau and in November submitted a lengthy *Denkschrift betreffend die Revolutionierung der islamischen Gebiete unserer Feinde* (Memorandum on Revolutionizing the Islamic Territories of Our Enemies). He outlined the methods of insurrection in the various Islamic colonies of the Entente, proposed to finance jihad propaganda adequately and have it accompanied by Turkish military actions. In November 1914, he established the Oriental News Bureau (Nachrichtenstelle für den Orient, NO) as a semi-official office of the AA.[354]

In view of his activities, it is not surprising that former research suggested that the jihad was not a Turkish idea, but 'made in Germany' and fabricated by 'Abu Jihad', the father of the jihad, as Oppenheim was called by some Arabs.[355] But Aksakal has convincingly proved that not only the Ottoman Empire had repeatedly declared the jihad during several wars of the nineteenth century but also that other Muslim peoples had used this appeal in their struggle against European colonial powers.[356] Furthermore, Sultan Abdul Hamid II had vigorously encouraged Pan-Islamic ideas and in order to intimidate the European powers, he had attempted to reinforce the Caliphate as the spiritual head and the defender of the Islamic world. In his *Pensées et souvenirs* (Thoughts and Memoirs) he wrote: 'Are England, France, Russia and the Netherlands not all in my power? One word of the Caliph would suffice to launch the jihad, and woe betide the Christian powers.'[357]

In November 1914 after Turkey had finally entered the war, the jihad proclamation was declared in several stages, with the argumentation that the Caliph, according to Sura 9.41 of the Holy Qur'an, has declared the holy war against the aggressors Russia, Britain and France. All Muslims were asked to take up arms even against their own governments.[358]

Even before this proclamation, Enver put his secret propaganda and sabotage organization TM at the service of the jihad. He had already created it in 1908 and trained it well in 1912 in the defence of Libya against Italian aggression. During the war, threatened by an Allied invasion, TM organized special cells of propaganda and resistance in Turkish areas. Outside of Turkey, especially in Libya and in the Caucasus region, it made revolutionary propaganda and organized volunteers for espionage, sabotage and guerrilla warfare against the Entente.[359]

The NO in Berlin was organized like the usual offices for propaganda abroad.[360] It had departments of Turkish, Arab, Indian, Persian and Russian affairs, and sections dealing with the following activities: analysing and translating the international press; preparing brochures, leaflets, posters and special newspapers for Germany, the Orient and neutral countries; compiling address lists of receivers and multipliers of propaganda; and recruiting agents and speakers. Oppenheim and his collaborators wrote articles in Turkish and Arabian newspapers, founded new newspapers such as the *Korrespondenzblatt* and *Der neue Orient* and took care of Muslim POWs and their correspondence.[361] Supported by their numerous Turkish, Arab, Indian and Tartar authors, they published roughly three million copies of 1,000 different publications in 24 languages.[362] The propaganda material was forwarded to Turkey, via neutral countries to Allied colonies, with German propaganda expeditions to Persia and Afghanistan, or smuggled over the borders to Egypt and the Maghreb, but the results were rather fortuitous. A good example is the *Open Letter to Asquith*, published in eight languages with 68,000 copies, which denounced British oppression in Egypt and demanded independence.[363]

Because of the difficulties of distribution in April 1915, Oppenheim left the direction of the NO to one of his collaborators and founded a new branch in Constantinople. From there he established throughout Turkey 70 newsrooms with newspapers and publications for the small elite. The German consuls had already established some newsrooms and continued to support them. They distributed the propaganda material not only there, but also in coffee houses, schools and hospitals, offered them to Mecca pilgrims and organized demonstrations with German flags and Arab and Turkish speakers praising the strength of Germany. One consul employed fairy-tale tellers for oral propaganda; another succeeded in obtaining enemy reports prior to their publication and could thus counter them rapidly with his own propaganda. The bribing of newspapers or the delivery of newsprint – which in Turkey was scarce and thus more valuable than money – in exchange for friendly news was also quite common.[364]

All jihad propaganda had to take into account that the great majority in the oriental countries was illiterate. For this reason, Oppenheim travelled the Arab provinces of Turkey and made jihad speeches in the mosques.[365] He also launched propagandistic picture stories. Their topics did not only use religious arguments but emphasized the economic exploitation of the Muslims in the Entente colonies and the military superiority of the Central Powers which were fighting for their liberation. Especially Kaiser Wilhelm was presented as a confidence-inspiring friend of the Muslims, even as a Muslim himself, who had converted to Islam and even made the *hadj*, the pilgrimage to Mecca. When the Egyptian government allegedly prohibited his propaganda name 'Hajj Wilhelm Friend and Protector of Islam', he was rebaptized 'Hajj Muhammad Guillamo'.[366] Some examples from the picture brochure *Tyranny and Justice* can demonstrate the particular propaganda approach: British soldiers carry huge sacks of money from Egypt to Britain; a Russian soldier stands on a large board carried by five Muslims; a starving Arab painstakingly ploughs the land while a well-nourished French soldier is comfortably looking on; an emaciated Indian holds a tiny coin in his hand, while a very big coin symbolizes the huge revenues of the British in India (Figure 36).[367] However, such propaganda against the Allied colonial regime did not bother Turks and Arabs too much in view of the problems in Turkey itself. Some people even went so far as calling the newsrooms 'sacks of lies'.[368]

Other leaflets appeal to Muslim solidarity with the Ottoman Empire and describe in detail the overwhelming success of the German and Ottoman armies against the Entente powers, for instance, at the Dardanelles. They describe the atrocities of the Russians and the crimes of the British in India. They condemn the religious persecution of the Muslims by the French and their sacrificing of Muslim soldiers at the European front. Arab deserters praise the good life in the German POW camps and advise their comrades to desert and to join them. They remind the Muslims of their glorious deeds during the era of the Prophet Muhammad and ask them to expel the French and the Russians from the lands of Islam. They promise all Arabs dying for the jihad the pleasures of paradise, and menace those fighting for the Allies with eternal punishment in hell.[369]

Jihad propaganda was supposed to be supported by military action. The first target was Egypt, formally an Ottoman province with Abbas Hilmi II as the Khedive (viceroy) at its head, but in fact under British rule. The Khedive had already in August 1914 offered the Turks his support against the British and promised an uprising in Egypt in case of a Turkish attack. However, neither he nor the Egyptian nationalists had made any preparations to stir up the masses let alone to collect arms and munitions, and the Turkish government did not trust them.[370] On the military scale, Enver had already envisaged in the beginning of August a Turkish-German attack against the Suez canal and had a few useless agents with some propaganda material cross the Suez Canal but the results were nil.[371] At least Ahmed Djemal Pasha, Minister of Marine and governor of Syria, in an attempt to give the attack a truly jihadist character, raised a 'Saviour Islamic Army of Egypt' with Libyan, Circassian, Kurdish, Arab and even Bulgarian Muslims joining the Turkish troops.[372] However, in January 1915 Turks, Germans and 'saviours' were easily repulsed by British-Indian troops, and there was not even a shadow of an uprising of the Egyptian population.[373]

The most active propagator of jihad outside Turkey was Sheikh Sayyd Ahmed ash-Sharif, the leader of the Muslim sect of the Senussi in Libya. Calling himself the representative of the Caliph in North Africa, he sent propaganda messages to Ali Dinar, the Sultan of Darfur, and to various Arab and Indian Muslim leaders, asking them to declare the jihad and to fight against the British. After he had routed the Italian army in Libya, German and Turkish ships and submarines could land there and deliver arms, money and propaganda material. However, neither Dinar's 2,600 riflemen and his four field guns nor the more numerous and better-equipped Senussi warriors had a chance against British troops reinforced by Australian and Indian army units.[374]

Members of a Persian committee in Berlin financed by the AA made propaganda in Teheran and Shiraz against British and Russian control. At the same time a small German expedition in Persia mobilized a few tribal warriors and the gendarmerie with propaganda and money and nearly won over the Shah for an alliance with Germany. But finally Russian troops arrived and completely crushed a German inspired revolt. A projected alliance with Habibullah, the Emir of Afghanistan, was finally not concluded either.[375] More successful was revolutionary propaganda in the Russian Caucasus where the oil fields of Baku could be damaged and in the former Turkish provinces of Kars and Ardahan where the population rose against the Russian regime.[376]

The Germans also launched propaganda appeals to Morocco and, with the help of arms and money sent with submarines and fishing boats from Spain, they could provoke some local unrest, but as Graham A. Cornwell has rightly pointed out, it was quite paradoxical that at the same time over 445,000 Moroccan 'volunteers' fought for the French in Europe and another 40,000 worked as labourers there.[377]

Efforts to stir up mutiny among Indian troops in Mesopotamia had a very limited effect while propaganda for an uprising in Bengal failed completely, despite the financing of the Indian newspaper *Ghader* and the shipment of propaganda and armaments from the United States to India organized by the German military attaché in Washington, Franz von Papen. British counter-espionage was simply too efficient. [378]

Although very early in the war Enver had created a special office for the coordination of propaganda activities with the Germans, quite a few problems and frictions turned up from time to time.[379] Above all both allies did not have the same war aims. The Germans wanted to liberate the Muslim peoples from colonial rule, while the Turks wanted to integrate them into the Ottoman Empire.[380] However, neither Egyptians nor Persians wanted to be governed by Turkish pashas, and moreover the Shiite Persians did not like the Sunnite Turks. When Turkish troops invaded the Persian province of Azerbaijan and announced its annexation, they counteracted the propagandistic activity of the German expedition there.[381] Besides neither the Turks nor the Austrians trusted the Germans. Talaat found the Germans 'overbearing and insolent' and was convinced that they wanted to reduce Turkey 'to a colony in disguise' according to the model of Egypt. Enver complained several times about the inept propaganda of the German consuls. Even a German brochure about *Georgia and the World War* was forbidden by Turkish censorship because it concerned an area belonging to the Turkish sphere of interest. Enver had also secretly placed members of his TM in the German NO who informed him about its propaganda projects and tried to steer them according to Turkish interests. The Austrian propaganda directed by the military attaché Joseph Pomiankowski did not support the jihad and competed with the Germans in economic and cultural propaganda affairs.[382] When in occupied Serbia 8,000 Muslims volunteered for the jihad, the Austrian Foreign Office blocked their military deployment.[383]

Furthermore, the Germans committed serious blunders in their propaganda war: The AA assigned the journalist Max Roloff (a giaour!) to go to Mecca and to recruit pilgrims there for the jihad – an enterprise which 'would have caused outrage in the Islamic world'.[384] Fortunately he quietly stayed in a German village and sent only fictional reports to the AA.[385] Despite Enver's warnings, Oppenheim in May 1915 paid 5,000 Turkish pound, the equivalent of 100,000 mark (€380,000), for jihad propaganda to Hussein, the Sharif of Mecca, one month before the latter started negotiations with the British about his insurrection.[386]

Several historians have criticized the lack of money for the jihad. According to Tilman Lüdke the whole jihad propaganda cost only 0.06 per cent of the total war expenditure or as much as was spent to finance the whole war for one single day.[387] It is doubtful, however, if more money would have produced better results in view of the lack of jihad enthusiasm of most of the Arabs, even in Turkey itself.[388]

One of the greatest handicaps of jihad propaganda was the fact that the Central Powers could not sufficiently deliver arms and munitions for wide-scale revolts in the Islamic colonies of the Entente. As Hew Strachan puts it so well: 'The power of the sword was mightier than the pen.'[389]

German propagandists were also busy at the Western Front where the French and the British had stationed numerous Muslim soldiers from their colonies. Leaflets were thrown over the trenches; a Tunisian agent, Muhammad Sâlih ash-Sharîf at-Tûnisî, invited them by megaphone to desert and to join the jihad, and a few Algerian soldiers deserted indeed after the Germans had shown them a holy flag and informed them about the proclamation of the Caliph.[390] German planes also dropped special leaflets over Indian troops, either appealing them to join the Holy War, unfortunately in Hindi which the Muslims did not understand, or prepared by the Ghaderites, a group of Indian revolutionaries in exile around the San Francisco weekly *Ghader* (Mutiny) urging them to kill their British officers and raise the standard of revolt in Hindustan.[391]

Once the Muslims had deserted or were taken prisoner, the Germans put them into special propaganda camps, the Crescent Moon Camp (Halbmondlager) at Wünsdorf for POWs from the French and British colonies and the Vineyard Camp (Weinberglager) at Zossen for POWs from Russia, besides Muslim Tatars also Christian Georgians and Armenians.[392] In these camps, situated near Potsdam, the Germans built mosques, served halal food, employed imams and organized Islamic celebrations. Muslim and German propagandists attempted to win them over for military engagement in favour of jihad and national liberation. A two-weekly with the title *El Dschihad* was published in Arabic, Tatar and Russian; other newspapers were *Kaukasien* for the Georgians and *Hindostan* in Hindi and Urdu for the Indians.[393] However, the style of the articles was often too high-brow, and most prisoners were illiterate anyway.[394] Georgians and Armenians usually repudiating independence propaganda had to be moved to other camps, and after the abdication of the tsar, the Tatars as well saw no more reason to fight against Russia. Despite generous promises to grant jihad fighters land and houses in Anatolia after the war, the success of propaganda was rather limited. At the turn of 1916–17, only 2,000 volunteers were sent to Turkey, but as they were badly treated, most of them deserted and finally ended up in Turkish POW camps. 'To rely on the jihad, which has never raged,' wrote the German ambassador in Constantinople, Paul Graf Wolff Metternich, to the chancellor on 15 March 1916, 'was a failure'.[395] Finally in spring 1917 jihad indoctrination was stopped, and most POWs were employed outside the camps for agricultural and industrial labour.[396]

Jihad propaganda is usually considered a failure.[397] This is true if one compares its results with the great expectations at the outset of the war. On the other hand, the fear of jihad, which at certain moments even degenerated into widespread panic among British leaders, obliged the Allies to engage important troop contingents in North Africa, Persia and North West India – troops which were desperately lacking at the European fronts.[398]

The British reacted very effectively to the jihad threat. They transformed Egypt into a British protectorate and on 18 December 1914 deposed the unreliable khedive by his more docile uncle Hussein Kamel with the title of Sultan. They also proclaimed martial law, arrested Turkish and Egyptian agitators, interned Germans and Austrians on the island of Malta, expelled unreliable princes and sheikhs or put them under house arrest. Furthermore, they moved the Egyptian troops to the South and replaced them by more reliable soldiers from India, Australia and New Zealand until their garrison consisted of roughly 100,000 men. In India, they distributed propaganda leaflets, inserted friendly articles into the newspapers and obliged maharajas and other dignitaries to sign statements of loyalty. They even had the Aga Khan, the spiritual leader of the Islamic sect of the Ismailis, come to Egypt and speak to the Indian troops.[399]

In August and October 1914, the British administration in Egypt already established contacts with Arabs eager to liberate themselves from the Turkish yoke. The British were especially interested in stirring up Hussein ibn Ali, the influential Sharif and Emir of Mecca. But he was cautious and told them, that he 'could not break with the Turks immediately and that he was awaiting a colourable pretext.'[400]

So far British propaganda had been rather modest, limited to a few leaflets dropped over Arab areas with the appeal to join the separatists and to kill all German and Turkish officers.[401] When in December 1915 Marc Sykes, member of the Committee Advising the Government about Near Eastern Affairs, found out about this state of neglect, he suggested to create an Arab Bureau in Cairo and entrust them with the task of making counter-propaganda against German and Turkish jihad indoctrination. This was rapidly established on 1 January 1916 under the direction of Gilbert Clayton, and now British propaganda took a new vigour. For instance, ulemas from the famous Al-Azhar University in Cairo told the Arab soldiers in the Ottoman army that the Turks had deceived them and stolen from them the Caliphate and the Qur'an. In May 1916, the Egyptian newspaper *Al-Ahram* reprinted an article from *The Times* of 9 April about alleged anti-Islamic orders of the former governor of the German colony of East Africa.[402] From March 1918, MI7(b)3 directed the propaganda in the Near East.[403]

The Arab Bureau was not the only example of efforts made towards trying to win over the Arabs to the Allied cause; the India Office also sent propaganda material to local tribes, made its own negotiations, for instance with the sheikdoms at the Persian Gulf and concluded an anti-Turkish alliance with Sayyd al-Idrissi of Asir. The aims of the India Office, however, were different from those of the Arab Bureau: It wanted to annex Mesopotamia to the British Empire whereas the Arab Bureau favoured at least an autonomous status.[404]

Finally Hussein, frightened by a secret project of Wahib Bey, the Turkish governor of Medina, to depose him, decided to throw in his lot with the British.[405] On 20 June 1915, he started serious negotiations about an Arab insurrection with Sir Henry McMahon, the British High Commissioner in Cairo, and on 10 June 1916 the insurrection broke loose. The British had promised Hussein an independent Arab state, with the exception of Aden, Kuwait and the Syrian coast demanded by the French. They also delivered him modern weapons and financial subsidies of £50,000 per month, which was later increased to £100,000 and in 1917 to £200,000 (£2.1 million, £4.3 million and £8.6 million, respectively). All in all the British spent for the Arabs, at the outrage of the treasury office, the enormous sum of £11 million (£473 million), while the German expenditure for propaganda and expeditions in all neutral and enemy countries together until 30 January 1918 amounted to 380 million mark (€1.4 billion) only.[406] Despite these huge costs, the military support of the Arabs was, in the view of contemporaries and historians alike, rather negligible if not even a failure. The war was not decided by the tribal warriors but by the most efficient Anglo-Indian troops of General Edmund Allenby.[407]

But even its propagandistic value was rather limited if not counterproductive. Most Arab officers in the Ottoman army fought loyally until the end of the empire, and quite a few of them later even joined the Turkish Republican Army.[408] Most Arabs outside of the Hejaz remained ambivalent or hostile to the revolt. The leader of the Shamar, Ibn-Rashid, and the Imam Yahya of Yemen – who attacked the British naval base of Aden and delivered food for the beleaguered city of Medina, respectively – continued to support the Turks.[409] The Arab revolt never grew into a mass movement. In the Maghreb, people either did not believe the news about the revolt or considered it as an enterprise stirred up by the Christians. In India, the revolt of the Sharif was unanimously condemned, his name cursed in the mosques, and in several Indian cities the Muslims demonstrated against him.[410]

Turkish propaganda reinforced this negative impression. In August 1916, Haidar, the successor of Hussein appointed by the Turks, proclaimed that the treacherous alliance with Britain against the Caliph would lead to the occupation of the holy sites by the British giaours; Djemal in Damascus had the leading ulema pass a fatwa (religious decree) with the following text:

> What befits a person who has been hyped with the good will of the Caliph and who has been elevated to the highest of honour, when that person betrays the Caliph by joining the latter's enemy? Answer: deposition and death.

Muftis of other Syrian and Palestinian towns signed further fatwas against Hussein, and Damascus with the Arab newspapers *Al-Sharq* and *Hijaz* became the centre of anti-separatist press propaganda.[411]

Hussein did what he could: In a proclamation *To the Muslim World* he accused the Turks of having 'departed from the precepts of the Coran [...] and sapping the foundation of the Caliphate'. He also published a propaganda weekly denouncing the execution of dozens of Arab dignitaries by Djemal and accused the Young Turkish Party of having introduced secular reforms.[412] The British officers – among them the legendary Thomas E. Lawrence who was not more active than his comrades but was immortalized after the war by the indefatigable marketing of the American publicity manager Lowell Thomas – did their best to indoctrinate the Arabs under their command by promising them the golden realm of independence.[413] However, as Lawrence later wrote in a suppressed chapter of his memoirs *Seven Pillars of Wisdom*, which was only reinserted much later: 'It was evident from the beginning that if we won the war these promises would be dead paper.'[414] His Arab followers got a foretaste of how reality would differ from propaganda, when on 6 December 1917 Djemal informed the population in a speech in Beirut about the projected partition of the Arab provinces of Turkey between Britain and France, according to the secret Sykes–Picot Agreement of 16 May 1916, which was concluded approximately three weeks before Hussein had started his revolt for Arab independence. Did the tribal warriors lay down their weapons after this alarming news? Certainly not, they found out only after the war that they had been betrayed by British propaganda. The Sharif, furious about the Paris Peace Conference, refused to ratify the Treaty of Sèvres. A few years later, he even lost his country after an invasion by the Saudis. The British government did not lift a finger to help him. Hussein spent the rest of his life in exile, in Amman, a thoroughly embittered man.[415]

Chapter 7

SELECTED PROPAGANDISTS – EIGHT PROFILES

Alfred Lord Northcliffe (Great Britain)

Winning the war became his mission.[1]

Born under the modest name of Alfred Harmsworth, but ennobled – in various steps from baronet over baron to viscount – Lord Northcliffe (1865–1922) was not only the most powerful newspaper tycoon of all war-faring countries who controlled around 40 per cent of the British dailies but also one of the most courageous personalities of the whole war. He consistently denounced the weaknesses and failures of the British war effort emphatically demanding from the government to cancel censorship and tell people the truth. Defying the censors' complete blackout on news from the battlefield, Northcliffe's *Daily Mail* was the first paper to publish an unvarnished article about the hasty retreat of the British soldiers after the defeat in the Battle of Mons. To the great surprise of the journalists, the director of the PB, Fredrick E. Smith (later Lord Birkenhead), not only let the article pass but even made a favourable comment about it. This created a triple sensation: for the first time the public was informed about the desperate situation at the front; Smith was fired, but no disciplinary measures were taken against the newspaper or Northcliffe himself. It was probably this event that made him conscious of his great power, and he subsequently transformed all his papers, especially *The Times* and the tabloid paper *Daily Mail*, into a strong power factor in British politics with the unique aim to win the war at all costs (see motto above). Whenever the government accepted his views he would go along, if not he would attack it mercilessly. For instance, in harsh headlines such as 'The 22. A Conspiracy of Silence' the *Daily Mail* editorial of 19 October 1915 claimed that the 22 cabinet members were deceiving the people by their exaggerated suppression of news. For this acrimonious criticism, in all other belligerent countries Northcliffe would have spent the rest of the war in prison, but not so in Merry Old England where freedom was always respected when combined with power. The censors, however, complained time and again that despite the rights conferred to them by DORA they could do nothing against Northcliffe, because the political leaders were afraid to interfere with him. But it was also his personal skill and his talent for political intrigue which helped him along. Cleverly exploiting controversies inside the cabinet, the tycoon had the uncanny knack of playing off one cabinet minister against the other. For instance, allied with Lloyd George and the British General Sir John French, he reproached Kitchener of being responsible for the insufficient supply of shells and bombarded him with headlines in the *Daily Mail* such as 'Tragedy of the shells. Lord Kitchener's grave error.' Although he could not have Kitchener ousted, at least he had his way when in May 1915 Lloyd George was nominated Minister of Munitions and, after the death of Kitchener one month later, Minister of War. But Asquith remained prime minister and Northcliffe practically acted as some sort of an extra-parliamentary opposition reproaching the authorities of not doing enough in order to win the war.

After the shell controversy, Northcliffe turned to the issue of conscription. Even before the war, he had supported a campaign to introduce conscription face to the menacing German 'Nation in Arms'. Now in view of the dramatic decline of volunteers he pushed for conscription by pointing at the German propaganda argument: while Germany will fight until the last German soldier, Britain would only fight until the last Frenchman. While Kitchener and Asquith preferred to delay conscription, Lloyd George agreed with him that the nation's resources in manpower had to be more vigorously exploited. Although Asquith survived the conscription crisis, he was finally forced to resign on 1 December 1916 by an intrigue of Northcliffe and Lloyd George who, considered as Northcliffe's 'godchild', became prime minister.

As a propagandist, Northcliffe was unrivalled. Considering already before the war the aggressive policy and the military build up of Germany as a threat for the British Empire, he had his newspapers fulminate against German militarism, publish stories about invasion and war, for instance the ill-famed serial *The [German] Invasion of 1910* by William Le Queux, and he did not hesitate to print the most unbelievable information about the Germans so that even Kaiser Wilhelm II himself once bitterly complained about the *Daily Mail's* canards.[2] During the war, the Northcliffe press even increased its hateful campaign against Germany, flooding the public with the atrocities of the 'Huns', calling the sinking of the *Lusitania* a 'premeditated murder', categorically refusing any peace by negotiation and insisting on total victory. The Germans feared him so much that they had a warship shell his country house in Broadstair on the coast of Kent – fortunately he was not there at that moment – and intended to launch an anti-Northcliffe-*Daily Mail*.

Due to the unrestricted submarine warfare of the Germans, Britain as well ran into food shortage. Northcliffe called for strict rationing, but when he complained about the failure of the Admiralty to keep the submarines in check and divulged its use of decoy vessels, the *Daily Mail* was censored for the first time. After the declaration of war by Washington, Northcliffe was dispatched there from June until December 1917 with the task of launching a vast propaganda campaign and squeezing the American Treasury for huge financial contributions to bankrupt Britain. He lavishly distributed propaganda material to the press, brought veterans and even a German submarine over to America, and successfully brainwashed even the people in the Midwest, a region settled by many German-Americans.

After his return to Britain, Northcliffe criticized the government for its insufficient propaganda, which in his view was responsible for the defeat of Italy at Caporetto and the defection of Russia. Lloyd George therefore decided to reorganize British propaganda and appointed Lord Beaverbrook (Max Aitken) as head of the Ministry of Information and Northcliffe, who refused a subordinate position, head of the independent Department of Enemy Propaganda directly responsible to the prime minister. He would direct propaganda against Germany and Austria while Beaverbrook would take care of all other foreign countries.[3] Already three and a half years ago, by October 1914, Northcliffe had realized the value of dropping leaflets over the German front (see p. 113), and in autumn 1916, he convinced the Commanding General Haig to authorize this propaganda instrument which was then successfully applied by MI7(b)4 under Cockerill. Although Northcliffe's achievements in destabilizing the Austrian and German fronts by leaflet propaganda have been exaggerated in older research, he nonetheless contributed to the weakening of the morale of the enemy soldiers and later said modestly: 'We have to some extent hastened the end.'[4] After the end of the war, Northcliffe propagated a harsh treatment of the Germans in order to prevent them from starting another war, but could not realize all his aims. With his health rapidly deteriorating, he died in 1922 at the age of 57.

George Creel (United States)

Weld the people of the United States into one white-hot mass instinct with fraternity, devotion, courage, and deathless determination [and forge] the war-will, the will-to-win [which] depends upon [consecrating] body and soul and spirit in the supreme effort of service and sacrifice.[5]

Creel's widespread activities as the civilian chairman of the American propaganda organization CPI have already been discussed in the previous chapters. Thus I shall concentrate here on some biographical aspects typical for his personal approach in that matter.

Until the war, George Creel (1876–1953) worked as a freelance journalist and newspaper editor. Politically he was a devote follower of Wilson. Already in 1905, in his newspaper *Independent,* he proposed Wilson as president, in 1910 he supported his campaign for the governorship of New Jersey and finally in the presidential election of 1912 he advertised him as the 'hope of the nation'. In the 1916 election, he justified neutrality and enthusiastically praised Wilson as the man who 'kept us out of war'. When one year later, on 14 April 1917, he was appointed chairman of the CPI, he presented a very different Wilson: the man who 'wants to make the world safe for democracy'. In order to achieve this, there was in his view only one way: to crush Germany, and Creel's objective was, as he had put it himself, to 'sell the war'.[6] He had to convince the American people of the necessity to fight by suggestive slogans (see motto). How to explain such a sudden change of mind? Creel had no personal conviction except 'Right or wrong – my president'. As the main title of his memoirs *How We Advertised America* suggests, he considered himself not as a politician but as a public relations expert who today would advertise Coca Cola as the best American brand and tomorrow ridicule it as an abominable drink which even a man dying from thirst in the desert would refuse. But this drive to jump at any opportunity to sell and also his ability to pick up the right men without long pondering was perhaps the reason why Creel succeeded in a very short time in creating the most efficient propaganda organization of all war-faring nations. Let me give an example: At the end of April 1917, an unknown young man walked into Creel's office and presented him a rather unusual project – to organize voluntary speakers for propaganda talks during the four-minute intervals in movie theatres all over the country. As a cautious French or German official, Creel would have carefully examined this proposition and not taken a decision until the end of the war, but as a dynamic sales agent he appointed the young man director of the new organization on the spot: the famous 'Four Minute Men' who throughout the war delivered 7,555,190 speeches, not only in movie theatres, but also in churches, labour unions, schools and even assemblies of Indian tribes (see pp. 60, 103).

In his memoirs, Creel explained his rapidity by the fact that he was pressed for time, but I would consider it as a basic feature of his personality reflecting the very American motto of 'Time is money'. It is all the more impressive as he had to fight a staunch Republican opposition in Congress which not only alimented the CPI parsimoniously but cited him time and again to hearings where he had to defend himself against the most denigrating criticisms. Not very helpful either were the officials in the various administrations who, ignorant as they were of the most basic psychological aspects of propaganda, insisted on tedious posters such as 'Save More Coal!' and tried to hamper an excellent group of illustrators which Creel had brought together. The military as usual was of no help either, for instance by refusing that war correspondents accompanied the army, but Creel pushed his demand through, although heavy sanctions prevented 'unhelpful' reporting (see p. 23).

Creel's most important instrument of propaganda was his monopoly on news only limited by the press offices kept by some minor branches of the administration. According to his early suggestion to the president, all channels of communication in and out of the country, be it by letter (through the post offices), cable or wireless, were efficiently controlled and censored and after such a 'purge' exclusively distributed to the press by CPI so that only 'positive' communication useful to the Allied war effort existed. Although Creel maintained that the CPI was an alternative to censorship, it was 'in fact an alternative form of censorship' as Alan Axelrod puts it.[7]

The public indeed considered him as the chief censor of the country – a reproach he passionately tried to rebuke later.[8] It may sound incredible, but before the declaration of war Creel had asked the president to avoid government censorship with their ugly blanks, which he might have found in French and Austrian newspapers. As we have seen, he pleaded instead for a voluntary self-censorship of the journalists, but in reality 'in the matter of censorship [...] Creel lived a sort of Jekyll and Hyde–existence',[9] as Mock and Larson put it. Although he was a member of the Censorship Board and could have offending journalists persecuted by the Attorney General or even cut off the supply of newsprint, he only rarely used these powers and let pass quite a few infringements on important regulations (see p. 177).

Creel was proud of his highly centralized CPI and mocked at the multitude of propaganda organizations in France and Britain which in his view resulted in 'confusion and failure' and financial squandering.[10] Nevertheless, he cooperated quite well with the French and Italian offices but not at all with the British ones. Most impressive is also the scope of mobilization. The CPI employed 150,000 people and mobilized a wide range of communication specialists: journalists, scholars, filmmakers, actors, painters, photographers, cartoonists, women, students – all of them contributing to Creel's propaganda network.

The CPI was also the only propaganda organization of the war that set up a special division for the minorities. On Independence Day, 4 July 1918, it organized a demonstration of 37 national minorities including 'enemy aliens' such as the American Friends of the German Republic in order to show the world, especially the Central Powers, their overwhelming support for America's war. This demonstration had been suggested by Will Irwin, one of the collaborators of Creel, and it was typical for him to approve this initiative despite his initial doubts – an excellent example of how this gifted manager motivated people.

As far as the content of Creel's propaganda is concerned, it was much less ingenious than his organization. The arguments were copied from the British and the French and concentrated on the aggressions and barbarities of the Germans and their plots and intrigues in America. He accused the 'medievally organised Prussian militaristic state' of dominating Germany and of threatening the world. Time and again he pointed at the mighty resources and military achievements of the United States, preached the 'gospel of Americanism', that is their democratic freedoms, and quoted from Wilson's speeches being considered as 'our most effective weapons'.[11]

On 1 November 1918, the CPI was dissolved, and in September 1919, Creel's protector Wilson had a stroke, could not resume his activities anymore and died five years later. Creel had no further opportunity to use his extraordinary organizational talents and resumed his writing of magazine features.

Henri Barbusse (France)

I must admit that I make propaganda.

We've got to give all we have, our strength and our skins and our hearts, all our life and what pleasures are left us […] so as to come out on top, and win.

Continue this war until the end of the war, […] sacrifice yourself and give the utmost so that one day your children won't have to do what you did.[12]

Until the war Henri Barbusse (1873–1935) was a journalist and a not too successful writer.[13] In August 1914, he volunteered for the front, although he was already 41 years old. His motivation explained in a letter to the chief editor of *L'Humanité* was nothing but an echo of the official French war propaganda: 'This war is directed against our old infamous enemies: militarism and imperialism [...]. Our victory will destroy the main den of the Caesars, the Kronprinz, the lords and mercenaries who imprison a people and would like to imprison others.'[14] In January 1915, Barbusse was fighting at the front and participated in the extremely bloody Battle of Crouy. Subsequently he was employed in the rear and finally worked as a secretary of the General Staff of the 21st army corps. Often sick, he was finally demobilized on 1 January 1917.

When in July 1915, Gustave Téry, the editor of the newspaper *L'Oeuvre*, asked Barbusse for 'Impressions' from the front, he soon began to collect material for a whole novel with the title *Le Feu* (Under Fire), and his manuscript was completed in the middle of 1916. It started to appear in the feuilleton of *L'Oeuvre* in August 1916 and was edited as a book at the end of 1916. What was its special message?

Until its publication, the French war novels played down and idealized the reality of war like for instance *Gaspard* by René Benjamin. Barbusse, however, embellishes nothing but shows the war as it really is: the miserable vegetating of the soldiers in the mud of the trenches, their shameful exploitation by the shopkeepers, their terrible injuries and their dreadful deaths. For this reason the book was considered for a long time a pacifist work. But will this experience turn the soldiers into pacifists? Will they throw away their gun? No, certainly not! There are two reasons for this: first a deep hatred for the Germans, 'the dirty Boche race', with officers who are 'not men, they're monsters [...] a specially filthy sort of vermin [...] microbes of the war [...] calf-heads [...], snouts like snake', and as prisoners they are kicked into the mud or stabbed in the back.[15] The Kaiser is considered 'a stinking beast to have brought this war on', whereas the constantly warring Emperor Napoleon I is praised as 'a great man'.[16] With such alleged quotes from *poilus*, Barbusse does not really convey a correct impression of the French soldiers' parlance, but perfectly emulates French and British war propaganda which represented the Kaiser as the embodiment of evil and the Germans as animalized monsters.

Above all, Barbusse purveys a special and much more subtle message which is particularly emphasized in the chapters 'Under Fire' and 'The Dawn'. In 'Under Fire', one of the characters in the novel, the corporal Bertrand, condemns the war, but emphasizing that it is necessary for the future, he orders his soldiers to carry on. In 'The Dawn' we read:

> There will be no more war, when there is no more Germany. [...] We must fight, if we've got to make such a sacrifice, it's because we're fighting for progress [...] war must be killed in the belly of Germany.[17]

In the second motto given above, the nature of the sacrifice is clearly defined: The soldiers must give all they have, including their lives. By promising that after the destruction of German militarism there would be no more wars, Barbusse effectively counters the main pacifist argument discovered by postal control: continuing this hopeless war is an absurdity. He gives the war a sense acceptable to the common soldier, that permanent peace and progress are worth all the sacrifices: 'If the present war has advanced progress by one step, its miseries and slaughter will count for little.'[18]

Regardless of the possible propagandistic value of *Le Feu*, the French censors, the most severe of all war-faring nations, intervened as usual, suppressed a few lines and once even had Barbusse's home searched and one chapter confiscated. But suddenly they stopped their interventions, at the great surprise of Barbusse who ironically wrote to his wife that Anastasia 'is suffering from hemiplegia'.[19] It was not until 1935 that the former censor Paul Gsell revealed why censorship had been so benign: It was him who prevented his colleagues from suppressing *Le Feu* by reading aloud some of its passages. Consequently, when Barbusse published his novel as a book after reinserting parts formerly deleted by the censors, he got away with it. Probably Gsell continued to protect him – there were several other examples for such 'censor patronage' (see p. 178), and the Office of the Prime Minister complained time and again to the Ministry of War that certain publications were not censored or that sanctions were not applied. It could also be that the censors took it for granted that the book version would be identical with the already censored newspaper version. Be that as it may, *Le Feu* won the coveted Goncourt Prize and became a great success. In only four months, 100,000 copies of his book were sold, and full of pride, the author heard from young *poilus* that they considered him as a kind of spiritual guide: When reading *Le Feu* they understood 'the necessity of sacrificing themselves' at the front.[20] Government circles were also very satisfied with this unexpected and free contribution to French war propaganda. High officials of the War Ministry and of the Ministry of the Interior congratulated Barbusse for his book and invited him to give speeches for soldiers, for instance, through the Association Propaganda and Education by Word and Theatre under the joint tutelage of the Ministries of War and of Education. Barbusse, who knew from the very beginning that he wrote a propagandistic book (first motto above), indefatigably continued with several appeals to the 'liberators' from 'German militarism' such as *Pourquoi te bats-tu* (Why Do You Fight?), published shortly after the repression of the mutinies in the French army, and *Jusqu'au bout* (Until the End) (third motto above), a quotation of the famous war cry of Clemenceau who demanded to continue the war until the complete defeat of Germany. Accordingly, Barbusse, although he later became a fanatical communist and a good friend of Stalin, strongly condemned the fact that the Bolshevists made peace with the Germans and denounced it as a deadly split.

So we see that the alleged pacifism of Barbusse was nothing but a myth, behind which Barbusse hid his real face: a Clemenceau of propaganda who refused a peace of compromise with the 'krauts' and, armed with chimerical visions of the future and the war motto *Jusqu'au bout*, pushed the exhausted and demoralized soldiers of the 'Grande nation' to more and bloodier sacrifices. His novel *Le Feu* was nothing but the last trump card of French war propaganda, whose old slogans – abolition of militarism, last war – were repackaged in a more seductive way. They had already been refuted at the Zimmerwald and Kienthal Conferences and also by deputies of the SFIO and PSI (see pp. 163–4).

My reinterpretation of the alleged pacifism of Barbusse and his novel *Le Feu* published in 2000 in *Guerres mondiales et conflits contemporains* (*GMCC*) was accepted in Germany[21] but passed over in silence in France because it contradicts the old Jacobin myth according to which France makes war only for peace and progress – an attitude which Lenin had already qualified as a fundamental error.

Gabriele D'Annunzio (Italy)

Blood begins to drop from the body of the fatherland […] the killing begins […] blood fumes at the feet of an invisible greatness, […] we have no other worth but that of our blood to be shed.[22]

As a young man, Gabriele D'Annunzio (1863–1938) was more interested in women than in politics – a typical Latin lover who besides his wife (until their separation in 1890) had an official mistress and so many other cocottes that one of his biographers wondered how he found the time to take care of all of them.[23] He became the most popular Italian writer – one of his specialities was to compromise his lovers by divulging the secrets of the alcove in newspaper articles or in whole books such as *Il Fuoco* (The Fire) – and from the end of the 1880s committed himself to propaganda for the Italian Irredentists still living under the suzerainty of Austria-Hungary. As the poet of the *Risorgimento* (Revival of Italy), he wanted to transform the Adriatic Sea into a *mare nostrum* (our [Italian] sea). Owing to his luxurious lifestyle, he accumulated so many debts that in 1910 he had to flee from his creditors to Paris where he lived quite well as the gigolo of a wealthy Russian countess who paid him 30,000 francs (€81,000) per year. When the war broke out and Italy remained neutral at the outset, D'Annunzio launched a flamboyant appeal to his compatriots asking them to join the Allies: *Aux Italiens. Un Italien* (To the Italians from an Italian) was published on 30 September and 1 October 1914 simultaneously in French and Italian newspapers. When on 12 and 13 February 1915 he was invited to a conference for the defence of the Latin civilization, he recited an *Ode à la résurrection latine* (Ode for the Latin Resurrection) which was published in several French newspapers and made him the symbol of Italian bellicosity. Apart from his numerous propagandistic appeals, he also supported the Legion Garibaldi, a troop of roughly 2,000 Italian volunteers fighting at the French front.

The majority of the Italian people was opposed to the war, but a very active group of interventionists, most of them from the nationalist bourgeoisie, agitated for an intervention on the Allied side. On 26 April 1915, the Italian government concluded a military pact with the Entente, but because of strong opposition in the parliament preferred to keep it secret for a while. At about the same time the city of Genoa invited D'Annunzio to give a speech on the occasion of the 55th anniversary of the liberation of Italy from the reign of the Bourbons. With his debts finally paid for by his editors, D'Annunzio accepted and, being enthusiastically welcomed in Genoa by a large audience of interventionists, he compared the wars of liberation of the nineteenth century with the current war. With a religious fervour worthy of a Catholic priest, this master of dramatic mass communication expressed his political appeal in religious terms and terminated his homily with an imitation of the sermon on the mount:

> Blessed be those who, having opposed the event [war] will accept in silence the supreme necessity and will want to be, not the last but the first one [to sacrifice themselves]. Blessed be the youth who hunger and thirst for glory for they will be sated. [...] Blessed be the pure of heart, blessed be those who will return victorious, for they will see Rome's new visage, Dante's forehead crowned anew, Italy's triumphant beauty.[24]

He later gave more speeches in Genoa and also in Rome, and on the day of the formal declaration of war on 23 May 1915, he told an enthusiastic crowd in Rome that the killing would now begin and they would have the splendid occasion to shed their blood for the fatherland (see motto above). For him, the supreme aim of this war was not so much victory, but blood and death.

Despite his advanced age of 52, D'Annunzio voluntarily enlisted, but famous as he was, obtained important privileges: He would neither march nor sit in lice-infested lorries, but use his own car with an army chauffeur at his service. Furthermore, he would not freeze for months in the icy trenches of the Alps, but continue his lavish life style in his luxurious villa and join the front only now and then for a short time as a sort of a holiday warrior, sometimes with the infantry, bus mostly away from the crowds on board of an aeroplane. Besides he was the only person authorized to give propagandistic speeches in an army under the Commanding General Cadorna, who usually allowed only the priests to speak at the front and tried to reinforce the crumbling war spirit not by propaganda but by summary mass executions for the most trivial failures (see p. 105). Only once Cadorna was dismissed after his catastrophic defeat in the Battle of Caporetto in October 1917 did the army appoint official propaganda officers, amidst them D'Annunzio as well, who gave speeches and distributed propaganda material amongst soldiers and civilians.

In his propaganda speeches at the front, D'Annunzio continued his politico-religious approach which nowadays sounds quite pathetic but was probably well adapted to an army predominantly consisting of peasants accustomed to ecclesiastical guidance. He conjured the '*cameratismo triomfante*', the comradeship among the soldiers and their participation in the national fight for victory. He called them all admirable warriors and heroes who have the will to win and perform an act of love for the fatherland. As he put it, only those ready to die for this love belonged to the Italian nation and would be honoured as martyrs with their corpses sanctifying the conquered soil.

He was also one of the first to use aeroplanes for launching leaflets with propaganda messages over the cities of the enemy. Thus he exhorted his compatriots in the irredentist cities Trieste and Trent to hold out and promised them their rapid liberation from the Austrian yoke. In February 1918 he directed three torpedo boats to Bakar (Buccari), the Austrian naval headquarters, and launched insulting messages in bottles. But his most noteworthy exploit and the most famous single propaganda action of the whole war was his flight to Vienna on 9 August 1918. On this day, eight Italian aeroplanes roamed the sky over the surprised population of Austria's capital which so far had never experienced an Italian air attack and was without any air defence. Luckily the Italians did not throw bombs but launched leaflets with the following message:

> We do not wage war with you, but only with your cruel government which cannot give you neither bread nor peace. Since you have put on the Prussian uniform the whole world is up in arms against you. Do you want to continue fighting? Go on if you want to commit suicide. The decisive victory promised by the Prussian generals is like the bread from Ukraine: one dies before it arrives. Cheers for liberty, cheers for Italy, cheers for the Entente.[25]

After the war D'Annunzio qualified the peace treaty with Italy as a *vittoria truncata* (a truncated victory) and tried to establish a fait accompli in September 1919 by occupying Fiume (now Rijeka in Croatia) with 2,000 irregular troops. As the Italian government refused to incorporate the city, he proclaimed there the Italian regency of Carnaro, the first fascist state with himself as *Duce*, but had to surrender the city in December 1920. In strong competition with Benito Mussolini, he tried to be appointed prime minister by the King but after an assassination attempt, which left him heavily injured, he retreated to private life in a splendid villa on Lake Garda which he had confiscated before.

Juozas Gabrys (Russia/Lithuania)

The aim which I wanted to achieve: A free Lithuania among the liberated nations of Europe.[26]

Juozas Gabrys (1880–1951) was a Russian citizen but a Lithuanian national.[27] He had already played a leading role in the Revolution of 1905, but when the tsarist repression set in again in 1906 he went into exile and finally settled down in Paris, the favourite place of revolutionaries from Eastern Europe. Paris was expensive, and he soon succeeded in combining financial and patriotic activities in order to make a living. For instance, he edited Lithuanian books and was royally paid by Lithuanian emigrant organizations in the United States. From 1911 on he advocated the liberation of the European nationalities and became an 'Ethnic Entrepreneur'. In May he founded the Lithuanian Information Bureau (LIB) and had it financed by donations from Lithuania and especially from the Society of Lithuanian Patriots in the United States; in October, together with the French journalist Jean Pélissier, he established the Union des Nationalités (UdN). While the task of the LIB was to mobilize European public opinion against Russian oppression in Lithuania and to obtain autonomy for this country, UdN was supposed to give to all the oppressed nationalities of Europe a common platform to express their grievances and problems. From 1912 appeared the periodical *Annales des Nationalités* as an organ of the UdN with many special issues on various nationalities usually paid for by their representatives. When World War I broke out, Gabrys was on a fundraising tour in America. Convinced that this war would offer the Lithuanians a unique chance to become independent, he asked the Lithuanian emigrants for their support and was finally authorized by a Lithuanian congress to spread propaganda for his country in Europe and to represent Lithuania in a future peace conference. A National Assistance Fund (Tautos Fonda) was set up which collected $14,000 (today $336,000) right on the spot for Gabrys's activities and spent another $120,000 ($2.8 million) for him during the entire war.

Back in Paris, Gabrys organized a congress of nationalities, but as France was allied to Russia he had to play 'a loyal comedy' in favour of the Allies, and any propaganda for the liberation of Lithuania was impossible. When in summer 1915 the Germans conquered Poland and a large part of Lithuania, it seemed evident that the future of these countries was in their hands. Thus in July 1915 Gabrys moved from Paris to Lausanne in neutral Switzerland. There he immediately contacted the German envoy Gisbert Baron von Romberg, who employed him as an agent of the AA with the code name 'Käufer' against a monthly remuneration of 1,000 mark (€3,800) and further payments for special services like the editing of the German propaganda periodical *Litauen* and the organization of propaganda conferences like the Third Congress of Nationalities in June 1916 in Lausanne (see p. 62). For the editing of the conference papers alone he got 40,000 mark (€152,000).

In Lausanne, Gabrys continued editing the *Annales*, created the new propaganda periodical *Pro Lithuania*, probably financed by the French, and founded several new institutions, first of all the Supreme National Council (Auksciausia Lietuviu Tautos Taryba, ALTT) as the political organ of the Lithuanians, its Permanent Legation which elevated Gabrys to the dignity of a 'proto-diplomat', and several money-collecting organizations. The most important financial contribution came in after the proclamation of the Lithuanian Day by Pope Benedict XV on 20 May 1917. On this day, collections were organized in favour of the Lithuanian war victims in the Catholic churches throughout the whole world. All the money – several millions of Swiss francs – was transferred to Gabrys's account and made this ethnic entrepreneur one of the richest men in Switzerland. It goes without saying that the war victims never saw a penny of it.

All the money was used for Gabrys's widespread propaganda activities: salaries for his seven employees, a gigantesque press campaign in favour of Lithuanian liberation covering nearly all the dailies of France, Germany and Switzerland, travels, conferences, brochures and periodicals. Sometimes Gabrys had to bribe journals in order to place articles in favour of Lithuania, for instance, for a certain period he paid 5,000 French francs (€13,500) per month to the editors of the influential French daily *Le Temps*.

In his Lithuanian memoirs, Gabrys claimed to have decisively contributed to the creation of the Lithuanian Council (Taryba) set up by the German occupation authorities in September 1917 in Vilnius, but this is highly doubtful. It may be correct that the Germans offered him the presidency of the Taryba, but he preferred to stay in Lausanne, to organize conferences with members of this council in Switzerland and paid them travel expenses and sometimes even salaries.

Although he acted as a German propaganda agent in close cooperation with Ropp (see pp. 122–3), he never broke off his contacts with French politicians and, according to his own words, 'juggled' between both sides, not only in his negotiations with diplomats, but also in the *Annales* where a pro-Allied article about the cruelty of the German occupation regime in Lithuania was followed by a pro-German article about the Flemish activists in Belgium. His sharp criticism of the German army in Lithuania was tolerated by the AA which disapproved of the harsh occupation regime there.

After the official recognition of the Lithuanian State by Germany on 23 March 1918, the Taryba changed its name to Lithuanian State Council and refused to accept Gabrys's ALTT as the highest Lithuanian authority. In the last Lithuanian conference in September 1918, the delegation of the renamed council under the later president Antanas Smetona insisted on its sovereignty and was not prepared to concede any political rights to Gabrys. After all, he had committed a grave blunder by not organizing a political following in the country and refusing German propositions to become president of the Taryba. After the war, several of his initiatives to get a foothold in Lithuania with the help of his French friends, especially as a member of a French military mission in March 1919, came to nothing, and a propaganda campaign against the Lithuanian government with the help of a fake news agency and five issues of a poorly made newspaper had no success either. As a last resort Gabrys supported by Ropp raised a battalion of mercenaries in Lithuania and tried twice, in August and October 1919, to come to power through a putsch, but failed completely.

Alfred Weber (Germany)

Our position in the centre of Europe necessitates [the creation] of a federation of Central-European states as the basis of our existence and our Weltpolitik in the Balkans and Asia Minor.[28]

The most active propagandists in Germany were university professors and schoolteachers. One of them was Alfred Weber (1868–1958), from 1903 until 1907 a professor of political economics at the German University of Prague, thereafter at Heidelberg University. Until the war he was opposed to the Kaiser's imperialistic aspirations and his craving for colonies.[29] In an article about German trade with the colonies of the other European powers, published in 1904, he convincingly demonstrated that Germany did not need political expansion, let alone colonies, in order to sell its products abroad. Instead he advocated a customs union between

Germany and Austria-Hungary to which other European states could adhere at a later date.

On 26 July 1914 when the outbreak of the war was imminent, Weber told his friends:

> The European peoples will be called to slaughter each other for nothing at all because neither in France nor in Russia the people want to make war; nobody except our enemies will be able to profit from it.[30]

Nevertheless after joining a patriotic manifestation on 1 August 1914, he was filled with enthusiasm and, in spite of his advanced age of 46, he voluntarily enlisted and, until May 1916, served as a captain at the Alsatian front. During this time, he wrote the memorandum *Bemerkungen über die auswärtige Politik und die Kriegsziele* (Remarks about Foreign Policy and the War Aims) and published the propaganda brochure *Gedanken zur deutschen Sendung* (Ideas about the German Mission). In both treatises, he discussed Germany's geographical and strategic position after the war and propagated his own version of 'Mitteleuropa' (see p. 119): a federation of German satellite states stretching from western Russia to the Balkans. But unlike other propagandists he insisted on the free self-determination of the 'smaller European nations which should voluntarily and intrepidly join Germany.'[31] Numerous letters, for example, by Thomas Mann, Sombart, Scheler and many soldiers congratulated Weber on his brochure. He also sent the memorandum about his war aims to several Reichstag deputies and organized three conferences with them but could not reach an agreement on these points.

In May 1916, tired of the monotonous life in the trenches, he became an adviser in the Treasury Office in Berlin, where he soon acted in favour of the practical realization of 'Mitteleuropa'. In June, he was unofficially authorized by Zimmermann to win German and Polish politicians for the establishment of an autonomous Polish state, limited, of course, to the Russian province of Poland. In July, Weber met Ropp, the leader of the League of the Alien Peoples of Russia (see pp. 122–3), and both closely cooperated in the Polish and later in the Lithuanian affairs.

Weber was especially active in mobilizing influential politicians and high-ranking civil servants: For instance his superior at the Treasury Office, State Secretary Siegfried Count Roedern, who personally intervened with the chancellor and promised to establish a National Bank for the Poles, the Reichstag deputies Naumann and Eduard David and the publicist Ernst Jäckh. Weber also co-founded the German-Polish Society and organized receptions with Polish delegations and German VIPs at the Hotel Adlon and in the DG where Ropp, Łempicki and Prince Radziwiłł made propaganda for the Polish state.

A few months after the establishment of the Kingdom of Poland on 5 November 1916, the government started negotiations about a similar project for Lithuania (see p. 123). In order to support the chancellor against the opposition of the Annexationists, Ropp, Weber and the influential Reichstag deputy of the Catholic Centre Party, Erzberger, launched an intensive propaganda campaign. On 30 November 1917, together with various politicians, bankers and professors, they founded the German-Lithuanian Society (Deutsch-Litauische Gesellschaft), and Weber became its vice-president. The principal task of this association and of its official newspaper, *Das Neue Litauen*, was to win over public opinion in Germany and Lithuania for the establishment of a Lithuanian state under German control. Through his personal contacts and articles in *Das Neue Litauen*, Weber emphasized the advantages of creating an autonomous Lithuanian state against two opposing forces: The German Annexationists like General Ludendorff who wanted to annex the country and left-wing politicians in Lithuania such as Steponas Kairys who insisted on complete independence. In his article 'Litauen vor der Entscheidung', Weber emphasized that 'Lithuania can only prosper economically when it closely joins the German Reich'.[32] Finally, under German pressure, the opposition in Lithuania was forced to acquiesce, and on 23 March 1918, a semi-independent Lithuanian state with close ties to Germany was proclaimed in Berlin. During the reception that followed, Weber explained to the Lithuanian delegation why they were tied to Germany. He said that

> the self-determination of the peoples is determined by the realities of life and that [...] you [the Lithuanians] as a healthy nation with a great future and as a vigorous state can only live in close affiliation with us and with our strong support and [...] offer us also guarantees for our security in the East.[33]

The Lithuanian politicians present at this ceremony, completely indoctrinated by German propaganda, praised with emphasis the rather limited independence of their country. The cleric Konstantinas Olšauskas spoke of the 'resurrection of Lithuania', and Augustinas Voldemaras, who in November 1918 became the first Lithuanian prime minister, acclaimed the German reorganization of Eastern Europe as 'leadership without domination'.[34]

While this pillar of 'Mitteleuropa' was gloriously established, the complete fiasco of the German war aims policy was on its way: On 21 March 1918, General Ludendorff had started his all-out attack on the Western front which after initial success was answered by a mighty Allied counteroffensive obliging the Germans to retreat and finally to ask humbly for an armistice. Poland and Lithuania became really independent, the dream of 'Mitteleuropa' was over.

Even in December 1917 Weber had expressed sincere doubts about Ludendorff's hazardous project of an offensive and was implicated in the propaganda campaign of Hahn and Prince Max von Baden in favour of a separate peace with Britain – a campaign somewhat played down in a recent biography of the prince.[35] Although Lloyd George's speech on 5 January 1918 seemed to have thwarted the rather timid peace appeals of Lord Lansdowne and Max von Baden (see p. 68), Weber and the other political friends of the Prince did not give up. Hahn wrote a memorandum for the government which Ludendorff upon recommendation of Haeften, director of the MAA, submitted to Count Hertling on 14 January. A bit later Weber gave a speech at the influential political club Wednesday Evening (Mittwochabend), extended it to a memorandum, had it signed by several politicians, industrialists and trade unionists, and submitted it to Ludendorff on 11 February. He warned the general against the revolutionary agitation which had just triggered the strikes of January and desperately asked him not to jeopardize the realization of Germany's most important war aim, 'Mitteleuropa', but to make possible peace negotiations with Britain by the assurance to restore the sovereignty of Belgium after the war. [36] On 16 February, an interview of Heinrich Mantler, director of Wolff's news agency, with Prince Max appeared in many German newspapers – an interview which, however, never took place, but was prepared by the Prince beforehand in close cooperation with Hahn.[37] It proclaimed very moderate German war aims such as the freedom of the seas, mentioned in Britain 'men of all political convictions looking for a way out [of the war]', but complained that their proposals of peace negotiations had just been rejected by the Allied Council at Versailles. However, the crucial question of restoring the independence of Belgium was again passed over in silence, and in Britain the media resonance was limited to the *Morning Post* and the pacifist daily *The Nation*.[38]

On 18 February, Prince Max travelled to the military headquarters at Bad Kreuznach and, referring to Weber's memorandum, tried to convince Ludendorff personally to renounce the offensive and allow the declaration about Belgium. However, the general flatly refused, specified as war aim the temporary occupation of Liège and strong economic ties with Belgium and insisted on his offensive. When the Prince asked him what would happen in case of a defeat, he coldly answered: 'Then Germany will have to perish.'[39] The next day Max returned to Berlin and discussed Ludendorff's reaction with his political friends. Weber congratulated the Prince on his interview with Mantler and underlined the importance of the German war aim of Mitteleuropa. Having received another critical memorandum from the German-Swiss military expert Hermann Stegemann, the Prince travelled again on 21 February to Bad Kreuznach in the hope of convincing Ludendorff this time.[40] However, he was probably not received, as he did not mention this meeting with Ludendorff in his detailed memoirs. Undauntedly, a few days later, Prince Max commissioned from Hahn and Weber a new memorandum with the title 'Ethical Imperialism', supposed to serve as a basis for a future understanding with Britain.[41] When it was handed over to the Kaiser and chancellor on 20 March, it was, as Prince Max put it, only of 'historical value' because Ludendorff's offensive started one day later. Nevertheless the Prince believed that one day it might dominate the war policy of the government.[42] Indeed, on 2 October 1918 Max von Baden was appointed chancellor, but it was far too late for any honourable peace agreement.

Hugo von Hofmannsthal (Austria-Hungary)

In [foreign] officials one has to arouse as much as possible the understanding of the political importance of Austria in the world.[43]

Until the war, Hofmannsthal (1874–1929) led a peaceful and comfortable life as a famous Austrian writer and librettist. When on 26 July 1914 he was mobilized for the Territorial Army, he immediately contacted one of his influential acquaintances,

Josef Redlich, deputy of the Austrian Reichsrat, and asked him to intervene so that he could avoid wasting his time in such a strenuous, uncomfortable and maybe even deadly occupation.[44] Redlich indeed procured him the *Superarbitrierung*, as the Austrians called the exemption, and on 12 August he was transferred to office service and appointed director of the Press Bureau of the KFA. Following Talleyrand's well-known advice *Pas trop de zèle* (Don't overdo it), Hofmannsthal worked in his office only on Monday and Tuesday and spent the long weekend in his private residence in the pleasant Vienna suburb of Rodaun. It is not known if he ever contacted journalists; in any case articles about the KFA are hard to find in Austrian newspapers. But as this bureau did not only handle charitable work, but also organized war propaganda, he wrote at least one article per month, usually in the Vienna newspaper *Neue Freie Presse*, until April 1915 when he left the KFA.

His first articles, however, ran counter to official war propaganda. He condemned the boycott of foreign words in the German language and the appeals for parsimony. On the contrary, he asked the Austrian upper class to spend lavishly in order not to ruin the artisans, and he set a good example himself by having his home redecorated in neoclassical style. Furthermore, he warned against contemporary war literature and recommended the lecture of certain classical German and Austrian authors, all of them presented in an expensive anthology edited by himself.[45]

Under the influence of the Tuesday Association (Dienstagsverein), he finally embarked on more substantial war propaganda from November 1914. The aim of this association was to develop an Austrian identity and to strengthen the Danube Monarchy against the overpowering German Empire.[46] In his preface to the statutes of the Tuesday Association, Hofmannsthal called for 'combating chronic pusillanimity' and reinforcing courage and tenacity. In an article on 'Die Bejahung Österreichs' (Consent to Austria) in the *Österreichische Rundschau* of 1 November he took up the lie of the 'defensive war', praised the 'political and moral unity' of the army, and compared its achievements against Russia with the brilliant advances of Field-Marshal Prince Eugene of Savoy against the Ottoman Empire in the eighteenth century. This article was reprinted four times in German periodicals and collective propaganda books.[47] The main recurrent themes of Hofmannsthal's propaganda until its end in summer 1917 were to downplay the bad performance of the Austrian army on the Eastern front and to create a specific Austrian identity and tradition based on the myth of famous Austrian leaders such as Empress Maria Theresa and Prince Eugene of Savoy, 'the greatest Austrian', whose French origins, however, were slightly inconvenient.

In his articles about the battles in Galicia and the Carpathians, where the Austrians cut a very sorry figure and were finally saved only by the intervention of German troops, Hofmannsthal praised the Austrian army as 'the most invincible one which has ever fought under the double-headed eagle since the days of Prince Eugene', considered its performance much more heroic than all the Punic wars together and justified their defeats either as 'a grandiose strategic decision' or a 'victorious retreat'.[48]

When he was 'looking for the sense of the war and a higher necessity' – a typical topos in many literary reflections[49] – he invented a European mission for Austria as a defence against the Asiatic onslaught and against the renewed French menace in the tradition of Louis XIV. He also praised the multinational Dual Monarchy as a model for a new European harmony.[50]

Although in the beginning of 1915 Hofmannsthal's superiors had allowed him to limit his work for the KFA even more, he wanted to get completely away from his duties because in view of the imminent declaration of war by Italy he was afraid to be transferred to active military service – a procedure which menaced quite a few shirkers in the offices, for instance, also Stefan Zweig who was employed in the KA and also dabbled in propaganda.[51] Thus, on 6 April 1915, Hofmannsthal once again asked Redlich for help who, together with two high officials of the Foreign Ministry, went to see Minister-President Karl Count Stürgkh.[52] Due to his intervention, Hofmannsthal was again exempted from military service, but only for a 'non-specified period' and against the obligation to spread patriotism in public relations. Thus he had to continue his propaganda in case of a check by the very active Commission of Control of Exemptions. As Hofmannsthal enjoyed travelling abroad, he decided to visit old friends in Germany, in occupied Poland and in Belgium, and combine this with conferences and some networking. His friends in the Foreign Ministry facilitated his trips by procuring him visas and travel permits.[53]

His first journey took Hofmannsthal to the part of Russian Poland occupied by the Austrian military administration. He was well received, wined and dined, and published a very favourable report in the *Neue Freie Presse* praising to the skies the Austrian efforts to reconstruct the ruined country.

In Berlin, Hofmannsthal visited the DG and there he met important politicians and civil servants. Refusing the German project of 'Mitteleuropa' which would reduce the Dual Monarchy to a German satellite state, he tried to bring home to them Austria's importance as a connecting link to the Balkans and the Near East (see motto above).

In his conferences in Berlin, Warsaw, Leipzig, Zurich, Stockholm and Oslo, he compared the achievements of Austria in literature with its military strength and presented its European mission which would terminate the epoch of nationalism. In his speech on 'Our War' in January 1916 in Berlin, he welcomed the war against Italy and exclaimed: 'Now the fight for Austria's honour has come and everybody [except him!] has joyfully hurried to join this war.'[54]

In April 1917, all exemptions from military service were subject to a revision. Hofmannsthal was summoned as well, but his friends in the Foreign Ministry pointing at his successful propaganda missions in Poland, Sweden and Norway obtained his definite exemption. When two months later Hofmannsthal found out that in Prague nobody cared for his 'Austrian Idea', he put an end to his propagandist activity. In any case his achievements in this field were of doubtful value. The Foreign Ministry somewhat distrusting him did not send him on official mission except in 1918 for an exhibition in Switzerland; the audiences applauded the famous writer but were not convinced by his arguments because of his cumbersome style and his inability to make the point clear. Last but not least, his Austrian fellow writers did not appreciate a shirker making war propaganda. Karl Kraus wrote in *Die Fackel*: 'This man is one of the most outstanding examples of the army of literati mustered in order to glorify events which they do not want to live through at any price.'[55] When Arthur Schnitzler read his enthusiastic speech about 'Our War', he commented: 'It is repugnant that somebody does everything in order not to be sent to the front and to be exempted, and then gives a brilliant speech about our war against Italy.'[56] Stefan Zweig, himself a shirker turned propagandist, made similar remarks.[57]

Louis Raemaekers (The Netherlands)

Looking through the cartoons again, I feel that you [Raemaekers] have done more to arouse English people to the real nature of the Huns than the combined efforts of all our orators and newspapers. (Lord Northcliffe in 1916).[58]

Louis Raemaekers (1869–1956) was a Dutch painter and from 1906 a political cartoonist.[59] When the war broke out, he was shocked by the atrocities of the German army during their invasion of Belgium. In order to incite his country to join the war on the Allied side, he published propaganda cartoons in the Dutch newspaper *De Telegraaf* which was resolutely pro-Entente.

In his cartoons he depicted real or invented atrocities by German soldiers or drew up hate cartoons with ugly Germans, even the Kaiser, in disgusting postures, both in a very expressive style (see also p. 40). Raemaekers was very skilled in depicting emotions such as hatred, anger or despair. However, he was not able to differentiate: In one of his cartoons Allied soldiers marching over dead bodies look as cruel and fanatical as their German counterparts.[60] Furthermore, he presented sadistic violence even in cases which did not really fit. When, in March 1916, a German submarine sank nine neutral ships, he commented this break of neutrality with the cartoon of a gorilla called 'The German Beast' sitting on the corpses of two violated women.[61]

It is clear that his cartoons aroused fanatic hostility against the Germans, not only in the Netherlands, but also all over the world. The German Consul General in Amsterdam attributed to them 'a particularly spiteful and poisonous impact, especially because they convey the ideas better than the written words and [...] also because they are by an artist of exceptional talent'.[62] And in a later German monograph on British World War propaganda the author wrote: 'The cartoons of Raemaekers had more propaganda value than several volumes of English propaganda pamphlets put together'[63] (see also the motto above).

As the German envoy in The Hague protested several times against Raemaekers's cartoons and accused the Dutch of infringing upon their neutrality, finally they were not only obliged to confiscate his drawings several times but even to arrest once Kick Schröder, the editor-in-chief of *De Telegraaf*. Finally in November 1915,

Raemaekers left his country and settled in Britain where he was received with open arms. His cartoons were published in Northcliffe's *Daily Mail*, exhibited in London galleries and sold at exorbitant prices. At the end of 1915, Wellington House published albums of his cartoons, one of them in 18 languages, and had them distributed widely, including to each British soldier. In France as well, his cartoons were exhibited in 25 cities and published in the leading magazines, sometimes in special issues. In both countries, the cartoonist was enthusiastically celebrated and received by leading statesmen such as Asquith and Poincaré. It was again Wellington House who started the most successful cartoon campaign, launching Raemaekers in the United States shortly after their declaration of war to Germany – an enterprise which, after some initial problems, led to the flooding of the American press with millions of his cartoons.

After the war the interest in Raemaekers waned because people had enough of his hate cartoons, and it also turned out that the most terrible atrocities were pure inventions. Raemaekers continued publishing his cartoons in *De Telegraaf* but settled down in Brussels, fled before the beginning of World War II to America and after his return to Brussels spent the last three years of his life in his home country.

Chapter 8

ANTI-WAR PROPAGANDA

In August 1914, the overwhelming majority of the political parties and other organizations in all war-faring countries wholeheartedly supported the declaration of war of their governments and had their parliamentary fractions vote for the war credits. The same happened in countries such as Italy and the United States which joined the war later. Only a very tiny minority stayed aloof: The Bolshevik and Menshevik fractions in the Russian Duma and the two-man fraction of the Socialist Party in the Serbian parliament either voted against or left the hall prior to the vote, and the Bolsheviks in exile under the leadership of Vladimir I. Lenin even appealed to 'transform the imperialistic war into a civil war for socialism'.[1]

However, when the war did not end as quickly as most people had expected, some organizations split over the war issue, new anti-war groups were founded, and from 1917 more and more people desired peace. Yet it must be emphasized that anti-war activists were hopelessly outnumbered and their activities in favour of peace were either consistently impeded or vigorously suppressed by the authorities. The following sections will discuss the development of the anti-war organizations, analyse their arguments, agitation methods and the techniques of two caricature magazines which refused or ridiculed official war propaganda.

How was anti-war propaganda organized?

Some political parties which publicly supported the war effort and voted the war credits were not as monolithic as they appeared. This was the case of the Social Democratic Party of Germany (Sozialdemokratische Partei Deutschlands, SPD), which soon after the first vote against the war credits by Liebknecht on 2 December 1914 split into the MSPD, 'M' signifying 'Majority'; 'Die Internationale', later called 'Spartakus'; and the Social Democratic Working Group (Sozialdemokratische Arbeitsgemeinschaft), later constituted as Independent Social Democratic Party of Germany (Unabhängige Sozialdemokratische Partei Deutschlands, USPD). Although most Spartakists formally adhered to the USPD, their aims were different: The USPD accepted the defence of the country, but refused the war credits because of the annexationist aims of the government. The Spartakists following the line of Lenin completely refused the war and appealed to struggle against the government according to Liebknecht's slogan 'Civil war, not civil truce'. However, both the USPD and the Spartakists were rather weak and outside Berlin, Leipzig and the industrial Ruhr area were 'just an underground sect', as David Morgan puts it.[2] In two by-elections for the Reichstag the candidates of the USPD were handsomely beaten.[3] Nevertheless, according to several witnesses, Liebknecht was the most popular politician not only in the German but also in the French trenches.[4]

The Italian Socialist Party (Partito Socialista Italiano, PSI) split in two parts: A group around Mussolini and the trade unions had switched over to the interventionist side already in October 1914 and was expelled from the party.[5] After the Italian declaration of war, the PSI adopted the policy of *né aderire né sabotare* (neither support nor sabotage) meaning that it would neither support the war nor fight against it. However, the party was divided between a majority 'reformist' wing indirectly supporting the war effort by cooperation with local administrations and commissions, and the 'intransigents' being in favour of revolutionary action.[6]

The various Russian socialist parties were also divided about the war issue. The 'defencists' wanted to halt revolutionary action during the war while other groups issued anti-war proclamations. Even some Bolsheviks denounced Lenin's position as 'defeatism'.[7] The controversy about the war issue was not settled by the February Revolution of 8 March (23 February) 1917; it grew more complicated with two new players in the game: the Provisional Government bent on continuing the war, and Lenin having returned to Petrograd and propagating immediate peace negotiations.

The British Labour Party was some sort of an umbrella organization consisting of the Trade Unions, the Fabian Society and the ILP. Only the latter one refused the war and the recruiting campaign, joined anti-war demonstrations and demanded peace by negotiation. But unlike the German USPD, it voted the war credits – a decision still confirmed by a vote of 198 against 61 at its conference at Leeds in April 1917.[8] One wonders if through this attitude in parliament the ILP did not jeopardize its own propaganda for a negotiated peace.

It was not easy to agitate against the war in France, a country which despite its alliance with Russia had remained neutral and was attacked and partly occupied by the German army. Hence only three deputies of the French Socialist Party (Section française de l'Internationale Ouvrière, SFIO) – the schoolteachers Brizon, Alexandre Blanc and Jean-Pierre Raffin-Dugens – voted against the war credits on 24 June 1916. Together with 28 other deputies they constituted the anti-war minority of the SFIO, which issued several appeals against the war, explained their views in some letters to their followers at the front, but did not actively support anti-war activities in the country. Despite a formal interdiction by their party, they also attended the international socialist conference at Kienthal, and Brizon elaborated the essential draft of its anti-war resolution.[9] More active were the leaders of the Metallurgic Workers' Federation (La Fédération des Métaux), Alphonse Merrheim and Albert Bouderon. In November 1915 they founded the Committee for International Action (Comité d'action internationale), later replaced by the Committee for the Renewal of International Relations (Comité pour la Reprise des Relations Internationales, CRRI). It stood at the forefront of anti-war agitation, sometimes in cooperation with another trade union organization, the Social Defence Committee (Comité de défense sociale, CDS). Other groups limited their agitation to a special audience.[10]

In Austria, the Social Democratic Workers' Party (Sozialdemokratische Arbeiterpartei, SDAP) under the leadership of Viktor Adler supported the war for fear of the Russian peril, but the Czech, Slovakian and Italian sections of the party refused to join its campaign. Furthermore, Adler's own son Friedrich, attacking the patriotic course of his father, expressed his sympathies for the 'Zimmerwald Left' (see p. 164) and in March 1916 founded the Association Karl Marx (Verein Karl Marx). A few months later, on 21 October 1916, he shot the Austrian Minister-President Stürgkh as a sign of protest against the policy of the SDAP and the Austrian war regime. From November 1916, the SDAP demanded negotiations about a peace without annexations and indemnities.[11]

Many other organizations were also divided over the war issue. Traditional pacifist associations, such as the German Peace Society (Deutsche Friedensgesellschaft, DFG), the French Association for a Legal Peace (Association de la paix par le droit) or the British National Peace Council, supported the war and even published patriotic appeals, but at least the DFG moderated its support for the government from 1915 and condemned annexations.[12] In Britain and Germany, new peace groups were founded: Already in August 1914, Liberals and Socialists founded the UDC and in November the NCF. Both organizations not only fought conscription but also demanded negotiations about a compromise peace.[13] In Germany in November 1914, the BNV was founded, which unveiled the myth of the war of defence, but instead of mobilizing the masses, it tried to influence higher officials in the AA and abroad. Nevertheless, its small number of around 100 members and its modest agitation irritated the authorities so much that in November 1915 they suspended their newspaper *Völkerfriede* and in February 1916 prohibited all other activities of the BNV. Therefore in July 1916 the BNV was replaced by a new organization, the Central Office for International Law (Zentralstelle für Völkerrecht, ZfV).[14]

Women's organizations split even more. In Britain, the war even divided a whole family devoted to the women's liberation movement, the Pankhursts. While Emmeline Pankhurst, the leader of the Women's Social and Political Union, and her eldest daughter Christabel stopped all suffragette activities and appealed for 'vigorous national defence against the German peril', the younger daughter Sylvia campaigned against the British entanglement with the war.[15] Smaller anti-war organizations were the Women's Peace Crusade with only 5,000 members and the East London Federation of Suffragettes.[16]

The League of German Women's Associations (Bund Deutscher Frauenvereine, BDF) under the leadership of Gertrud Bäumer organized the National Women's Service (Nationaler Frauendienst), a sort of social agency taking care of soldiers' families, organizing war work for women and teaching them how to adapt home economics and cooking to food shortages. The German Union for Women

Suffrage (Deutscher Verband für Frauenstimmrecht) under Marie Stritt also supported the war, whereas Anita Augspurg and Lida Gustava Heymann from the local branches of both associations in Hamburg-Altona condemned the war and participated in the great women's anti-war conference in April 1915 in The Hague. When they were expelled from the BDF they co-founded the German Women's Committee for a Permanent Peace (Deutscher Frauenausschuß für dauernden Frieden).[17]

In France, the National Council of French Women (Conseil national des femmes françaises) wholeheartedly supported the war and expelled pacifist members like Gabrielle Duchêne who founded small anti-war groups such as the Committee of Socialist Women's Action for Peace and against Jingoism (Comité d'action féminine socialiste pour la Paix contre le Chauvinisme), led by Louise Saumoneau, and the French Section of the International Women's Committee for Permanent Peace (Section française du Comité international des Femmes pour la Paix permanente).[18]

Even the international anarchist movement split: One smaller fraction, led by Jean Grave and Pierre Kropotkine, in March 1916 published the *Manifesto of the Sixteen* supporting the aim of the Entente to fight until complete victory, but the majority around Alexander Schapiro and Errico Malatesta, having already published a manifesto against the war in 1915, now passionately rejected this new appeal and demanded a world congress of the working class or a revolution to impose peace.[19]

The American anti-war organization Industrial Workers of the World had no chance to agitate against the war. Their meeting halls were raided, their propaganda material confiscated and around 100 activists condemned to prison terms of up to 20 years. Others were convicted for not having bought war bonds, fined by the courts and turned over to the Ku Klux Klan for tarring and feathering.[20]

What were the principal arguments?

The sophisticated agitation in favour of the war has been analysed in Chapter 3: from patriotic appeals for duty and sacrifice to vague promises of future rewards, from frightening warnings against the enemy's cruel intentions to exaggerated atrocity stories and downright lies – the panoply of their agitation was as various as it was ingenious. Anti-war activists, on the contrary, did not need to invent such far-fetched arguments: The horrors of war spoke for themselves. The different arguments will be summarized according to the manifestos of the conferences of Zimmerwald (5–9 September 1915), Kienthal (24–30 April 1916)[21] (see p. 164) and various other appeals.

Often evoked were the enormous casualties: Europe had become a gigantic slaughterhouse with millions of corpses, cripples, widows and orphans, with ruins piled on ruins, with misery and privation, malnutrition and disease.[22] In France and Turkey demographic arguments were mentioned: It would not be possible to make up for the heavy losses of human life.[23]

Of particular acuity were comparisons between the millions dying in the trenches and the warmongers and capitalists 'thriving in warmth and prosperity behind your backs'.[24] A cartoon in the *Worker's Dreadnought* showed an exhausted labourer with a gun and two war profiteers with their money bags sitting behind him, accompanied by the text: 'Aren't they worth defending?'[25] Complaints about lack of food and outright hunger were more typical for countries with bad supply: Germany, Russia, Austria and Italy.[26]

In order to finance the war, all countries were obliged to resort to domestic borrowing (see pp. 91–6). Quite early the question arose of who would pay for interests and reimbursement. The propagandists in both war camps promised that the defeated enemy would pay for this – an argument which was especially put forward in France so that the slogan '*L'Allemagne paiera*' (Germany will pay) became proverbial and is sometimes used nowadays as well.[27] The anti-war activists easily dissipated such illusions. They pointed out that it would be impossible to extort huge indemnities from the ruined enemy and prophesied that the workers would have to pay 75 per cent of their wages in order to reimburse the national war bonds.[28] Neither now nor later will be any money available for the people's welfare and social reforms.[29]

The war aims of the 'Hold out politicians' such as national defence, democracy and the liberation of oppressed nationalities were contrasted with the fact that they were actually destroying the liberties of their own peoples and the independence of other nations. USPD-leader Käthe Duncker called this the 'downright deceit of the people'.[30] On 20 February 1917, during a peace debate in the House of Commons several liberal and Labour MPs, all of them militants of the UDC, attacked the war policy of the government: Arthur Ponsonby compared the recent assurance of the prime minister that 'we are not fighting a war of conquest' with Britain's actual and projected annexations of approximately 1.5 million square miles. Philip Snowden compared the modest size of the German colonies with the possessions of the British who actually ruled one-fifth of the surface of the world.[31] Trevelyan suggested that the Allies, before fighting for the liberty of small nations, should liberate their own oppressed nationalities in Russia, Morocco, Ireland, India and North Africa – a view shared by many other anti-war activists.[32] Liebknecht, the Italian socialist deputy Oddino Morgari and some French socialists as well denounced the projected annexations by Italy and Germany.[33]

The question of who had started the war was also hotly disputed. Instead of accusing a single country, numerous activists from the Bolsheviks to the members of the UDC, referring either to Lenin's or to John A. Hobson's theory of Imperialism, blamed the capitalists of all countries who competed and finally fought with each other in order to dominate and to exploit the whole world.[34] A particular argument circulated among anarchists and French soldiers: The European elites afraid of the emancipation of the working class and of the 'red wave' had started the war in order to knock down the working class.[35]

Prussian militarism and German war crimes were not excused but related to French and Russian militarism; British navalism; and the French, British and Belgian crimes in their African colonies.[36] Furthermore, enemy propaganda had accused the Russians as well as the British during the Crimean and the Boer War, respectively, of the same crimes.[37] To pretend that after victory over Germany there would be no more wars was considered a monstrous lie. In their speeches at the respective parliaments in Paris and Rome, the socialist deputies Brizon and Morgari prophesied with nearly the same words: 'This war as well will produce new wars; the defeated country will brew vengeance.'[38] The French feminist Saumoneau found it even necessary to refute the assertion of some French propagandists that the Germans were 'a people of barbarians and idiots'.[39]

What was the principal demand of the anti-war activists? All above-mentioned organizations and many non-organized women crying 'We need our husbands' propagated time and again the same aim: armistice and immediate negotiations about a 'peace without annexations and indemnities' according to the famous formula of the Petrograd Soviet (see p. 170).[40] In Russia, France, Germany and Italy, such demands were sometimes combined with calls for a revolution.[41]

How did the agitation function and how did the authorities react?

The methods of the anti-war activists closely resembled those of the war propagandists: Public appeals, demonstrations and petitions to parliaments, conferences, meetings and fundraising activities, and speeches and appellations in the parliaments were their main activities while newspapers, brochures and leaflets, posters, cartoons and writings on walls were their principal instruments. In Italy and Germany, banknotes were stamped with slogans like 'No peace without revolution'.[42] However, they had no propaganda gadgets at their disposal such as children toys or household items, but disposed of a particular weapon of their own: political strikes. The conferences will be discussed at first, followed by the strikes and other agitation means.

International conferences were possible only in neutral countries. In September 1915, April 1916 and September 1917, the anti-war socialists organized three international propaganda conferences in the Swiss villages Zimmerwald and Kienthal, and in Stockholm, respectively. The German socialists were always represented whereas delegations from Britain and France participated only partially or not at all because of prohibitions by their parties or passport restrictions. The manifesto of the first conference condemned the war in strong words, but an appeal to vote against the war credits was prevented by the German delegate Georg Ledebour. The resolutions of the so-called Zimmerwald Left around Lenin and the Polish delegate Karl Radek to transform the civil truce into civil war by 'a revolutionary struggle against the capitalist governments' were not accepted either. The manifesto of the second conference went further and demanded a vote against war credits and 'an immediate peace without annexations'. It was in Stockholm that the most radical manifesto was passed calling for simultaneous mass action, especially an international strike in order to overthrow the governments and to enforce peace.[43]

However the propagandistic effect was not equally achieved in all countries. In Britain, the manifestos could be published in the *Labour Leader* of the ILP. In Italy, the Zimmerwald manifesto in the socialist newspaper *Avanti* was at first suppressed, but after a vigorous protest by the PSI it was published four months later. The German censors suppressed all information about Zimmerwald, but the *Vorwärts*, organ of the SPD, finally published extracts from *Avanti*. French censors initially let pass some information about Zimmerwald, but later imposed a complete black out, whereas the Kienthal resolution could be published by *L'Humanité*. The British, French and Italian delegations could not come to Stockholm because of passport refusals, and the organizers were so disappointed that they did not even invite the press. Hence the last manifesto was only rarely published and remained practically unknown.[44]

The most active forces next to the socialist organizations were splinter groups of the feminist movements. At the end of March 1915, the German feminist and social democrat Clara Zetkin organized the International Conference of Socialist Women in Bern, where Lenin's wife Nadezhda Krupskaya tried in vain to win the delegates for a resolution in favour of a revolutionary class struggle. But even the rather modest peace manifesto condemning the war as an imperialistic aggression for capitalist motives was forbidden in Germany and Zetkin jailed for having circulated it.[45] A second women's conference in Bern three years later, in April 1918, appealing to all women to refuse any physical or intellectual war work had no propagandistic success at all.[46]

In late April 1915, another women's conference was organized in The Hague. However, most of the 1,126 delegates were suffragettes from the Netherlands, their French and Russian colleagues were not allowed to attend, in Britain the Foreign Office refused 156 passports, and even the remaining 24 delegates but three were finally prevented by the naval authorities to cross the channel. Furthermore, the jingoist British press calling the delegates 'peacettes' mocked at 'this shipload of hysterical women'. Despite all these harassments, the conference was a great success. Its resolution stipulated the establishment of a permanent conference discussing peace feelers and negotiating peace conditions. In May and June, 13 delegates submitted this resolution to nearly all European governments, but only Knut A. Wallenberg, the Swedish Minister of Foreign Affairs, contemplated the idea of hosting such a conference.[47]

Speeches and interpellations in parliament were another cornerstone of propaganda. The task was not to convince the government to make peace but to rally support from the people by publishing them as leaflets.[48] Three examples might suffice here: On 14 December 1915, the Spartakist Liebknecht asked the chancellor: 'Is the government ready to enter into peace negotiations on the basis of renouncing all sorts of annexations, if the other belligerent parties consent to do the same?'[49] On 20 February 1917, the liberal MP Trevelyan demanded the same in the House of Commons and said: 'We too shall have to settle by a negotiated peace, and not by a dictated peace, and why, in Heaven's name, are we not negotiating now?'[50] On 1 July 1916, the socialist deputy Oddino Morgari set the convocation of a peace conference as agenda for the session of the Italian parliament and said: 'One thing is certain: if the war continues for another year, 3 or 4 million men more who have the right to live, will perish, and all war-faring states will go bankrupt.'[51]

The reaction to such speeches differed from country to country. While in Britain and Italy the governments and the deputies of the ruling coalition listened and answered politely, but quietly continued their war all the same, in Germany a multitude of other tactics was employed: The interpellations were not admitted, the representatives of the government replied evasively or even refused to answer, speeches were blocked by procedure tricks like announcing the 'end of debate', by constantly heckling the speaker as a 'traitor to our country' and in two cases even by physically assaulting him.[52]

A special weapon against the war were political strikes supposed not only to halt war production but also, combined with mass demonstrations, to force the ruling elites to make peace. However, in order to prevent strikes, to regulate wages and working conditions and to restrict the workers' mobility, the war-faring states, usually with the consent and the support of the trade unions, sooner or later introduced some sort of an 'industrial conscription', as the Austrian deputy Redlich dubbed it. In Austria from 1914 and in Germany from 1916 all men, albeit and naturally with the exception of the bourgeoisie, were obliged to work, could be sent elsewhere for work and could not quit their jobs. However, in Austria, the application of the War Labour Act (Kriegsleistungsgesetz) varied because not all factories were involved. Some men had a special status, and from March 1917 workers could appeal to arbitration commissions. In Britain and Italy, only workers in war-related industries were concerned, and in France only those who had been called back from the front. In Italy throughout the war, and in Germany and Austria at certain times, such factories were militarized, that is the workers were directed by officers, subordinated to military discipline and guarded by a military unit; in Germany in this case all the workers liable to military service were theoretically paid military wages of only 53 pfennig (€2.01) per day plus a food allocation of 2.10 mark (€7.24).[53] In Russia it was not necessary to adjust the labour conditions to the war, because workers had practically no liberties, and police and army regularly intervened in strikes.[54] In at least one case, one country even copied from the other: The British Munitions of War Act of 2 July 1915 was the model for the German Patriotic Auxiliary Service Law (Vaterländisches Hilfsdienstgesetz, VHD) of 6 December 1916, hatefully called 'Law of Compulsory Work'. Thus as Gibelli puts it, the working force in all or in the concerned factories was transformed into an 'army of labour'.[55]

It is not possible in the context of this book to analyse all the strikes in detail. Only the general course of events in the various countries with special consideration of anti-war agitation and the reaction of the authorities is discussed here. In Italy, Roberto Bianchi writes: 'the intensity of the events was unparalleled in other Western countries'.[56] Despite the severe regulations of the Industrial Mobilization (Mobilitazione industriale) in autumn 1916 and throughout 1917, tens of thousands of strikers, many of them women, accompanied by adolescents and children, spontaneously demonstrated all over the country 'against the war and for peace', with 500 demonstrations alone taking place between 1 December 1916 and 15 April 1917.[57] Many of these demonstrations degenerated into armed uprisings reaching their climax in August 1917 in Turin: The houses of both rich 'signori' and of war propagandists, such as schoolteachers, were attacked, town halls occupied, shops plundered and destroyed, fire arms were put to use and barricades erected. However, the reformist majority of the PSI remained true to its program of 'neither support nor sabotage' and refused to transform the disturbances into organized revolutionary action.[58] Only in Turin the propaganda of the 'intransigent' faction of the PSI was effective enough to push the uprising close to an outspoken revolt, but the authorities were well prepared. They had already banished militant anti-war propagandists to faraway places, put them in prison, in Sardinian camps or sent them to the front.[59] Besides, the government had put the war zones and all industrial areas under the control of some sort of a military dictatorship. In Turin, army units equipped with machine guns mowed down 50 demonstrators, injured hundreds, court-martialled 12 socialist agitators for 'indirect treason' and incarcerated thousands without even questioning any of them. Attempts of the demonstrators to fraternize with soldiers and appeals like 'Do not shoot your brothers' usually failed.[60] Having crushed the uprising in Turin, the government issued decrees against defeatism which punished any act intended to 'lower public morale and lessen the resistance of the country' with imprisonment for up to 10 years and fines up to 10,000 lire (€27,500) – the double of an average yearly income. The result was a wave of denunciations and a 'hunt for the defeatists', and all the desperate people, who after the disastrous defeat at Caporetto in October 1917 expected a revolution and eagerly waited for the Austrians and Germans to come and to govern the country, waited in vain.[61]

In Germany, the *Vorwärts* and *Der Wahre Jacob* were in the hands of the MSPD, and the USPD and Spartakus could only count on the support of some local papers such as the *LV*, and were otherwise obliged to resort to the haphazard distribution of brochures and leaflets. Besides, their organizations were infiltrated by police informers eager to obtain up to 36,000 mark (€136,800) for denunciations. Two disciplinary measures – dispatching to the front or 'protective custody' (Schutzhaft), in reality preventive custody during months or even years without any verdict – were time and again imposed by the authorities not only to leaders like Rosa Luxemburg, but also to simple members.[62] When for instance on 2 February 1918 the authorities in Wilhelmshaven laid hand on the membership list of a local group of the USPD, they jailed the older activists and dispatched all the 60 younger men to the trenches.[63] In some cases strikers acquitted by tribunals were thereafter put in protective custody[64] – a procedure reintroduced by the NS-Regime in 1933.[65]

The first political strike broke out in June 1916 as a protest against the prison sentence of Liebknecht.[66] The mass strikes of April 1917 were not initiated by the USPD or the Spartakists, but erupted spontaneously because of misery and hunger, after the authorities had announced a reduction of the bread rations. Only in Leipzig the workers demanded peace negotiations as well and the cancellation of the VHD.[67] The tiny group of Spartakists was not able to coordinate the strikes or even to convert them into revolutionary action, and their appeals for demonstrations in favour of peace without annexations and indemnities according to the proclamation of the Petrograd Soviet were prohibited; the few demonstrators who dared to come were easily dispersed by the sabres of mounted police.[68] The leaders of the USPD on the other hand were, as the Reichstag deputy Wilhelm Dittmann later explained, opposed to 'revolutionary gymnastics' and 'putsch tactics' which in their view would only endanger the lives of their followers.[69]

In January 1918, however, anti-war agitation came to a height. Incited by the Spartakists and revolutionary activists in the factories, approximately half a million men put down their tools and demonstrated for an immediate peace with Russia, more food and the abolition of the VHD. However, like in Italy, the army in Berlin had the soldiers of four machine gun battalions ready to intervene and to shoot their fathers and brothers, as Kaiser Wilhelm had already told recruits in 1891. Fortunately, the intervention of a massive contingent of police, accustomed to ruthlessly shooting strikers and demonstrators for decades, was sufficient to restore 'law and order'. In the end the 'hold out politicians' of the MSPD joined the strike committee and rapidly succeeded in stopping the strikes. Finally dozens of demonstrators ended up dead or injured, 150 were jailed and 3,500 dispatched as cannon fodder to the front with the label 'B' on their uniform so that they were placed in the most exposed trenches.[70]

This crushing defeat seemed to have broken the back of the German anti-war movement for quite a while. Although activists continued to distribute leaflets, even for the soldiers at the front, and Spartakus intended to equip the workers with arms and munitions, no major actions were signalled. Even appeals to demonstrate for peace on 1 May 1918 were not followed at all, as the KPA triumphantly reported.[71] Perhaps the rapid advance of the German offensive from March reinvigorated the hope that the war might rapidly be won. After the military defeats in July and August, propaganda for a revolutionary fight and a general strike in favour of peace started again, but strikers only demanded less working hours and better food supply. On 5 September 1918, the Spartakist Ernst Meyer wrote to Lenin: 'Unfortunately we cannot report major actions at present or in the near future. But there will be more projects in winter.'[72] Only when negotiations about an armistice were already under way, the USPD under Eisner agitated in Munich and on 7 November overthrew the government while the revolution in Berlin was achieved by the spontaneous actions of the German sailors.

In France the scope of the protest movements was limited to certain areas.[73] As the overwhelming majority of the French socialists supported the war, strikes and peace demonstrations were instigated by the trade unions, but for ideological reasons they did not cooperate with the deputy Caillaux and his Republican League (Ligue républicaine) which also militated in favour of a compromise peace. Although from December 1914 in Paris individuals distributed numerous anti-war leaflets and brochures, for instance in the metro, in churches and tramways, in public toilets and house entrances, this did not lead to organized action.[74] After some isolated anti-war meetings from December 1915 onwards,[75] in spring

1917 the CRRI and the CDS organized a conference and a strike in Paris with slogans such as 'Down with the war', 'Down with the Republic' and 'Long live the Russian Revolution'. Workers also went on strike in the provincial centres, but the very efficient censorship suppressed or falsified all information so that activists sometimes resorted to travelling in order to spread the news.[76] In spring 1918 it was again the CDS, this time supported by the General Confederation of Labour (Confédération générale du travail, CGT), which called for demonstrations and 'strikes until armistice'. Especially in the Loire area workers even tried to close down armament factories. Following the example of desperate wives, fathers and youngsters, they also prevented soldiers from mounting on trains to the front. In both years the authorities suppressed the strikes either by cavalry, gendarmes or colonial troops, a total of 1,700 suspects were arrested, hundreds of leading activists court-martialled and sent either to the front or to forced labour in the colonies.[77] However, Clemenceau did not only rely on brutal force; he also succeeded in disqualifying the trade unions. He had agents provocateurs infiltrate the strikers and produced fake documents about the unions' connections with the German secret service, so that the anti-war movement dried up quite rapidly.[78] The mighty German spring offensive also deterred some trade unionists like Merrheim to join the strikers because they did not want to be blamed as defeatists.[79] In any case, as Charles Sorrie puts it, 'the majority of French citizens were never attracted to efforts at prematurely ending the war'.[80]

'A whole country with the emperor at its head wants peace, but is forced to continue fighting', wrote Stefan Zweig on 27 April 1918.[81] Indeed, the desperate efforts of Karl I, Emperor of Austria-Hungary, and his ministers to open peace negotiations with France were not only blocked by Poincaré and his prime minister, Alexandre Ribot, but even passed over in silence for one year, so that it only became known in April 1918 by an indiscretion of Clemenceau.[82] Thus, all anti-war agitation in the Dual Monarchy came to nothing except for one case: When on 12 January 1918, the peace negotiations in Brest-Litovsk reached a deadlock because of the inflexible position of the German military, more than 700,000 workers went on strike demanding immediate peace and an improvement of the desperate supply situation. Although the AOK was prepared to clamp down on the strikers with 50 battalions of the field army, the authorities preferred to make far-reaching concessions: They facilitated peace with Russia by renouncing all territorial demands, reformed the food distribution and alleviated the militarization of the enterprises.[83]

The Russian socialists were much better accustomed to underground combat than were their German and French counterparts and did their best to stir up the workers and undermine the armed forces. By 14 August 1914, the Russian Social Democratic Labour Party (Bolshevik), following Lenin's appeal, distributed a leaflet refusing the imperialist war and advocating the establishment of a republic.[84] There was some agitation in the factories, however, and most of the numerous demonstrations and strikes – in the first seven weeks of 1917, there were 268 strikes in Petrograd alone– were not directed by the socialists but broke out spontaneously. Economic and political motives, hunger and the demand for peace were closely intertwined.

As Joshua Sanborn writes: 'Food was the top political issue of the day in February 1917' – a statement well illustrated by a contemporary police report, 'Resentment is felt worse in large families, where children are starving in the most literal sense of the word, and where no other words are heard except, "Peace, immediate peace, peace at all cost".'[85]

Unfortunately this desperate wish was not granted so rapidly. After the February Revolution had removed the tsar, a 'Dual Regime' was established. The insurgents created the 'Petrograd Soviet', a council of workers and soldiers which on 28 February (14 March 1917) published its famous *Appeal to the Peoples of the Whole World*, known worldwide under the slogan 'Peace without annexations and indemnities'.[86] The conservative and liberal elites represented in the Duma established the 'Provisional Government' whose Minister of Foreign Affairs, Milyukov, denounced the appeal of the Soviet as a 'German peace', and declared to fight until a 'decisive victory'.[87] The government supported by the social revolutionaries and the Mensheviks in the Petrograd Soviet confirmed this view and in May started an offensive which failed completely.[88]

This bellicose attitude ignoring the widespread demand for peace and land reform sealed the fate of the Provisional Government. The Bolshevik Central Committee, reinforced by Lenin who in April had returned from his exile in Switzerland, denounced the 'naked imperialist character' of Milyukov's declarations, and now a vast peace campaign broke loose. More important than their numerous newspapers and leaflets was, in view of the high percentage of illiteracy in the country, oral propaganda in small discussion groups and mass meetings. Every day Lenin addressed the crowds from the balcony of a ballerina's villa exhorting them to stop fighting and to take control of the lands of big landowners. The Bolsheviks trained hundreds of professional agitators and stepped up their propaganda for immediate peace and land reform in the recently established factory committees.[89] Above all they created numerous agitation cells in the armed forces, according to Lenin's demand in his 'April Theses' read on 4 April (17 April) in front of the Petrograd Soviet, that 'the most widespread campaign for this view [peace and the abolition of capitalism] must be organised in the army at the front' (Figure 37).[90] They also concentrated on certain convincing topics and supplied their agitators with elaborate model speeches such as 'What gave us the February Revolution in seven months?', 'How to end the war?', 'The actual situation of the Red Guards and their tasks', and 'The situation of the working class and its role'. But as words alone would not overthrow the government, the Bolsheviks trained workers militarily and created their own combat units, the 'Red Guards', which were equipped with arms and munitions by the factory and the regiment committees.[91] In the evening of 24 October (6 November) 1917, the coup d'état started. As the Provisional Government had failed to bring in reliable troops in sufficient numbers, it took the Bolsheviks little more than 24 hours to seize power. It was typical for the confused situation in Russia that the order of the new government to open immediate negotiations about an armistice met with opposition at the Stavka, where General Nikolai Dukhonin tried to jeopardize it. Finally the Bolsheviks had to rely on German propaganda leaflets informing the soldiers' committees about their orders.

Dukhonin was lynched, and the soldiers themselves negotiated the armistice with German officers.[92]

In Britain, the unions were quite patriotic and the workers so much intimidated that a simple threat to send them to the front stopped strikes immediately.[93] There were very few political strikes and none against the war.[94] In the United States as well, nobody went on strike for peace.

There were many other varieties of anti-war agitation depending on local circumstances. In Britain, apart from numerous activities in favour of a negotiated peace,[95] heavy agitation evolved around conscription and the 'conchies' issue. Britain was the only combatant country that until 1916 not only allowed propaganda against conscription, but even thereafter recognized 16,500 conscientious objectors. Contrary to the other belligerent countries, police did not harass or prohibit the anti-war conferences and demonstrations of the UDC, NCF or ILP, but did not protect them either against the violent aggressions organized by 'patriotic' organizations. For instance, the Discharged Soldiers and Sailors Federation, usually well informed in advance about UDC meetings by the jingoist press, employed young hooligans or soldiers from the dominions and the colonies in order to disturb anti-war activities and to destroy propaganda material.[96] After the introduction of conscription in 1916, propaganda in favour of a negotiated peace was more and more obstructed (see p. 13) but not prohibited, while any agitation against recruiting was punishable by DORA. Hence police informers infiltrated all anti-war organizations, police arrested people who distributed brochures, raided dozens of offices, sometimes even without a search warrant, confiscated propaganda material and destroyed printing equipment, but not really in a consistent manner.[97]

The 'conchies' issue also led to heated controversies. The conchies were obliged to do civilian service for the army which in Britain was quite harmless but could be very dangerous when they had to dig trenches and extend barbed wire at the front. A total of 1,350 hardliners who refused to support the war in any way were put in jail, 35 of them sentenced to death by the military tribunals. Here anti-war propaganda found a long running issue. Russell, university lecturer at Cambridge and a militant of the UDC, organized demonstrations, a press campaign and at the head of a deputation even met Prime Minister Asquith personally. Under this pressure the authorities gave in, and the death sentence was commuted to forced labour.[98] Later Russell became editor of the anti-war magazine *Tribunal*, wrote a pamphlet against the unjust punishment of conchies and assisted them in the tribunals. Nevertheless, approximately 70 of them died of bad treatment.[99]

In order to prevent the declaration of war by Wilson, in 1917 American anti-war agitators started publicity campaigns in newspapers proposing a conference of neutrals to settle the German-American dispute. Women's organizations staged rallies in favour of a referendum, canvassed for peace in front of the Capitol and on 24 April 1917, the day of the vote, in a last ditch effort personally tried to convince deputies to vote against the war.[100]

Anti-war groups also prepared conspicuous propaganda events like the voyage of Ford's peace ship which sailed on 4 December 1915 from New York to Stockholm with 5,000 women activists on board – an important enterprise which could not be suppressed by censorship. When the women arrived there, on 8 February 1916, they organized a conference to propose peace terms to the belligerent countries, but nothing came out of it.[101] Even the assassination of Stürgkh served propaganda purposes: The murderer declared, 'I wanted to demonstrate for a peace without annexation and indemnities and [...] also in favour of revolutionary tactics.'[102]

Rolland was just in Switzerland when the war broke out, and he decided not to return to France. He published his famous anti-war treatises *Au-dessus de la mêlée* (Above the Battle) and *Aux peuples assassinés* (To the Assassinated Peoples), and became a sort of rallying point of pacifists not only from France but also from Germany and Austria. Less known but at least equally active was the Italian pacifist Enrico Begnami, who was already living in Swiss exile since 1889. In the column *Guerra alla Guerra* (War against War) of his periodical *Coenobium* (Printed in Italy), he published information about peace congresses and anti-war reflections by Leo Tolstoi, Norman Angell, Schnitzler and feminist activists such as Saumoneau and Marguerite Gombat. He had also anti-war publications smuggled to Italy until in 1918 *Coenobium* was suppressed and the author deprived of his passport. Henri Guilbeaux, who had founded *Demain*, was accused in France of spying for Germany and sentenced to death in absentia. When the Swiss authorities jailed him, he was freed by Lenin who declared him a Russian citizen and had him brought to Moscow.[103]

The German pacifist groups limited themselves to harmless appeals, meetings and publications which did not reach the masses. But even the modest leaflet *Shall We Annex?* of the BNV of July 1915, which was directed against the Annexationists and distributed to politicians and officials only, led to the intervention of police happily confiscating the remaining three copies. From November 1915 on, the BNV was more and more reduced to silence by the authorities with arrests, house searches and interdictions to meet, to travel, to publish and to communicate with foreigners, until in February 1916 all activities were formally prohibited.[104] Nevertheless, in March 1916 Mina Cauer and other female members of the BNV distributed to the clergy 30,000 copies of a peace prayer by the Anglican Archbishop of Canterbury, Randall Davidson, who condemned the war and asked for a peace of understanding. They were fined by a tribunal for 'having considerably worried the public'. The principal activities of the ZfV, the successor organization of the BNV, consisted of propaganda against the various annexationist organizations, appeals to the Reichstag and public support for Bethmann Hollweg's peace offer of 12 December 1916. Like the BNV the ZfV as well was prejudiced to popular agitation and never organized mass meetings in favour of peace.[105]

It is remarkable that even some of the teachers to whom especially in France and Germany a preponderant role in war propaganda had been assigned, protested against the war. In August 1915, representatives of the French teachers' unions signed a declaration proclaiming 'This is not our war'. In 1917, several teachers refused to distribute the usual hate propaganda at school and insisted on speaking about the Russian Revolution in class. The authorities reacted swiftly: their mail was opened, their homes were searched, they were dismissed from school, expulsed from their apartments and jailed for several months.[106] A famous case, characterized as a new Dreyfus Affair, was the nursery schoolteacher Hélène Brion, general secretary of the teacher's union and member of the CRRI. She had distributed posters and brochures against the war, with titles such as *Enough Men Killed – Peace* and *Peace without Annexations and Conquests*. Due to the pressure of Clemenceau who insisted on an exemplary punishment, she was calumniated as a defeatist and a German spy by an orchestrated press campaign, and finally in March 1918 condemned by a military tribunal to a suspended sentence of three and a half years.[107] In Germany teachers acted individually and, it seems, not at school. For instance, in Hamburg in May 1917, a militant of the USPD asked women at an assembly of her party to go on strike in order to compel the government to make peace. A policeman in civilian clothes was present and took note of her appeal. She was immediately dismissed from school and arrested as 'a danger for the security of the Reich.' Another teacher showed his aversion to war propaganda in the obligatory and lengthy report to the School Board by writing only two sentences: that he had informed students and adults about the war, but that 'there were no new viewpoints'.[108]

Let us not forget courageous individuals protesting against the war, for instance, the highly decorated British officer Sassoon. After a convalescent leave, he refused to resume duty, joined anti-war publishers, published poems about the suffering at the front and in July 1917 wrote a manifesto denouncing the 'war of aggressions and conquest [...] for which the fighting men are sacrificed'. When he submitted it to his colonel, Sassoon was threatened with a lunatic asylum and finally sent to a war hospital with the diagnosis 'shell shock'. After his 'treatment', he returned to the front and fought with some interruption in France until he was wounded in July 1918.[109] When the painter and non-commissioned officer Heinrich Vogeler sent the Kaiser a letter criticizing the peace of Brest-Litovsk as a dictated peace, he was interned in a lunatic asylum for 63 days.[110] Russell did not only help conchies but also tried to travel to Washington hoping to stir up President Wilson against the war mongers in Britain. In order to prevent this trip, the Foreign Office asked the Home Office to convict him under DORA so that it could refuse a passport. He was indeed condemned by a tribunal to pay a fine of £100 (£4,300), and as he could or would not pay, his belongings were sold, he lost his position in Cambridge and the passport was refused. In December 1916, he supported the German peace proposal and had an open letter to Wilson smuggled out of the country. In winter 1918, he was finally jailed for six months.[111] Georg Nicolai, a medical officer in the German army, signed together with Albert Einstein, the pacifist Wilhelm Foerster and the writer Otto Buek the *Aufruf an die Europäer* (Appeal to the Europeans) condemning the jingoist Appeal to the Civilised world (see p. 38). When in a lecture at the University of Berlin he condemned the war, the lecture was cancelled, he was demounted in his rank and sent to a small garrison. There he wrote the anti-war tract *Biologie des Krieges* (Biology of War), smuggled the manuscript to Switzerland and had it published there. When he was finally asked to stop all pacifist activities and threatened to be sent to the trenches, he captured a plane and fled to Denmark.[112]

How did cartoonists fight against the war: Le Canard enchaîné *and* Glühlichter

Le Canard enchaîné, founded on 4 September 1915, is the only satirical war magazine that still exists today.[113] Their editors explained that contrary to other newspapers they would publish only false news and 'un-scuff the skulls'. In 1917 they asked their readers to elect the greatest skull-stuffer: 5,653 of them voted for Hervé, editor of the chauvinist newspaper *La Victoire*, closely followed with 5,402 for Maurice Barrès, leader of the League of Patriots and author of a daily propaganda column in *L'Echo de Paris*.[114]

The special strategy of the magazine consisted in ridiculing French war propaganda by exaggerating its nationalistic arguments. For example: In February 1918, after a heavy German bombardment of Paris which killed 56 people, Hervé tried to calm down the excitement of the population by arguing that while London had been bombarded so many times by the Germans, the French felt humiliated that Paris had been spared for such a long time. The *Canard* wrote: 'Yes, the families of the 56 dead felt, like the others, extremely humiliated. But now, they are no longer humiliated at all. They are very happy. Like Hervé. Very happy.'[115] The magazine also invented Hervé's reaction: 'I know well that there were victims, but they were a ridiculously tiny number. And, further, one cannot make an omelette without breaking eggs. The essential thing is to have a big cellar like mine, not to be an egg and to eat the omelette.'[116]

In September 1915, the *Canard* reported that Hungarian war profiteers had cheated the army by selling cheap cattle at exaggerated profits and commented ironically: 'It is certainly not the suppliers of the French army who would act in this way.' In reality, fraudulent French businessmen had acted like their Hungarian colleagues and pocketed commissions of up to 700,000 francs (€1.9 million) in a sale of horses to the army.[117] The magazine even dared to ridicule one of the main topics of Allied propaganda, the atrocity stories. In an article on the cut hand, the author describes his search for a boy whose hand has been amputated by the German barbarians. After a time-consuming investigation, he finally finds the boy with a huge bandage around his hand, but his mother explains that he has caught his finger in a door.[118]

In cartoons as well the magazine ridiculed war propaganda, for instance, the frequent promises that victory is near: Two little boys foresee that as adults they will join their daddies in the trenches, and under the title 'Don't worry' a *poilu* says to another: 'During the Hundred Years' War they all died of old age.'[119]

Under the title of each issue of the *Canard,* a small duck says to huge scissors, the symbol of censorship: 'You will have my feathers, but not my skin.' In 1915, the censors suspended the magazine for a while, but from 1916 on despite a few interventions they became surprisingly tolerant and even accepted jokes about themselves. In one of them a charwoman tells her employer: 'The wife of the censor, you know, this guy who makes the white spaces, she has just produced a black baby.'[120] And when in autumn 1916 Prime Minister Alexandre Ribot promised the abolition of political censorship, a cartoon depicts the censor of the *Canard* committing suicide.[121]

Glühlichter was an Austrian socialist cartoon magazine, comparable to *Der wahre Jacob* in Germany. In all of its texts and also in some of its caricatures, it closely followed German and Austrian war propaganda. For instance, it depicted Belgian francs-tireurs on the gallows or German soldiers helping French farmers to plough.[122] On the other hand, *Glühlichter* was the only cartoon magazine that published cartoons severely condemning war and advocating peace: In a cartoon called *Mobilisierung* (Mobilization), by the famous artist Alfred Kubin, a huge terrifying man jumps over towns and villages. In another one, a grandfather tells his little grandson: 'Yes, my boy, soon we both shall be conscripted as well.'[123]

War itself was represented in an apocalyptic cartoon as an armed monster driving a cart, accompanied by furies called murder, fire, pest, hunger and death, with jackals, hyenas and vultures following them (Figure 38). In another cartoon, one sees a huge library with the lists of the casualties.[124] Besides, *Glühlichter* published social cartoons sharply criticizing the lack of solidarity and the unequal distribution of commodities in Austrian society. Topics include the landlord who on 1 August 1914 embraces the departing soldier but on 1 February 1915 evicts his widow and her small children, the delivery of huge sacks of coal to a stately mansion angrily observed by a poor worker's family obviously lacking this commodity, and two undernourished old men who look at the dining table through a magnifying glass and explain: 'After all, one wants to see what one eats.'[125] However, from April 1915 a new censor, Dr. Mager, suppressed more and more articles and cartoons in every second issue. The journalists fought back mocking at him in a caricature, a shadow figure and a comic strip.[126] As this did not placate him, he even started confiscating articles by classical authors such as Christoffel von Grimmelshausen, Johann Wolfgang von Goethe and Adolf Glassbrenner. Finally from 1916 the magazine ceased publication with the editor explaining on 30 December 1915 in a note to the readers, 'that a social democratic humour magazine is impossible under the actual censorship.'[127]

Chapter 9

HOW SUCCESSFUL WERE CENSORSHIP AND PROPAGANDA?

How was censorship outwitted?

I would like to emphasize that censorship in general succeeded in keeping the people in utter ignorance and thus proved to be the indispensable prerequisite of successful propaganda. However, especially in France, censorship was often also quite successfully circumvented. A relatively mild method was to blackmail the censors by threatening either to complain to the prime minister about the blank spaces or to have the article read out in parliament. In rare cases, censors would either reduce their orders substantially or agree to postpone their decisions.[1] Another method was used by Clemenceau. He systematically mailed his articles to political personalities and other VIPs before they were censored. Other newspapers would send their subscribers special editions containing all censored articles of the previous weeks or months.[2] Very courageous papers would ignore censorship instructions, not submit articles or photos to the censorship office or simply keep censored articles.[3] This happened even in the United States despite their very repressive regulations: Newspapers criticized the administration, published articles about highly sensitive topics such as the French tanks and the secret Allied treaties and got away with it.[4] In France, it was also possible to publish two versions of the newspaper: one censored with blank spaces, kindly forwarded to the censors, and another comprehensive version destined for sale.[5] For this reason, suspicious censors sometimes bought three copies of a newspaper at a stand in order to verify whether their order had been executed.[6] The French PB complained that from July 1916 to July 1917, out of 1,076 censored articles, 319 were published anyway.[7] On the other hand, the Office of the Prime Minister frequently complained to the Ministry of War that the censors had failed to suppress dangerous articles.[8] Contrary to the German censors, their French colleagues had no special instructions about photos and could rely only on the general guidelines, but their interventions were ignored by 50 per cent of the newspapers and magazines. An extreme case was *La Bataille* which accepted only 1 or 2 cuts out of 27 and got away with only one warning.[9] As far as film censorship was concerned, it could be outwitted by replacing on the permission card the title of the authorized film with a film without visa.[10]

Personal connections also proved helpful. At a time when even the use of the word 'peace' was strictly forbidden, a book by a certain August Schvan, *Les bases d'une paix durable* (1917) (The Bases of a Durable Peace), was passed by the censor, his close friend, with the argument that it was simply a philosophical construction.[11] Such old friends' networks spared certain authors trouble with censorship[12] (see p. 145 and below).

In Germany, editors were asked to present a copy of all publications to the local police, and they usually complied with the orders. In cases of litigation they could also come to an arrangement. When a German caricature of the Pope's peace proposal was not accepted, the cartoonist presented it again, without the pontiff, and obtained approval.[13] Censor's protection existed as well. The Armenian massacres committed by Germany's ally Turkey from April 1915 were put under preventive censorship and all articles were completely suppressed. Whereas the Reverend Lepsius, who was an eyewitness, could not place his report on this question in a single newspaper, Max Roloff, a less important journalist, succeeded in publishing a highly provocative article in *Die Hilfe*, the influential periodical of Naumann. It seems that Jäckh, a collaborator of *Die Hilfe* and renowned expert on Turkey, who at that time worked in the censorship office, let the article pass.[14]

Another trick was to say things indirectly. Gerlach was a specialist in this method. As he could not criticize in his *Welt am Montag* the war heroes Hindenburg and Ludendorff or the submarine war, he completely passed them over in silence. As he was not allowed to praise German left-wing socialists for refusing the war credits, he did honour to the Italian socialists for the same action, and his readers knew whom he meant. Since he could not criticize the vast annexation program of the military and right-wing circles, he resorted to historical articles: condemning Napoleon I who had annexed half of Europe and was finally exiled to St. Helena, and praising former Chancellor Otto von Bismarck who, after the Prussian victory of 1866, renounced all annexations of Austrian territory. Heinrich Mann used the same method. On November 1915, in an article about Emile Zola in the pacifist periodical *Die Weißen Blätter* he severely criticized the Empire of Napoleon III:

An Empire which is only based on force and not on freedom, justice and truth, an Empire where one only gives orders and obeys, makes money and exploits others, but does not hold men in respect – such an Empire cannot win even if it sets off to battle with superhuman might.

Every reader knew that he meant the German Empire, the censors were furious, but could do nothing about it.[15]

Censors were supposed to suppress all information about the infidelity of soldiers' spouses but did not succeed because it happened too often and the consequences kept tribunals and separate allowance authorities busy. In some cases a soldier on leave did not find his home anymore because his wife had left with her lover and all of the furniture, and in another case a soldier killed his spouse and her lover.[16] In Britain the authorities from 1916 had to investigate 40,000 cases, found one-third of the spouses guilty and stopped paying them separate allowances. After the war, quite a few veterans divorced.[17] Jokes as well slipped through censorship control.[18] Even the serious catholic periodical *Monika – Katholische Zeitschrift für Mütter und Frauen* published, with utter indignation of course, the following story: In a cinema, during the projection of a film, the director suddenly climbs the scene and says: 'Outside is an armed soldier on leave wanting to surprise here his wife with her lover. As I want to avoid any scandal I ask the concerned couple to leave by the side door.' As a result not less than 23 couples leave the hall. However, the same story circulated as well in Britain.[19]

As newspapers, because of censorship and self-censorship, became less and less credible, in Germany, Austria, France and in the occupied territories alternative news were spread orally through rumours, gossip and jokes in a 'black market of information', as Maureen Healy puts it. Information about strikes and riots was also transmitted by flyers, billboards, broadsheets, leaflets and graffiti.[20] In occupied Serbia, the Austrian occupation authorities had gathering places observed by spies and rumour-mongers arrested. In autumn 1918, several military commanders in Germany penalized the dissemination of false rumours with one year in prison or a fine of 1,500 mark (€5,700).[21]

When the war ended, censorship continued, except in Turkey and in Germany. Turkey was the first country to abolish it on 11 June 1918.[22] In Germany, it ended with the revolution. However, 15 years later it was imposed again. In Britain, it continued until June, in France until September 1919. In Italy, it ended on 29 June 1919, was re-established on 3 October 1919 and was abolished on 1 April 1920; five years later it was reintroduced by Mussolini. In Russia, censorship continued under the Soviets but became far more stringent than before. In the United States, the restrictions were removed on 25 June 1919, but 30 federal states promulgated new sedition laws which surpassed the former regulations in theory and practice alike, only replacing the German spy with the Bolshevik revolutionary. So most Americans, having fought 'to make the world safe for democracy', did not get their former democratic freedoms back for more than 25 years.[23]

How did people react to propaganda?

Several historians such as Nicolas Reeves, Trevor Wilson and Alexander Watson have queried the influence of propaganda in World War I or at best conceded to it only a secondary importance.[24] Winter categorically writes:

> Did propaganda help shorten the war? Almost certainly not. Germany capitulated when its army was beaten in the field and for no other reason. [...] Attempts to divert attention from this fact gave Great War propaganda military significance it did not deserve.[25]

All critics consider only patriotic propaganda, while anti-war as well as defeatist propaganda are not even mentioned. In the first part of this chapter, I shall deal with patriotic propaganda at the home front under the following aspects: the quality of propaganda, the receptivity of the addressees and the impact of propaganda over time. A short summary of the influence of the various propaganda instruments and its support by the disciplinary measures of the authorities will follow. Then the difficult position of anti-war propaganda between its limited resources and the surveillance and prosecution by the authorities will be analysed. Finally the situation at the military front and the reaction of the soldiers to patriotic and defeatist propaganda will be discussed.

First of all one has to distinguish between bad and good propaganda. Bad propaganda makes statements which have low credibility and cannot be confirmed by independent witnesses.[26] An example is the allegation in French newspapers: 'Half the German shells are made of cardboard, they don't even burst.'[27] Good propaganda is not necessarily true but should look credible: for example, the German atrocities in Belgium and Northern France reported by the refugees. Even if their information was not correct in all cases, they were considered reliable eyewitnesses, and thus the credibility and the propaganda value of their reports were extremely high. Even more successful was the propagandistic exploitation of the sinking of the *Lusitania* and the execution of Miss Cavell, because the Germans could not deny these facts. Good propaganda also depends on catchy slogans. The famous word of a *poilu* about the civilians in a French cartoon, 'Let's hope that they will hold out', was quoted approximately 30 times and even applied to advertisements for shoes or mattresses.[28]

All marketing experts agree that publicity succeeds only if people are receptive to it. A non-smoker convinced of the harmful effects of tobacco on his health will not be seduced by the most extravagant cigarette posters. An inveterate smoker will not be prevented from smoking by notices on the packages such as 'Smoking can be deadly'. The same distinction refers to propaganda. All propaganda messages pass through three filters determined by the preconceived ideas and convictions of the addressees:

• Selective exposure: People prefer to expose themselves to propaganda which 'is consistent with their attitudes, congruent with their beliefs, and supportive of their values', and they tend to avoid or even reject information that is contrary to them.
• Selective perception: 'Even in a heavily censored country there is still a wealth of information, and people will screen out those parts of propaganda which impress them most, provided that they are congruent with their opinion and reject or refute other aspects.'
• Selective retention: People will remember more easily propaganda which fits their ideas, even for a long time, but rapidly forget propaganda which does not fit.[29]

Now a few cases about the success of these three filters will be presented.

Selective exposure: In Britain a school inspector complained: 'It is always the same people [...] already won over, who form the audience [at propaganda speeches].'[30] In Baden 'the patriotic meetings of the bourgeoisie attracted only those whose national convictions did not need to be strengthened.'[31] A German soldier refused to read the propaganda paper *DK* and called it a 'central swindle' – a typical reaction to the hated propaganda flooding.[32] As the social democratic cartoon magazine *Der wahre Jacob* spread official propaganda throughout the war, half of its readers contemptuously calling it *Durchhalte-Jacob* (Jacob Hold Out) later cancelled their subscription.[33] In October 1914, quite a few Germans had taken subscriptions of war brochures. By June 1915, they did not want them anymore and threatened the messenger to throw him down the staircase. Two months later the production of these brochures was cancelled.[34]

Selective perception: The Scottish miners leader Bob Smillie ignored the shame message of the infamous poster 'Daddy, what did you do in the great war?' and said that he would answer: 'I tried to stop the bloody thing, my child.'[35]

Selective retention: Two less-known episodes, one of them even tragic, demonstrate the success of atrocity propaganda. One is told by the French music-hall star Mistinguett. When her lover Maurice Chevalier was taken prisoner by the Germans, 'well informed people' assured her that his hands had been cut and his eyes gouged out.[36] In autumn 1917, the German cruiser SMS *Brummer* successfully attacked a British convoy near the Shetland Islands and sank several British war and commercial ships. When the cruiser offered to take aboard surviving sailors and passengers, they panicked, preferred to swim away and drowned.[37]

Long-lasting selective retention: When in September 1918 the German government was obliged to ask for an armistice, chauvinists remained under the sway of Ludendorff's former propaganda slogan that the war had practically been won and did not accept that their troops had been beaten. Thus they believed in the stab-in-the-back myth which maintained for a long time that the victory had been prevented by treacherous socialists and defeatists at home.

An example of an extremely long-lasting selective retention of German war propaganda is Hitler.[38] Before and after the American declaration of war, the German authorities inculcated in soldiers and civilians alike the conviction that the Americans were incapable of intervening in any decisive way in the conflict. The Prussian Minister of Finance Oskar Hergt explained in the Prussian chamber: 'The great army across the sea cannot swim, it cannot fly, thus it will not come.'[39] On the military level, Ludendorff considered the United States weaker than the Netherlands, and Admiral Henning von Holtzendorff maintained that the submarines would sink most American troop ships before the end of the war. As a result the danger coming from America was underrated in Germany. British-born Princess Evelyn Blücher wrote that 'almost the whole country was making fun of and laughing at the idea of an American army'.[40] When in summer 1918 more than 500,000 American soldiers were fighting in Europe, censorship suppressed this news and German newspapers mentioned only a few failed American air attacks and maintained that submarines still sank tens of thousands of gross tons.[41] Such propaganda was accompanied by caricatures of American soldiers: an incompetent regiment of billionaires, cowboys riding on sea horses or even a load of tin soldiers.[42] Hitler was fully under the sway of German propaganda and like many other soldiers particularly enjoyed caricatures.[43] The result is impressive: throughout his life, he held the Americans in very low esteem. Albert Speer, his architect and, during World War II, Minister of Armaments, recalls Hitler making the following remarks in the 1930s:

> The Americans had not played a very prominent part in the war of 1914–18, he thought, and moreover, had not made any great sacrifices of blood. They would certainly not withstand a great trial by fire, for their fighting qualities were low.

As late as 1942, after the Americans had launched their successful landing in North Africa, Hitler described the United States as a country 'which did not have the necessary morale in order to win the fight for the new world order'. His ridiculing of Wilson as an 'apostle of peace' and his scoffing at American military utilities corresponded precisely to the arguments of German propaganda in the First World War.[44] No wonder that on 11 December 1941 he declared war on the United States, thereby sealing the German defeat.

The receptivity of the addresses was influenced by social categories such as class, gender, age, education, ethnic identity and, last but not least, by personal interests, that is 'whether holding opinions or taking actions can help to achieve rewards or avoid undesirable outcomes'.[45] Social class was a major factor. As Nicolas Mariot shows, the elites, the intellectuals and the middle classes in France were more receptive to war propaganda than employees, workers and peasants who were motivated neither by patriotism nor by propaganda. In Britain, 40 per cent of the professional and commercial classes voluntarily enlisted, against 27 per cent of the industrial workers and 22 per cent of the rural population. In Germany and Italy the results were comparable.[46] Consequently in the German trenches the conscripted proletarians considering the voluntary enlistment of enthusiastic middle-class people 'frivolous, stupid and senseless', contemptuously called these *Kriegsfreiwillige* (volunteers) *Kriegsmutwillige* (war wantons) and did what they could in order to bully them.[47]

The home front presented a similar image. People from bourgeois families readily accepted patriotic propaganda for the war. Especially privileged groups such as army suppliers, black marketers, shopkeepers and restaurateurs accepted it even more because the war coincided with their personal interests. A wholesale clothier and his employees at Tours were happy to see the war going on, owing to the high profits and the good wages they were receiving.[48] In Germany, Thomas Mann, himself a propagandist, believed in official propaganda until the end, and his children were shocked when they met a defeatist.[49] On the other hand, workers were less exposed to propaganda because they had neither the time nor the money to buy and to read newspapers or to acquire items and gadgets with propaganda messages.[50] Furthermore, at least in Germany, many of them distrusted official information, considered newspaper articles as lies and front reports as a laughing stock.[51] Already on 2 August 1914 one of them openly characterized the alleged French bombardment of Nuremberg as a lie and explained: 'Berlin is only looking for a reason to strike out at the French.'[52] In 1914 and 1915, an eight-year-old boy, son of a petty bourgeois in Nuremberg, heard time and again from relatives and other adults that newspapers were lying, that the Germans had lost the Battle of the Marne and might lose the war. In August 1916, after propaganda about alleged famine in Britain he concluded: 'Nobody believes in newspaper reports any more.'[53] It seems, however, that in France and Britain a more significant part of the working class and of the petty bourgeoisie was patriotic than in Germany, Russia, Austria and Italy.[54]

Receptivity also depended on age and gender. Smaller children fell easily prey to indoctrination because their critical capacities were quite underdeveloped. Children from bourgeois families accepted chauvinist slogans more readily than those from peasant and working-class families. The influence of the school type and of the teachers was also important. Children from secondary schools were more influenced by annexationist propaganda, whereas children in elementary schools were more ready to accept a negotiated peace. In 1917, the little daughter of an elementary school director told her father: 'It is the Kaiser who was responsible for the war, he must be the first to be beheaded.'[55] Gender also played a role. Girls were far less receptive to propaganda than were boys, and teachers complained of how difficult it was to indoctrinate them.[56] In Germany, Italy and France, women were in the forefront of anti-war agitation. The influence of ethnic factors having been sufficiently analysed on pp. 120 and 122–37 does not need to be discussed here again.

Another aspect has to be considered: Acceptance and refusal of war propaganda fluctuated in time from early acceptance in 1914–15 over passive ignorance to hate of propaganda and the establishment of a counter-public with rumours, gossip and criticism in 1916–18.[57] The reaction to the campaigns for military enlistment in Britain is a good example.

In 1914, British atrocity propaganda was at its height and heavily influenced the extent of enlistment. Until January–May 1916, there was no conscription there. Of the five million men fit for military service, approximately 2.5 million – that is roughly half of them – enlisted voluntarily, and one-fifth of them did so in the enthusiasm of the first six weeks of the war.[58] However, quite a few of these 'volunteers' were forced to join the colours due to outside pressure by landowners, corporations, social aid authorities and even theatre managers refusing engagement to young actors.[59] Thus the number of volunteers was less impressive than some authors would have it, but the recruiters had an indefatigable supporter: 'The Germans were', as John M. Bourne puts it, 'in many ways the perfect enemy [...] galvanising public opinion in support of the war effort.'[60] Their first and greatest blunder was the invasion of Belgium followed by Bethmann Hollweg's qualification of the international treaty on Belgium's neutrality, signed also by Germany, as a 'scrap of paper' and his admission in the Reichstag that the Germans had indeed broken international law. This fact was immediately exploited by British propaganda with facsimiles of the treaty and songs and posters like *The Scrap of Paper, Enlist To-day*.[61] Even more impressive upsurges of enlistment figures corresponded exactly to the next German atrocity cases: the destruction of Louvain, the bombardments of the British coast, the sinking of the *Lusitania*, the *Bryce Report* and the execution of Miss Cavell, although in the case of Louvain the defeat at Mons also played a role (see the organograms on p. 212).

But by autumn 1915, war enthusiasm was already on the wane, despite frequent propaganda rallies of the PRC.[62] As the number of volunteers was insufficient, the so-called Derby Scheme was adopted, under which civilians could attest to be willing to serve. Some people formally signed in the hope that in this way the voluntary system would at least be preserved. However, as only 24.59 per cent of the men signed, conscription was introduced in 1916: in January for bachelors and childless widowers between 18 and 41, in May 1916 also for married men, and from April 1918 the age was raised to 50 or even up to 56 if necessary. But even then men could appeal for exemption to tribunals, which practically everybody did. Other conscripted men successfully shirked: either they did not enlist, did not turn up for enlistment or bribed clerks in order to be removed from the recruitment files, so that throughout summer and autumn 1916 the authorities were obliged to round up apt-looking men in the streets, in railway stations, football fields, theatres and other entertainment places, even in a travelling circus. Between March 1916 and March 1917, 370,000 men were enlisted whereas 780,000 were either exempted by complacent tribunals or got away with forged exemption certificates. As tribunals granted numerous exemptions, their total number finally amounted to 2,740,000 men; the number of conscripts was slightly higher (2,770,000). The conclusion is clear: Neither 'feather' blackmail nor poster propaganda nor the rallies of PRC and NWAC brought enough Britons into the trenches, only atrocity propaganda succeeded temporarily, and almost half of the men, unimpressed by propaganda, even successfully thwarted the Military Service Act.

In the United States, the situation was not better. As only 70,000 volunteers turned up in the first six weeks after the declaration of war, military service had to be introduced rapidly. And even then most Americans dutifully registered for the draft and afterwards asked for exemption.[63] Widespread opposition to the war had to be crushed by the drastic Espionage Act of 15 April 1917 persecuting people who dared to criticize conscription (see pp. 8–9).

Even among children, the most malleable propaganda activists, the impact of propaganda slowed down. In 1917, French enquiries concluded that education had failed to mobilize the children.[64] In Germany and Britain, school compositions and lessons were criticized as 'mechanically repeating' or 'mere reproductions of newspapers headings',[65] and in Germany, honest teachers admitted that some of their students bluntly refused war propaganda.[66] With the 'saturation of everything military' came a sort of 'pacifist turn': children's books either returned to classical adventure stories or shifted from describing the joys of war to 'a solemn rite of sacrifice and duty'.[67] By the end of the war, the 'school front' also deserted.[68] The war diary of a 12-year-old German school girl convincingly indicates the changing attitude from 1914 to 1918. On 3 August 1914, she noted that her school mates were happy about the war against France, the hereditary enemy. One year later, after a school festivity, she wrote: 'I was sad again because as a girl I could not volunteer for the front.' On 1 February 1918, she was completely disillusioned: 'We must not believe any more the lies of the older people. We were children, students, and all of us in the school, lead by the director and the teachers, had cried: Hurrah.'[69]

The receptivity to propaganda could also brusquely change at short notice. Police reports about the mood of the population in Berlin show a clear relationship between emotions and the military situation. Usually rather depressed from autumn 1915 because of the never-ending food crisis, the people's state of mind temporarily improved after each success: the breakdown of the Allied offensives in April 1916, the victory at Caporetto in October 1917, the armistice in the East in December 1917 and the enormous advance of the German army during Ludendorff's offensive in spring 1918, but it reached its lowest point after the German defeats in summer 1918.[70] In the Allied countries, public sentiment reached its lowest ebb in 1917, *l'année de l'angoisse* (the year of anxiety) as the French termed it, and in the first months of 1918.[71]

The influence of the various propaganda instruments also varied over time (see pp. 83–4, 87). Quite successful until the end of the war were the campaigns for the sale of war bonds, although in some countries such as Austria and Britain additional pressure had to be applied. Propaganda by postcards and exhibitions also continued to be well received while the circulation of cartoon magazines dropped in 1917, stage plays and films already from 1915 switched back to traditional amusement, and militaristic children toys were soon no longer in demand. Allied atrocity propaganda had its heyday in 1914–15, but was also later presented at certain times. British propaganda in the United States contributed to an active support of this country to the Allied cause from the very beginning.

When despite all the propaganda in the second half of the war an increasing part of the civilians did not want to suffer any more for the annexationist aims of the ruling elites and demanded immediate peace negotiations, not only in Germany but also in the Allied countries, severe sanctions were applied.[72] The result was fatal: Instead of crushing Prussian militarism, the Italian, French, American and to a lesser extent the British elites introduced Prussianism in their own countries. Imitating the incarceration of numerous socialist activists like Liebknecht and Luxemburg in Germany, the Allies as well started an 'epidemic of prosecutions', as Millman puts it. They not only punished striking workers and embittered war widows but also above all decapitated the protest movements by jailing prominent leaders: the former Minister of Finance Caillaux in France, the philosopher Russell and the journalist Morel in Britain, the socialist leader Costantino Lazzari in Italy and the socialist politician Eugene V. Debs in the United States, the latter being condemned to 10 years of prison one week after the armistice.[73] The shrewd combination of state propaganda and police oppression was most clearly recognized by the liberal British newspaper *The Nation*:

The government is to push its own propaganda of opinion by press and public meetings and circulars, using public money for the purpose, but opposing opinions are to be crushed by fines and imprisonments. That is one way of getting national unity. But what is worse than a unity based upon ignorance, silence, and repression?[74]

Patriotic propaganda, however, justified this quite ambiguously: If oppression occurred in the enemy country, it was considered as 'a proof of German tyranny', but at home 'it was accepted as evidence of our sturdy defence of liberty'.[75]

In contrast to these efficient measures, anti-war propagandists cut a sorry figure. They were a small minority hopelessly outnumbered by powerful 'patriotic associations' such as the German Fatherland Party with 1.5 million and the French UGACPE with 11 million members. In Britain UDC, ILP and NCF were not even able to defend their meetings against attacks by hired thugs. Furthermore, an impressive panoply of disciplinary measures allowed the authorities to keep down the anti-war activists throughout the war. In Germany at certain times, the workers did not even dare to demonstrate fearing to be shot by police. Spartakist plans to arm themselves and to infiltrate the army could not be realized. More often than not a crisis was triggered by spontaneous actions of the population, but as Giovanna Procacci puts it for Italy, 'no practical force capable of rendering it operational existed'.[76] That means that the anti-war activists were not able or not willing to transform militant protest into a revolutionary challenge that would force the government to open peace negotiations – a statement also true for France, Britain and Germany.

Only in Russia the situation was different. The Bolsheviks had found in Lenin a most ingenious propagandist who not only identified with the principal desire of the peasants for peace and land reform but was also able to infiltrate the army and to get the support of soldiers and workers through a very skilled multi-faceted campaign. But words and demonstrations alone never make a revolution. In contrast to the other countries, the Bolsheviks mobilized as well the might of weapons. They organized arms and munitions, formed and trained their own military units, the 'Red Guards', and won the day. Without such propaganda and the concomitant military preparations, the October Revolution would not have taken place and the Provisional Government and the Stavka would have continued the war (see p. 170).

How did the soldiers react to propaganda? Their correspondence gives us ample information about their attitude towards the war. Unfortunately it is usually available only in a sanitized form. It was subject to postal control, and in order not to be punished most soldiers carefully avoided compromising remarks (see pp. 13–14). Nevertheless one can see which arguments were neglected and which were retained. According to several studies, the correspondence of most German and British soldiers did not refer to the war aims and the patriotic propaganda concepts of the elites. They did not fight for Kaiser, king and fatherland neither for democracy or the ideas of 1914, and even less for Mitteleuropa, Alsace-Lorraine or the freedom of the smaller nations, but accepted only to do their duty by defending their country and protecting home and family.[77] According to Annick Cochet, French soldiers' correspondence was characterized by a fatalistic attitude expressed by *résignation et la volonté defensive* (resignation and defensive will).[78] Especially in 1917 and 1918, French and German letters show that a great majority of the soldiers did not care for victory, wanted immediate peace, hated the *jusqu'au boutistes* (to the enders) and sometimes even agitated against official propaganda.[79]

In Italy, the archives of the police contain numerous anonymous letters to the Royal family in which desperate soldiers and civilians offend and menace the king and the ruling elites for having started this war.[80] In stage plays written and performed by soldiers Baumeister recognizes the language of victimization and not of propagandistic pathos.[81]

Especially revealing are letters which have escaped postal control. When the French socialist deputy Brizon in his speech on 16 June 1916 explained why he and his two colleagues voted against the war credits, he received 154 letters, all of them congratulating him for his courage. Eighty-four came from the front but had circumvented the postal system of the army. Although they do not constitute a representative sample, they show at least a frankness absent from controlled letters: the soldiers wrote that they were 'desperate', felt 'abandoned in the carnage', and 'all had enough of the war'. Instead of 'war culture', patriotism and hate of the enemy, one encounters only hate of the war, of the officers and even more of the elites, the deputies and propagandists who insist on continuing the war: They were called 'sinister bloodthirsty bandits', 'blood mongers' and 'murderers of the people'.[82] In the memoirs of the Alsatian peasant Dominik Richert, one can find a similar expression: He was 'full of deadly hate against all those who in exchange for high payment force the deplorable soldiers to stay at the front and to meet certain death'.[83]

In the British army, the situation was not much better. In his memoirs, a British officer characterized the atmosphere in June 1915 in his platoon as follows: 'There was no patriotism in the trenches [...] they [the soldiers] don't believe in the war, they don't believe in the staff.'[84] In the following years, the mood seems to have improved. Nevertheless conscripted soldiers either considered war as a 'waste of life' or proudly claimed later that they 'have never been of any use to them [the military]' – rather modest remarks compared with the hate tirades of their German and French counterparts.[85]

A particular nuisance was the enormous difference in the food supply of the continental armies.[86] Officers received larger and better rations and could also buy additional food because of their higher salaries – a simple soldier in Germany received 15.90 mark (€60.42) per month, in France 150 sous (€20.25); a German lieutenant however received 310 mark (€1,178). A popular slogan was: '*Gleiche Löhnung, gleiches Essen, und der Krieg wär' längst vergessen*' (With equal pay and equal food the war would have been long over).[87] The situation acerbated in Germany from 1916 when rations destined for the soldiers were systematically embezzled and redistributed to the officers; some of them even stole packets arriving from the soldiers' families.[88] Numerous letters smuggled home complained that officers were dining sumptuously whereas the soldiers got only rotten food – conditions which undermined all propaganda efforts.[89] The Bavarian Minister of War once commented: 'Such letters have a worse effect than all the news spread by the enemy.'[90] Mark Cornwall comments on the relation between hunger and propaganda in Austria: 'Hungry troops were less receptive to Austrian propaganda.'[91]

But how to explain that despite all this criticism only 1 per cent of the soldiers deserted?[92] Should one not conclude that after all the defence myth combined with permanent 'hold out' propaganda was successful? As it turns out, deserting was very difficult, especially in trench warfare. The aforementioned Alsatian soldier already wanted to desert in 1914 but had to wait for such an opportunity until July 1918.[93] A German letter of August 1918 compares the wish to desert with the lack of opportunity:

> I'd like to say that the entire infantry wants to desert, if they only always could. [...] Many soldiers want to defect to the enemy and don't have the opportunity, [...] you cannot imagine how relieved the enemy prisoners are when they come over to us. It is the same with our soldiers, they are happy when they get over there.[94]

Deserters ran the risk of being shot by either side and some were even shot by the enemy when they surrendered (see p. 116).[95] One should also not forget the vast array of disciplinary measures: at the front operated close surveillance was conducted by NOCs, officers, and soldier sentries; in the French army even by some special informants of the GQG who 'made it their business to stop desertion attempts'.[96] Behind the lines, military police arrested suspect soldiers and while in 1914 in the British army there was one policeman to every 3,306 soldiers, in 1918 one policeman kept 292 of them under surveillance. According to a certain definition of 'heroism' 'the fear of the military police in the rear must be greater than the fear of the enemy at the front'.[97] Not all, but some deserters were also executed in front of the troops.[98]

In Germany, it was relatively easy to jump from a train transporting soldiers from the Eastern to the Western front, and in summer 1917, 10 per cent of them did it. They were well received by members of secret organizations which gave them forged papers and rationing cards and showed the way to the Danish or the Dutch borders.[99] In the Austrian army, deserting seems to have been frequent, because in 1918, 250,000 deserters hid in the hinterland.[100] When in spring 1918 the soldiers of a whole Hungarian division refused to attack at the Piave, they were transported to the German Western front, with the result that they ran over to the French.[101]

Those who wanted to evade the trenches had two other possibilities: exemption and fraudulent hospitalization. However, both were not so easy to realize. Quite a few qualified workers were indispensable for industrial production and were sometimes even recalled from the front. Shirkers without such qualifications looking for a quiet office job or some peaceful occupation in the rear had greater problems because they usually needed influential connections (see pp. 18–19, 184). In Great Britain, possibilities for exemption were much more numerous than on the continent.

Two doubtful methods to escape from the trenches were what the British called to get a 'cushy one' and the Italians *fare i matti* (behave as madmen).[102] A 'cushy one' was a shot causing a light wound but heavy enough as to incapacitate the soldier to continue fighting. One could get it by exposing an arm or a leg above the parapet of the trench or going on patrol at night when the enemy could not aim so well.[103] Simulating madness was easy. When the German NOC Vogeler was interned in a lunatic asylum, he discovered that it was full of simulating soldiers, but they terribly suffered from the barbaric medical treatment of the doctors.[104] Other methods were self-mutilation like shooting one's foot or taking drugs and dangerous drinks which provoked sickness. Once they arrived at the hospital, soldiers were reported sobbing and begging doctors not to be sent back to the front or tried to procure medical certificates about serious maladies.[105] In France in September 1915, a whole network of fraudulent hospitalization was discovered where with the complicity of doctors thousands of valiant *poilus* were discharged from service.[106]

It is evident that none of these soldiers consented to war as the theory of 'war culture' would have it. But were they influenced by defeatist propaganda? One could point at the enemy's leaflets, at sporadic letters by Brizon to socialist comrades at the front and agitation by German socialists and political strikers dispatched to the front, but the most efficient anti-war propaganda came from the families at home: a wave of letters complaining about oppression, misery and foot shortage especially in Germany, Austria and Italy (see pp. 106, 187). And when soldiers on leave came home, they saw the situation with their own eyes. The authorities, quite aware of the negative results on the soldiers' morale, did what they could in order to stem the tide: postal censors tried to confiscate letters of complaint (see p. 13), and the civilians were time and again exhorted not to mention their problems in letters to the front. In order to keep soldiers even during their leave away from the defeatist influences of civilian society, the Italian authorities in December 1915 hit upon an ingenious idea: they authorized the priest Giovanni Minozzi and other clerics to establish several hundreds of comfortable Case del Soldato (Houses of the Soldier) where during a leave the soldiers could relax, get personal advice from the clergymen and remain under the sway of patriotic propaganda.[107]

It is clear that in such a situation efficient defeatist propaganda could rapidly destabilize the enemy's army. The most striking example concerns the situation on the Russian front in 1917. Immediately after the February Revolution, OHL and AOK organized a vast propaganda and fraternization campaign which later was supported by the Bolsheviks and lead to peace negotiations (see pp. 110–11, 170–1).

In spring 1918, the Italians launched such an enormous defeatist propaganda campaign against the Slav regiments in the Austrian lines at the Piave, that the AOK had to withdraw some of them, and its last offensive in June, the 'Battle of the Solstice', turned out to be a failure (see pp. 111–12).

In summer and autumn 1918, the German army had no chance against the Allied offensive based on a modernized weapon system with sophisticated artillery location and tanks which finally even succeeded in breaking through the formidable Hindenburg defence line. But the 'military strike', analysed by Wilhelm Deist and recently reaffirmed against critics by Ziemann,[108] also played a certain role: Roughly one million German soldiers deserted thereby weakening the German front considerably. One may assume that quite a few of them were influenced by the avalanche of French and British leaflet propaganda successfully undermining their morale (see pp. 112–15, 117).

I do not pretend that everybody hated the war. In all armies there were soldiers who did believe in the defence myth and identified with patriotic propaganda because it corresponded to their personal convictions. First of all there were the eternal lansquenets, 'the princes of the trenches', as Ernst Jünger called them.[109] One of their most outstanding examples was Jünger himself who already as a secondary school student had tried to join the French Foreign Legion. A Swiss volunteer of the French army later remembered: 'I felt ill at ease as long as we were not back to the fire-line.'[110] After the war, such people in Germany joined the free corps and later the SA; in Britain and France they engaged in the various colonial wars.[111] The military situation also played an important role: In summer 1918 the successful Allied troops were in such high spirits that the British army dropped its project of 'political education' (see p. 109). Let us not forget the privileged 'base-wallahs' who did not risk their lives at all and lived quite comfortably in the rear or, if they were Germans, even more comfortably in the occupied territories.[112] No wonder that in the French army between January 1916 and January 1918 their number increased from 19.7 to 28 per cent, in absolute numbers to 730,000 non-combatants versus 1,870,000 combatants.[113]

I hope to have made it clear that one has to differentiate between several reactions to war propaganda, be it of the patriotic or the defeatist variety. Ernst Jünger wrote: 'After all everybody experienced their own war.'[114] I would add: Everybody responded to propaganda in their own way depending on the various factors I have tried to analyse. Nevertheless in this context propaganda still had an indispensable task: to reinforce individual attitudes to war and, sustained by efficient organization, channel them towards appropriate action. The numerous examples discussed here demonstrate how important this was.

Chapter 10

STILL GOING ON: THE LEGACY OF WAR CENSORSHIP AND PROPAGANDA

After 1918, some heated discussion developed about the usefulness, importance and justification of Allied war propaganda. There was a curious reversal of opinion. Whereas in the Allied countries it was heavily criticized, the Germans praised it highly. The war's military loser, General Ludendorff, maintained that he was not beaten on the battlefield but instead owed his defeat to the ruthless Allied propaganda which had successfully broken Germany's will to hold out further.[1] The former Lance-Corporal Hitler went even further than Ludendorff. In *Mein Kampf*, he condemned German propaganda as insufficient and 'psychologically erroneous' and expressed great admiration for the atrocity stories of the Allies which provoked hatred and mobilized world opinion.[2] From 1928 until 1942, German students wrote several doctoral dissertations about Allied propaganda, perhaps in order to improve German propaganda for World War II.[3] On the other hand, it was revealed in Allied countries that many atrocity stories about the Germans were pure inventions and that public opinion had been deceived. In the United States, one year after the war, the former collaborator of the CPI Will Irwin remembered his war activity as preparing 'an age of lies'.[4] In Britain, Ponsonby, who had permanently condemned the war, proved in 1928 that Allied propagandists had ignominiously, and often consciously, spread innumerable lies.[5] In France, Lucien Graux published seven volumes of propaganda lies; in 1927, Julien Benda accused the intellectuals of having ceded to jingoist passions; and in 1934, Jean Guéhenno denounced them as members of a 'profitable undertaker's company', luring poor soldiers into their tombs.[6] As a consequence, official pronouncements were no longer trusted. During World War II, most people did not believe information about German concentration camps, brushing it aside as a fabricated atrocity story from Allied propaganda.

When the Great War ended, indoctrination continued. The Allies, especially the French, used propaganda to ensure punishment of the war-guilty Germans. The Germans refuted the war guilt and demanded equal treatment.[7] After the Treaty of Versailles, the war between historians started, both sides blaming the other for the responsibility of the war's outbreak.[8]

But the World War had a more lasting repercussion. The ruling elites had discovered that such massive manipulation of public opinion allowed them to realize their aims without too much opposition. Therefore the twentieth century saw the institutionalizing of censorship and propaganda by government and business, most conspicuously in Fascist Italy, Soviet Russia, and Nazi Germany. In the context of this book I must limit myself to a few examples: the interwar period in the Soviet Union, and the contemporary period in modern Russia, China, France and Germany.

In the Soviet Union, all publications were subjected to *Glavlit*'s preventive censorship. In the 1930s, several huge propaganda planes were constructed, these included a radio set and leaflet dropping machinery. Especially prominent are Stalin's photo falsifications.[9]

In Putin's Russia, old Stalinist practices have been revived. History textbooks are cleaned of unpalatable facts about Soviet history and filled with the ideology of 'Putinism' composed of nationalism, orthodoxy, autocracy, and militarism.[10] Most of the media is under government control, and on television Allied atrocity stories of World War I enjoy a gloomy comeback (see p. 38). Modern techniques have refined the old tactics. Anyone who searches the internet for 'Ukraine' will be overwhelmed by Russian 'cyber-warriors' and their defamation campaign against the Ukrainian President Petro O. Poroshenko and the Western powers.[11]

The effectiveness of censorship activity is demonstrated by the silence about Mao Zedong's murderous 'Great Leap Forward'; in 1962 this campaign cost the life of 45 million people. Even Western statesmen congratulated Mao on the 'success' of his policy. Although Western scholars have been allowed to study the documents, the Chinese government still hesitates about publishing the truth at home.[12]

Recent press decrees issued by the Chinese authorities not only allow deep insights into how indoctrination works, but also demonstrate how close it is to techniques from World War I. Thus it is formally forbidden for journalists (a) to publish in China or abroad 'state secrets or other information not yet formally authorised'; (b) to publish critical reports without formal permission from their superiors; (c) to copy 'unauthorised news from foreign media or websites'. Furthermore, the Central Office for Propaganda regularly informs journalists which information is acceptable or must not to be published at all.[13]

Western democratic countries are also open to charges of indoctrination. In France the white spaces in newspapers returned in both World War II and the Algerian liberation war (1957–62), and 'subversive' chansons such as the song *Le Déserteur* were also forbidden.[14] A comparison between French information policy in 1899 and 100 years later is also revealing. In 1899, when President Félix Faure died in the arms of a prostitute because of an aphrodisiac overdose, journalists were free to report this. But, when President François Mitterrand died in 1996 from the consequences of prostate cancer and his doctor revealed the character of his sickness – something kept secret since 1981 – a court jailed him for four months, fined him 260,000 francs (€40,000) and confiscated his book. At least the public was then informed about the president's mistress and illegitimate daughter living in a spacious Parisian apartment and protected by a special guard – at taxpayer expense. Leading journalists in the capital knew about this but had not dared to report it – self-censorship just as in World War I.[15]

Propaganda from companies is called advertising, and for some people this is so disturbing that they plaster their mail boxes with signs 'No Advertising Please,' and pay for technical devices to suppress this nuisance in television sets. The fact that companies also keep secret information about the health dangers of their products – be it drugs, foodstuffs, or earlier, asbestos, and that the authorities more often than not stand by and support them – is well known and does not need to be documented here.

What about press freedom nowadays? Every year the association Reporters without Frontiers publishes the press freedom index. Of course, authoritarian countries such as China, North Korea, Russia, Iran and Turkey are at the bottom of the list, but in democratic countries the authorities also try to undermine press freedom as much as they can. In February 2017, Germany was revealed in place 16, far behind the Scandinavian countries; France fared even worse at place 39 after Ghana and Namibia. Why is Germany in place 16? In this country journalists are in some cases controlled by the German Secret Service (Verfassungsschutz); the administration repeatedly withholds information, and journalists are attacked by right-wing extremists and Salafists. As since 2013 everybody including the blind and the deaf is obliged to pay heavily for public service broadcasting, newspaper subscriptions are in free fall.[16] Furthermore, the admission of more than one million Arab refugees without consultation of the parliament by Chancellor Angela Merkel in autumn 2015 has triggered a heated controversy in public opinion. Public broadcasting and the national newspapers wholeheartedly supported the chancellor's decision and quite a few people accused them of distorting reality by using self-censorship and publishing biased reports and even downright lies. Furthermore, journalists and professors criticizing immigration policy saw their books removed from bookseller's shelves, were denounced as right-wing extremists and received many anonymous threats so that they had to give their lectures under security protection and now publish further articles abroad or in online-blogs.[17] At present some people do not read German newspapers anymore and prefer to subscribe to special German editions of Swiss and Austrian dailies available online from July 2017 (NZZ-Perspective and DerStandard.de). The details of what happened since cannot be discussed here.

One of the most outrageous cases of censorship occurred in July 2014 but was only disclosed in April 2015. Two days before Russian soldiers in Ukraine shot down a Malaysian passenger plane with a BUK rocket, the German government and probably some other governments were officially informed about the dangerous situation in the Ukrainian airspace after a successful Russian rocket attack on a high-flying Ukrainian military plane. Instead of obliging their national carriers to change routes immediately, officials suppressed this information, probably in order not to antagonize Putin, and, as a result, 298 people died.[18]

Chapter 11

ORGANOGRAMS OF CENSORSHIP AND PROPAGANDA

The following organograms graphically represent the simplified structure of the organization of censorship and propaganda in the seven principal war-faring countries, indicating the responsibilities, activities and the interconnections of the various branches of civilian and military administration operating in these fields. A special section, the organization of theatre censorship in Paris and Berlin, will be presented in detail. All these organograms have been created by Nathalie Chamba. Finally two special organograms will indicate the influence of atrocity propaganda on the number of British recruits from August until October 1914 and of British volunteers from October 1914 until December 1915. I thank Martin Schramm for the permission to reprint the latter from his book (Schramm 2007: 403 and 406).

List of organograms

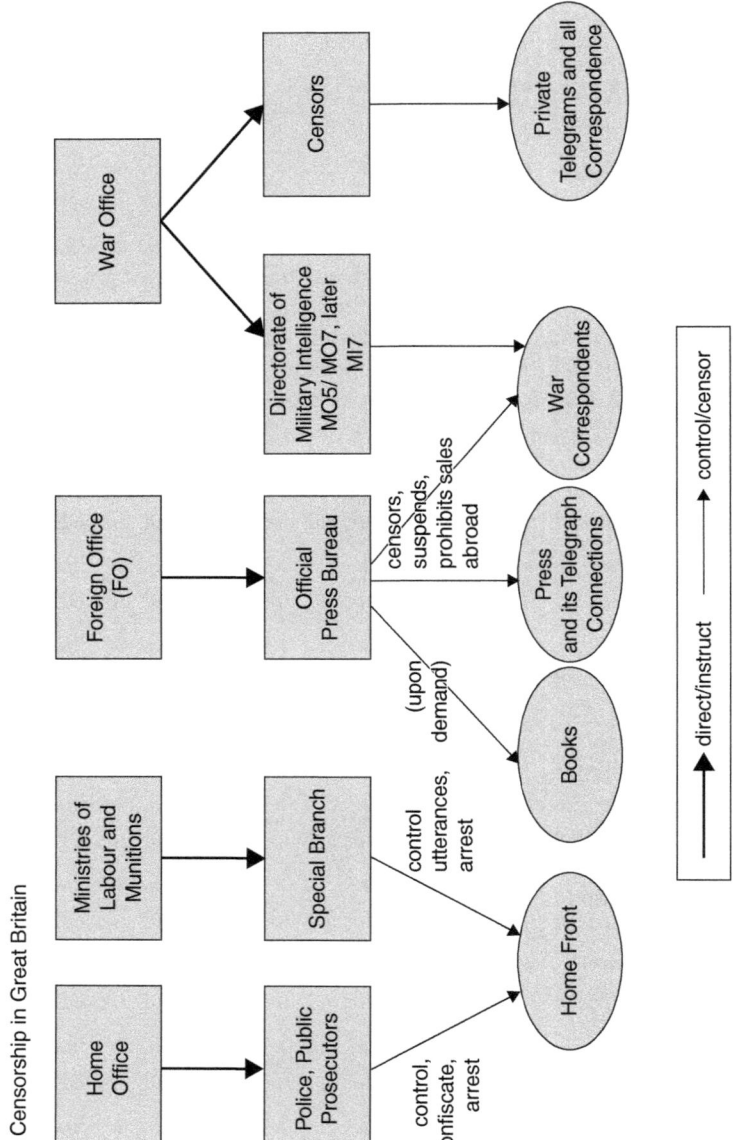

1. Censorship in Great Britain

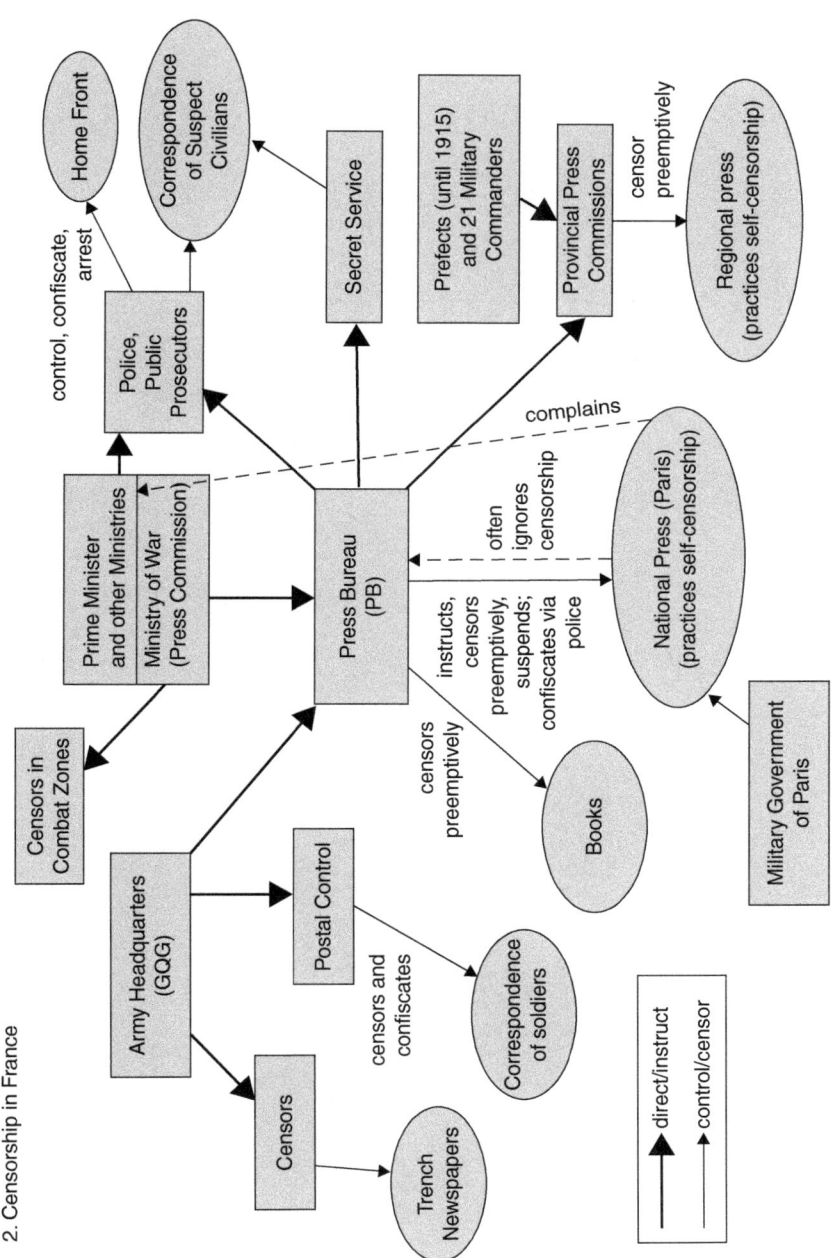

2. Censorship in France

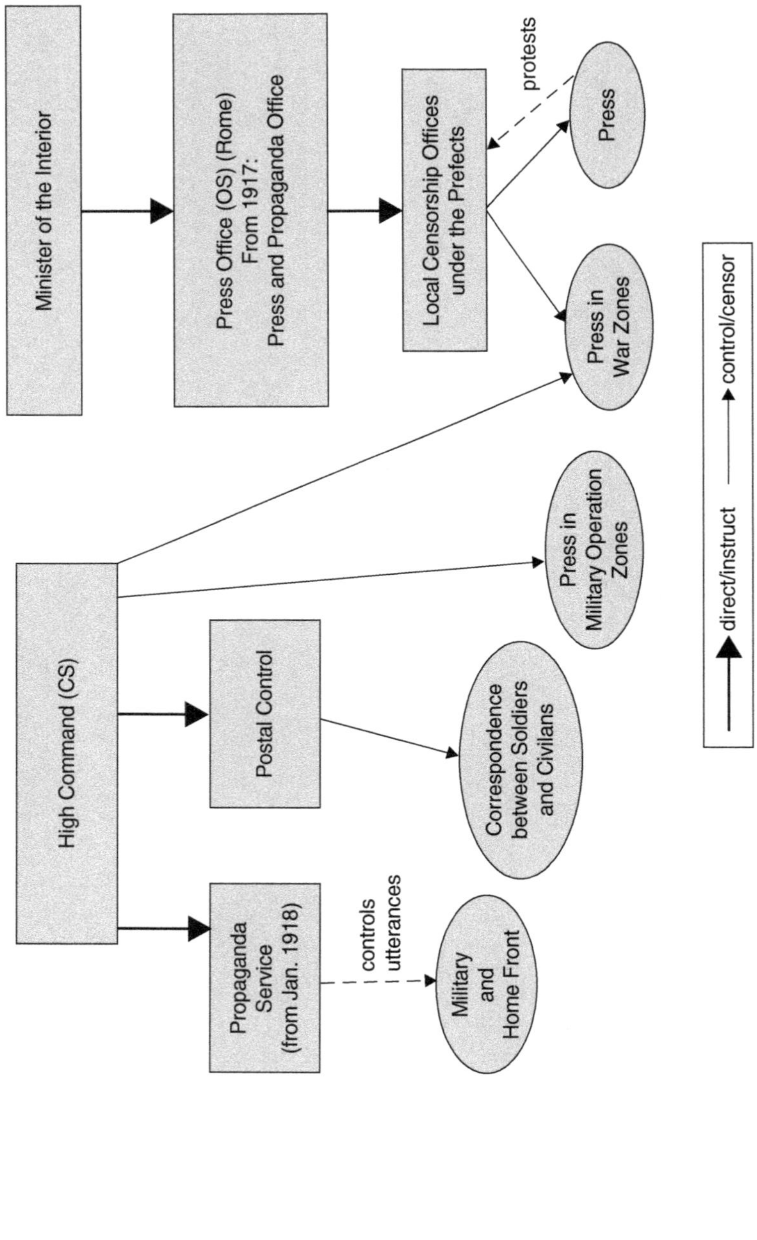

3. Censorship in Italy

Minister of the Interior

Press Office (OS) (Rome)
From 1917:
Press and Propaganda Office

Local Censorship Offices
under the Prefects

Press

protests

Press in
War Zones

High Command (CS)

Press in
Military Operation
Zones

Postal Control

Correspondence
between Soldiers
and Civilians

Propaganda
Service
(from Jan. 1918)

controls
utterances

Military
and
Home Front

direct/instruct   control/censor

4. Censorship in Russia

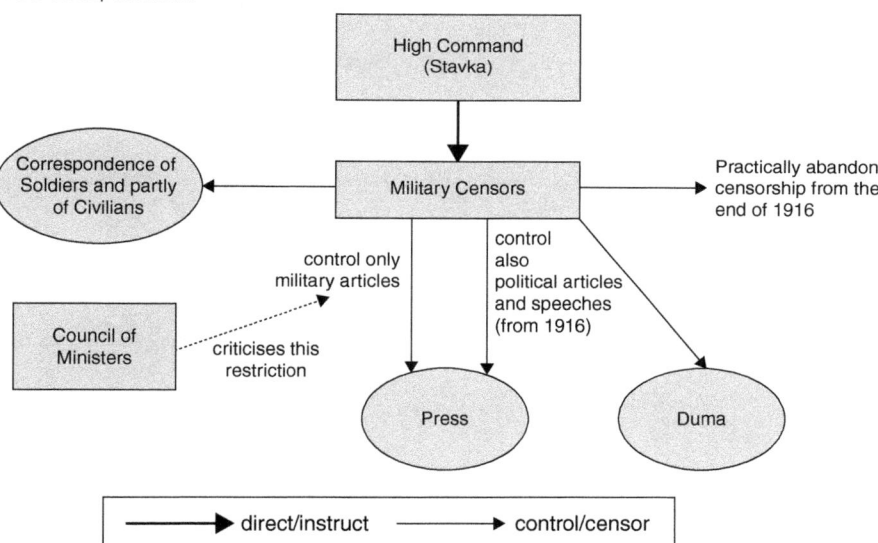

5. Censorship in the United States

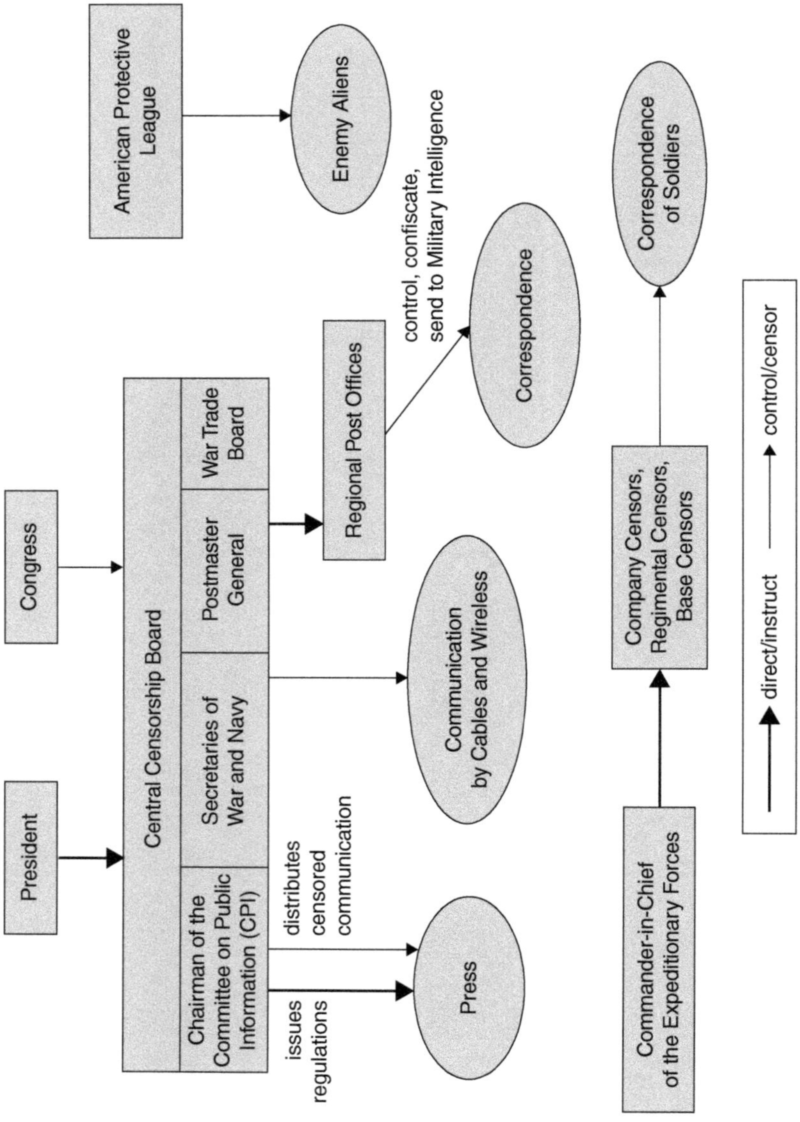

President

Congress

American Protective League → Enemy Aliens

Central Censorship Board

Chairman of the Committee on Public Information (CPI)

Secretaries of War and Navy

Postmaster General

War Trade Board

issues regulations

distributes censored communication

→ Press

Secretaries of War and Navy → Communication by Cables and Wireless

Postmaster General → Regional Post Offices

control, confiscate, send to Military Intelligence

Regional Post Offices → Correspondence

Correspondence of Soldiers

Company Censors, Regimental Censors, Base Censors → Correspondence of Soldiers

Commander-in-Chief of the Expeditionary Forces → Company Censors, Regimental Censors, Base Censors

→ direct/instruct

→ control/censor

6. Censorship in Germany

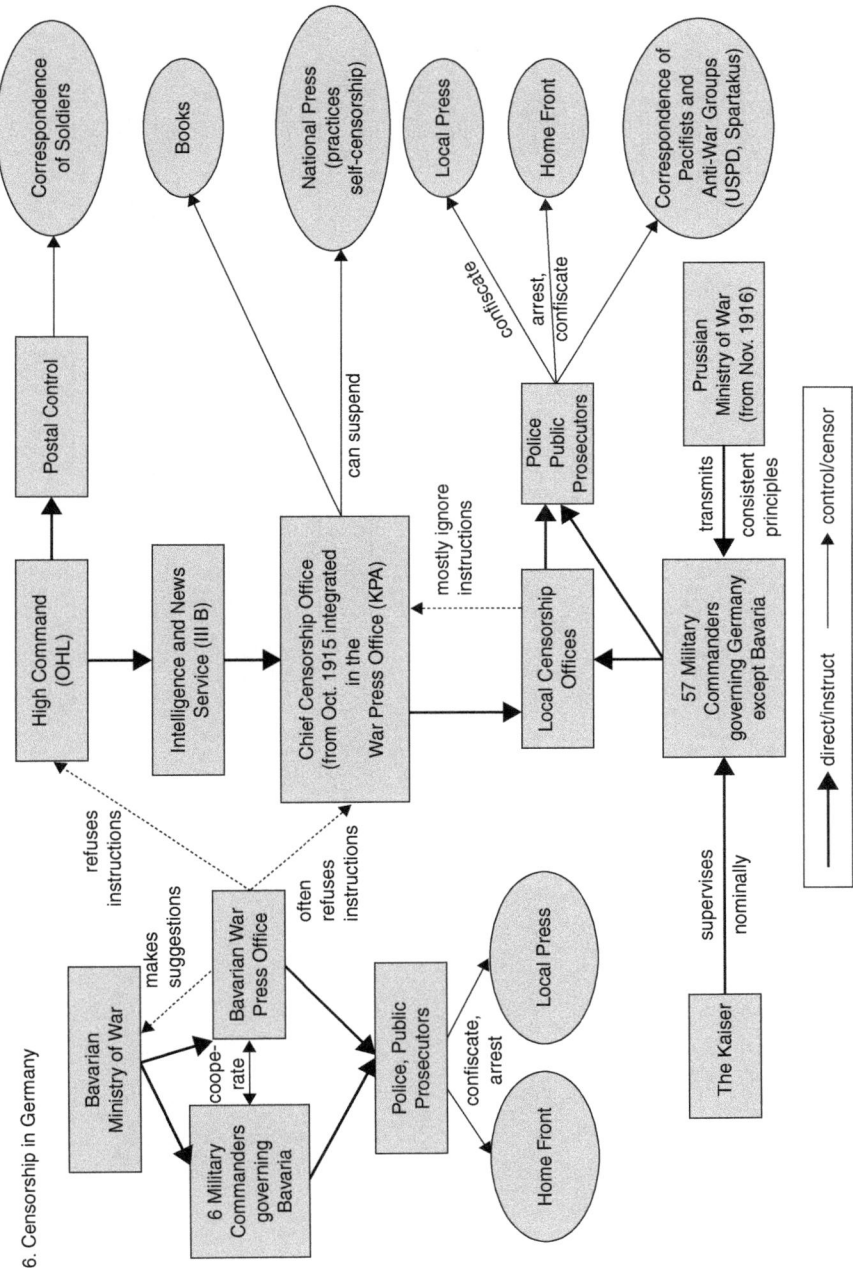

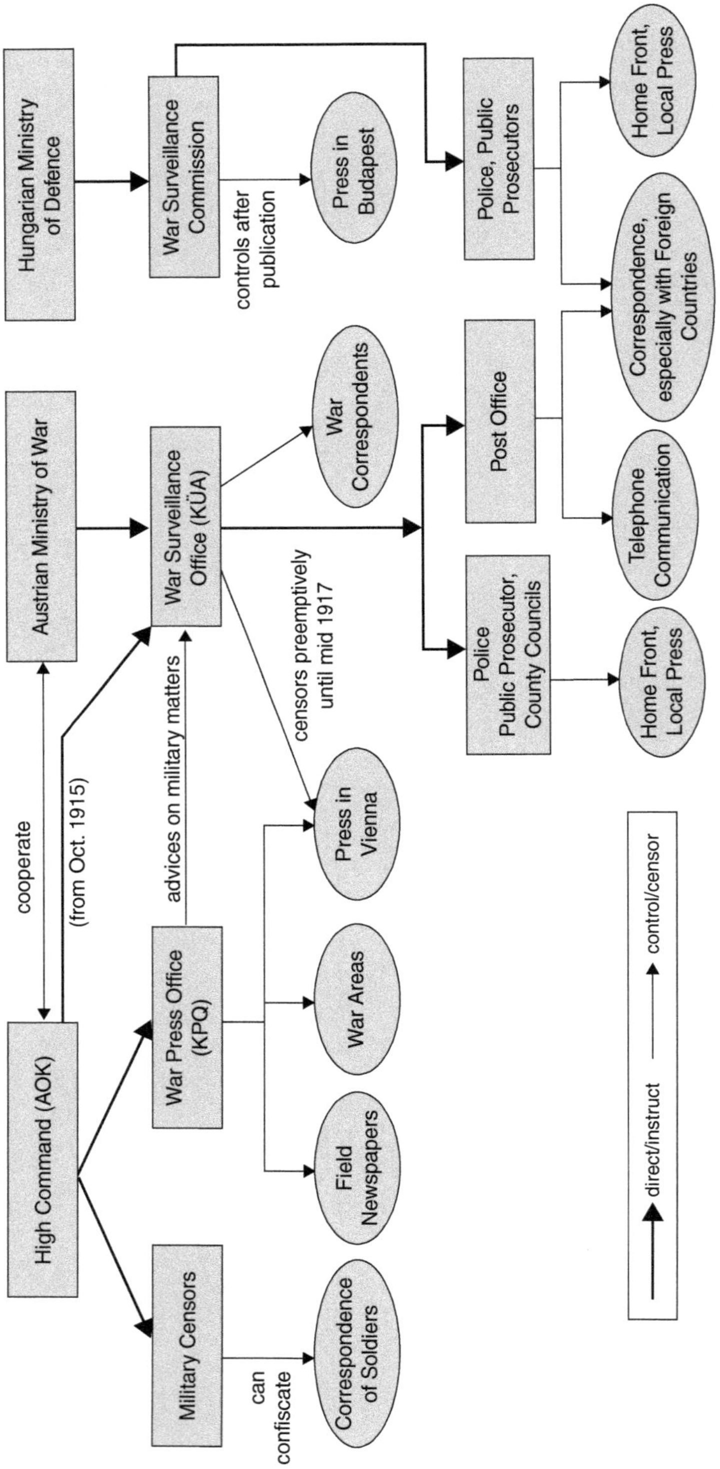

7. Censorship in Austria-Hungary

Hungarian Ministry of Defence → **War Surveillance Commission** → **Press in Budapest**

War Surveillance Commission — controls after publication

Police, Public Prosecutors → **Home Front, Local Press**

Police, Public Prosecutors → **Correspondence, especially with Foreign Countries**

Austrian Ministry of War → **War Surveillance Office (KÜA)** → **War Correspondents**

War Surveillance Office (KÜA) — censors preemptively until mid 1917

Post Office → Correspondence, especially with Foreign Countries

Post Office → **Telephone Communication**

Police Public Prosecutor, County Councils → **Home Front, Local Press**

High Command (AOK) — cooperate — Austrian Ministry of War

High Command (AOK) → (from Oct. 1915) → War Surveillance Office (KÜA)

War Press Office (KPQ) — advices on military matters → War Surveillance Office (KÜA)

High Command (AOK) → **War Press Office (KPQ)**

War Press Office (KPQ) → **Press in Vienna**

War Press Office (KPQ) → **War Areas**

War Press Office (KPQ) → **Field Newspapers**

High Command (AOK) → **Military Censors**

Military Censors — can confiscate → **Correspondence of Soldiers**

→ direct/instruct

→ control/censor

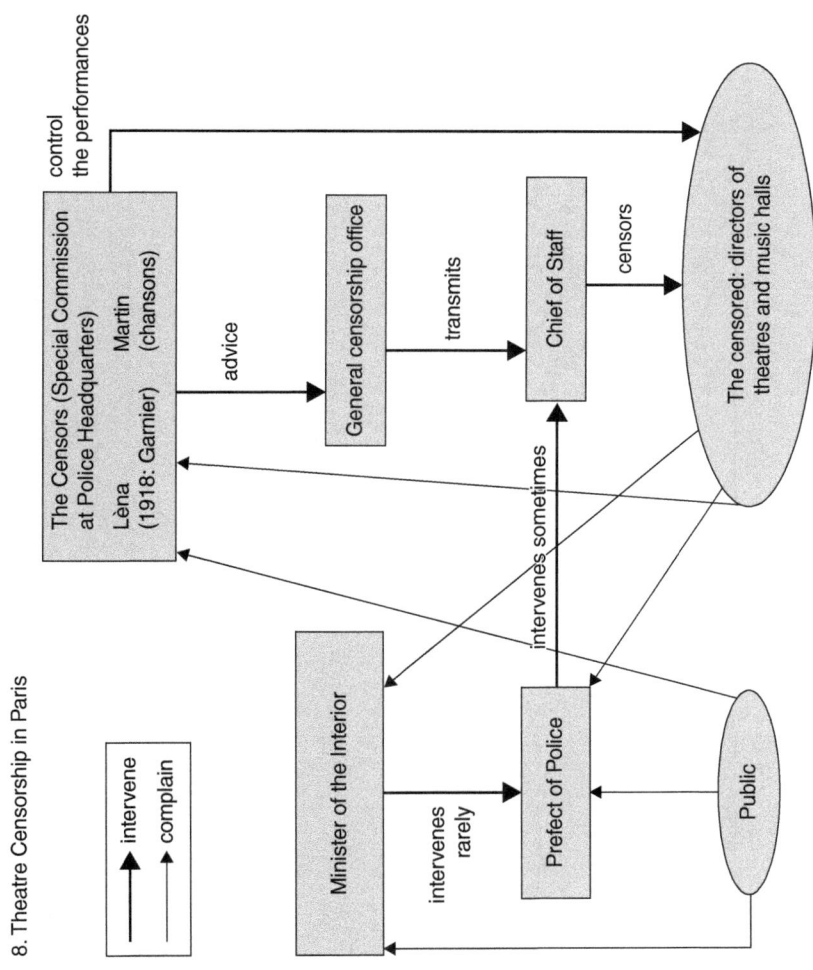

8. Theatre Censorship in Paris

intervene

complain

The Censors (Special Commission at Police Headquarters)

Lèna Martin
(1918: Garnier) (chansons)

control the performances

advice

General censorship office

transmits

Chief of Staff

censors

The censored: directors of theatres and music halls

Minister of the Interior

intervenes rarely

Prefect of Police

intervenes sometimes

Public

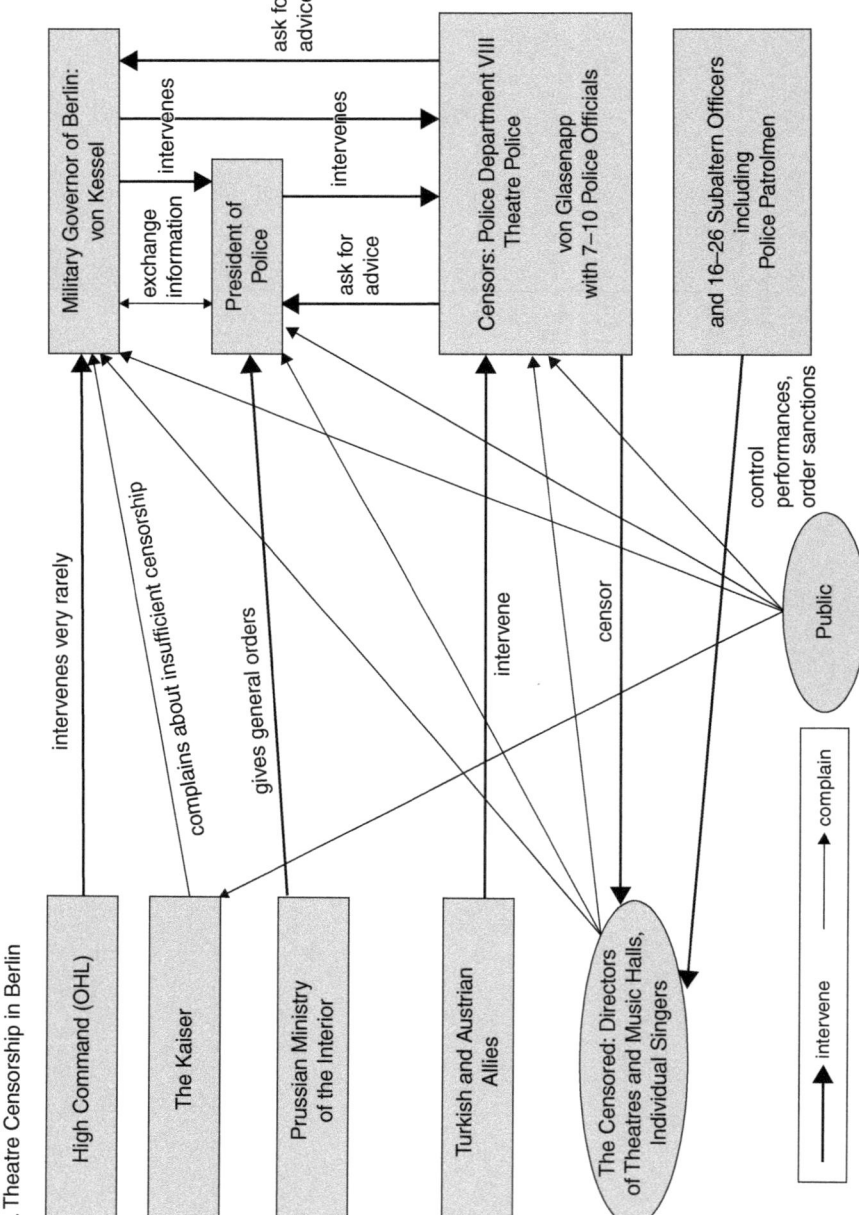

9. Theatre Censorship in Berlin

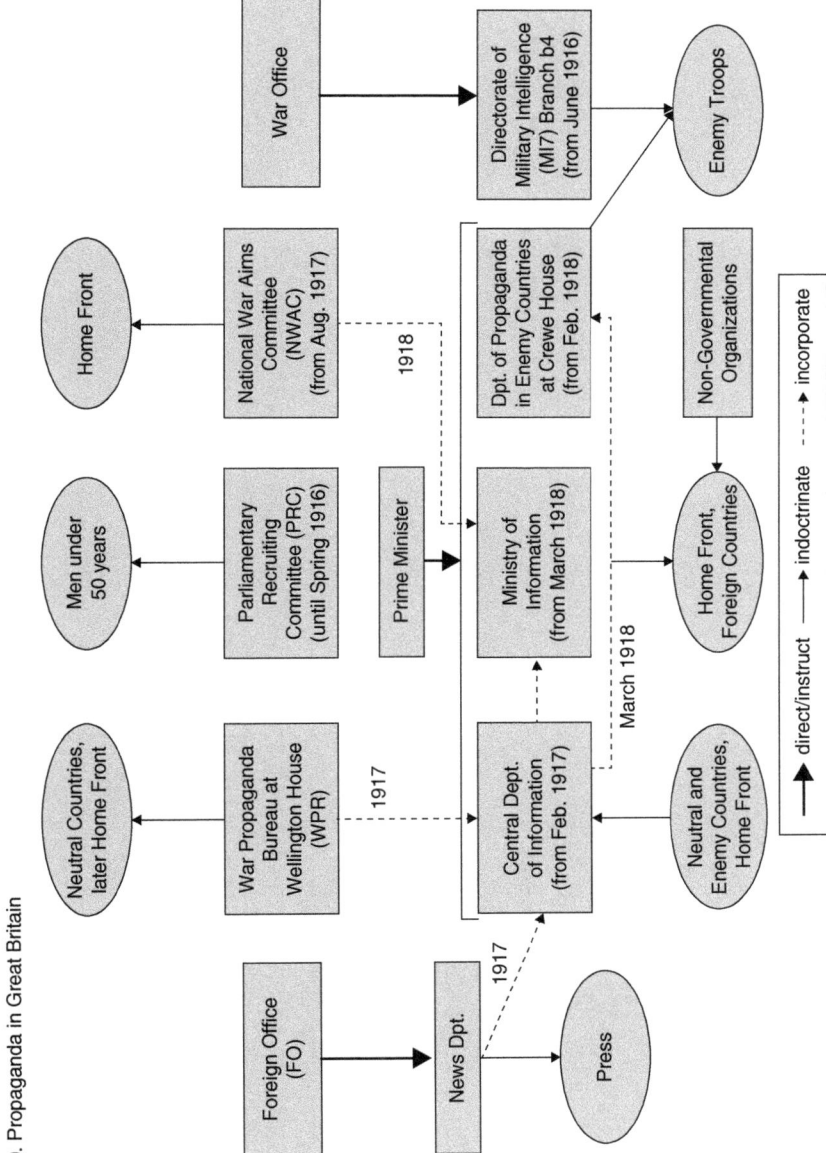

10. Propaganda in Great Britain

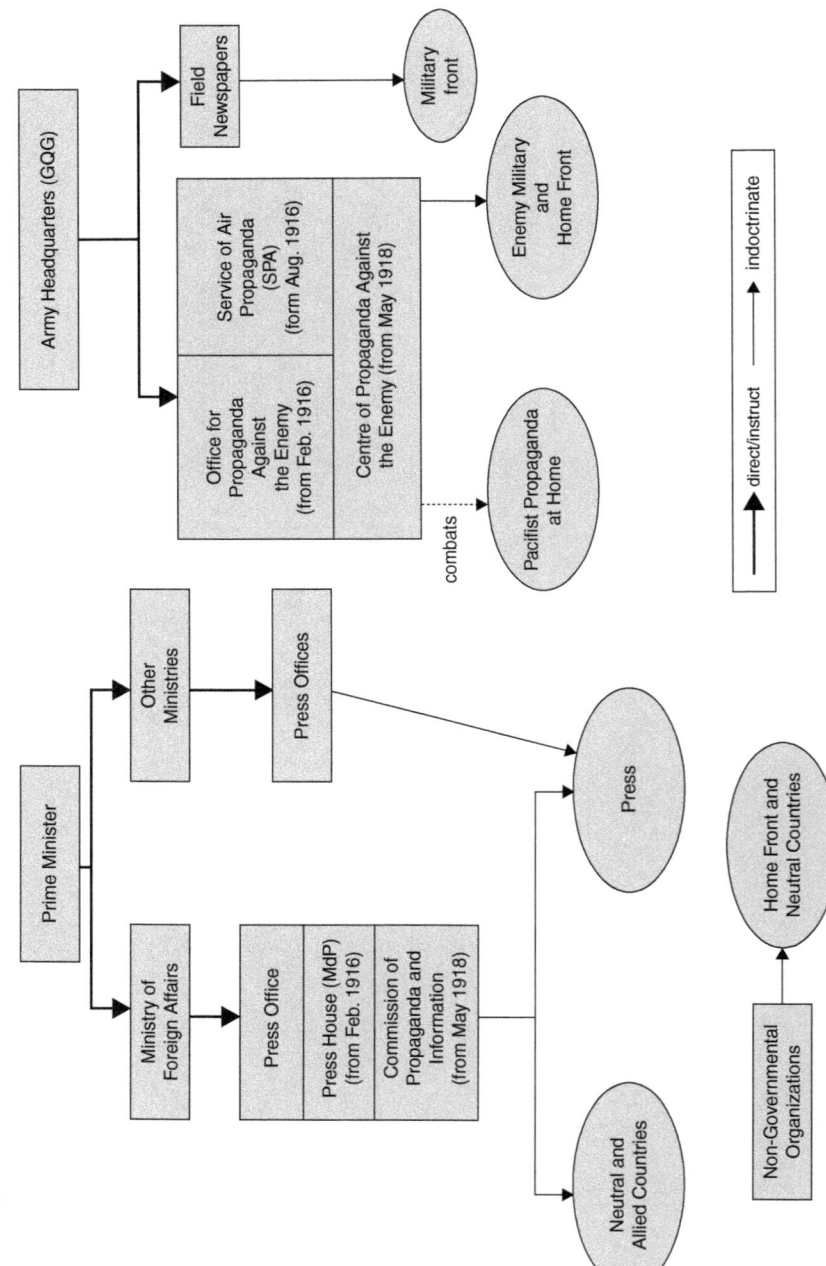

11. Propaganda in France

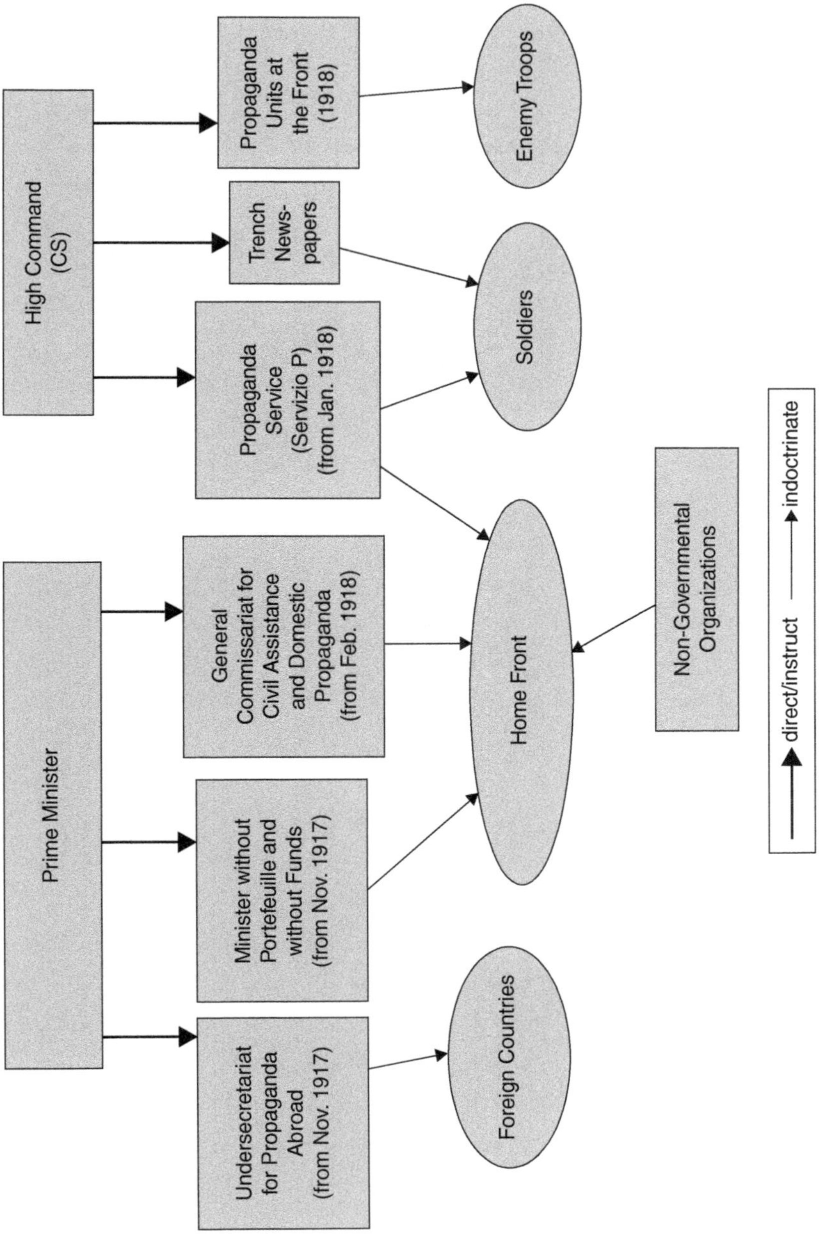

12. Propaganda in Italy

Prime Minister

Undersecretariat for Propaganda Abroad (from Nov. 1917)

Minister without Portefeuille and without Funds (from Nov. 1917)

General Commissariat for Civil Assistance and Domestic Propaganda (from Feb. 1918)

Foreign Countries

Home Front

Non-Governmental Organizations

High Command (CS)

Propaganda Service (Servizio P) (from Jan. 1918)

Trench News-papers

Propaganda Units at the Front (1918)

Soldiers

Enemy Troops

direct/instruct

indoctrinate

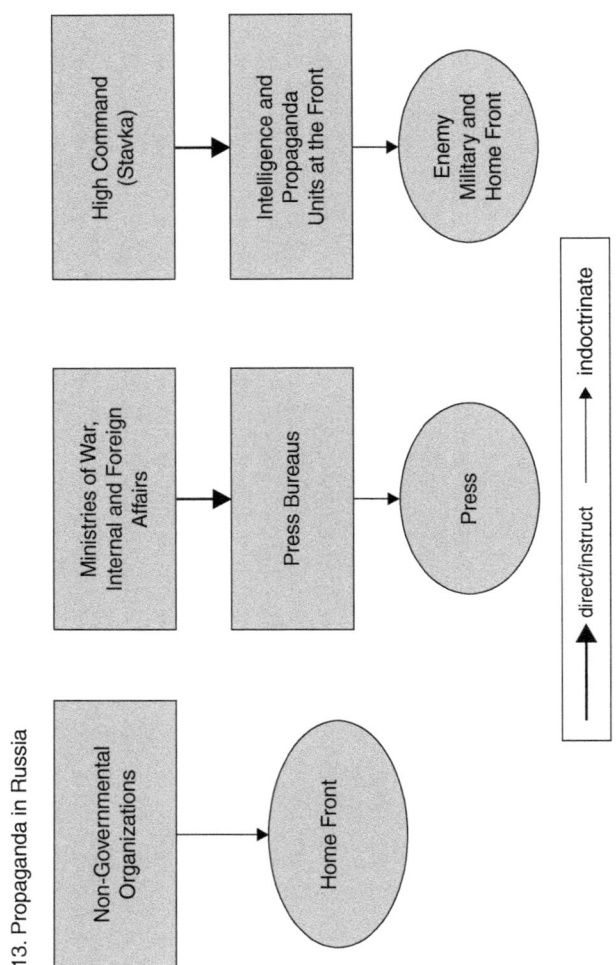

13. Propaganda in Russia

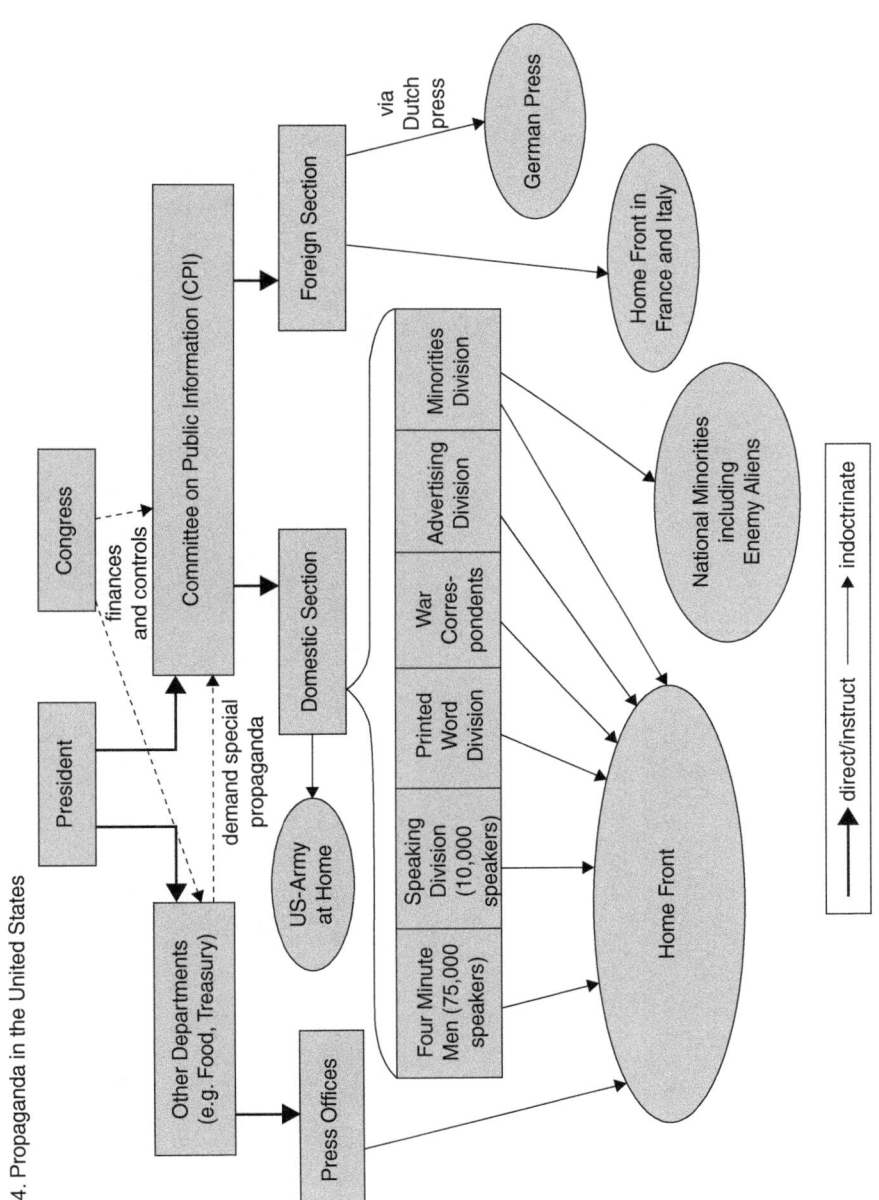

14. Propaganda in the United States

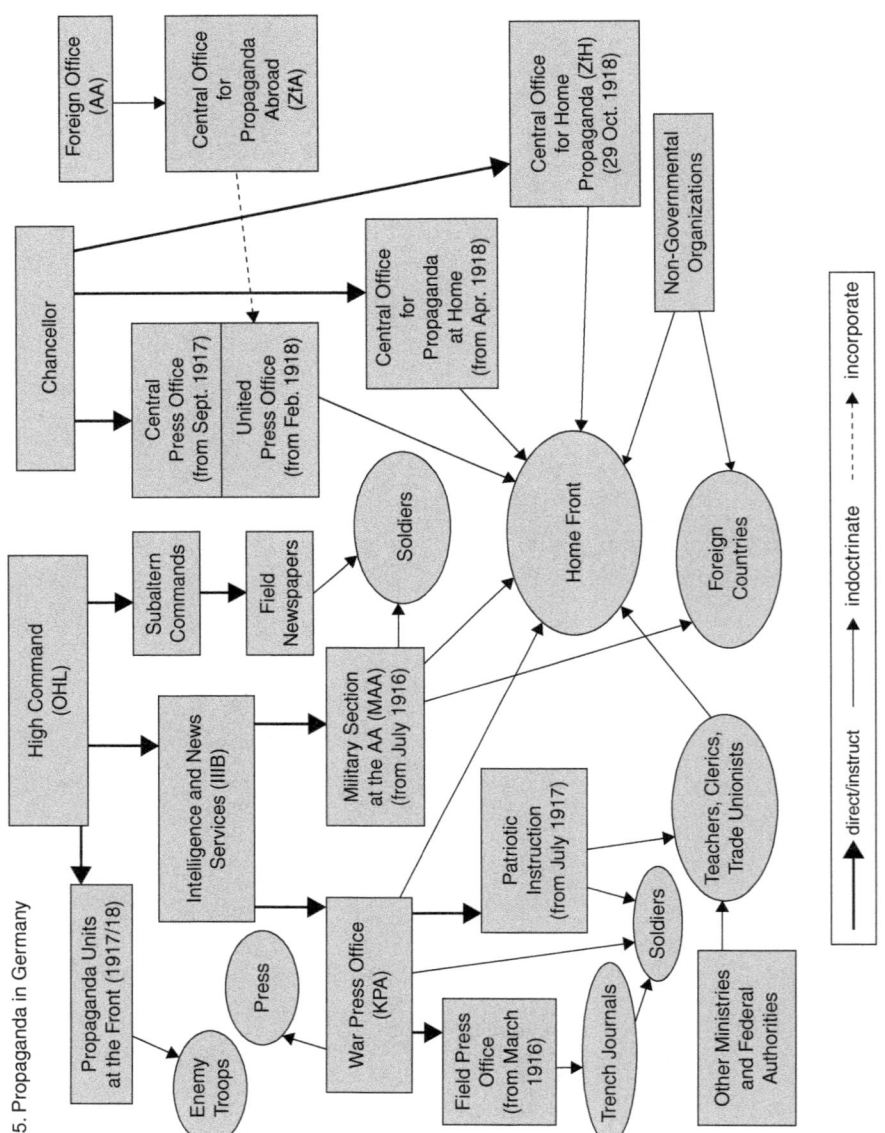

15. Propaganda in Germany

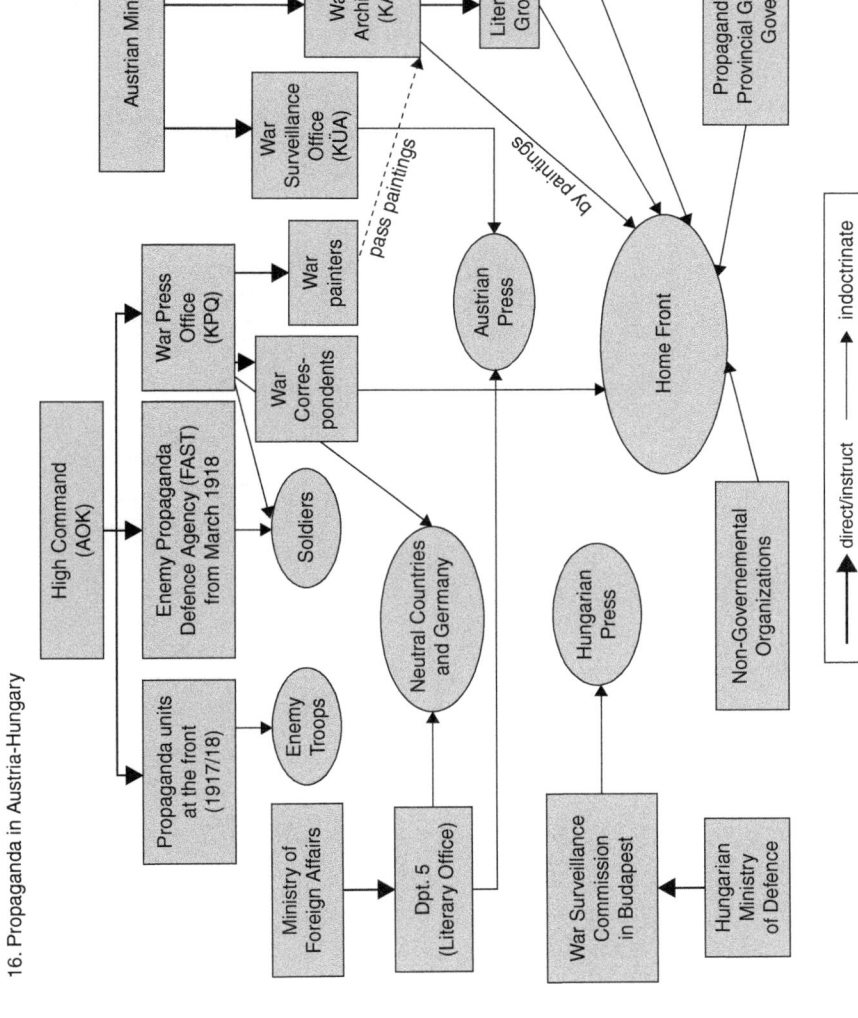

16. Propaganda in Austria-Hungary

Austrian Ministry of War

War Welfare Bureau (KFA)

Press Office

War Archives (KA)

Literary Group

War Surveillance Office (KUA)

War painters

Propaganda Offices of Provincial Governments, Governors

pass paintings

by paintings

High Command (AOK)

War Press Office (KPQ)

Enemy Propaganda Defence Agency (FAST) from March 1918

War Corres-pondents

Soldiers

Austrian Press

Home Front

Propaganda units at the front (1917/18)

Enemy Troops

Neutral Countries and Germany

Hungarian Press

Non-Governmental Organizations

Ministry of Foreign Affairs

Dpt. 5 (Literary Office)

War Surveillance Commission in Budapest

Hungarian Ministry of Defence

direct/instruct ⟶ indoctrinate

17. The influence of Atrocitiy propaganda on British military engagement 1914–15 (see p. 183)

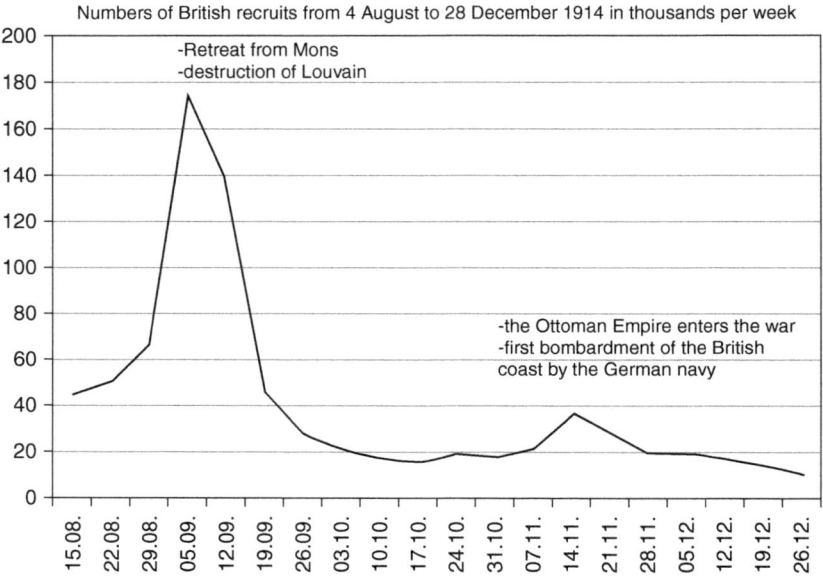

Numbers of British recruits from 4 August to 28 December 1914 in thousands per week

-Retreat from Mons
-destruction of Louvain

-the Ottoman Empire enters the war
-first bombardment of the British coast by the German navy

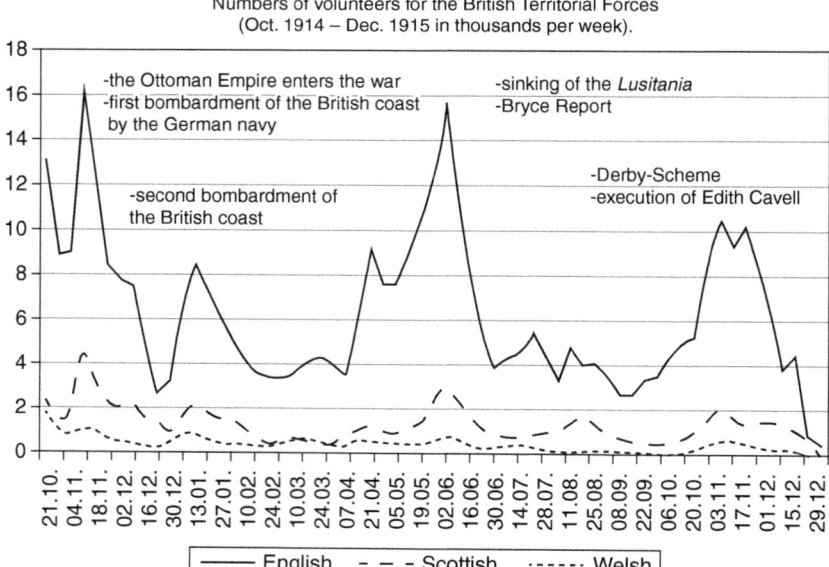

Numbers of volunteers for the British Territorial Forces
(Oct. 1914 – Dec. 1915 in thousands per week).

-the Ottoman Empire enters the war
-first bombardment of the British coast by the German navy

-sinking of the *Lusitania*
-Bryce Report

-second bombardment of the British coast

-Derby-Scheme
-execution of Edith Cavell

—— English   – – – Scottish   ······ Welsh

Chapter 12

ICONOGRAPHY: FIGURES 1 TO 38

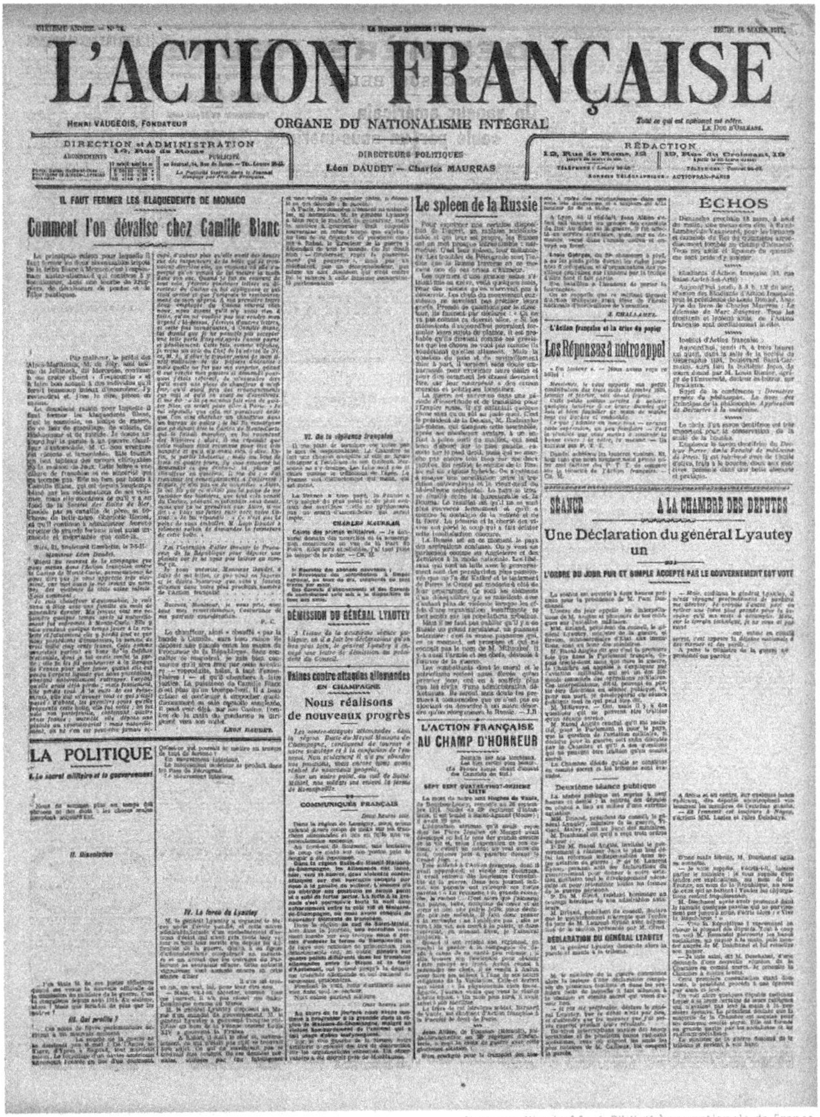

L'ACTION FRANÇAISE

Henri VAUGEOIS, Fondateur

ORGANE DU NATIONALISME INTÉGRAL

DIRECTION et ADMINISTRATION

DIRECTEURS POLITIQUES

Léon DAUDET — Charles MAURRAS

RÉDACTION

IL FAUT FERMER LES ELAQUEDENTS DE MONACO

Comment l'on dévalise chez Camille Blanc

Le spleen de la Russie

ÉCHOS

Les Réponses à notre appel

SÉANCE À LA CHAMBRE DES DÉPUTÉS

Une Déclaration du général Lyautey

DÉMISSION DU GÉNÉRAL LYAUTEY

Nous réalisons de nouveaux progrès

L'ACTION FRANÇAISE AU CHAMP D'HONNEUR

LA POLITIQUE

Figure 1 *L'Action française*, title page, 15 March 1917. Blank spaces: deleted by censorship. See p. 11.

Figure 2 *Ruy Blas*, 9 April 1916, title page. Cartoon and text deleted by censorship.
See p. 11.

Figure 3 André Gill: 'Madame Anastasie', *L'Éclipse*, title page, 19 July 1874. She is
the traditional French symbol of censorship. See p. 22.

Figure 4 Alfred Leete: 'Passed by the censor'. His caricature mocks at the delaying of information by censorship. See p. 24.

Figure 5 Edmund J. Sullivan: 'A deal with the devil', *The Kaiser's Garland*, London, 1915, p. 27. See p. 36.

Figure 6 'God punish England'. German propaganda coal. See p. 37.

Figure 7 Giovanni Capranesi: 'Sign the war loan'. Italian poster. See p. 40.

Figure 8 Louis Raemaekers: 'Mater Dolorosa', *La Baïonnette* 32, 10 February 1916. See p. 40.

Figure 9 Abel Faivre: 'German propaganda', *Echo de Paris*, 22 June 1915. The soldier: 'One would not believe that I killed the mother.' See p. 43.

Figure 10 Walter Trier: 'The Anglo-French gang of illusionists', *Lustige Blätter* 30, 3, 1915, pp. 8–9. See p. 36.

Figure 11 Bernard Partridge: 'The Potsdam Variety Troupe', *Punch's Almanach for 1917*, pp. 17–18. See p. 45.

Figure 12 Johann Bahr: 'In the British recruiting office', *Lustige Blätter* 47, 1915, p. 10. 'Nobody since eight days! The last person one week ago was the char woman!' See p. 46.

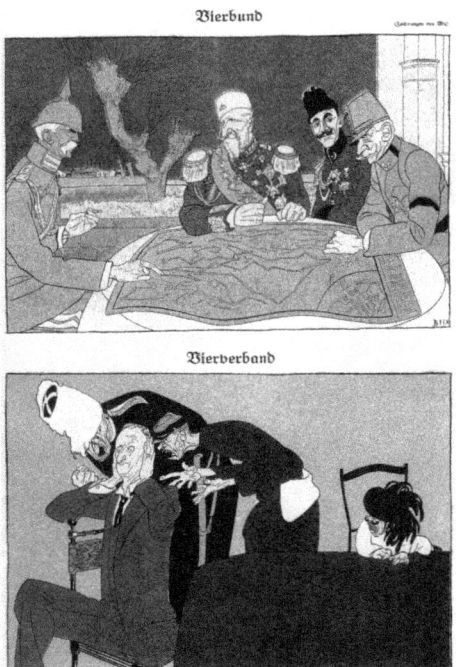

Figure 13 Ragnvald Blix: 'The Central Powers and the Allies', *Simplicissimus*, 30 November 1915. See p. 46.

Figure 14 Carlin: 'War profiteers', *Numero* no. 100, 21 November 1915. 'What have you done for the fatherland?' 'I have supplied the army with shoes.' On top of the drawing one sees the soldiers' feet. See p. 49.

Figure 15 Louis Oppenheim: 'Are we the barbarians?' This German poster of 1918 compares the cultural and social achievements of Germany, Britain and France: number of Nobel Prizes, patents and published books, percentage of literacy and social security benefits. See p. 52.

Figure 16 'Kultur or Death', *L'Europe anti-prussienne*, 20 February 1915 (reprint of an American cartoon). See p. 53.

Figure 17 Victor MacClure: 'Germania 1914 Germania 1918', British leaflet, July 1918. In 1914, the German people shown as a donkey, led by Germania, a general and a prince, follows the carrot called victory. In 1918, the donkey, completely emaciated, led by war profiteers, follows the carrot called Ersatz-victory. See p. 55.

Figure 18 Wilhelm Schulz: 'The last rat is mounting on the sinking ship of the Entente', *Simplicissimus*, 14 September 1916, vol. 21, p. 308. In August 1916, Romania had joined the Allies. See p. 55.

Figure 19 Rudolf Herrmann: 'Lead-pouring in St. Petersburg', *Muskete*, 31 December 1914, p. 107. The Tsar emulates the German New Year's Eve custom of fortune telling by pouring molten lead into water. In the cellar grenades are produced for the revolution. See p. 56.

Figure 20 Anton Hoffmann: 'We are challenged to fight till the very end'. This German poster of 1917 demonstrates the fate of the German people after the defeat: working as slaves under British and French control. See p. 57.

Figure 21 German plate 1914/15, Wilhelm II and Franz Josef I. See p. 73.

Figure 23 German iron watch chain. People were exhorted to exchange golden watch chains or other precious possessions into iron items and got badges with the inscription 'Gold for the defence – iron for the honour'. See p. 91.

Figure 22 Erich von Stroheim as a German officer. Poster for the American propaganda movie *Heart of Humanity* (1918). See p. 86.

Figure 24 'Who signs the war loan shortens the war'. German children as propaganda agents. See p. 93.

Figure 25 'Times are hard, but the victory is certain'. Hindenburg as war loan propagandist on a poster. See p. 94.

Figure 26 Madonna nail statue, Bolzano. A special way to extract money for the war in Austria and Germany: People would hammer nails costing up to 100 mark or kronen into wooden statues, in this case around the statue. See p. 95.

Figure 27 King Peter I of Serbia in a German war adaption of the children's book *Struwwelpeter*. See p. 101.

Figure 28 Wilhelm II in the British war version of *Struwwelpeter*. See p. 101.

Figure 29 Karl Olszewski: Marianne, the symbol of France, in the German war version of *Struwwelpeter*. In the German war version, Marianne, the symbol of France, plays with a match box called 'Ideas of Revenge' and burns to ashes while two friendly cats wearing German and Austrian helmets try to warn her. See p. 101.

Figure 30 Edward V. Lucas: *Swollen headed William*, 1914, pp. 4–5; the British version. In the British war version, the Kaiser plays with a match-box called 'world politics', and the two cats are his grand-father Wilhelm I and Bismarck. See p. 101.

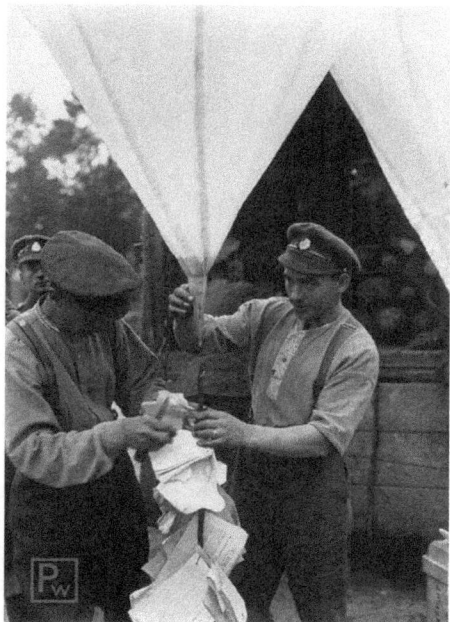

Figure 31 British balloon distribution of propaganda leaflets, September 1918. See p. 113.

Figure 32 French propaganda leaflets for the occupied areas. See p. 113.

Figure 33 'The first million', British leaflet, August 1918. See p. 115.

Figure 34 The good life of 'German prisoners in England', British leaflet, August 1917. See p. 116.

Figure 35 'Russia's Vampires', German propaganda poster for Russia 1918. Britain, France and America are sucking helpless Russia. See p. 121.

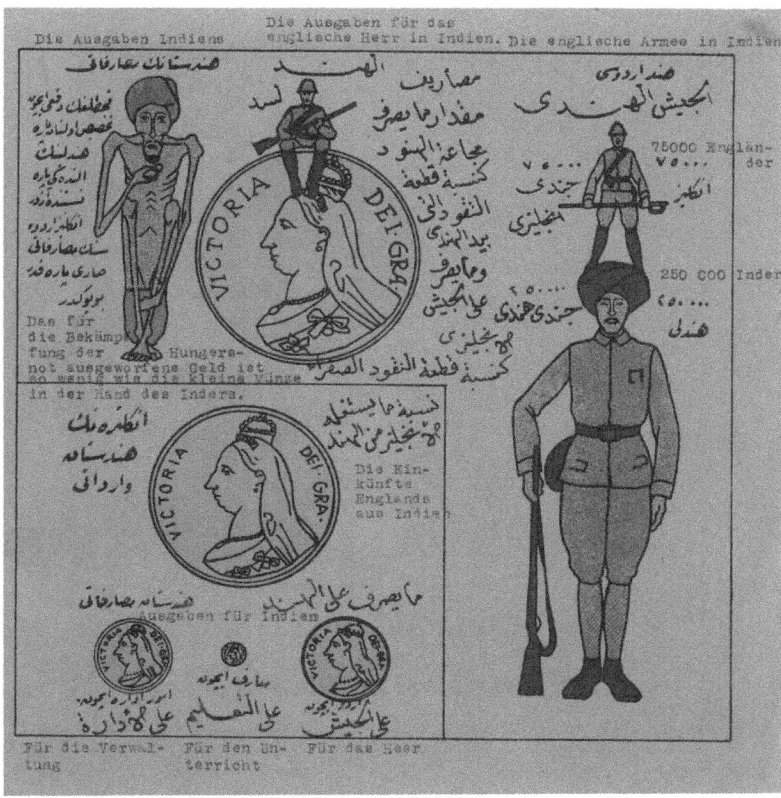

Figure 36 British revenues and expenditure in India. The revenues are much higher, most of the spending goes to the British administration and army, and the starving population gets very little. Page from a German propaganda booklet. See p. 131.

Figure 37 Lenin's speech in front of the Petrograd Soviet on 4 April (17 April) 1917. Among others he condemns the war and the Provisional Government which wants to continue it. See p. 170.

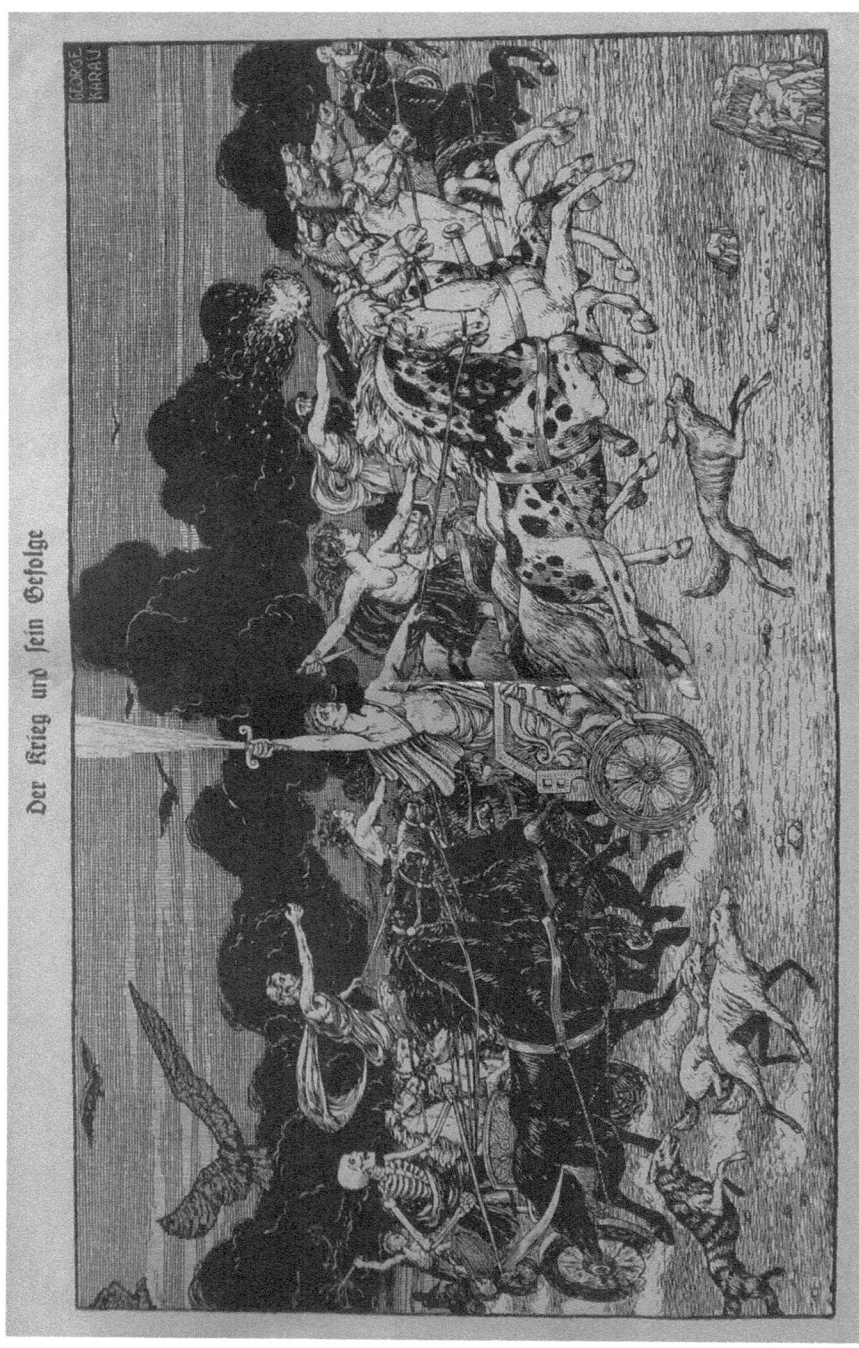

Figure 38 Georg Karau: 'The war and his retinue', *Glühlichter* 2, 14 January 1915, 4. See p. 175.

Appendix

APPROXIMATE CURRENCY CONVERSIONS
FROM 1915 TO 1999–2017

This comparison between the purchasing power of the various currencies is not a categorical statement of fact but can only serve as a general guide. The German mark is a special problem. Due to extremely inflated prices during the war, the buying power of the mark in 1915 was much lower than in 1914 and the coefficient therefore relatively inferior to the other currencies. The continental currencies were compared until their disappearance in 1999 and then converted to the Euros. In the text, all figures of 1915 will be followed in brackets by the corresponding figures of 2017.

£1 1915 = £43
www.nationalarchives.gov.uk/currency-converter/
$1 1915 = $24
www.dollartimes.com/inflation/dollars.php
1 mark 1915 = 5.9 dem 1999, €3.8
www.fredriks.de/hvv/kaufkraft.php#BSP1
1 French franc 1915 = 14.4 Francs 1999, €2.70
www.fr.wikipedia.org/wiki/évolution_du_pouvoir_d'achat_des_monnaies_
    françaises
1 Italian lira 1915 = 5,314 Lira in 1999, €2.75
www.commercialistatelematico.com/documenti/coefficienti.htm
1 Dutch fl. 1915 = 14.88 fl. in 1999, €6.75
www.iisg.nl/hpw/calculate-nl.php
1 Swiss franc 1915 = 9 CHF in 2017
http://www.portal-stat.admin.ch/lik_rechner/d/lik_rechner.htm

NOTES

Preface and acknowledgements

1 Lasswell 1971.
2 The following is based on Purseigle 2008: 9–14; Bauerkämper and Julien 2010a: 7–19; Julien 2014: 53–8.
3 Winter 2014; Véray 2014.
4 Audoin-Rouzeau and Becker 2000: 145; see for a more balanced view in the trenches Audoin-Rouzeau 1992: 163–72.
5 Julien 2014: 72.
6 Purseigle 2008: 11.
7 Lipp 2003: 311; Offenstadt 2010: 60, 72–3; Ridel 2014; Ulrich 1997: 94–5; Ulrich and Ziemann 2010: 179; Nelson 2011: 242; Nelson 2014; Fuller 1990: 39; Reimann 1997: 140–1.
8 Fuller 1990: 39.
9 Ashworth 1980: 24–6; Offenstadt 2010: 60, 72–4.
10 Ashworth 1980: 26–8; Weintraub 2001; Ziemann 1995: 101–2; Ziemann 1997a: 102–3; Christmas 1917: Pignot 2012: 249.
11 Ziemann 1997a: 99.
12 Bonzon and Robert 1989: 10, 17, 50, 63, 71; Wette 1995a: 132; Klemperer 1989: 372–4; Leed 1979: 109; Delvert 1918: 200 (quote).
13 Winter and Robert 2012a: 472–3; Nelson 2014.
14 Purseigle 2008: 13.
15 Quoted after Taylor Allen 1984: 11; see also Creel's statement on p. 78.

General introduction

1 Acemoglu and Robinson 2013: 79–82 and passim.
2 *Triumph des Willens*, dir. by Leni Riefenstahl (1935, UFA).
3 Juskobou (Pseud.): 'Le Bourre-crâne', in: Montant 1968: Appendix.
4 Monger 2012.
5 Lunzer 2016.

Chapter 1

1 Remark on 28 December 1917 to Charles P. Scott, in: Knightley 2002: 116–17.
2 In Bavaria constitutionally forbidden, but applied in practice: Schmidt 2006: 33; D. Fischer 1973: 10.
3 Berger and Allard 1932: 21–2; Navet 1994: 36; Forcade 2011: 71; Reeves 1999b: 30.

4 Section based on: Rajsfus 1999: 30–58; Forcade 1998: 116–236; Forcade 2004a: 35–47; Smith 2001: 75–95; Rose 1995: 42, 54; Rose 2001; Demm 2002j; Deist 1990; Creutz 1996: 110; Welch 2014: 27–30, 39–45; Mock 1972; Fiori 2001: 79–81, 92–3, 100, 283, 317; Sanders and Taylor 1982: 18–20, 51–4; Cook 1920: 27, 41–4, 58–9; Oberzensurstelle 1973; Axelrod 2009; Sorrie 2014.
5 Rose 2001: 2647; Wüstenbecker 2010: 227; Axelrod 2009: 70; Fiori 2001: 79–81.
6 Mock 1972: 57.
7 Cook 1920: 33–4, 47–54.
8 Fiori 2001: 92–1.
9 Scheer 2010: 82–5, 97; Cornwall 2016: 404–6, 424.
10 Moreau 2016: 95–6.
11 Fiori 2001: 283.
12 Sanders and Taylor 1982: 50; Nicolai 1920: 77; Pöppinghege 2006: 204.
13 Beaupré 2006: 89; Sorrie 2014: 56.
14 Creutz 1996: 52–3, 61–3; Deist 1990; Welch 2014: 39–41; Schramm 2007: 318; Forcade 2011: 74; Forcade 2004a: 40.
15 Deist 1970: 686–7, 693; Rose 1995: 43–5; Newton 2002: 32.
16 Fiori 2001: 79–81, 100.
17 Forcade 2004a: 39–40; Rajsfus 1999: 29–32.
18 Sorrie 2014: 48, 56.
19 Forcade 2004a: 43; Forcade 2011: 73; Rajsfus 1999: 51; Fiori 2001: 95; see organograms nos 1 and 2.
20 Welch 2014: 27–9; Deist 1990: 200–3; Deist 1991: 126–38; Chickering 2002: 46 (quote).
21 Deist 1970: LI; Deist 1991: 137.
22 Gerlach 1994: 80; Rajch 2007: 105–12.
23 D. Fischer 1973: 10, 172–3, 185, 227–8, 232–7, 245, 250–2; Deist 1970: 153; Deist 1991: 134.
24 Healy 2004: 123; Scheer 2010: 172–3.
25 Berger and Allard 1932: 95, 120, 197; Sorrie 2014: 58–9; Healy 2004: 133; Fiori 2001: 99.
26 Deist 1970: 73, 87; Deist 1990: 201–2; Flemming and Ulrich 2014: 63; Nicolai 1920: 73–5, 83; Pöppinghege 2006: 211.
27 Deist 1970: 110, 115, 119.
28 Marquis 1978: 476; Altenhöner 2008: 86–8; Rose 1995: 42–3; Rose 2001: 2647; Cook 1920: 84.
29 Axelrod 2009: 72 (quotes).
30 Axelrod 2009: 71–3; Mock 1972: 50 (1st quotes); Mock and Larson 1968: 81–2; Wüstenbecker 2010: 227 (last quote).
31 Smith 2001: 84 (2nd quote); Golder 1927: 183 (1st and 3rd quote).
32 Köroglu 2007: 13–14.
33 Section based on: Collins 2004: 208; Stark 2009; Williams 2005; Forcade 1998: 697–761; Forcade 2011: 72; Rajsfus 1999: 186–241; Krakovitch 1991; Baumeister 2005; Hiley 1990: 178; Healy 2004: 99; Robb 2002: 136; Demm 2018a: 360.
34 Stark 2009: 15–19; Krakovitch 1991: 333–5; Joseph 2000: 31.
35 Krakovitch 1991: 332–4; Healy 2004: 99; Robb 2002: 136.
36 Baumeister 2005: 33–5, 143–5, 178–80, 183–6; Rajsfus 1999: 186–7; Forcade 2011: 72; Joseph 2000: 29; Hiley 1990: 178; Krakovitch 1991: 334–6; Healy 2004: 99.
37 Krakovitch 1991: 334; Rajsfus 1999: 186.

38 LAB, A. Pr. Br. Rep. 030–05, no. 136: 79 (1914), no. 134: 247r (1917); Stark 2009: 41.

39 LAB, A. Pr. Br. Rep. 030–05, no. 28: 99r–100r.

40 LAB, A. Pr. Br. Rep. 030–05, no. 715: 333–4 (Hannover), 335 (Stettin), no. 134: 187–8 (Aix-la-Chapelle).

41 Letter of complaint by von Kessel to Prussian Ministry of War, 29 December 1914, LAB, A. Pr. Br. Rep. 030–05, no. 715: 333–4 (Hannover), 335 (Stettin),, no. 134: 62r; Stark 2009: 48 (quote).

42 LAB, A. Pr. Br. Rep. 030–05, no. 136: 136r–137v, no. 134: 6, 195, no. 63: 26, no. 1534: 72–3; Stark 2009: 108–9; see organograms nos 03 and 04.

43 Stark 2009: 52 (quote).

44 Krakovitch 1991: 337–9; LAB, A. Pr. Br. Rep. 030–05, no. 134: 38; Stark 2009: 49, 64, 224; Rajsfus 1999: 197–9; Williams 2005: 109–10, 162; Collins 2004: 212–13.

45 Stark 2009: 49.

46 Williams 2005: 162.

47 Koerber 1994: 66–7.

48 Section based on: Rose 1995: 49, 53–4; Rajsfus 1999: 29–68; Forcade 2004a: 40–3; Berger and Allard 1932; Koszyk 1973; BDIC, 'Consignes de censure données à la presse', F res 0270/C; Mock 1972: 80–1, 91, 134; Fiori 2001: 79–107.

49 Berger and Allard 1932: 9, 15; Rose 2001: 2647; Demm 2002j: 56.

50 Rose 1995: 42; Rose 2001: 2647.

51 Rose 1995: 42, 54; Rose 2001: 2647; Cook 1920: 43, 55–6.

52 Forcade 2004a: 40–1; Rajsfus 1999: 58.

53 Oberzensurstelle 1973; Cook 1920: 58–9; Kriegsüberwachungsamt 1916.

54 Demm 2000a: 49; Rose 1995: 49; Rose 2001: 2647; Holl 1988: 123–5; Shand 1975: 99–101, 103–4.

55 See also Fiori 2001: 96, fig. 4; Scheer 2010: 157–9; Cornwall 2016: 405–6.

56 See also *Arbeiterwille*, 9 August 1918.

57 E.g. *Vorarlberger Wacht*, 9 August 1918; Healy 2004: 130–1, 134.

58 Gerlach 1994: 59.

59 BDIC, F res 0270/C, 15–16 September 1917.

60 'Consignes de censure données à la presse', BDIC, F res 0270/C, and ASHAT, series 5 N; Préfecture de Police, Paris, Archives/Musée, l'annexe du 31 mai 1916 à l'instruction n° 1000 du 30 septembre 1915, série Bᴬ, carton 1712.

61 E.g. BDIC, F res 0270/C, 12 September 1917.

62 BDIC, F res 0207/C, 23 March 1915, 12 September 1917, 6 October 1917, 17 September 1917, 4 October 1917.

63 Oberzensurstelle 1973: 204–5, 208, 218, 222, 251, 262 (quotes).

64 Deist 1970: 88, 100, 151 note 30, 172.

65 Gerlach 1994: 58.

66 Deist 1970: 1155.

67 Fiori 2001: 358.

68 Blücher 1920: 173; Zhdanova 2017.

69 D. Fischer 1973: 155.

70 Beurier 2008: 315–16.

71 Cook 1920: 27; Rose 1995: 54.

72 Demm 2018e: 263–4.

73 Rajsfus 1999: 66 (quote); Montant 1968: 46–54; Montant 1990: 141–2; Bavendamm 2004: 186–7.

74 Papadia 2016; Fiori 2001: 201–5, 211.

75 Millman 2000: 11–12, 77, 82, 181–3; 188–90, 256 (quote); Pankhurst 1932: 263, 301; Carsten 1982: 176; Rose 1995: 51–4, 103; Swartz 1971: 189; Robb 2002: 112; Deist 1970: 1140.
76 Sorrie 2014: 178–201.
77 Section based on: Cabanes 2004: 55–75; Cochet 1986; Rajsfus 1999: 133–70; Jeanneney 1968; Corner and Procacci 1997: 227; Forcade 1998: 790; Healy 2004: 85, 124–5, 136; Ulrich 1997: 103; Mock 1972.
78 Englander 1997: 138; Demm 1988: nos 122, 124.
79 Healy 2004: 124–5, 136.
80 Gibelli 1999: 177; Corner and Procacci 1997: 227.
81 Healy 2004: 85.
82 Kennedy 2014: 26.
83 Kennedy 2014: 27–8.
84 Ulrich and Ziemann 2010: 124 (quote); Graves 1929: 154, 167; Hochschild 2011: 150.
85 Ulrich 1997: 103; Rollet et al. 2007: 329 (quote); Deist 1970: 995; Brocks and Ziemann 1994: 113.
86 Bonzon and Robert 1989: 42, 62, 97.
87 Bazzanella 1980: 344 (quote).
88 Ulrich and Ziemann 2010: 126; Jeanneney 1968: 217, 219; Mock 1972: 96, 100–2, 153–68; Ridel 2007: 278; Ulrich 1997: 78–80; Gibelli 1999: 149; Forcade 2004a: 50.
89 Bonzon and Robert 1989: 10.
90 Silber 1932: 106–8; 'Contrôle postal de Londres', BDIC, 4 Δ res 0016.
91 Mock 1972: 61–71.
92 Rajsfus 1999: 99, 161–71; Deist 1970: 262–3; Kirchner 1992: 86, 91, 94, 103, 111, 117, 128, 134; Koch 2015: 155.
93 Knežević 2018: 110–16.
94 E.g. Deist 1970: 397, 762, 1054–5, 1099.
95 Fiori 2001: 201–3, 291; Procacci 1989: 46–8; Gatti 2000: 71–9, 38, note 44 (quote), 116.
96 Englander 1987: 24–32, 29 (quotes).
97 Creel 1920: 69–70 (quote), 168–70, 179–81; Mock 1972: 32–4, 190–3, 198, 211–15; Capozzola 2008: 117, 184–5; https://en.wikipedia.org/wiki/East_St._Louis_Race_Riots.
98 Berger and Allard 1932: 57.
99 Schramm 2007: 322.
100 Graham 1917: 76–8.
101 Koszyk 1973: 176.
102 Fiori 2001: 155, 255.
103 *Le Temps* 19,418 and 19,419 of 5 and 6 September 1914.
104 Mock 1972: 88.
105 Calculated by Demm 2014: 123.
106 Rose 2001: 2648 (quote); e.g. *The Graphic* XCII: 183, 247; Oberzensurstelle 1973, List of Casualties: 269–70; Healy 2004: 131; Rajsfus 1999: 34, 44.
107 Rose 2001: 2648 (quote); Forcade 1998: 779; Fiori 2001: 126, 154.
108 *Journal officiel*, 14 November 1916: 3350, ASHAT, 5 N 344, fol. 62.
109 Demm 2018a: 366.
110 Rose 2001: 2648; Ulrich 1997: 145; Oberzensurstelle 1973, Letters: 208; Gerlach 1994: 58.
111 Rose 1995: 43–50; Rajsfus 1999: 94–132.
112 Forcade 1998: 228–9, 774, 800; Mock 1972: 203–4; Fiori 2001: 225–7; Oberzensurstelle 1973: 242, 270; Welch 2014: 143; Becker 1986: 45; Healy 2004: 131.

113 Forcade 2004a: 51–2; Rose 1995: 42–3.
114 Sorrie 2014: 198–245.
115 Deist 1970: 722.
116 Deist 1970: 11140–2, 1147.
117 Cook 1920: 25–6, 111–13.
118 Zweig 2001: 277.
119 Verhey 2000: 327.
120 Welch 2014: 143.
121 Deist 1970: 669; Oberzensurstelle 1973: 242–3.
122 Koszyk 1973: 171.
123 Fiori 2001: 250–2; Beneš 1928: 48; Healy 2004: 133.
124 Creel 1920: 156–8.
125 Hirschfeld and Gaspar 1982: 97–100.
126 Rajsfus 1999: 186–8, 197, 241; Demm 2018a: 368–9.
127 Healy 2004: 135.
128 Demm 1988: nos 287, 289, 290.
129 German cases in Demm 2014: 140–2.
130 Boulanger 1998: 87; Horne 1989: 203–4; Demm 2018a: 372.
131 Demm 2018a: 373.
132 Berger and Allard 1932: 251–3.
133 Cook 1920: 138.
134 Rajsfus 1999: 40; Montant 1989, vol. 8: 1647–8.
135 Oberzensurstelle 1973: 195, 214, 219, 230, 254, 264; Deist 1970: 148.
136 Fiori 2001: 366–8.
137 Ward 1981: 121–3.
138 Oberzensurstelle 1973: 201, 226.
139 Oberzensurstelle 1973: 272 and 242–3; Demm 1988: nos 212–15, 220–31.
140 Hiley 1990: 179; Millman 2000: 11.
141 Fiori 2001: 137.
142 Becker 1986: 62.
143 Oberzensurstelle 1973, Foreign Newspapers: 202; Lehmann-Russbüldt 1927: 62; Beneš 1928: 29–30; Demm 1988: no. 293; Deist 1970: 1275.
144 Deist 1970: 120–1; Deist 1990: 204; Berger and Allard 1932: 148, 184, 227; Fiori 2001: 211–12; Forcade 1998: 367–9, 786–8.
145 D. Fischer 1973: 163; Healy 2004: 140; Rauchensteiner 2014: 710–12.
146 For lack of detailed studies, only Paris, Berlin and sometimes Britain can be considered; section based on references in note 51; Krivanec 2012: 247; Rajsfus 1999: 194.
147 LAB, A. Pr. Br. Rep. 030–05, no. 681: 18, 79r–v, 81–83 (1st quote), 88; Jüllig 1994: 121; Proctor 2010: 8; Krivanec 2012: 109–11.
148 Krakovitch 1991: 349–51; Krivanec 2012: 247; Rajsfus 1999: 187, 192–6, 240; Stark 2009: 35, 209; Williams 2005: 108, 162.
149 LAB, A. Pr. Br. Rep. 030–05, no. 502: 85v (1st quote); Rajsfus 1999: 187 (2nd quote), 191.
150 Krakovitch 1991: 345; Rajsfus 1999: 194; LAB, A. Pr. Br. Rep. 030–05 no. 319: 212r–214v, 234, no. 530: 118r–119v, no. 810: 139.
151 Joseph 2000: 23; Krakovitch 1991: 343–4; Rajsfus 1999: 193.
152 Krakovitch 1991: 345; Rajsfus 1999: 187, 192–4, 240–1; Collins 2004: 207.
153 LAB, A. Pr. Br. Rep. 030-05, no. 134: Letters of 19 and 27 September 1914, fol. 31, 36, 8 October 1914, fol. 20–2, 23, 26–7, 11 August 1915, fol. 8r–v.

154 Collins 2004: 205; Williams 2005: 188, 193.
155 Krakovitch 1991: 335, 340, 345–7; Rajsfus 1999: 186, 196–9, 202.
156 LAB, A. Pr. Br. Rep. 030–05, no. 134: 195.
157 Demm 2018a: 360–2, 365–6.
158 Rajsfus 1999: 234.
159 Jeancolas 1994: 229; Rajsfus 1999: 202, 211.
160 Bub 1938: 110–11.
161 Welch 2014: 154.
162 Ward 1981: 116–19.
163 Mock 1972: 179–81; Wood 1990: doc. 117 and 118.
164 Stark 2009: 11–13.
165 First censored edition: Genevoix 1916, second complete edition: Genevoix 1925; Demm 2000a: 56–61.
166 Beaupré 2006: 82–8.
167 All suppressions of 9 May 1915 in Rajsfus 1999: 69–72.
168 Rajsfus 1999: 39.
169 Demm 2018a: 373–4.
170 Baumeister 2005: 179–81, 183–5; Jüllig 1994: 125–6; Hiley 1994: 213; Altenhöner 2008: 200; Krivanec 2012: 258; Joseph 2000: 33–4; Krakovitch 1991: 344; Read 1941: 14–15; Brocks 2008: 30–1; Metken 1994: 138; Collins 2004: 193, 203–5; Sorrie 2014: 49; Horne 1994: 136; Schulz-Besser 1915: 81; Berger and Allard 1932: 98; Watson 2014b: 814.
171 Rajsfus 1999: 19.
172 Berger and Allard 1932: 103.
173 Fiori 2001: 319–21; Knightley 2002: 101–6; Oberzensurstelle 1973: 239.
174 Knightley 2002: 139–40.
175 Knightley 2002: 133; Leab 2007: 167; Mock 1972: 153–5, 173–6.
176 Collins 2004: 208–9.
177 Sanders and Taylor 1982: 24.
178 Schramm 2007: 318–19.
179 Rose 1995: 53–4.
180 Rajsfus 1999: 66.
181 Koszyk 1973: 178–80, 160.
182 Fiori 2001: 427–30, 429 (quote).
183 Demm 2018a: 374 (quotes).
184 Berger and Allard 1932: 172.
185 Section based on: Bavendamm 2004: 180–205, Sorrie 2014: 190–5 and Forcade 1998: 775–7, 775 (quote).
186 Berger and Allard 1932: 237–9, 256–8.
187 Caillaux 1920: 68, 72–3; Allain 1981: 126–8; Forcade 1998: 481–4; Mock 1972: 185–6.
188 Demm 2002d: 365–6; Newton 2002: 16–18.
189 Deist 1970: 406–13; Stibbe 2001: 143.
190 Stibbe 2001: 143–57.
191 Deist 1970: 149.
192 Gutsche 1973: 202; Gerlach 1994: 137–9; Deist 1970: 782.
193 Gatrell 2005: 102.

Chapter 2

1 Quoted after Strachan 2001: 1115.
2 Demm and Sterling 2005: 941.
3 Beaupré 2014: 450; Schumann 1996: 222; Robb 2002: 145.
4 Raithel 1996: 276.
5 Becker 1977; Kruse 1991: 73–5; Raithel 1996: 235–40, 274–7; Watson 2008: 45.
6 Buchner 1930: 22.
7 Lerouge 2004: 38 (1st quote); Altrichter 1933: 122–3; Strachan 1996: 393–4, 393 (last quote); Winter 1988: 29; Buchner 1930: 22, 25.
8 Scott 1921: 131 (quote); Gooch 1996: 435; Corner and Procacci 1997: 223–40; Janz 2010: 201–2; Gatti 2008a: 281; Candeloro 1978: 164; Bazzanella 1980: 334–9.
9 Demm 2002e: 31 (quote); Robb 2002: 96.
10 Schwabe 1969; Bruendel 2003; Albes 1996: 251.
11 Schwalbe 1937: 9.
12 Taylor Allen 1984: 9–11; Demm 2018f: 321–3; Demm 2002e: 30–1.
13 Demm 2018f: 321 (also quote).
14 Demm 2018f: 321–2.
15 Weise 2004: 15 (quote).
16 Weise 2004: 29.
17 Schulte Strathaus 1938: 49.
18 Le Naour 2001: 266.
19 Schulte Strathaus 1938: 34–5 (quote).
20 Schulte Strathaus: 3.
21 *Weltspiegel,* 6 June 1916; Scheidemann on 9 November 1919.
22 Deist 1970: 337–8, 348–9; Kestler 1994: 39–46; Maurer 2015: 619.
23 Marwick 1991: 85.
24 Huber 1928: 26–51; Koch 2015: 51–2.
25 Tumanova 2014: 345–70.
26 Forcade 2004b: 458.
27 This chapter is based on Cook 1920; Sanders and Taylor 1982; Deist 1970; Stegmann 1972; Creutz 1996; Wilke 1997; Montant 1989, vol. 2: 177–330; Forcade 2004a: 35–47; Sorrie 2014; Cornwall 2000; Cornwall 2016: 408–35; Pisa 2015; Medyakov 2014; Squire 1935; Wells 2014.
28 Stites 1999: 9
29 Waltz and Tonnelat 1922: 11–16.
30 Mai 1977: 207–9, 211–13.
31 Cornwall 1997: 180 (quote); Cornwall 2016: 408, 415–17.
32 Mock and Larson 1968: 92; Wells 2014.

Chapter 3

1 Pressel 1967: 110, 120–2, 132–4, 211–15; Monger 2012: 95 and Hammer 1971: 325 (1st quote), 107, 126, 292; Kellermann 1915: 393–4; Senin 1993: 47; Graham 1917: 32 (last quote).
2 Pressel 1967: 110, 120–2, 132–5, 211–14; Seeber 1991: 235; Monger 2012: 95, 107, 126; Kellermann 1915: 393–4; Senin 1993: 47; Mommsen 2004: 170, 177; Gerlach

1994: 53–5; Hammer 1971: 292; Strachan 2001: 1115–17; Gatti 2008a: 284; Fuchs 2004: 305.

3 Pressel 1967: 177–87, 120 (quote); Weber 1989: 490; Mensching 1968: 34.
4 Hochschild 2011: 151 (quote).
5 Fuchs 2004: 305; Healy 2004: 127–9; Buchner 1930: 47.
6 Gregory 2008: 152–3.
7 Frevert and Schmidt 2011: 18–20; Demm 2002e: 43–4.
8 Rebentisch 2000: 204.
9 See also Rebentisch 2000: 207; Nolan 2004: 60 (quote); Schramm 2007: 383, 393, 413; Demm 2018a: 361.
10 Demm 1988: no. 31.
11 Sombart 1915; Demm 1988: no. 366.
12 Demm 1988: nos 53, 45.
13 Roshwald and Stites 1999b: 349; Kestler 1994: 128.
14 Demm 1988: no. 63; Überegger 2015: 275.
15 Gerlach 1994: 107–8; Jeismann 1992: 336; Demm 2002c: 18.
16 Weber 1999c: 182–6; Hartwagner 1942: 127; Schwabe 1969: 31; Demm 1988: no. 4.
17 Schulte Strathaus 1938: 131 (quote); Demm 1988: nos 176, 198.
18 APP, BA 773, fol. 3052, 29 July 1917; Krivanec 2012: 107; Demm 1988: nos 111, 187; Demm 2018a: 361.
19 Demm 1988: no. 368.
20 Courmont 2010: 38; Jeismann 1992: 350–2.
21 Orzoff 2004: 175.
22 Hartwagner 1942: 161.
23 Williams 1972: 32; Stibbe 2001: 18.
24 Times History 1916, VI: 243; 1917, XII: 231.
25 Author's translation; Johann 1973: 34–5; Stibbe 2001: 22.
26 Zweig 2001: 266.
27 Rickards 1968: 178.
28 Weber 1999b: 160; Schwabe 1969: 290; Demm 1988: no. 8; Demm 2002c: 19.
29 Sombart 1915; Stibbe 2001: 76–8; Demm 2000c: 118–19; Herf 1984: 130–51.
30 Horne and Kramer 2001; Horne 2014: 569–70.
31 Rolland 1983: I, 58 (1st quote); Winter 2014: 225 (2nd quote).
32 Ungern-Sternberg and Ungern-Sternberg 2013; Ungern-Sternberg 2016; Kellermann 1915: 86–99; Maurer 2013: 168–70; Maurer 2015: 264–73; Rasmussen 2014: 197–9; Schwabe 1969: 19–21; Read 1941: 76.
33 Wilson 1979: 371.
34 Bryce 1915: 5 (quote), 6–7.
35 Wilson 1979: 372–4; Knightley 2002: 88.
36 Welch 2014: 66.
37 Read 1941: 146–8; Horne 2014: 577.
38 Escudier and Richepin 1916; Schulte Strathaus 1938: 91–3; Demm 2016: 473.
39 Horne and Kramer 2001: 229–61; Horne 2014: 569–71; Peterson 1968: 53–5; Blücher 1920: 39; Demm 2018d: 351–4; Spraul 2016; Scianna 2017.
40 Zweig 2001: 275.
41 Greenhill 2008; Schramm 2007: 319–21, 385; Axelrod 2009: 57.
42 Hull 2014: 104–5; Read 1941: 210–12; www.wikipedia.org/wiki/Edith_Cavell.
43 Times History 1916,VI: 431 (quote); Beitin 2000: 277–9; Museum 2014: nos 85, 86; Robb 2002: 103.

44 Panayi 1989: 184–203; Robb 2002: 9.

45 Liulevicius 2000: 63–9; Schaepdrijver 2014: 111–13, 229–49; Rivas 1918; Read 1941: 168–70.

46 Read 1941: 178–82.

47 Kiefer 1999: 121–31, 131 (quote).

48 Rickards 1968: no. 180.

49 Topitsch 2000: 59–61; Demm 1988: nos 105, 114.

50 Avenarius 1918: 68–94; Demm 1988: nos 110, 200.

51 Zislin 1916.

52 Schulz-Besser 1915: 101–3.

53 'Cannon-Fodder – and after' by Leonard Raven-Hill, *Punch*, 25 April 1917: 267; Zislin 1916: 3.

54 Demm 1988: nos 381, 383.

55 Wood 1990: doc. 61.

56 Demm 1988: nos 15, 17–20, 21, 23, 27, 151, 345; cf. Demm 2018d: 346, 356 (ill.); Museum 2014: nos 90–6; Klemperer 1989: 238; Rebentisch 2000: 211–13.

57 Rebentisch 2000: 223.

58 Avenarius 1918; Schulte Strathaus 1938: 90–3; Topitsch 2000: 72.

59 Topitsch 2000: 74.

60 Avenarius 1918: 7–47.

61 Kaplan 2000: 95.

62 Horne 1994: 135–7; Kaplan 2000: 98–9, 111–13; Avenarius 1918: 158–66.

63 Demm 1988: no. 333 (quote).

64 Rebentisch 2000: 209–11, 220–3; Jahn 1995: 12–29; Demm 1988: nos 333, 326, 379; Rickards 1968: no. 65; Schramm 2007: 556, 560; Museum 2014: no. 43; Beaupré 2006: 156–9; Hirschfeld and Gaspar 1982: 512–13; Pisa 2015.

65 Schramm 2007: 418–20.

66 Beaupré 2006: 156–9; Demm 1988: nos 45, 326, 327; owl: Times History 1916, IV: 373.

67 Holzer 2008: 66–75, 112–17; Read 1941: 163; Überegger 2008: 269–71; Opfer-Klinger 2008: 285–6.

68 Wanderscheck 1936: 17.

69 Baralong Incidents, Zeppelin LZ 54: Wikipedia; Kestler 1994: 129.

70 Times History 1918, XVII: 377–8.

71 Kramer 1994: 151; Paddock 2004a: 124; Kessel 2008: 205; Demm 1988: nos 127, 128; Bernard Partridge: 'The Triumph of Culture', *Punch*, 23 August 1915.

72 Watson 2008: 793, 819.

73 Read 1941: 44, 48, 62, 78–80, 112–14, 136–9; Maß 2001: 22 (quote); Véray 2014: 488–90; Hirschfeld and Gaspar 1982: 508; Demm 1988: nos 127–8, 338–40, 342; Knightley 2002: 87, note ***.

74 Demm 1988: nos 340, 342, 339, 198, 197.

75 Demm 1988: nos 338, 341.

76 Times History 1917, XIII: 87.

77 Read 1941: 109, 131; Bernstorff 1920: 53, 259–60; Deist 1970: 159, 266; Huber 1928: 80.

78 Hirschfeld and Gaspar 1982: 404, 414–19; Knightley 2002: 86.

79 Lasswell 1971: 32–3 (quote); Read 1941: 215.

80 Véray 2014: 481; Demm 1988: nos 115, 116, 337; Lasswell 1971: 162; Demm 2018d: 349; Eisermann 2000, nos 103–5, pp.165–6.

81 Pignot 2012: 245–7.

82 Schulte Strathaus 1938: 119–20.

83 Schmidt 2006: 83–5, 113–14, 150–1, 156 (quote).

84 Afflerbach 2015a: 242, 250.

85 Isenghi 1977: 158–9.

86 Afflerbach 2015a: 247; Chickering 2015: 98.

87 Le Bon 1915: 291.

88 Blücher 1920: 117; Rolland 1983: II, 217.

89 Graham 1917: 74.

90 Holzer 2008: 66–75, 112–17; Leidinger 2014b: 161–2.

91 Holzer 2008: 124; Haste 1977: 87.

92 Sassoon 1931: 13.

93 Weinrich 2014: 665.

94 Marwick 1991: 258 (quote); Hochschild 2011: 149, 224–5.

95 Pyta 2007: 138, 150.

96 Pyta 2007: 120–50; Goltz 2010: 37–40, 45–8; Hoegen 2007: 77–9, 85, 94, 142–4,
    147–9; Museum 2014: no. 99; Rebentisch 2000: 128; Demm 1988: no. 32.

97 Goltz 2010: 39.

98 Ducatel 1978: 66.

99 Mann 1991: 34.

100 Nolan 2004: 58.

101 Überegger 2015: 274.

102 Véray 2014: 495; Demm 1988: no. 144.

103 Musner 2013: 523–5.

104 Kennan 1964: 52–3.

105 Véray 2014: 495.

106 Winter and Robert 2012a: 472–3.

107 Roukes 1997: 14–16, 120–2; cf. also Knieper 2002: 72–4 and Freud 1905: 933/1.

108 Cappiello: 'Le clownprince', *La Baïonnette*, 22 July 1915.

109 Demm 1988: no. 47.

110 Freud 1905: 933/6; Schneider 1988: 32; Schwalbe 1937: 9–11.

111 Demm 1988: no. 69.

112 Demm 1988: no. 2.

113 The other figures in the centre are from left to right: French General Joseph Joffre
    as a weightlifter with two hollow weights; Prime Minister David Lloyd George with
    a big money bag and silver bullets; Former French Prime Minister René Viviani
    conjuring a laurel wreath out of a hat; French President Raymond Poincaré holding
    back the Japanese ally who tries to run away.

114 The other figures from the left to the right: Alfred von Tirpitz, German Grand
    Admiral and until March 1916 Secretary of State of the Imperial Naval Office,
    singing the hymn of hate (see p. 37) under water; Tsar Ferdinand of Bulgaria,
    ironically called 'fearless Ferdie' because he hastily left Sofia after a British bomb
    attack; German Crown Prince Wilhelm as 'little Willie'; Sultan Mehmed V of Turkey
    as a weary tramp cyclist; Count Ferdinand von Zeppelin as Zeppelino, inventor of
    the Zeppelin air ships which bombarded British cities; King Constantin of Greece
    as Tino keeping his balance between Germany and the Allies; in June 1917 he was
    forced by the Entente to abdicate.

115 Demm 1988: nos 67–8, 129–31.

116 Demm 1988: no. 123.

117 Demm 1988: no. 286.

118 Demm 1988: nos 289–91.
119 Demm 1988: nos 191–3.
120 Stoff 2006: 30–2; Higonnet 2014: 144–6; Hirschfeld and Gaspar 1982: 195–7; Stockdale 2004: 84–5, 93–102.
121 Demm 1988: nos 101–4.
122 Demm 1988: no. 8.
123 Jahn 1995: 12–14, 29–31, 143–5, 158–61.
124 Gibelli 1999: 135.
125 Bir et al. 2000: 370–1.
126 Hewitson 2012: 216 (1st quote); Freud 1905: 933/2 (2nd quote); Le Naour 2001: 267–8.
127 Demm 1988: no. 166.
128 'Per la limitazione di consumi', BDIC, 4 Δ 0394.
129 For the following, see Deist 1970: 289–99; Mai 1977; Müller 1986.
130 *Freiburger Tagespost*, 6 August 1914, quoted after Geinitz and Hinz 1997: 29.
131 Altenhöner 2008: 194; Buchner 1930: 17.
132 Strachan 2001: 106; Altenhöner 2008: 200.
133 Williams 1972: 21.
134 Lohr 2003: 24–9.
135 Collins 2004: 183, 191; Robb 2002: 134–5, 168.
136 Jahn 1995: 160; Gibelli 1999: 224.
137 Ward 1981: 53–4.
138 Gerlach 1994: 29–31, 38.
139 Gerlach 1994: 38; Blücher 1920: 10 (quote).
140 Gulbransson 2001: 195–200.
141 Mihaly 1986: 19.
142 Pourcher 1994: 54; Bavendamm 2004: 66; Lerouge 2004: 40; Spears 1968: 537.
143 Panayi 2014: 221–9; Schramm 2007: 37–9; Healy 2004: 214; Altenhöner 2008: 192–5; Demm 1988: nos 312–13; Bavendamm 2004: 53–4; Robb 2002: 9; Lohr 2003: 31–4; Gatrell 2005: 180.
144 Robb 2002: 9.
145 Lohr 2003: 24–6, 31–3; Gatrell 2005: 180; Lohr 2004: 99; Tumanova 2014: 352–8.
146 Geinitz and Hinz 1997: 29–30.
147 Hiley 2007: 157–8; Demm 1988: nos 305, 300.
148 Waites 1987: 224.
149 Robert 1997: 117–18.
150 Demm 1988: no. 273.
151 Darmon 2002: 205–8; Bouloc 2008: 336–40; Gregory 2008: 136–9.
152 Healy 2004: 66–7.
153 Bir et al. 2000: 344; Deist 1970: 321.
154 Demm 1988: nos 295, 297.
155 Collins 2004: 200–1.
156 Ceadel 2014: 576–8; Kriegel 1964: 217–19; Demm 1988: nos 247, 249, 260–3.
157 Demm 1988: no. 265.
158 Ceadel 2014: 605.
159 Demm 2018a: 371.
160 Williams 1972: 201–2, 248, 262; Pourcher 1994: 210–12, 231–4.
161 Monger 2012: 114–16; Gregory 2008: 235–41; Wilson 1988: 741 (quotes); Bush 1984: 74; Hochschild 2011: 291; Robb 2002: 8–9; Williams 2005: 193.

162 Sombart 1915: 3 (1st quote); Troeltsch 1915: 209 (2nd quote); Lübbe 1969: 229; Demm 2002c.

163 Kellermann 1915: 302, 322–3; Demm 2018d: 345–6 (quotes).

164 Lasswell 1971: 216; Kellermann 1915; Thimme 1932; Monger 2012: 140–60.

165 Demm 2018a: 362.

166 Roshwald and Stites 1999b: 352.

167 Wells 1914; Demm 2002c: 7.

168 Mann 1968; cf. Demm 2000b: 211.

169 Ungern-Sternberg 2016; Demm 2002c: 15–16 (quotes).

170 Verhey 2000: 326.

171 Demm 1988: nos 43, 46, 51.

172 Thimme 1932: 235–42; Demm 2002e: 43 (1st quotes); Demm 2002c: 22–4; Demm 1998: 116–19.

173 Rossini 2008: 69; Lasswell 1971: 216 (quote); Messinger 1992: 21.

174 Demm 1988: nos 328, 334.

175 Orzoff 2004: 171–2; Demm 1988: no. 331.

176 Jahn 1995: 142; Vescovo 2008: 227; Frey 2003: 106–8.

177 Huber 1928: 92; Demm 1988: no. 370–1; Bub 1938: 99–100.

178 Jahn 1995: 142; Graham 1917: 31; Perreux 1966: 251; Gerlach 1994: 38–9; Proctor 2010: 80–1; Altenhöner 2008: 199; Williams 1972: 21, 33.

179 Jüllig 1994: 129; Demm 2002g: 63; Gerlach 1994: 39; Demm 1988: no. 373.

180 Sowerwine and Sowerwine1985 V, 6: 49.

181 Ridel 2014, ch. 3.2.

182 Gregory 2008: 69.

183 Burnett 1974: 117.

184 Rauchensteiner 2014: 127.

185 Paddock 2004a: 119.

186 Mombauer 2014: 96.

187 Fuchs 2004: 300; Loez 2014; Rickards 1968: no. 41, 43–5, 105, 108.

188 Winter 1991: 91 (quote); Monger 2012: 93; Cornwall 1997: 185–7; Oldenburg-Januschau 1936: 126; Audoin-Rouzeau 1992: 182; Watson 2008: 50–2; Watson 2010: 146–64; Reimann 1997: 140–1.

189 Robb 2002: 172.

190 Rudolph 1997: 289.

191 Hammer 1971: 244, 323.

192 Cochet 1986: 496.

193 Gregory 2008: 69, 111, 153–7; Horne 1989; Watson and Porter 2010: 154–9.

194 Fuchs 2004: 305; Mommsen 2004: 168; Jahn 1995: 40; Monger 2012: 107; Hammer 1971: 318; Schweitzer 2003: 151; Millman 2000: 37.

195 Moreau 2016: 98.

196 Watson and Porter 2010: 148; Roccucci 2007: 123.

197 Monger 2012: 94–6; Gregory 2008: 108–12.

198 Moule 1917: 41.

199 Gregory 2008: 152–7; Pressel 1967: 202–5.

200 Bessel 1997: 215.

201 Reutter and Reichardt 1914: 24.

202 Welch 2014: 27–8; Schramm 2007: 359; Rickards 1968, nos 25, 53, 85–6, 95, 105, 197; Ostermann 2000: 133–5.

203 Becker 1986: 36–9.

204 Blücher 1920: 32.

205 *The Graphic* XCII, 3 July 1915: 5.
206 Demm 1988: no. 90.
207 Demm 1988: nos 21, 27; Hirschfeld and Gaspar 1982: 545.
208 Demm 1988: no 50.
209 Gregory 2008: 69.
210 Lasswell 1971: 102; Welch 2014: 27; Peterson 1968: 42–3.
211 Bethmann Hollweg 1921: 51.
212 Mondini 2014: 187.
213 Demm 1988: no. 253.
214 Bush 1984: 73 (quote); Watson and Porter 2010: 161–3.
215 Gankin and Fisher 1960: 681
216 Monger 2012: 94; Wells 1914; Cooper 1972: 88.
217 Eilers 2000: 182–6, 186 (quote).
218 Ludendorff 1921: 274; Mai 1977: 218.
219 Monger 2012: 95.
220 See also Buchner 1930: 159 (23 January 1917); Deist 1970: 817.
221 Watson 2015: 233, 489; Rickards 1968: no. 181 (quote).
222 Mai 1977: 215, 220, 228–9; 'Wenn sie siegten', leaflet, BDIC, 4 Δ 0399, 4 Δ 0154 (quote).
223 Koszyk 1968: 143.
224 Deist 1970: 970.
225 Sassoon 1931: 61.
226 Paveau 2005: 247–57; Rauchensteiner 2014: 941; e.g. Times History 1917, X: 1–40; XII: 153–92, XIII: 361–96; 1918, XV: 217–52; XVI: 361–96, XVII: 397–432, 402 (quote); Bulletin nos 60–3.
227 Ridel 2007: 29.
228 Bruendel 2014; Shackelford 1998.
229 Graves 1929: 243; Robb 2002: 116; Gregory 2008: 153–7; Donson 2010: 99.
230 Procacci 1989: 54; Pisa 2015; Robb 2002: 120 (quote); https://en.wikipedia.org/wiki/Christopher_ Addison,_1st_Viscount_Addison#World_War.
231 Verhey 2000: 326; Monger 2012: 93, 199 (quote), 209; Gregory 2008: 177; Robb 2002: 73; Überegger 2015: 272.
232 Demm 2002c: 19–22; Demm 2009: 94; Bruendel 2003: 258–60; Monger 2012: 199, 207 (quote); Robb 2002: 80, 104; Magri 1997: 374–418.
233 RTP, 13 Leg., 1914/18, 4, 81st session, 27 February 1917: 2375 C, B.
234 Bihl 1992: nos 131, 147; 'Das gleiche Wahlrecht für Preußen', *BT* no. 350, 12 July 1917.
235 Monger 2012: 96; Rossini 2008: 64–9; Roccucci 2007: 121, 127.
236 Creel 1920: 299–301.
237 Ostermann 2000: 117; Albes 1996: 175, 185; Ponce 2014: 299.

Chapter 4

1 Burnett 1974: 115.
2 This chapter is partially based on Albes 1996; Ostermann 2000; Sanders and Taylor 1982; Peterson 1968; Will 2012; Rossini 2008; Masaryk 1925; Wells 2014; Rickards 1968; Demm 2009; Stuart 1920; Deist 1970; Gregory 2008.
3 Healy 2004: 127.

4 Deutsche Reden 1915; Hearnshaw 1979: 460–2; Köroglu 2007: 6; Maurer 2015: 537–56.
5 Gregory 2008: 75–6.
6 Sanders and Taylor 1982: 15–17, 103–6; Gregory 2008: 75–7; Hochschild 2011: 150–1.
7 Pourcher 1994: 56, 168.
8 Zweig 1984: 83.
9 Ward 1981: 31.
10 Creel 1920: 84–94; Mock and Larson 1968: 113–30; Axelrod 2009: 113–25.
11 Creel 1920: 6, 148–55.
12 Albes 1996: 251.
13 Ostermann 2000: 333–5.
14 Peterson 1968: 142–3.
15 Köroglu 2007: 74; Will 2012: 195.
16 Creel 1920: 294 (quote), 295–300; Rossini 2008: 81–99; Rossini 2007a: 47–50.
17 Mock and Larson 1968: 251.
18 Müller 1986: 353; Millman 2000: 235.
19 Wilson 1988: 734; Monger 2011: 333, 346; Monger 2012; Millman 2000: 229–37.
20 Monger 2015: 511–12 (quote).
21 Cabanes 2004: 67; Véray 2014: 494; Horne 1997a: 199–201, 204; Monger 2011: 332–4, 334 (quote); Demm 1988: nos 389, 391–3.
22 Monger 2015: 524–6
23 Welch 2014: 217–18; Mai 1977: 213–17; Deist 1970: 806–21, 865–6, 809, note 16; Koch 2015: 89–90.
24 Deist 1970: 823, 831, 937–41.
25 Deist 1970: 806 (quote), 821, 865, 970; Mai 1977: 208, 214, 227; Müller 1986: 337, 346.
26 Demm 2002g: 69.
27 Demm 2002g: 61 (quote), 69; Buchner 1930: 145.
28 Goebel 2012b: 231.
29 Gatti 2000: 71–9, 129–30; Gatti 2008b: 299; Corner and Procacci 1997: 228–9; Fiori 2001: 107, 256, 344.
30 Thimme 1932: 52–118; Ernst 1933: 26–7; Deist 1970: 1179; Sanders and Taylor 1982: 214–16.
31 Demm 2002i: 188–90; Demm and Nikolajew 2013: 171–7.
32 Tosi 1977: 183; Masaryk 1925: 217; Stuart 1920: 206.
33 Gerlach 1994: 121–4 (quote).
34 Gerlach 1994: 125–7.
35 Sanders and Taylor 1982: 38–41; Hochschild 2011: 148; Robb 2002: 97.
36 Deist 1970: 343, 740, note 10, 807–8, 929.
37 Creel 1920: 8, 72, 224.
38 Wilson 1988: 737; Ward 1981: 29.
39 Knightley 2002: 92–4; Lindner-Wirsching 2006: 118.
40 Swinton 1940: 48–121.
41 Artinger 2000: 163.
42 Reeves 1999b: 30; Knightley 2002: 101–3; Lindner-Wirsching 2006: 118, 120–3.
43 Deist 1970: 867–9.
44 Džambo 2003a: 11–12, 19–21; Cornwall 2016: 408–10.
45 Knightley 2002: 122.
46 Fiori 2001: 319–40.
47 Creel 1920: 297.

48 Wilke 1997: 87–9, 94–7; Kestler 1994: 51–68; Montant 1989, vol. 2: 177–80, vol. 3: 409–25; Sanders and Taylor 1982: 38–43.

49 Albes 1996: 145–6, 392; Ostermann 2000: 332; Ponce 2014: 303–4; Demm and Nikolajew 2013: 260–3.

50 Sanders and Taylor 1982: 115.

51 Ostermann 2000: 155–6, 172, 333–5; Ponce 2014: 301–6; Albes 1996: 93–5, 145–6, 166–7, 189, 390–2, 397.

52 Ostermann 2000: 113, 247–8.

53 Albes 1996: 145; Demm 2002i: 175–6, 244.

54 Albes 1996: 190.

55 Albes 1996: 190; Ponce 2014: 303.

56 Fischer 1984: 130, note 81; Montant 1989, vol. 7: 1512.

57 Creel 1920: 11–12, 297–299.

58 Montant 1980; Montant 1989, vol. 7: 1416–44.

59 Ostermann 2000: 140, 286–399.

60 This section is based on Sanders and Taylor 1982: 168–72; Squire 1935: 45, 51, 65; Peterson 1968: 14, 17–18, 29–30, 151–7; Fulwider 2016: 51–75, 98–105, 122, 129–31.

61 Fulwider 2016: 168 (quote).

62 Dernburg [1914–15]: 21, 24.

63 Seymour 1926: II, 49.

64 'Die deutsche Presse über das Friedensangebot', *BT* no. 638, 13 December 1916; Scott 1921: 2–3; Kirchner 2014: 71, 79–88 (1917); Therstappen 2008: 89.

65 Scott 1921: 26–8, 27 (quote); 'Un piège diplomatique', *Le Temps* no. 20240, 14 December 1916; 'La manœuvre allemande pour diviser les Alliés', *Les Echos* no. 11807, 13 December 1916; Bavendamm 2004: 184.

66 Soutou 1917: ch. 8 (quote); Afflerbach 2015a: 250, 253.

67 Afflerbach 2015a: 249–50; Chickering 2015: 111.

68 Czernin 1919: 186.

69 Afflerbach 2015a: 253.

70 Ludendorff 1919: 4.

71 'Die Berliner Presse zur Antwort des Vierverbandes', *BT* no. 1, 2 January 1917.

72 This paragraph is based on Maier 1983: 47–87; Demm 2002d [1990!]: 365–79; Max von Baden 1968: 188–207, 225–67; Max von Baden papers available recently in the GLA.

73 Lansdowne: 'Coordination of Allies war aims', in: *Daily Telegraph*, 29 November 1917.

74 *Verhandlungen* 1918: 8–12; Max von Baden 1968: 192.

75 Prince Max Papers GLA FN A 5552, 6–7, quote retranslated from the German.

76 Wilson 1970: 324.

77 Scott 1921: 225–33; Newton 2002: 16–39, did not consult the fundamental article by Maier 1983, mentioned Demm 2002d [1990] en passant but does not seem to have read it.

78 PDHC 1917–1918, 5th series, vol. 103: 72–3, 143–4, 221 (quote).

79 Wils 2015: 229; RTP 1914/18, 6, 133rd session, 25 February 1918: 4041B–4141B.

80 Lansdowne: 'Lord Lansdowne and Count Hertling', in: *Daily Telegraph*, 5 March 1918: 7–8.

81 RTP 1914/18, 6, 142nd session, 18 March 1918: 4425A–4426A; Max von Baden 1968: 252.

82 Robbins 1976: 150–62.

83 Scott 1921: 296–7, 354–7, 386–97; Kirchner 2014: 182–4.
84 Deist 1970: 329–30, 350, 808.
85 Buchner 1930: 65–6.
86 Albes 1996: 134–5, 151–3; Ostermann 2000: 102; Peterson 1968: 19–30; Sanders and Taylor 1982: 36, 42–3.
87 Masaryk 1925: 85; Albes 1996: 397.
88 Albes 1996: 93–4.
89 Welch 2014: 24–5.
90 Kestler 1994: 29.
91 Rolland 1983: II, 228–9 (16 May 1916).
92 Montant 1968: 66–78 and appendices; 'Propagande germanophile', BDIC, 4 Δ 1543; Cornwall 2000: 175; Thimme 1932: 52–101.
93 Thimme 1932: 55–8; Kirchner 1992: 282 (1918); Ostermann 2000: 231–3; Ernst 1933: 26–30; Beneš 1928: 48–9; Koch 2015: 163.
94 Koch 2015: 150.
95 Thimme 1932: 65–101; Waltz and Tonnelat 1922: 16–18, 38–40; Ernst 1933: 8–9, 30; Huber 1928: 149; Buchner 1930: 64 (8 February 1915), 138 (8 July 1916), 166 (25 March 1917), 172 (30 April 1917), 179 (21 June 1917), 198 (26 September 1917); Lehmann-Russbüldt 1927: 46; Zuckmayer 1966: 272.
96 Will 2012: 212.
97 Creel 1920: 190.
98 Elizalde 2007: 30–1, 34–5.

Chapter 5

1 Robb 2002: 96; various articles in: Zühlke 2000.
2 I follow Peterson 1968, Sanders and Taylor 1982, Ponsonby 1928 and Holzer 2007.
3 Holzer 2007: 35–6 (quote).
4 Kiefer 1999: 116.
5 Ponsonby 1928: 21, 135–9; Peterson 1968: 240; Lasswell 1971: 206; Read 1941: 14; Wanderscheck 1940: part 6, p. 2.
6 Avenarius 1918; Koch 2015: 188–9.
7 Eisermann 2000: 253–7, nos 60, 62, 97, 99; Beurier 2008: 302.
8 Eisermann 2000: 141–3, nos 141, 92–4, 145–7, nos 66–9, 148–50 and photo no. 59; 246.
9 Beurier 2008: 318–21, 311, 296, 298 (quote); Eisermann 2000: 234–5.
10 Artinger 2000: 164–5; Eisermann 2000: 134–6, nos 84–5; *The Graphic* XCII, 4 September and 16 October 1915: 309, 487; *Weltspiegel* no. 97, 3 December 1916; Dewitz 1994: 175.
11 Artinger 2000: 158–9, plate 36.
12 Eisermann 2000: 137, nos 86–8; 'rolls of honour' in each issue of *The Graphic*.
13 Noll 1994: 263–71, with a striking example: 266; Lindner-Wirsching 2006: 124; Holzer 2013: 489.
14 Malvern 2004: 13, 25–7, ill. 16–18.
15 Malvern 2004: 18–21; Fox 2015: 105–7, plate 2 and fig. 4.9.
16 Artinger 2000: 86, 92, 95–6, 125–8, 127 (quote), 135, 260–1.

17 Robichon 1994: 287–97; Becker 2014: 512–14; Weight 1994: 276–83; Steinlen 1978: 229–55; Artinger 2000: 206–7.
18 Artinger 2000: 169–70, 195–209; Cornwall 2016: 417–18.
19 Artinger 2000: 225–9; Goebel et al. 2012a: 176–7; Malvern 2004: 50–2.
20 Artinger 2000: 135, 260–1.
21 Malvern 2004: 69–90.
22 This paragraph is based on Metken 1994, Flemming 2007, Brocks 2008, Pust 2008a.
23 Row 2002: fig. 26–7.
24 Holzer 2013: 488–9.
25 Pust 2008b.
26 Denscher 2013: 495; Creel 1920: 133.
27 Creel 1920: 138; Wells 2014; Fox 2015: 70; Hiley 1990: 177 (quote).
28 I follow Rickards 1968, Museum 2014, Hiley 1997, Denscher 2013 and Smith 2008.
29 Museum 2014: nos 35, 37; Hiley 1997: 44–5; Rickards 1968: nos 6, 14.
30 Smith 2008: 229–31; Rickards 1968: 39.
31 Witkop 1933: 7 (quote); Ulrich 1995: 113.
32 Watson 2008: 51.
33 Kessel 2012: 82.
34 Schulte Strathaus 1938: 26.
35 Hiley 2007: 148.
36 Calculated after Schwalbe 1937: 39, I have added the circulation of *Ulk* (250,000); Hewitson 2012: 218.
37 www.punch.co.uk./about/ retrieved 8 August 2016; Krollpfeiffer 1935: 42; Hartwagner 1942: 64–5, 72.
38 Hartwagner 1942: 96; Schulte Strathaus 1938: 39; Topitsch 2000: 72; Le Naour 2001: 266.
39 Ranitz 2014: 142, 166; Hartwagner 1942: 101–2.
40 Hartwagner 1942: 97–9; Ranitz 2014: 130–4, 172–3.
41 Navet 1994: 35; Navet 2000: 7 (quote).
42 Demm 1988: nos 212, 215, 221, 224–7, 231.
43 Weise 2004: 185–9; Hartwagner 1942: 62–3; Weber 1981: 73–82; Kessel 2012: 83.
44 Stibbe 2001: 45; Kessel 2012: 86.
45 Ranitz 2014: 154–6.
46 Hiley 2007: 164.
47 Ranitz 2014: 200, note 107 (quote); Creel 1920: 226; Mock and Larson 1968:108–9.
48 Ranitz 2004: 96–7; Albert Hahn, 'Zijns meesters stem', *Notenkraker* no. 11, 5 May 1917: 8, Demm 1988: no. 323.
49 Kessel 2008: 199–201; Kessel 2012: 82; Hiley 2007: 148–50, 155.
50 Scheler 1917: 402.
51 Hiley 2007: 155, 160.
52 The exception: 'The Triumph of Culture' by Bernard Partridge, *Punch* 23 August 1915, see Topitsch 2000: 53–4.
53 Ranitz 2014: 126–8; Hiley 2007: 168–73.
54 Demm 1988: no. 236.
55 Demm 1988: nos 203–5; further examples Demm 1988: nos 147–8, 326, 328.
56 See for instance 'Nouvelle Armée du Salut', *Europe antiprussienne*, 20 February 1915 (reprint of an American cartoon), Demm 1988: no. 335.
57 Demm 1988: nos 185–6.

58 'Elles tiendront' by Léonnec, *La Baïonnette* no. 124, 15 November 1917: 728–9.

59 'Les femmes aux urnes', *Le Canard enchaîné* 2, no. 35, 28 February 1917.

60 LAB, A. Pr. Br. Rep. 030–05–02, no. 6146; Baumeister 2005: 152–5.

61 Schwalbe 1937: 47.

62 The chapter is based on APP, BA 770–782; LAB, A. Pr. Br. Rep. 030–05, Th 28, Theaterzensur 1913–1930; Baumeister 2005, Krivanec 2012, Krakovitch 1991, Joseph 2000.

63 Robb 2002: 134–5; Collins 2004: 189–90.

64 Collins 2004: 189–91; *The Graphic* XCII: 94 (quotes).

65 Collins 2004: 183–92, 214–15, 221; Williams 2005: 8 (quote), 11.

66 APP, BA 770: 80, BA 773: 3052, 3090, BA 787: 1006.

67 APP, BA 771: 960, 1010; BA 773: 3090; BA 787: 1021, 1035, Rip (Georges G. Thénon), L'école des civils, BA 822.

68 Krivanec 2012: 160.

69 Otto Reutter and Max Reichardt, '1914', in: LAB, A PR. BR. Rep. 030–05–02, no. 6049; Baumeister 2005: 69–71, 111, 126–8, 150–2; Jüllig 1994: 126–8; Krivanec 2012: 158–60; *La revue tricolore*, APP, BA 770.

70 APP, BA 771: 56, 1086; Stark 2009: 108–9.

71 Rüger et al. 2012: 125.

72 Baumeister 2005: 61–9, 61 (quote); Jüllig 1994: 128; Collins 2004: 7.

73 Krivanec 2012: 95–7, 139–41.

74 Krivanec 2012: 97–8.

75 Krivanec 2012: 149–50.

76 Joseph 2000: 27–8 (quotes), 35; Krakovitch 1991: 343; APP, BA 787: Les adieux de Marie-Louise; APP, BA 770: 70.

77 APP, BA 822, Rip, BA 840: Les sult-âneries, BA 841: 1006; Krivanec 2012: 236–8, 245–6.

78 Joseph 2000: 35.

79 https://archive.org/details/immerfestedruffv00koll, retrieved 22 December 2015; Krivanec 2012: 117, 230–1; Rüger et al. 2012: 135–6.

80 Williams 2005: 193 (quote).

81 Collins 2004: 192.

82 Rip 1915.

83 APP, BA 822.

84 Baumeister 2005: 147–65; Krivanec 2012: 248–50.

85 LAB: A Pr. Br. Rep. 030–05–02, nos 6049 and 6787; Rüger et al. 2012: 134 (1st quote) Baumeister 2005: 163–7 (2nd quote)

86 Baumeister 2005: 185–7; Krivanec 2012: 258–9, 293–4.

87 Baumeister 2005: 269–90; Artinger 2000: 153–5.

88 Baumeister 2005: 134, 140–2; Jüllig 1994: 134; Goebel 2014: 369; Jahn 1995: 143; Krivanec 2012: 187–90.

89 Herzfeldtheater to Abteilung VIII, 9 December 1914, LAB, A. Pr. Br. Rep. 030–05, no. 779, fol. 240.

90 Robb 2002: 135; Collins 2004: 212.

91 Krivanec 2012: tables nos 30–5.

92 Sanders and Taylor 1982: 124 (quote).

93 Wilson 1988: 737 (quote); Reeves 1999a: 23; Jeancolas 1994: 227–8.

94 This chapter is based on Winter 1999, Welch 2014, Bir et al. 2000, Oppelt 2002, Véray 1994, Véray 2014, Jahn 1995, Hiley 1994, Ballhausen and Kren 2003, Baumeister 2005, Jelavich 1999, Jeancolas 1994, Rother 1994b, Demm 2018a, Sorlin 1999, Sanders and Taylor 1982.
95 Véray 2014: 477; Sorlin 1999: 121.
96 Sanders and Taylor 1982: 123–30.
97 Jelavich 1999: 39 (quote); Welch 2014: 56; Bir et al. 2000: 335, 355–6; Rother 1994a: 199; Vitelleschi 1999: 163; Sorlin 1999: 120; Jeancolas 1994: 229; http://www.earlycinema.uni-koeln.de/films/view/25754 and 29518.
98 Vitelleschi 1999: 164.
99 Gibelli 1999: 225; Faccioli 2008: 871; Vitelleschi 1999: 163.
100 Faccioli 2008: 872; Bir et al. 2000: 350–2; Sorlin 1994: 239; Vitelleschi 1999: 165–7.
101 Jahn 1995: 155–62, 157 (quote); Gatrell 2005: 88.
102 Bir et al. 2000: 341–4; Hiley 1994: 219–21; Paris 2014; Véray 2014: 490; Reeves 1999b: 35–7; Hochschild 2011: 226–7.
103 Vitelleschi 1999: 162–3.
104 Bir et al. 2000: 352–3; Sorlin 1999: 122; Faccioli 2008: 874; Reeves 1999b: 41 (quote); Vitelleschi 1999: 164.
105 Véray 2014: 478; Faccioli 2008: 874.
106 Creel 1920: 120–8.
107 Wilson 1988: 737–8.
108 Sorlin 1999: 123; Véray 2014: 478 (quote), 494; Vitelleschi 1999: 164.
109 Bir et al. 2000: 365; Millman 2000: 245 (quote).
110 Jahn 1995: 160–2.
111 Ward 1981: 36–9.
112 Véray 2014: 497; DeBauche 1999: 140, 143 (quote); Ward 1981: 53–6.
113 https://www.filmothek.bundesarchiv.de/video/580591?q=propaganda+first+world+war; Bub 1938: 98–9.
114 Bub 1938: 80.
115 Jelavich 1999: 37; Bir et al. 2000: 336–7; Toeplitz 1979: 137–8; Robb 2002: 85 (quote); Audoin-Rouzeau 1993a: 75.
116 Bub 1938: 78.
117 Petrone 1998: 100.
118 Jelavich 1999: 38; Bir et al. 2000: 341, 353, 364; Oppelt 2002: 144; Jahn 1995: 158; Rother 1994a: 200; Jeancolas 1994: 231; Sorlin 1999: 120; Gibelli 1999: 226–7.
119 Bub 1938: 91.
120 Leidinger 2014a: 324.
121 Toeplitz 1979: 154.
122 Hiley 1994: 218.
123 Holzer 2007: 40–2; Lindner-Wirsching 2006: 127–30; Schwarz 2013: 520.
124 Véray 2014: 477–80; Bub 1938: 95; Lindner-Wirsching 2006: 130–1; McKernan 2017.
125 McKernan 2017.
126 Healy 2004: 101.
127 Koerber 1994: 70–2, 133; Bub 1938: 96; Karlsch 1994: 161–3.
128 Bir et al. 2000: 365; Jeancolas 1994: 234; Véray 2014: 486–7; Holzer 2007: 41; Horne 1997a: 207; Reeves 1999b: 29; Hochschild 2011: 290.
129 Monger 2015: 514–18.

130 Rossini 2008: 98–9.
131 This chapter is based on Goebel et al. 2012a; Lange 2003; Beil 2004; Healy
     2004: 88–91, 107–21; Sommer 2013.
132 Artinger 2000: 153–5.
133 Brandt 1993: 249; Lange 2003: 89 (quote); Sommer 2013: 505.
134 Brandt 1993: 249; Goebel et al. 2102a: 147 (quote); Lange 2003: 17.
135 Museum 2014: 97 and no. 78; Rickards 1968: no. 154; Beurier 2008: 320; Perreux
     1966: 316; Goebel et al. 2012a: 151.
136 Artinger 2000: 199, 210, 225–6, 228; Goebel et al. 2012a: 167–8.
137 Tumanova 2014: 350.
138 Denscher 2013: 501.
139 Sonderausstellung 1915; Goebel et al. 2012b: 203, 230–1; Donson 2010: 66.
140 Goebel et al. 2012b: 231.
141 Creel 1920: 142–6.

Chapter 6

 1 Flemming and Ulrich 2014: 112.
 2 *DK* no. 60, 26 March 1917: 2; Jorio et al. 2008: 17.
 3 Bruendel 2010: 90; Vorsteher 1994: 160.
 4 Bub 1938: 99–100.
 5 Besier 1984: 147–8; APP, B A 771, fol. 1010; 787 (quote).
 6 Fox 2015: 63.
 7 Strachan 2004: 115–17; Ullmann 2014: 417–20.
 8 Renz and Sauvage 2008: 62.
 9 Deist 1970: 348–9; e.g. Kurth 1937: 14–15, 39; this and most of the following is based
    on Jorio et al. 2008, Kilian 2008 and Berg 2015.
10 Ulrich and Ziemann 2010: 139; Rauchensteiner 2014: 574–8; Koch 2015: 89–90.
11 Hammer 1971: 300.
12 Times History 1916, VII: 252.
13 Times History 1919, XVIII: 158–9; Collins 2004: 45, 221; Goebel et al. 2012b: 217,
    215 (quote), 216.
14 Monger 2015: 520–2.
15 Jorio et al. 2008.
16 Berg 2015: 12.
17 Bruendel 2010: 87.
18 Berg 2015: 9, 14.
19 Reichsbank 1916.
20 Müller 2008: 246; Collins 2011: 236; Buchner 1930: 96 (25 October 1915); Audoin-
    Rouzeau 1993a: 161–3; Healy 2004: 244; Rolland 1983: III, 392 (5 April 1918).
21 Buchner 1930: 121 (11 March 1916).
22 See also Buchner 1930: 133–4 (10 July 1916); Donson 2010: 110.
23 Gibelli 1999: 229.
24 Véray 2014: 484.
25 Buchner 1930: 96 (25 October 1915), 162 (19 February 1917, quote), 171 (30 April
    1917); Collins 2011: 78–9; Denscher 2013: 499.

26 Kennedy 2014: 125, 144; Audoin-Rouzeau 1993a: 160–3; Achs 2013: 424–5; Demm 2002h: 88–9; Hämmerle 1993: 195; Fava 1997: 62; Fava 1993: 187, 195; Goebel et al. 2012b: 215–17; Healy 2004: 244; Collins 2011: 167–8.

27 Collins 2011: 152–3.

28 Koszyk 1968: 140.

29 Bruendel 2010: 85–8.

30 The following analysis is mostly based on the collection of Rickards 1968.

31 Rickards 1968: nos 25–6, 30, 33, 35, 36, 38; Museum 2014: no. 153; Row 2002: fig. 16.

32 Rickards 1968: nos 28, 62, 72, 74, 75, 81, golden coin: nos 51 and 54; Bruendel 2010: 88–90; Museum 2014: nos 156–7.

33 Rickards 1968: nos 91, 93; Denscher 2013: 496.

34 Rickards 1968: nos 63–4; Artinger 2000: 177 with plate 37; Denscher 2013: 498 (quote).

35 See also Goltz 2010: 39–42; Hoegen 2007: 208–10; Vorsteher 1994: 161.

36 Rickards 1968: nos 5, 9, 29, 66, 86.

37 Rickards 1968: 67, 73.

38 Rickards 1968: nos 7, 10; Row 2002: fig. 17.

39 Rickards 1968: nos 20, 26, 29, 66, 69, 71, 80, 84, 160, 166, 175, 163, US: 33, 49, 50, 61, 73, 172, 174.

40 Rickards 1968: nos 5, 29, 36, 52, 186, 197, 223.

41 Rickards 1968: nos 29, 195.

42 Rickards 1968: nos 26, 68.

43 Véray 2014: 484.

44 Véray 2014: 485; Rother 1994a: 199, 205.

45 Vitelleschi 1999: 170.

46 Ward 1981: 49–52; Bir et al. 2000: 367–70; DeBauche 1999: 146.

47 Schneider 2013; Pust 2014: 211–24; Goebel et al. 2012a: 152–8.

48 Buchner 1930: 132 (29 May 1916); Mihaly 1986: 94.

49 Darmon 2002: 130; Museum 2014: no. 140.

50 Times History 1919, XVIII: 175–8.

51 Goebel et al. 2012a: 157–62, 161 (quote); Hochschild 2011: 290; Robb 2002: 110.

52 Bruendel 2010: 105.

53 Kilian 2008: 158; Berg 2015: 15.

54 Kilian 2008: 140, 156.

55 Gatti 2000: note 44 on p. 38 (quote).

56 Creel 1920: 180–1; Mock 1972: 121; Collins 2011: 152–3.

57 Times History 1919, XVIII: 161–3.

58 Rauchensteiner 2014: 574–8, 574 (quote).

59 I define children according to contemporary use as persons of up to 14 years of age. This chapter is a modified and extended version of Demm 2018g.

60 Key 1902: 261.

61 Christadler 1978.

62 Quoted after Lemmermann 1984: 272.

63 Düding 1986: 108; Watson 2008: 45; Schubert-Weller 1998: 25; Donson 2010: 53–5 (quote).

64 Bendick 1999: 66–70; Donson 2010: 47–8, 58.

65 Gerard 1998: 40, 45; Bendick 1999: 49–51; Amalvi 1998: 65 (quote).

66 Paris 2004: XIV, XVIII–XIX; Müller 2008: 242–3, 252.

67 The only reference in vol. 35, 1912–13: 107.

68 Gerard 1998: 42; Paris 2004: XVII; Watson 2008: 45–6; statistics in: *The Boy's Own Annual* 37, 1914–15: 713.

69 Achs 2013: 421; Kuprian and Mazohl-Wallnig 1998: 106, 108 (1st quote), 114–16, 120 (2nd quote).

70 Fava 1997: 67.

71 Audoin-Rouzeau 1993a: 24–5; Goebel et al. 2012b: 201; Kuprian and Mazohl-Wallnig 1998: 105, 107, 122; Donson 2010: 63; Kennedy 2014: 131; Corner and Procacci 1997: 227–9; Fava 1997: 54; Fava 1993: 147; Pisa 2015.

72 Arbeitsbericht 1920; Donson 2010: 181–3, 66; Demm 2002h: 75; Goebel et al. 2012b: 203.

73 GLA 235/16167/A 5230.

74 Welch 2014: 216, 245; Donson 2010: 184.

75 Collins 2011: 82–3; Creel 1920: 91–2, 111.

76 Donson 2010: 9; Pisa 2015; Corner and Procacci 1997: 227–8; Fava 1997: 54–7.

77 Audoin-Rouzeau 1997: 41.

78 Demm 2002g; Peureux 1972: 79–81.

79 Kennedy 2014: 133–5; Demm 2002h: 76; Demm 2002g: 62–6; Fava 1993: 182; Audoin-Rouzeau 1993a: 176–7.

80 Nipperdey 1986: 16–7; Kennedy 2014: 130; Donson 2010: 8.

81 Audoin-Rouzeau 1993a: 176; Zunino 2014: 321.

82 Witzenmann 1998: 47, 34, 19; Demm 2018b: 273.

83 Donson 2010: 81.

84 Zunino 2014: 322.

85 Kennedy 2014: 136; Collins 2011: 227–8.

86 Audoin-Rouzeau 1993a: 176.

87 Peureux 1972: 57; Rühlmann 1918: 103–4.

88 Peureux 1972: 92; Buchner 1930: 36 (24 September 1914); Collins 2011: 87.

89 Kluger 1993: 110; Fava 1997: 60; Demm 2002g: 65; Peureux 1972: 92.

90 Demm 2002g: 65; Audoin-Rouzeau 1993a: 83–5; Kennedy 2014: 131.

91 Gibelli 1999: 233–4.

92 Demm 2002g: 64–5.

93 Demm 2002g: 65 (quote).

94 Demm 2002g: 65–6, 68; Goebel et al. 2012b: 228–30; Donson 2010: 69; Kennedy 2014: 136; Audoin-Rouzeau 1997: 42; Fava 1997: 56; Lerouge 2004: 99–100, 185, 321; Gibelli 2014.

95 Mihaly 1986: 59.

96 Donson 2010: 116–18, 120, 198; Paris 2004: 27; Buchner 1930: 47, 90; Collins 2011: 101; Kennedy 2014: 104–6; Walker 2007; Peureux 1972: 115.

97 Liebknecht 1966: 535 (quote).

98 Hoffmann 1997: 331; Cohen 2002: 39–40; Audoin-Rouzeau 1993b: 160; Kennedy 2014: 51.

99 Mihaly 1986: 349.

100 Kennedy 2014: 51; Demm 2002h: 109; Hirschfeld and Gaspar 1982: 480; Buchner 1930: 29, 39, 76; Donson 2010: 171–2; Cohen 2002: 44; Audoin-Rouzeau 1993a: 158.

101 Donson 2010: 170.

102 Hoffmann 1997: 334; Müller 2008: 253.

103 Hoffmann 1997: 334; Müller 2008: 253; Paris 2004: 8–10; Zollinger 2013: 430–1.

104 Hoffmann 1997: 330.
105 Müller 2008: 237–42; Kennedy 2014: 62–4; Audoin-Rouzeau 1993a: 43–6.
106 Müller 2008: 237, 240.
107 Lemmermann 1984: 295–9; 295, 844 (quotes).
108 Kennedy 2014: 79 (quote), 134.
109 Lemmermann 1984: 333, 916.
110 Demm 2018a: 361, 368.
111 Buchner 1930: 19, 31, 45; Mann 2000: 68–9; Healy 2004: 223; Audoin-Rouzeau 1993a: 38–41.
112 Audoin-Rouzeau 1994: 175; Audoin-Rouzeau 1993a: 40–1; Briemle 1915; Laloux 2005.
113 Zunino 2014: 339 (quote).
114 Demm 2002h: 76–7; Audoin-Rouzeau 1993a: 52–5, 57–8.
115 Collins 2012; Kingsbury 2010: 169–217.
116 Collins 2011: 229–32, 237–6, 267 (quote).
117 Loparco 2011: 145, 193–7; Gibelli 1999: 230.
118 Kutzer 1915; Demm 2002h: 80–4; Zunino 2014: 207–15.
119 Demm 2002h: 79–81; Müller 2008: 244; Audoin-Rouzeau 1993a: 80–3, 85–7.
120 Demm 2002h: 81–2; Paris 2004: 65–7; Zunino 2014: 164–6; Robb 2002: 114.
121 Loparco 2011: 197.
122 Demm 2002h: 77; Zunino 2014: 152–4.
123 Demm 2002h: 82; Gellert 1915: 18 (quote).
124 Gellert 1915: 83; Donson 2010: 100.
125 Paris 2004: 39.
126 Müller 2008: 248; Kennedy 2014: 74–5; Paris 2004: 129–31; two late examples: 'Yaseen the Spy', *The Boy's Own Annual* 40, 1917–18, 605–9; 'The Flying Claws', no. 41, 1918–19, 361–4.
127 A.L. Haydon, 'For England and the Right. A Tale of War in Belgium', *The Boy's Own Annual* 37, 1914–15, 258 (quote).
128 Paris 2004: 129; Müller 2008: 247; Kennedy 2014: 76–7; Demm 2018a: 368–9; Zunino 2014: 343; Smith 2008: 233–8.
129 Audoin-Rouzeau 1993a: 70–2, 176; Paris 2004: 27; Donson 2014; Donson 2010: 90.
130 Demm 2002h: 84; Zunino 2014: 332–5, 347–50; Paris 2004: 127; *The Girl's Own Annual* 38, 1917, passim, 389.
131 Audoin-Rouzeau 1993a: 160–7; Donson 2014; Gibelli 2014; Pignot 2014; Demm 2002h: 85–6; Schumacher 1915: 54–6, 67, 79, 121.
132 Gibelli 1999: 228.
133 Gibelli 1999: 18–20, 176; Kennedy 2014: 144; Demm 2002h: 85; Pignot 2012: 83–4; Lemmermann 1984: 273–5; Collins 2011: 175–6; Gibelli 2014.
134 Collins 2008: 10.
135 Goebel et al. 2012b: 201 (quote).
136 Mostert 1918: 132 (quote).
137 Demm 2002h: 85; Zunino 2014: 335 (quote).
138 Audoin-Rouzeau 1993a: 163–5; Kennedy 2014: 83, 113, 120–1, 126; Demm 2002h: 85–7; Fava 1993: 181, 192; Collins 2011: 120–4; Goebel et al. 2012b: 218–22; Domonkos 1993: 83; Kluger 1993: 110; Bernard 1993: 144; Healy 2004: 75, 241–7; Kuprian and Mazohl-Wallnig 1998: 105.
139 Peureux 1972: 121.
140 Kennedy 2014: 83–7, 116, 123–6; Gibelli 2014; Times History 1918, XIV: 262, 279, 2 87.

141 Donson 2010: 95, 109–11, 123, 130–3; Demm 2002h: 85–8; Healy 2004: 75, 241–7; Rickards 1968: nos 217–22, 226, 232, 234, 236; Brenner 2013: 146.

142 Saul 1983: nos 32, 157.

143 Audoin-Rouzeau 1993a: 160–1.

144 Collins 2011: 47–8 (2nd quote), 175, 178–80, 237–8; Kingsbury 2010: 191 (1st quote), 195.

145 Fava 1993: 146, 191, 194–5; Kennedy 2014: 125; Demm 2002h: 88.

146 Rickards 1968: nos 44, 47, 49, 56–7, 60, 137–41, 143, 175, 220, 226–7, 229; Paddock 2014: 10; Gibelli 2014.

147 Creel 1920: 91–2; Collins 2011: 57.

148 Kennedy 2014: 125, 127; Peureux 1972: 97–8.

149 Demm 2014: 147–8.

150 Gibelli 2014; Audoin-Rouzeau 1993a: 85–9.

151 Demm 2002h: 82–3; Audoin-Rouzeau 1993a: 111–29; Kennedy 2014: 72; Zunino 2014: 322–5; film: http://www.earlycinema.uni-koeln.de/films/view/25754.

152 Higonnet 2014: 124.

153 Beyrau and Shcherbinin 2010: 161; Schumacher 1915: 52–5; Demm 2002h: 82–3, 110–11; Zunino 2014: 332–3; Audoin-Rouzeau 1994; Audoin-Rouzeau 1993a: 129–31, 133; Higonnet 2014: 124; Graham 1917: 85; Gibelli 2014; 'Mikey's Drum. A Story of the Great War', *The Boy's Own Annual* 40, 1917/18: 540–5, 660–5.

154 Ruggenberg 1994 (quote); British examples: Pankhurst 1932: 300.

155 Audoin-Rouzeau 1993a: 146–50; Horne and Kramer 2001: 311.

156 Goebel et al. 2012b: 227–8.

157 Graham 1917: 85.

158 Healy 2004: 218–28.

159 Fava 1993: 187–90; Fava 1997: 62.

160 Demm 2002h: 110–11.

161 Pappola and Lafon 2005: 309.

162 Schweitzer 2003: 64.

163 Watson 2014a: 191–2; Cornwall 1997: 184; Gatrell 2005: 64, 89 (1st quote); Graham 1917: 81 (2nd quote); Stiaccini 2015; Gatti 2000: 50–4, 62 (note 39); Senin 1993: 46; Houlihan 2012: 171; Boniface 2008: 137–9; Schweitzer 2003: 63–4; Madigan 2008: 75.

164 Houlihan 2012: 169 (quote), 172.

165 Graves 1929: 242; Schweitzer 2003: 65, 163–5; Madigan 2008: 62–89; see Times History 1916, VIII: 313, 326, 343

166 Houlihan 2012: 178, note 36; Ziemann 1997b: 131.

167 Fontana 1997: 26 (quote), 32–3; Times History 1916, VIII: 319.

168 Mondini 2014: 157–8.

169 Bianchi 2005: 237–46; Guerrini 2008: 229–35; Candeloro 1978: 165–7; Gibelli 1999: 121–3, 131, 134; Corner and Procacci 1997: 229–31; Row 2002: 141–3; Gooch 1996: 438–42, 442; Janz 2010: 203 (1st quote), 205–7; Bazzanella 1980: 344 (last quotes); Mondini 2014: 144–60.

170 Bulletin nos 108–10; Schaepdrijver 2014: 185.

171 Moreau 2016: 96.

172 Ridel 2014; Kurth 1937: 12–77, 123–72; Deist 1970: 343.

173 Heise 1999: 190–1, 208.

174 Cornwall 1997: 184; Cornwall 2000: 277.

175 Monger 2011: 335–46; Koch 2015: 32.

176 Creel 1920: 91.
177 Lipp 2003: 313; Kurth 1937: 14–15; *DK* no. 71, 25 April 1917: 4 (quotes).
178 Kurth 1937: 14–15, 24, 33, 39–43; *DK* no. 92, 15 June 1917: 2–3, 5–6; Lipp 1996: 283.
179 Koch 2015: 149.
180 Höffler 1997: 76–80; Gerlach 1994: 145; Demm 2014: 158.
181 *Karnisch-Julische Kriegszeitung*: 20 June 1917, 14 August 1918.
182 Lipp 2003: 57.
183 Nelson 2011; Nelson 2014; but see Audoin-Rouzeau 1992: 3, 10; Collonges and Picaud 2008: 104–5; Koch 2015: 106.
184 Nelson 2011; Nelson 2014; Audoin-Rouzeau 1992: 3–10, 36–91; Schulte Strathaus 1938: 50–2; Roshwald and Stites 1999b: 350–2; Ridel 2014; Kurth 1937: 215–16; Demm 1988: no. 111 (quote); Collonges and Picaud 2008: 105–7.
185 Fuller 1990: 14 (quote); Nelson 2011: 240; Nelson 2014.
186 Nelson 2014: introduction and note 2; Lipp 2003: 307.
187 Audoin-Rouzeau 1992: 173–82, 23 (quote); Fuller 1990: 35.
188 Audoin-Rouzeau 1992: 20.
189 Lipp 2003: 19–22, 48–57; Collonges and Picaud 2008: 105–6.
190 Gibelli 1999: 134–5; Isnenghi 1977: 40–52, 42 (quote); 'Journaux des tranchées italiens', BDIC, 4 Δ 0411.
191 Isnenghi 1977: 79–103.
192 Isnenghi 1977: 186, caricatures between 134 and 135.
193 Baumeister 2005: 211–27; Vescovo 2008: 820–9; Loubat 2016.
194 Koch 2015: 111.
195 Baumeister 2005: 218–20, 223–7, 232–5, 243; Fuller 1990: 94–110, 99 (quote); Murmann 1992: 27–49; Koch 2015: 112–13.
196 Vescovo 2008: 820–9.
197 Murmann 1992: 49–50.
198 Rickards 1968: 22 (quote); Becker 1986: 217–35.
199 Watson 2014a: 192.
200 Ludendorff 1921: 273 (quote); Welch 2014: 217–21.
201 Meinecke 1969: 287.
202 Demm 2009: 91, 95.
203 Cramer 1997: 116; Jahr 1998: 268; Ulrich and Ziemann 1997: 154; Zuckmayer 1966: 210; Fischer 2014: 207; Hirschfeld and Gaspar 1982: 460.
204 Watson 2010: 1147–57.
205 Cornwall 1997: 185–8; Cornwall 2000: 272–87.
206 Rauchensteiner 2014: 887–3.
207 Rauchensteiner 2013: 45; Rauchensteiner 2014: 944–54; Healy 2013b: 155–7; Grandner 2013: 562–4; Healy 2004: 54–6, 81–3; Healy 2013a: 138–9.
208 Corner and Procacci 1997: 229; Gatti 2000: 71–3, 129–30.
209 Gibelli 1999: 134–5, 134 (quote).
210 Englander 1997: 140–1; Watson 2008: 80.
211 Golder 1927: 37; Kirchner 2014: 102 (1914).
212 Nachtigal 2006: 173; Cornwall 2000: 41; Kirchner 2014: 393 (1914).
213 Kirchner 2014: 54 (1916); Jahr 1998: 268.
214 Komarnicki 1957: 80.
215 Cornwall 2000: 4, 41; Waltz and Tonnelat 1922: 14.
216 Szymczak 2015: 45–6; Kirchner 1992: 155–6, 166; 308, 310, 316, 322.
217 Cornwall 2000: 43–4.

218 Golder 1927: 385 (quote).

219 Times History 1917, XIII: 441.

220 Cornwall 2000: 43–9; Kirchner 2014: 71, 79–88 (1917).

221 Kirchner 2014: 116 (1917).

222 Cornwall 2000: 63–6, 74–8.

223 This paragraph is based on Cornwall 2000: 84–111 and Überegger 2015: 278.

224 This paragraph is based on Cornwall 2000: 174–80, 202–56, 209 (quote); Cornwall 1997: 182–3, 188; Thompson 1999: 189; Gatti 2008b: 303.

225 Nicolai 1920: 71–2; Thimme 1932: 39.

226 Koch 2015: 203.

227 This paragraph is based on Monballyu 2012: 9–11, 87–90; Wils 2015: 227–8, 232; Schaepdrijver 2014: 192–211.

228 Creutz 1996: 149–52; Kestler 1994: 78.

229 Kirchner 2014: 365–6; Schmidt 2006: 220–1.

230 Koch 2015: 221.

231 Waltz and Tonnelat 1922: 16–20, 36–43.

232 Kirchner 1985: XVII–III; Cornwall 2000: 7; Stuart 1920: 52; Sanders and Taylor 1982: 237.

233 Blankenhorn 1919: 48.

234 Kirchner 1992: XXI–III; Kirchner 1985: XXV; Creel 1920: 286.

235 Sanders and Taylor 1982: 228.

236 Thimme 1932: 36–7; Kirchner 2014: 158; Stuart 1920: 51; Swinton 1940: 65.

237 Koch 2015: 167–213, 243; Cornwall 2000: 4, 150–1; Waltz and Tonnelat 1922: 14; Wilkin 2016: 233.

238 Koch 2015: 32, 61, 203, 212; Sanders and Taylor 1982: 211; Waltz and Tonnelat 1922: 10; Thimme 1932: 36; Wilkin 2016: 235–6.

239 Kirchner 1985: XVIII–XIX; Kirchner 2014: 33, 364; Thimme 1932: 39, 48; Kestler 1994: 85–90.

240 Stuart 1920: 93; Thimme 1932: 49.

241 Kirchner 1992: 36–9, 194–5.

242 Kirchner 1992: 4–5 (Dec. 1914), 16 (Sept. 1915), 53, 60–1, 67, 97 (1916), 10–12 (1915), 70–1, 79–80 (1916), 133 (1917).

243 Kirchner 1992: 86, 91, 94, 103, 111, 117, 128, 134; Waltz and Tonnelat 1922: 41; Thimme 1932: 8–9, 165; Ulrich 1997: 167.

244 For instance *Feldpost*: Kirchner 1992: 34 (February 1916).

245 For the following see Bliembach 1992: 468–533.

246 Kirchner 1992: 487, 476.

247 Therstappen 2008: 90.

248 Kirchner 1992: 226 (March 1918); Kirchner 2014: 15; Ulrich and Ziemann 2010: 177; Ulrich 1997: 94–5 (quote); Altrichter 1933: 114–15; Thimme 1932: 121.

249 Wette 1995a: 132.

250 Koch 2015: 50–1 (1st quote); Stuart 1920: 94 (2nd quote).

251 Kirchner 1985: 235 (June 1918), 320–32 (September 1918).

252 Kirchner 1985: 310 (September 1918).

253 Kirchner 1985: 216 (August 1918).

254 Alfred Weber to Else Jaffé, 28 September 1918, BArch K, A. Weber papers 80: 9.

255 Kirchner 2014: 224 (November 1916).

256 Kirchner 2014: 24 (1914), 34, 50 (1915), 55 (1916), 77, 122 (1917).

257 Kirchner 2014: 30 (1914); Koch 2015: 241.

258 Kirchner 2014: 29, 159 (1914), 47, 49–53, 159–61 (1915), 169, 236 (1917), 181, 264–5 (1918); Überegger 2015: 278.
259 Kirchner 2014: 50, 159 (1914), 34 (1915), 55, 63, 163, 166 (1916), 77 (1917); BDIC, 4 Δ 1543, 4 Δ 0405; Montant 1968: 68–70, 84; Überegger 2015: 278; Koch 2015: 176, 184.
260 Kirchner 2014: 293–5, 314–22 (1918).
261 See also Kirchner 1958: 5–176 (1917–18), 259–303, 374–97, 457–73 (1918); Kirchner 1992: 2–3, 5 (1914), 8–9, 30 (1915), 41, 49 (1916), 105, 109 (1917); Stuart 1920: 53; Bruntz 1938: 107–12; Altrichter 1933: 116.
262 Kirchner 1985: 295.
263 Pöppinghege 2006: 133; Buchner 1930: 43 (29 October 1914), 50 (9 December 1914), 152 (9 November 1916); Mihaly 1986: 141.
264 Mihaly 1986: 141.
265 Jones 2014: 275; Materna and Schreckenbach 1987: 170 (January 1917); Koch 2015: 125, note 564 (quote).
266 Times History 1917, XII: 251–2.
267 Mostert 1918: 110; Gellert 1915: 87–98, 144–54.
268 Oberzensurstelle 1973: 239.
269 Kirchner 1992: 20–3; Kirchner 1985: 33 (1917); Walz and Tonnelat 1922: 11; Thimme 1932: 37.
270 RTP, 13. Leg., 1914/18, 4, 85th session, 1 March 1917: 2446; Graves 1929: 175–6, 234–7; Rolland 1983: II, 291, 555; Watson 2008: 71; Darmon 2002: 419–20; Ferguson 1998: 367–71.
271 Watson 2008: 221.
272 Kirchner 2014: 28, 29 (1914), 43, 162 (1915), 164 (1918); Horne and Kramer 2001: 348–51; Jones 2014: 271; Richert 1989: 404.
273 Huber 1928: 180–4; Times History 1917, XII: 243–4.
274 Ball 2017: 34–5; Times History 1917, XII: 243 (quote).
275 Times History 1917, XII: 230–3 and passim; Schmidl 2016: 374–5.
276 Times History 1917, XII: 236–9, 245–6.
277 Kirchner 2014: 23, 29 (1914), 35, 38, 43, 51, 162 (1915), 65 (1916), 12 8, 153, 233 (1917), 164 (1918); Mihaly 1986: 52–4, 127–30, 174; Times History 1916, VI: 243; 1917, XII: 248–62; Kachulle 1982: 160–2; Sanborn 2014: 133–4.
278 Kirchner 2014: 128.
279 Darmon 2002: 420–2; Sanborn 2014: 136–7; Times History 1917, XII: 244.
280 Sanborn 2014: 130–1.
281 Kirchner 1985: XXIX–XLV; Koch 2015: 138–42.
282 Lipp 2003: 194–6.
283 Ulrich and Ziemann 2010: 154–5.
284 Kirchner 2014: 369; Thompson 1999: 209.
285 Pöppinghege 2006: 135–47, 183–90.
286 Lein 2011: 418; Nachtigal 2006: 189; Gatrell 2005: 185; Lein 2014; Watson 2014a: 186; Jones 2014: 288; Cornwall 2000: 52
287 Nachtigal 2006: 183–5, 192.
288 Jahr 1998: 268–73; Nachtigal 2006: 192–3.
289 Szymczak 2015: 45–6.
290 Uyar 2013: 541–2.
291 Steuer 2014: 169–71; Jones 2014: 287; Pöppinghege 2006: 143; Monballyu 2012: 97; Times History 1916, VIII: 407–8 (quote).

292 Cornwall 2000: 128–9; Tortato 2008: 257.
293 Fisch 2010: 144–6.
294 This paragraph is based on Gatzke 1950: 56–60; Mommsen 2004: 103–5; Naumann 1915; Deutschland 1968: 363–5; Deutschland 1970: 35–7; Fischer 1984: passim; Demm 1990: 161–8.
295 Lowe 2014 [1967].
296 PA AA, R 20986: 90; R 20987: 113–15, 124, 126–8; R 20988: 16, 128, 132; R 20990: 1, 4; R 20992: 39, 66, 68–71, 122, 123; R 20993: 74–6, some in Zeman 1958: nos 3–4, 7–13.
297 PA AA, R 20983, 8 August 1914.
298 PA AA, R 20984, 3 November 1914.
299 PA AA, R 20990, 17 May, 11 August 1915; R 20991: 135; R 20992: 61–3, 75; R 20993: 84–7, 92–5.
300 Jalonen 2014.
301 Zeman 1958: nos 15–45, 51–3.
302 Zeman 1958: no. 32.
303 PA AA, R 20493: 62–6.
304 McKeene 2017: 133–4; Pipes 1990: 411.
305 'Berliner Börse', *BT* no. 117, 5 March 1914: 6; *BT* no. 114, 2 March 1916: 7; *BT* no. 110, 1 March 1917: 6. The exchange value of enemy currencies was not indicated during the war.
306 Pipes 1990: 597–603.
307 Fischer 1984: 130, note 81; Baumgart 1966: 213–14, note 19; Pipes 1990: 411, note*.
308 See also Kirchner 2014: 135–9 (1918).
309 Komarnicki 1957: 100–11, 109; Szymczak 2015: 38; Michael 2010: 26–7.
310 *BT* no. 570, 6 November 1916: 4 (1st quote); 'Polens Schicksalsstunde', *NDAZ* no. 307, 5 November 1916: 1 (2nd quote); Demm 1988: no. 351.
311 'Le coup de la Pologne', *Le Matin* no. 11941, 6 November 1916 (quote); 'Un aveu décisif', *Le Temps* no. 5211, 6 November 1916; Demm 1988: nos 352–3.
312 Kirchner 2014: 149–50 (1916); Szymczak 2015: 41–2; Polsakiewicz 2015: 78–80, 72–5, 149–52; Komarnicki 1957: 115–16.
313 This paragraph is based on Zetterberg 1978; Demm 2002a; Demm 2002b; Demm 2002i; Demm and Nikolajew 2013; Demm 2015.
314 Demm 2014: 145–6.
315 Lehmann 1996: 161–2.
316 Demm 2002f.
317 Demm 1988: nos 350, 354–5.
318 This paragraph is based on Wils 2015: 220–9; Schaepdrijver 2014: 157–84, 271–304; Dolderer 1989: 80–3.
319 Yammine 2013: 15–39.
320 Monballyu 2012: 77–80.
321 Cornwall 2000: 41; Nachtigal 2006: 173; Tumanova 2014: 361–4.
322 Healy et al. 2016.
323 Szlanta 2014; Szymczak 2015: 37–8; the following is based on Komarnicki 1957: 49–55, 147–74; Szymczak 2015: 44–6; Szlanta 2014 and Perdelwitz 1939: 127–94, 214–22.
324 Mueggenberg 2014: 66; the following is based on Mueggenberg 2014, Beneš 1928 and Masaryk 1925.
325 Masaryk 1925: 82–3.

326 Beneš 1928: 87.
327 Masaryk 1925: 273; Peterson 1968: 151–3.
328 Zeman and Klimek 1997: 28–31.
329 Quoted after Zeman and Klimek 1997: 23.
330 Sanders and Taylor 1982: 224.
331 Demm 1988: no. 357.
332 Fischer 2014: 207, 213; Kirchner 1992: 81, 84, 129 (1917).
333 Rajsfus 1999: 111; Waltz and Tonnelat 1922: 120; Klemperer 1989: 366; Mai 1977: 356–7.
334 Naumann 1913: 153.
335 *Staatsbürger Zeitung* no. 153, 24 June 1908, BArch B, R 8034/II, no. 6035: 95 (quote); *Schlesische Zeitung* no. 454, 1 July 1908, no. 153, 24 June 1908, BArch B, R 8034/II, no. 6034: 94; Demm 2018e: 261.
336 Kössler 1981; Schöllgen 1981; 'Die Bilanz der Kaiserreise', *Die Welt am Montag*, 21 November 1898, BArch B, R 8034/II, no. 6029.
337 Demm 2018e: 257 (quote); Schöllgen 1981: 142–3.
338 Kössler 1981: 91–3; Trumpener 1968: 9.
339 Kröger 2014: 91–2.
340 Demm 2018e: 255.
341 Kampen 1968: 66, 75.
342 Demm 2018c: 213–18; Gencer 2002: 50–4.
343 Bernhardi 1913: 111–12, 118; Bernhardi 1912: 148–9.
344 Aksakal 2008: 85–90.
345 Djemal 1922: 102–13.
346 Djemal 1922: 111–13, 113 (quote).
347 Aksakal 2008: 90 (quote)
348 Aksakal: notes 141–2.
349 Documents 1936: Note du Département de la main de M. de Margerie, 13 juillet 1914, no. 504, 727–9, 727 (quote).
350 McKale 1998: 47–50; Weber 1970: 62–5; Neulen 1994: 26 (quote); Morgenthau 1918: 32; Gencer 2002: 56–7; Trumpener 1968: 15, 20, 23, 28–9, 45–7.
351 Kröger 1994: 371 (both quotes).
352 Bihl 1975: 101–5; McKale 1998: 50–2; Hanisch 2014a: 103–6; Hanisch 2014b: 13–15.
353 Hanisch 2014a: 105; Hanisch 2014b: 22–5; PA AA, Orientalia Generalia 9, no. 1, R 14556–1, vol. 3: 0016–0018.
354 McKale 1998: 50–1; Bihl 1975: 101–77; Oberhaus 2007: 265–8; Hanisch 2014a: 103; Hagen 1990: 35–6; Bragulla 2007: 18.
355 E.g. Lüdke 2005: 1, 48–54; Hanisch 2014a: 103
356 Aksakal 2011: 187–9; Will 2012: 313.
357 Abdul Hamid 2007: 170.
358 Aksakal 2011: 186; Kahleyss 2000: 15.
359 Köroglu 2007: 86–8; Will 2012: 205–6; McKale 1998: 49–50; Oberhaus 2007: 160–1; Lüdke 2005: 75–82.
360 Bihl 1975: 101–5; Hanisch 2014a: 207–10; Kröger 1994: 373–5; McKale 1998: 67–70; Strachan 2001: 702–5.
361 Bragulla 2007: 19; Kahleyss 2000: 12–14.
362 Strachan 2001: 708–10; Bihl 1975: 108–10; McKale 1998: 68; Oberhaus 2007: 139, 146; Will 2012: 197–200; Kröger 1994: 373.
363 Bragulla 2007: 43; Moreau 2016:81.

364 Will 2012: 75–7, 135–8, 190–4, 213; Lüdke 2005: 125–33; Strachan 2001: 712.
365 Kröger 1994: 373; McKale 1998: 67, 107–10.
366 Köroglu 2007: 87; Lüdke 2005: 81; Weber 1970: 94; Jäckh 1916: 244; Oberhaus 2007: 141–3; Kirchner 2014: 326.
367 See also Kirchner 2014: 342–50.
368 Bragulla 2007: 84–5.
369 Hagen 1990: nos 8,1; 8,3; 8,5; 8,7; 8,12; 8,24; 8,25; 8,28; 8,30–32; 8,45; 8,58–60;10,5–6; Bihl 1975: 104; Bragulla 2007: 97–105.
370 Oberhaus 2007: 268–71; McKale 1998: 53–4; Lüdke 2005: 90–101.
371 McKale 1998: 97–100.
372 Kayalı 1997: 189.
373 Weber 1970: 98–100; McKale 1998: 86, 100–3; Will 2012: 212; Oberhaus 2007: 200–5.
374 McKale 1998: 145–7, 192–3; Times History 1916, IX: 319–20.
375 McKale 1998: 129–31, 144.
376 Bihl 1975: 41; Badem 2014.
377 Strachan 2001: 761–3; Bihl 1992: 23–7; Cornwell 2014: 257.
378 Strachan 2001: 791–3; McKale 1998: 76–8, 120–3.
379 McKale 1998: 49–50.
380 Strachan 2001: 813; McKale 1998: 134; Lüdke 2005: 186, 195.
381 McKale 1998: 81, 133–5.
382 Morgenthau 1918: 34, 145 (1st quote); Weber 1970: 257; Yalman 1957: 52–3 (2nd quote); McKale 1998: 108, 114–15; Bihl 1975: 110; Will 2012: 117–19, 124–6, 318 (last quote); Oberhaus 2007: 161–2; Bragulla 2007: 83.
383 Rauchensteiner 2014: 733.
384 Strachan 2001: 708.
385 Kröger 1994: 382; Demm 2018e: 265.
386 Lüdke 2005: 136.
387 Lüdke 2005: 187; Will 2012: 312.
388 McKale 1998: 98, 106.
389 Strachan 2001: 712 (quote), 812.
390 Hagen 1990: 40–3; Marc 1990: 403; Moreau 2016: 82.
391 Times History 1915, II: 337–8.
392 Bihl 1975: 83–5; Kahleyss 2000: 16–18.
393 Kahleyss 2000: 18–19.
394 Bragulla 2007: 84.
395 PA AA, R 21255.
396 Kahleyss 2000: 32–3; Cornwell 2014: 257.
397 E.g. Bihl 1975: 44; Will 2012: 301.
398 Will 2012: 312; Hagen 1990: 7; McKale 1998: XI; Oberhaus 2007: 268–70.
399 McKale 1998: 71–2, 90–2; Will 2012: 216.
400 McKale 1998: 72; Kayalı 1997: 185–9.
401 Will 2012: 196.
402 McKale 1998: 170; Will 2012: 208–9, 218–20.
403 Koch 2015: 33.
404 McKale 1998: 84; Lüdke 2005: 204.
405 Kayalı 1997: 189–90; Bihl 1975: 161–5; McKale 1998: 109–11.
406 Kayalı 1997: 111; McKale 1998: 161, 174, 205; Will 2012: 232; Thorau 2014: 189; Fischer 1984: 130, note 81.

407　Will 2012: 309; Thorau 2014: 185–6.
408　Uyar 2013: 537–8.
409　Kayalı 1997: 197; Bihl 1975: 164; Hagen 1990: 5–7.
410　Will 2012: 224–5.
411　Yalman 1930: 181 (quote); Moreau 2016: 97.
412　Kayalı 1997: 196–200; Lüdke 2005: 137; Times History 2018, XVII: 3 (quote).
413　Thorau 2014: 181–3.
414　Lawrence 2015: Introductory chapter, last but one paragraph.
415　Kayalı 1997: 197–8, 197 (quote); McKale 1998: 213–14.

Chapter 7

1　This section is based on Thompson 1999; Thompson 1999: 25 (quote).
2　Röhl 2008: 825.
3　Taylor 1972: 178–9.
4　Quoted after Sanders and Taylor 1982: 241.
5　Creel 1920: 5 (quote). This section is based on Creel 1920, Mock and Larson 1968 and Axelrod 2009.
6　Creel 1920: 225.
7　Axelrod 2009: 105.
8　Creel 1920: 6, 16–27.
9　Mock and Larson 1968: 84.
10　Creel 1920: 299 (quote).
11　Creel 1920: 106 (1st quote), 60 (2nd quote), 288 (3rd quote).
12　Barbusse 1937: 237, letter to his wife, 26 October 1916 (1st quote); Barbusse 1917: Chapter 24 'The Dawn' (2nd quote); Barbusse, 'Jusqu'au bout', in: *Journal mensuel des combattants*, 10 September 1917 (last quote), quoted after Demm 2000a: 56.
13　This section is based on Demm 2000a.
14　Demm 2000a: 46.
15　Barbusse 1917: chapter 2 'In the Earth' (quotes) and chapter 18 'A Box of Matches'.
16　Barbusse 1917: chapter 20 'Under Fire'.
17　Barbusse 1917: chapter 24 'The Dawn'.
18　Barbusse 1917: chapter 24 'The Dawn'.
19　Barbusse 1937: 231 (letter to his wife, 25 October 1916).
20　Demm 2000a: 55 with note 77.
21　Müller 2005: 131–2, 138; Müller 2016.
22　Speech on 25 May 1915, quoted after Bonadeo 1995: 74.
23　This section is based on Vogel-Walter 2004, Bonadeo 1995 and Gibelli 1999.
24　Quoted after Bonadeo 1995: 73.
25　Quote after Vogel-Walter 2004: 81.
26　Gabrys 1920: 43.
27　This section is based on Gabrys 1920, Demm 1990, Demm 2002h, Demm and Nikolajew 2013.
28　Weber 1999b: 170; Weber 1999d: 110.
29　This section is based on Weber 1999a: 109–228, Demm 1986, Demm 1990, Demm 2002d, Demm 2002b, Demm 2014, Demm 2015.

30 Demm 2014: 117 (quote).
31 Weber 1999d: 113.
32 Weber 1999a: 220.
33 Weber 1999a: 224.
34 Demm 2002b: 309.
35 Machtan 2018: 334–40, 347–54; the following paragraph is based on Max von Baden 1968: 188–207, 225–267; Demm 1990: 236–47; Demm 2002 [1990]: 5–20 and the Max von Baden papers available recently in the GLA.
36 Zwei Vorschläge zu einer deutschen politischen Offensive im Jahre 1918. Denkschrift A, 14 January 1918, in: Ludendorff 1921: 473-8 with asterisk on p. 473; Stegmann 1972: 88, note 91; Deutschland 1969: 239; Weber 1999e: 212–17.
37 Max von Baden papers, GLA FA N 5557, 2–5; text: 'Prinz Max von Baden über Krieg und Frieden', in: *BT* no. 86, 16 February 1918: 4.
38 Max von Baden papers, GLA FA N 5552, 6–7.
39 Max von Baden 1968: 242 (quote); Demm 2002d: 374.
40 Alfred Weber to Else Jaffé, 21 February 1918, BArch K, A. Weber papers 83: 195.
41 English translation in: Demm 1998: 84–120.
42 Max von Baden 1968: 253 (quotes).
43 This section is based on Hofmannsthal 2011 (quote: 279) and Lunzer 1981.
44 For the biographical aspects: Lunzer 1981; see also Redlich 2011/I: 19.
45 Hofmannsthal 2011: 98–106.
46 Hofmannsthal 2011: 119–20; Mionskowski 2016: 278.
47 Hofmannsthal 2011: 109–12 (quotes).
48 Hofmannsthal 2011: 144, 150-1, 163 (quotes)
49 Hofmannsthal 2011: 128; Vondung 1980a: 17–19.
50 Hofmannsthal 2011: 130, 135, 143, 159.
51 Zweig 1998: 137, 319–20; Überegger 2015: 265.
52 Redlich 2011/II: 35, 37.
53 For the following also Mionskowski 2016: 283–9.
54 Quoted after Lunzer 1981: 180.
55 Kraus 1916, quoted after Zweig 1998: 320.
56 Quoted after Lunzer 1981: 181.
57 Zweig 1998: 110, 175; Zweig 1984: 86.
58 Ranitz 2014: 115, note 1.
59 This section is based on Ranitz 2014.
60 'Le chemin de la victoire. Pour la France et pour la civilisation', in: Stopford 1916: 87.
61 'La bête allemande', in: Avenarius 1918: 174.
62 Ranitz 2014: 87, note 46 (quote).
63 Wanderscheck 1935: 171.

Chapter 8

1 Nation 1989: 33–5.
2 Nation 1989: 35, 55–7; Morgan 1975: 62–75, 75 (quote); Miller 1974: 124–32.
3 Times History 1920, XXI: 266.
4 Deist 1970: 300, note 4; Bonzon and Robert 1989: 58, 107 (quote); Barbusse 1917: chapter 20; Demm 2000a: 53.
5 Sbordone 2008: 150–3.

6   Procacci 1992: 152; Nation 1989: 53; Rosmer 1936: 328–9; Candeloro 1978: 173–5.

7   Melancon 1990: 62–71, 174–6; Nation 1989: 35.

8   Swartz 1971: 69, 85; Carsten 1982: 167.

9   *Journal officiel*, 60ème séance, 24 June 1916: 1442–3; Sowerwine and Sowerwine1985 VI, 2, 3 etc.; Gankin and Fischer 1960: 410.

10 Sowerwine and Sowerwine 1985, VII, table of contents; Rosmer 1959: 195–201; Gankin and Fischer 1960: 320–5, 407–10.

11 Nation 1989: 118; Rauchensteiner 2014: 201, 605.

12 Holl 2007: 170–2; Holl 1988: 120; Ingram 2005: 78; Shand 1975: 97.

13 Swartz 1971: 69; Marwick 1991: 120.

14 Deutschland 1970: 446; Holl 1988: 114–16, 123–5; Shand 1975: 98.

15 Hochschild 2011: 98–100; Wiltsher 1985: 39 (quote).

16 Carsten 1982: 170.

17 Demm 2014: 119–23; Watson 2015: 217–18; Wiltsher 1985: 57; Holl 1988: 117–19.

18 Ingram 2005: 80; Sowerwine and Sowerwine 1985. II.

19 Sowerwine and Sowerwine 1985, IV, 3 and 5; Malatesta 1915.

20 Industrial Workers of the World, https://en.wikipedia.org/wiki/Industrial_Workers_of_the_World, retrieved 1 November 1917.

21 Gankin and Fisher 1960: 329–33, 419–21.

22 Wiltsher 1985: 128; Carsten 1982: 149; Millman 2000: 186; Speech of Brizon at the French Chamber, 60ème séance, 24 June 1916, *Journal officiel*: 1442–3.

23 Sowerwine and Sowerwine1985, VI, 2, 222–5; Yalman 1930: 198; Bonzon and Robert 1989: 88, 90.

24 Melancon 1990: 78 (quote); Procacci 1989: 41.

25 Robb 2002: 74.

26 Liebknecht 1966: 613; Geyer in: RTP, 13. Leg., 1914/18, 1, 25th session, 21 December 1915: 507C; 8, 191st session, 13 July 1918: 6146A; Carsten 1982: 149; Melancon 1990: 213; Procacci 1992: 162, 172; Ullrich 1982: 68–70.

27 Rauchensteiner 2014: 565; Kilian 2008: 102; Huber 1928: 234–5.

28 Speech of Haase, RTP, 13. Leg., 1914/18, 2, 37th session, 24 March 1916: 843CD; Demm 2009: 95; Sowerwine and Sowerwine 1985, II, 2: 5, 7; IV, 8: 21–2.

29 Sowerwine and Sowerwine 1985, V, 6: 48; Gankin and Fisher 1960: 329–33, 419–21.

30 Miller 1974: 186.

31 Speech of Ponsonby, PDHC 1917–1918, 5th series, vol. 90, 20 February 1917: 1179–90, 1178 and 1183 (quotes); Speech of Snowden : 1224.

32 Speech of Trevelyan, PDHC 1917–18, 5th series, vol. 90, 20 February 1917: 1188–91, here 1190; Sowerwine and Sowerwine 1985, II, 2: 3; II, 3: 3–4; II, 4: 5; VI, 2: 19; VII, 1.

33 Liebknecht 1966: 204; Sowerwine and Sowerwine 1985, V, 6: 48, 51–2; VI, 2: 20.

34 Kriegel 1964: 198; Liebknecht 1966: 225–7, 230, 614; Sassoon 1931: 244; Sowerwine and Sowerwine 1985, IV, 3: 55, 58; IV, 8: 2; Swartz 1971: 151–2; RTP, 13. Leg., 1914/18, 8, 191st session, 13 July 1918: 6145C; Sowerwine and Sowerwine 1985, III, 1: 12–13.

35 Sowerwine and Sowerwine 1985, IV, 1: 7; IV, 8: 2; Bonzon and Robert 1989: 66, 93, 104, 107–8.

36 Sowerwine and Sowerwine 1985, II, 4: 8; III, 1: 11–13; VI, 2: 6.

37 Sowerwine and Sowerwine 1985, III, 1; Speech of Snowden, PDHC 1917–1918, 5th series, vol. 90, 20 February 1917: 1219.

38 Gankin and Fisher 1960: 330, 419; Speech of Brizon at the French Chamber, 60ème séance, 24 June 1916, *Journal officiel*: 1442–3 (quote); Sowerwine and Sowerwine 1985, V, 6: 49 (quote).

39 Sowerwine and Sowerwine 1985, VII, 3.

40 Swartz 1971: 69–71; Miller 1974: 166; Carsten 1982: 150; Kriegel 1964: 150; Meyer 1927: 36–7, 151; Wiltsher 1985: 138–9; Robb 2002: 118; Ledebour in: RTP, 13. Leg., 1914/18, 4, 82nd session, 23 February 1917: 2366D; Lehmann-Russbüldt 1927: 52; Sowerwine and Sowerwine 1985, VI, 2: 31; VII, 1; Pourcher 1994: 230–1 (quote); www.fr.wikipedia.org/wiki/hélène_brion; Williams 1972: 214; Rajsfus 1999: 94–112.

41 Melancon 1990: 78, 213–14; Pourcher 1994: 214, 224, 228, 235; Sowerwine and Sowerwine 1985, IV, 6: 4–5; VII, 4; Dokumente 1957: 630–3; Procacci 1989: 42; Procacci 1992: 148; Rajsfus 1999: 108.

42 Koch 2015: 151.

43 Gankin and Fisher 1960: 329–33, 419–21, 680–3.

44 Nation 1989: 85–7, 119–20, 136–8, 179–81; Sowerwine and Sowerwine 1985, III, 1: 21–3; Gankin and Fisher 1960: 680 and note 140.

45 Deutschland 1970: 292–5; Patterson 2014.

46 Wiltsher 1985: 188–90.

47 Wiltsher 1985: 84–9, 88 (quotes).

48 Carsten 1982: 150; Liebknecht 1966: 428–30; Miller 1974: 121, 300, 309–10; Nettl 1967: 592, 614.

49 Liebknecht 1966: 428.

50 Speech of Trevelyan, PDHC 1917–1918, 5th series, vol. 90, 20 February 1917: 1195.

51 Sowerwine and Sowerwine 1985, V, 6: 48–9.

52 Liebknecht 1966: 428–32, 438–41, 442–4, 600–4.

53 Deutschland 1970: 474; Flemming and Ulrich 2014: 196; Redlich 1929: 57–8; Rauchensteiner 2014: 148–9, 202–3, 727–8; Wrigley 1976: 119–21; Deutschland 1969: 159; Hardach 1973: 195; Deist 1970: 637, 1159–60, 1188; Procacci 1989: 34–5; Procacci 1992: 155–7; Gibelli 1999: 178–81; Scheer 2016: 440–68; Bonzon 1997: 164–95.

54 Hardach 1973: 232.

55 Gibelli 1999: 181.

56 Bianchi 2016.

57 Gibelli 1999: 213–15.

58 Procacci 1992: 152, 175; Gibelli 1999: 217–19.

59 Ceschin 2008: 220–2.

60 Gibelli 1999: 177, 219; Gatti 2008a: 283.

61 Pisa 2015; Bianchi 2016; Procacci 1989: 31–3, 37, 41–3, 51–4; Candeloro 1978: 172–3 (1st quote); Procacci 1992: 148–50, 154–5 (2nd quote), 161–5, 173.

62 Ullrich 1982: 118–20, 134–6; Kachulle 1982: 212, Anm. 35; according to RTP, 13. Leg., 1914/18, 3, 69th session, 28 October 1916: 1881.

63 Deutschland 1970: 451; Deutschland 1969: 286.

64 'Die Schutzhaft für freigesprochene Streiker', BT no. 91, 19 February 1918: 2–3.

65 Fraenkel 1941.

66 Morgan 1975: 57; Deutschland 1970: 442.

67 Miller 1974: 295; Morgan 1975: 83.

68 Dokumente 1958: 19–20, 23–4, 26–30.

69 Dokumente 1957: 682–3.

70 Deist 1970: 1157–66, 1169, note 2, 1183, 1187; Luban 2008: 23; Carsten 1982: 132–4, 141; Deutschland 1969: 145–7, 172–3; Dokumente 1958: 48–51, 67–70, 91, 113–14; Morgan 1975: 87–9.

71 Dokumente 1958: 122–3, 137–8, 139–41; Deutschland 1969: 297; Deist 1970: 752–3.

72 Dokumente 1958: 171–3, 178–80, 182–4, 191–4, 195 (quote).
73 Kriegel 1964: 213; Sorrie 2018: 1–39.
74 Rajsfus 1999: 94–7, 113–32.
75 Rosmer 1959: 28.
76 Kriegel 1964: 213; Robert 1992: 37–9.
77 Kriegel 1964: 158–60, 195, 207–15; Williams 1972: 213, 218, 269; Haddad 2014
    (quote); Becker 1986: 206–7, 209; Sorrie 2014: 236–9; Pourcher 1994: 236.
78 Kriegel 1964: 213–15, 218–19.
79 Haddad 2014; Robert 1992: 41–2; Pourcher 1994: 235; Sorrie 2014: 237.
80 Sorrie 2018: 30.
81 Rolland 1983: III, 378.
82 Rauchensteiner 2014: 898–904.
83 Healy et al. 2016; Rauchensteiner 2014: 871–5; Deutschland 1969: 145–6.
84 Sobolew et al. 1972: between 8 and 9.
85 Melancon 1990: 64, 214, 191, 198, 218, 225; Sanborn 2014: 191 (quote).
86 Sanborn 2014: 193, 197.
87 Sanborn 2014: 201; Sobolew et al. 1972: 30–1, 47–8.
88 Scott 1921: 95–6, 102–3; Golder 1927: 397–8.
89 Sanborn 2014: 202–3; Sobolew et al. 1972: 53–5; Times History 1917, XIII: 441.
90 Daly and Trofimov 2009: 71.
91 Sobolew et al. 1972: 110–12.
92 Sanborn 2014: 225–7; Sobolew et al. 1972: 310–11; Cornwall 2000: 58; Watson
    2014a: 193–4.
93 Millman 2000: 267.
94 Carsten 1982: 124–6, 172; Millman 2000: 264; Bush 1984: 84.
95 Swartz 1971: 71.
96 Swartz 1971: 105–7; Marwick 1991: 122; Millman 2000: 85–6; Wiltsher 1985: 130–2;
    Carsten 1982: 171; Williams 1972: 71; Pankhurst 1932: 304–5.
97 Bush 1984: 57; Millman 2000: 5, 80, 97, 178–9; Robb 2002: 120; Rose 1995: 43–5;
    Swartz 1971: 121; Pankhurst 1932: 301.
98 Ryan 1988: 56.
99 There are different figures. Marwick 1991: 121–2; Pankhurst 1932: 290–3, 314, 334–
    5; Millman 2000: 193–4; Robb 2002: 118; Rolland 1983: III, 265.
100 Wiltsher 1985: 164–6, 171.
101 Wiltsher 1985: 158–60.
102 Rosmer 1959: 201.
103 Bianchi 2008: 133–5; Zweig 2001: 309–31.
104 Holl 1988: 123–5; Shand 1975: 99–101, 103–4.
105 Deutschland 1970: 445–50, 445 (quote).
106 Sowerwine and Sowerwine 1985, II, 3: 3 (quote); II, 4: 3–5, 8; II, 7.
107 www.en.wikipedia.org/wiki/Hélène_Brion, Sowerwine and Sowerwine 1985, II,
    5: 6–8, 23–5, 30–2; Wiltsher 1985: 128; Kriegel 1964: 197.
108 Demm 2002g: 66, 69.
109 Sassoon 1931: 148–9, 230–2, 262–3 (quote), 283–5; Robb 2002: 117.
110 Vogeler 1989: 204–10.
111 Ryan 1988: 55–7.
112 Deutschland 1968: 479; Shand 1975: 102–3.
113 The first part is based on the magazine and on Douglas 2002; for the second part
    I could only consult the year 1915 of *Glühlichter* online.

114 'Coin!Coin!Coin!' *Canard enchaîné* (*CE*) 1,1, 10 September 1915; La Rédaction: 'Re-Présentation', *CE* 1 (sic), 1, 5 July 1916; Douglas 2002: 51–5.

115 Douglas 2002: 56, after *CE* 84, 6 February 1918: 3, 'Le point de vue du fumiste.'

116 Douglas 2002: 56, 'À travers la presse déchaînée', *CE* 85, 13 February 1918: 4.

117 Douglas 2002: 84 (quote); Sowerwine and Sowerwine 1985, IV, 8: 11.

118 'La main coupée. Conte à dormir debout', *CE* 1, 4, 15 October 1915: 4.

119 'Doux espoirs', *CE* 2, 28, 10 January 1917: 2; 'T'en fais pas', *CE* 2, 29, 17 January 1917: 1.

120 'C'est bien fait !', *CE* 1, 9, 20 August 1916: 3.

121 'Suicide dramatique du censeur du Canard Enchaîné', *CE* 2, 39, 28 March 1917: 1.

122 'Der Franktireur' in: *Glühlichter* XIX, 2, 14 January 1915: 2; 'Im Felde da ist der Mann noch was wert', 4, 25 February 1915: 1.

123 'Der Franktireur' in: *Glühlichter* XIX, 2, 14 January 1915: 3; 'Zwei, an die man nicht gedacht hat' by D.R. Andre, 2, 14 January 1915: 1.

124 'Bibliothek der Verlustlisten' by Corvin, *Glühlichter* XIX, 4, 11 February 1915: 4.

125 'Der Hausherr 1. August, 1. Februar' by Rudolf Hermann, *Glühlichter* XIX, 3, 28 January 1915: 8; 'Da schau, Mutter – Kohlen!', 2, 14 January 1915: 7; 'Man will doch auch sehen, was man ißt' by Corvin, , 5, 25 February 1915: 4.

126 *Glühlichter* XIX, 10, 6 May 1915: 5; 18, 26 August 1915: 4; 21, 7 October 1915: 8.

127 *Glühlichter* XIX, 27, 30 December 1915: 2.

Chapter 9

1 E.g. BDIC, F res 0270/C, 21/22 and 23 September 1917.

2 ASHAT, series 5 N 341, Ministry of War to Prime Minister, 25 July 1916.

3 Beurier 2008: 315.

4 Mock and Larson 1968: 87–9.

5 Rajsfus 1999: 41.

6 BDIC, F res 0270/C, 12 September 1917.

7 BDIC, F res 0270/C, 19 September 1917.

8 ASHAT, series 5 N 341, 22 December 1916; 8 January 1917.

9 Beurier 2008: 318; Navet 1994: 40.

10 Rajsfus 1999: 207.

11 Berger and Allard 1932: 114.

12 Forcade 2004a: 44.

13 Demm 2002e: 30.

14 Demm 2018e: 264–8.

15 Gerlach 1994: 69–70; Mann 2012: 180 (quote).

16 Cronier 2013: 130–2.

17 Hanna 2014: 24; Winter 1988: 264.

18 Hirschfeld and Gaspar 1982: 104, 112, 117, 318.

19 Hirschfeld and Gaspar 1982: 98–9; Williams 2005: 49.

20 Healy 2004: 126, 132 (quote), 141–8; Altenhöner 2008: 217; Materna and Schreckenbach 1987: 179; Welch 2014: 215–16.

21 Knežević 2018: 115; Deist 1970: 1259.

22 Köroglu 2007: 14.

23 Mock 1972: 213–22.

24 Wilson 1988: 743–4; Watson 2014a: 194; Reeves 1999b: 38.
25 Winter et al. 2014: 224–5.
26 Hovland et al. 1974: 269–70.
27 Becker 1986: 36–9.
28 Schulte Strathaus 1938: 117; Illustration 'Le sommier de Mimi et la guerre' by Lucien Laforge, in: *CE* 1, no. 9, 30 August 1916.
29 The theoretical aspects are based on Hovland et al. 1974: 250–1, 260, 270–1, 289; Perloff 2010: 66–7, 71–2; and Heath and Bryant 2008: 175–7, 347–8, 176 (quotes).
30 Horne 1997a: 208.
31 Müller 1986: 335.
32 Lipp 2003: 57 (quote); Watson 2008: 75.
33 Hiley 2007: 171; Hartwagner 1942: 72; Schulte Strathaus 1938: 9.
34 Buchner 1930: 65–6 (20 March 1915), 177 (26 June 1915), 83 (7 August 1915).
35 Robb 2002: 124–5 (quote).
36 Mistinguett 1954: 111.
37 Weise 2004: 134.
38 See partly for the following Demm 2002e: 51–2; Demm 2018f: 333.
39 'Die Etatrede des preußischen Finanzministers', in: *NDAZ* no. 30, 17 January 1918: 5.
40 Blücher 1920: 237.
41 Based on: *BT, NDAZ* and *LV* 15–22 July and 9–16 August.
42 Demm 1988: nos 77–9.
43 Krollpfeiffer 1935: 86–8; Schulte Strathaus 1938: 117, 121, 194; Hartwagner 1942: 66; Kessel 2012: 86; Kessel 2008: 203–4; Hiley 2007: 153; Hitler 1933: 204; no information in: Weber 2011.
44 All quotes in Demm 2018f: 333–4.
45 The theoretical aspects are based on Perloff 2010: 66–7, 71–2; and Heath and Bryant 2008: 175–7, 347–8, 176 (quote).
46 Mariot 2013; Loez 2014; Strachan 2001: 160.
47 Zuckmayer 1966: 214–19, 219 (1st quote); Klemperer 1989: 277 (2nd quote); Ulrich 1995: 115–17.
48 Williams 1972: 219.
49 Cf. Mann 1991: 34–5, 53; Mann 2000: 82.
50 Altenhöner 2008: 85; Gregory 2004: 15; Müller 2008: 241; Audoin-Rouzeau 1993a: 64.
51 Müller 1983: 252; Buchner 1930: 32–4, 55, 77, 144, 213, 223.
52 Mihaly 1986: 16.
53 Buchner 1930: 32–4, 55, 77, 144 (quote).
54 Millman 2000: 97–9; Kriegel 1964: 220–2.
55 Höffler 1997: 74.
56 Demm 2002h: 117–18; Donson 2010: 191; Audoin-Rouzeau 1993b: 169.
57 Bäumer 1930: 49; Altenhöner 2008: 217; Welch 2014: 206.
58 Strachan 2001: 160.
59 Gregory 2008: 74–5; DeGroot 1996: 52; Williams 2005: 9.
60 Bourne 1989: 210.
61 Gullace 1997: 717–19; Huber 1928: 167.
62 This paragraph is based on Gregory 2008: 101–6; Winter 1988: 39–40; Beckett 1990: 339–55.
63 Keene 2014: 518; Knightley 2002: 131.
64 Audoin-Rouzeau 1993a: 61, 178–9.
65 Kennedy 2014: 136 (2nd quote); Demm 2002h: 116 (1st quote).

66 Demm 2002h: 117.
67 Audoin-Rouzeau 1993b: 164; Donson 2010: 192 (quotes).
68 Hämmerle 1993: 299.
69 Mihaly 1986: 17, 187, 314.
70 Materna and Schreckenbach 1987: 13 April 1916: 199; 13 November 1917: 226; 17 December 1917: 235; 15 April 1918: 272; 20 June 1918: 279; 19 August 1918: 284–5.
71 Englander 1997: 141; Ziemann 2015: 122–4.
72 Afflerbach 2015a: 241
73 Deutschland 1970: 441–2; Millman 2000: 255–6 (quote); Ryan 1988: 55–7, 63; Axelrod 2009: 72–3; Caillaux 1920: 74–5, 161; Fiori 2001: 264–5.
74 'The Assassination of Opinion', *The Nation*, 24 November 1917, quoted after Monger 2012: 233.
75 Carsten 1982: 169.
76 Procacci 1992: 175.
77 Strachan 1996: 391; Reimann 1997: 140–1; Baumeister 2005: 241; Buschmann 1997: 221; Watson 2008: 49–51, 83; Ulrich and Ziemann 2010: 179
78 Cochet 1990: 365.
79 Becker 1986: 225; Cochet 1990: 362; Bonzon and Robert 1989: 63, 66, 78, 88, 109, 117; Reimann 1997: 143, 149; Lipp 2003: 22; Lipp 1996: 284–6; Ziemann 2015: 122.
80 Gibelli 1999: 149.
81 Baumeister 2005: 257.
82 Bonzon and Robert 1989: 10, 17 (1st quotes), 50, 63, 71 (last quotes).
83 Wette 1995a: 132; see also Klemperer 1989: 372–4.
84 Graves 1929: 151–2.
85 Beckett 1990: 349 (quotes); see also Leed 1979: 109.
86 Watson 2008: 127–9.
87 Ulrich and Ziemann 2010: 115.
88 Ziemann 1997a: 141; Kruse 1996: 541–3; Klemperer 1989: 373–4; Hobohm 1995: 136–8; Vogeler 1989: 196; Bonzon and Robert 1989: 39, 43, 64–5, 79, 91, 95.
89 Lipp 2003: 22.
90 Deist 1970: 296 (quote), 300, 306.
91 Vavro 1996: 408; Cornwall 1997: 182–3, 188–9, 187 (quote); cf. also Pietri 1990: 316.
92 Jahr 1998: 155.
93 Wette 1995a: 134.
94 Ulrich and Ziemann 2010: 150.
95 Mommsen 2004: 144; Hirschfeld and Gaspar 1982: 433, 434; Watson 2008: 60, 71.
96 Rajsfus 1999: 141; Watson 2008: 61 (quote).
97 Hirschfeld and Gaspar 1982: 434.
98 Jahr 1998: 202–3; Watson 2008: 58–60; Watson 2014a: 178–81; Ziemann 1997a: 205–7; Offenstadt 2010: 74.
99 Altrichter 1933: 122–3; Strachan 1996: 393–4.
100 Rauchensteiner 2014: 944–54.
101 Vavro 1996: 408.
102 Graves 1929: 151; Gibelli 1999: 120.
103 Graves 1929: 150–2, 174.
104 Vogeler 1989: 208.
105 Sassoon 1931: 217–18; Glaeser 1929: 289–90; Dorgelès 1919: 362–3; Bazzanella 1980: 342; Artinger 2000: 85; Watson 2008: 142, 146; Ziemann 1997a: 200–2, 225; Offenstadt 2010: 60, 71–2; Ulrich and Ziemann 2010: 176; Kruse 1996: 551.

106 Ridel 2007: 62, 270–2.
107 Gibelli 1999: 131–3, 131 (quote); Pluviano 2008.
108 Deist 1996; Ziemann 2015: 134–52.
109 Jünger 1937: 240.
110 Binet-Valmer 1918: 75; Cronier 2013: 250.
111 Mommsen 2004: 151; Kruse 1996: 535, 537; Leed 1979: 201–2.
112 Jünger 1937: 57.
113 Horne 1989: 203–4.
114 Quoted in Mommsen 2004: 150.

Chapter 10

1 Ludendorff 1919: 349, 360–9.
2 Hitler 1933: 204.
3 E.g. Huber 1928; Wanderscheck 1936; Schulte Strathaus 1938; Hartwagner 1942.
4 Irwin 1919: 23–5, 54–6; see King 1989.
5 Ponsonby 1928.
6 Graux 1918–20; Benda 1927; Guéhenno quoted after Ory and Sirinelli 1986: 66.
7 Dreyer and Lemcke 1993.
8 Julien 2014: 20–3.
9 King 1997.
10 Fareed Fakaria, 'The Rise of "Putinism"', *Washington Post*, 31 July 2014; Kathrin Hille, 'Patriotic Games. Russia Putin's Use of Soviet-era Symbolism Has Alarmed Those Already Fearful for the Future of the Country's Democratic Institutions', *Financial Times*, 17 April 2014.
11 Ulrich Clauss, 'Putins Trolle ziehen in die Propagandaschlacht. Im Internet organisieren Aktivisten Kampagnen gegen Russlandkritiker', *Die Welt*, 13 June 2014; Ulrich Clauss, 'Anatomie des russischen Infokrieges. Vom Kreml gesteuerte Cyberkrieger infiltrieren soziale Netzwerke und bilden Propaganda-Allianzen mit Links- und Rechtsradikalen', *Die Welt*, 2 June 2014.
12 Dikötter 2014.
13 Mark Siemons, 'Journalisten! Ihr müsst Auge und Ohr und Zunge der Partei sein! China setzt die Zensur der Presse in drastischer Weise durch', *Frankfurter Allgemeine Zeitung*, 29 July 2014.
14 *Action française*, 10 October 1939; Rajsfus 1999: 254.
15 Coignard and Wickham 1999: 32–41, 134–43.
16 Reporter ohne Grenzen, Rangliste der Pressefreiheit 2017, www.reporter-ohne-grenzen.de; Grandt 2018.
17 Anna Samarina, 'Bestseller "Kontrollverlust" vom Buchhandel boykottiert – Auch in den Medien wird zensiert', *Epoch Times*, 10 November 2017, www.epochtimes.de; Anne L. Mösken, 'Die neue allgemeine Verunsicherung', *Berliner Zeitung*, no. 264, 11/12 November 2017, Magazin: 1–2; Wolf 2015.
18 Demian von Osten et al., 'Luftverkehr: Bundesregierung hatte Hinweis auf Abschussgefahr über der Ostukraine', *Süddeutsche Zeitung*, 27 April 2015; www. spiegel.de/video/todesflug-mh17-die-geschichte-eines-Kriegsverbrechens-video-1547968.html.

BIBLIOGRAPHY

Sources

Archival sources

APPArchives de la Préfecture de Police, Paris: Cabinet du préfet, série B A.
ASHATArchives du service historique de l'armée de terre, Vincennes : série 5 N.
BDICBibliothèque de Documentation Internationale Contemporaine, Nanterre: Guerre mondiale 1914–1918.
BArch BBundesarchiv Berlin: Press archives of the Reichslandbund; Filmothek.
BArch KBundesarchiv Koblenz: Alfred Weber papers.
BDIC Bibliothèque de Documentation Internationale Contemporaine, Nanterre: Guerre mondiale 1914–18.
GLAGenerallandesarchiv Karlsruhe: Ministerium für Unterricht und Kultus; Max von Baden papers.
LABLandesarchiv Berlin: Polizeipräsidium Berlin, Theaterzensur, A. Pr. Br. Rep. 030-05.
PA AAPolitisches Archiv des Auswärtigen Amtes, Berlin: WK 11c: Unternehmungen und Aufwiegelung gegen unsere Feinde; WK 11s: Gefangenenlager; WK 2: Vermittlungsaktionen, Friedensstimmung und Aktion zur Vermittlung des Friedens; Orientalia Generalia.

Printed sources

Newspapers and magazines

Berliner Tageblatt (http://zefys.staatsbibliothek-berlin.de/list/title/zdb/27646518/)
Bulletin des Armées de la République (http://gallica.bnf.fr/ark:/12148/bpt6k110075 q?rk=21459;2)
Deutsche Kriegsnachrichten
Die Welt (http://www.welt.de/)
Europe antiprussienne
Financial Times (http://www.ft.com/)
Glühlichter (http://anno.onb.ac.at/cgi-content/anno?aid=glu&datum=1915&zoom=33)
Journal officiel de la République française (http://gallica.bnf.fr/ark:/12148/cb328020951/ date)
Karnisch-Julische Kriegszeitung (http://anno.onb.ac.at/cgi-content/anno?aid=kjk)
La Baïonnette (http://labaionnette.free.fr/1916/page1916.htm)
Le canard enchaîné (http://digital.staatsbibliothek-berlin.de/werkansicht?PPN= PPN784951896)
Le Matin
Le Temps (http://gallica.bnf.fr/ark:/12148/cb34431794k/date)

Leipziger Volkszeitung (http://digital.slub-dresden.de/werkansicht/dlf/141582/)
Lustige Blätter (http://digi.ub.uni-heidelberg.de/diglit/lb)
Muskete
Norddeutsche Allgemeine Zeitung (http://zefys.staatsbibliothek-berlin.de/list/title/
    zdb/28028685/)
Simplicissimus (http://www.simplicissimus.info/index.php?id=5)
Süddeutsche Zeitung (http://www.sueddeutsche.de/)
The Boy's Own Annual
The Girl's Own Annual
The Graphic
The Punch (https://www.punch.co.uk/index)

Printed books, articles and series

Abdul Hamid (2007 [1914]). *Avant la débâcle de la Turquie: pensées et souvenirs de l'ex-sultan Abdul-Hamid*. Paris.
Arbeitsbericht 1915 bis 1918 (1920). In: *Jahrbuch des Zentralinstituts für Erziehung und Unterricht 2*.
Avenarius, Ferdinand (1918). *Das Bild als Narr. Die Karikatur in der Völkerverhetzung.* Munich.
Ball, Richard (2017). *Wilhelm der Letzte. Bilanz über 25 Jahre Regierungszeit Wilhelms II*, ed. by Nathalie Chamba and Eberhard Demm. Nordhausen.
Barbusse, Henri (1917). *Under Fire. The Story of a Squad*. New York. http://www.greatwar.nl/books/lefeu/underfire.html.
Barbusse, Henri (1937). *Lettres d'Henri Barbusse à sa femme, 1914–1917*. Paris.
Bäumer, Gertrud (1930). *Heimatchronik während des Weltkrieges*. Berlin.
Beneš, Eduard (1928). *My War Memoirs*. London.
Berger, Marcel and Allard, Paul (1932). *Les secrets de la censure pendant la guerre*. Paris.
Bernhardi, Friedrich von (1912). *Unsere Zukunft. Ein Mahnwort an das deutsche Volk*. Berlin.
Bernhardi, Friedrich von (1913 [1912]). *Deutschland und der nächste Krieg*. Berlin.
Bernstorff, Graf Johann Heinrich (1920). *My Three Years in America*. New York.
Bethmann Hollweg, Theobald von (1921). *Betrachtungen zum Weltkriege*. Vol. 2. Berlin.
Bihl, Wolf Dieter (ed.) (1991). *Deutsche Quellen zur Geschichte des Ersten Weltkrieges*. Darmstadt.
Binet-Valmer, Jean-Auguste G. (1918). *Mémoires d'un engagé volontaire*. Paris.
Blankenhorn, Heber (1919). *Adventures in Propaganda: Letters from an Intelligence Officer in France*. Boston and New York.
Blücher, Evelyn Princess (1920). *An English Wife in Berlin. A Private Memoir of Events, Politics, and Daily Life in Germany Throughout the War and the Social Revolution of 1918*. London.
Bonzon, Thierry and Robert, Jean-Louis (1989). *'Nous crions grâce' – 154 lettres de pacifistes juin–octobre 1916*. Paris.
Briemle, Theodosius (1915). *Kinderkreuzzug in Deutschland und Österreich zur Erlangung von Sieg und Frieden*. Paderborn.
Bryce, James (1915). *Report of the Committee of Alleged German Outrages*. London.
Buchner, Ernst (ed.) (1930). *1914–1918. Wie es damals daheim war. Das Kriegstagebuch eines Knaben*. Leipzig.

Burnett, John (ed.) (1974). *Useful Toil. Autobiographies of Working People from the 1820s to the 1920s*. London.

Caillaux, Joseph (1920). *Mes prisons. Devant l'histoire*. Paris.

Cook, Edward (1920). *The Press in War-Time. With Some Account of the Official Press Bureau*. London.

Cooper Willis, Irene (1972 [1919–21]). *England's Holy War. A Study of Liberal Idealism during the Great War*. New York and London.

Creel, Georges (1920). *How We Advertised America. The First Telling of the Amazing Story of the Committee on Public Information That Carried the Gospel of Americanism to Every Corner of the Globe*. New York and London. https://archive.org/stream/ howweadvertameri00creerich#page/n9/mode/2up

Czernin, Ottokar Count (1919). *In the World War*. London et al.

Daly, Jonathan and Trofimov, Leonid (eds) (2009). *Russia in War and Revolution 1914–1922. A Documentary History*. Indianapolis and Cambridge.

Deist, Wilhelm (ed.) (1970). *Militär und Innenpolitik im Weltkrieg 1914–1918*. Düsseldorf.

Delvert, Charles L. (1918). *Histoire d'une compagnie*. Paris.

Demm, Eberhard (1988). *Der Erste Weltkrieg in der internationalen Karikatur*. Hannover.

Demm, Eberhard (ed.) (1998). 'Kurt Hahn's memorandum on the subject of ethical imperialism 1918', *War in History* 5: 84–120. [German ed. 1990]

Demm, Eberhard and Christina Nikolajew (eds) (2013). *Auf Wache für die Nation. Erinnerungen. Der Propagandaagent Juozas Gabrys berichtet (1911–1918)*. Frankfurt/ Main.

Dernburg, Bernhard [1914–15]. *Germany and the War. Not a Defense but an Explanation*. New York.

Deutsche Reden (1915). *Deutsche Reden in schwerer Zeit*. Vols. 1–3. Berlin.

Djemal Pascha, Ahmed (1922). *Erinnerungen eines türkischen Staatsmannes*. Munich.

Documents (1936). *Documents diplomatiques français (1871–1914)*, ed. by Ministère des Affaires Étrangères, Commission de publications des documents relatifs aux origines de la Guerre de 1914, Series 3: 1911–14. Vol. 10: 17 March–23 July. Paris.

Dokumente (1957). *Dokumente und Materialien zur Geschichte der deutschen Arbeiterbewegung*, Serie II. Vol. 2, ed. by the Institut für Marxismus-Leninismus beim Zentralkomitee der Sozialistischen Einheitspartei Deutschlands. Berlin.

Dokumente (1958). *Dokumente und Materialien zur Geschichte der deutschen Arbeiterbewegung*, Serie II. Vol. 1, ed. by the Institut für Marxismus-Leninismus beim Zentralkomitee der Sozialistischen Einheitspartei Deutschlands. Berlin.

Dorgelès, Roland (1919). *Les croix de bois*. Paris.

Escudier, Paul and Richepin, Jean (1916). *Le livre rouge des atrocités allemandes d'après les rapports officiels des gouvernements français, anglais et belge par image*. Paris.

Gabrys, Juozas (1920). *Vers l'indépendance lituanienne. Faits, impressions, souvenirs 1907–1920*. Lausanne.

Gellert, Georg (1915). *Im Granatfeuer der Schlachtfelder. Erzählung aus dem Völkerkriege 1914/15*. Berlin.

Genevoix, Maurice (1916). *Sous Verdun*. Paris. [censored edition]

Genevoix, Maurice (1925). *Sous Verdun*. Paris. [complete edition]

Gerlach, Hellmut von (1994 [1922]). *Die große Zeit der Lüge. Der Erste Weltkrieg und die deutsche Mentalität (1871–1921)*. Bremen.

Glaeser, Ernst (1929 [1928]). *Jahrgang 1902*. Potsdam.

Golder, Frank A. (ed.) (1927). *Documents of Russian History 1914–1917*. New York and London.

Graham, Stephen (1917). *Russia and the World: A Study of the War and a Statement of the World-Problems That Now Confront Russia and Great Britain*. London.

Graux, Lucien (1918–20). *Les fausses nouvelles de la Grande Guerre*. 7 vols. Paris.

Graves, Robert (1929). *Good-bye to All That. An Autobiography*. London.

Gulbransson, Grete (2001). *Meine fremde Welt. Tagebücher. Vol. 2. 1913–1918*, ed. by Ulrike Lang. Frankfurt/Main.

Hagen, Gottfried (1990). *Die Türkei im Ersten Weltkrieg. Flugblätter und Flugschriften in arabischer, persischer und osmanisch-türkischer Sprache aus einer Sammlung der Universitätsbibliothek Heidelberg*. Frankfurt/Main.

Hitler, Adolf (1933). *Mein Kampf*. 23rd edition. Vol. 1. Munich.

Hofmannsthal, Hugo von (2011). *Sämtliche Werke, vol. XXXIV. Reden und Aufsätze vol. 3*, ed. by K. E. Bohnenkamp et al. Frankfurt/Main.

Jäckh, Ernst (1916). *Der aufsteigende Halbmond*. 6th edition. Stuttgart and Berlin.

Jünger, Ernst (1937 [1920]). *In Stahlgewittern. Ein Kriegstagebuch*. Berlin.

Kachulle, Doris (ed.) (1982). *Die Pöhlands im Krieg. Briefe einer sozialdemokratischen Bremer Arbeiterfamilie aus dem ersten Weltkrieg*. Köln.

Kellermann, Hermann (1915). *Der Krieg der Geister. Eine Auslese deutscher und ausländischer Stimmen zum Weltkrieg 1914*. Weimar.

Key, Ellen (1902). *Das Jahrhundert des Kindes*. Berlin.

Kirchner, Klaus (ed.) (1985). *Flugblattpropaganda im 1. Weltkrieg. Europa, vol. 1: Flugblätter aus England 1914–1918*. Erlangen.

Kirchner, Klaus (ed.) (1992). *Flugblattpropaganda im 1. Weltkrieg. Europa, vol. 2: Flugblätter aus Frankreich 1914–1918*. Erlangen.

Kirchner, Klaus (ed.) (2014). *Flugblattpropaganda im 1. Weltkrieg. Europa, vol. 3: Flugblätter aus Deutschland 1914–1918*. Erlangen.

Klemperer, Victor (1989). *Curriculum Vitae. Jugend um 1900*. Vol. 2. Berlin.

Kraus, Karl (1916). 'Gruß an Bahr und Hofmannsthal', *Die Fackel*, 18 May.

K. und K. Kriegsüberwachungsamt (ed.) (1916). *Protokoll über Zensurweisungen 1914–1916*. Vienna.

Kutzer, Ernst (1915). *Lustiges Kriegskinderbuch*. Nuremberg.

Lawrence, Thomas E. (2015 [1935]). *Seven Pillars of Wisdom*. http://gutenberg.net.au/ebooks01/0100111h.html.

Le Bon, Gustave (1915). *Enseignements psychologiques de la guerre européenne*. Paris.

Liebknecht, Karl (1966). *Gesammelte Reden und Schriften, vol. 8, August 1914 bis April 1916*. Berlin.

Lucas, Edward V. (1914). *Swollen Headed William*. London.

Ludendorff, Erich (1919). *My War Memories*. Vol. 1. London. https://babel.hathitrust.org/cgi/pt?id=mdp.49015000156399;view=1up;seq=9.

Ludendorff, Erich (ed.) (1921). *Urkunden der Obersten Heeresleitung über ihre Tätigkeit 1916/18*. Berlin.

Malatesta, Errico (1915). *International Manifesto against the War*. London. https://kslnotes.files.wordpress.com/2017/03/manifest_scan.pdf.

Mann, Golo (1991). *Erinnerungen und Gedanken: eine Jugend in Deutschland*. Frankfurt/Main.

Mann, Heinrich (2012). *Essays und Publizistik. Kritische Gesamtausgabe*, ed. by Wolfgang Klein, Anne Flierl and Volker Riedel. Bielefeld.

Mann, Klaus (2000 [1932]). *Kind dieser Zeit*. Reinbek.

Mann, Thomas (1968 [1918]). 'Betrachtungen eines Unpolitischen', in: Hans Bürgin (ed.). *Politische Schriften und Reden*, Vol. 1. Frankfurt/Main.

Masaryk, Tomàs G. (1925). *Die Weltrevolution. Erinnerungen und Betrachtung 1914–1918.* Berlin.

Materna, Ingo and Schreckenbach, Hans Joachim (eds) (1987). *Berichte des Berliner Polizeipräsidenten zur Stimmung und Lage der Bevölkerung in Berlin 1914–1918. Dokumente aus geheimen Archiven, Band 4.* Weimar.

Max von Baden (1968). *Erinnerungen und Dokumente,* ed. by Golo Mann and Andreas Burckhardt. Stuttgart

Meinecke, Friedrich (1969). *Autobiographische Schriften. Werke. Vol. 8,* ed. by Eberhard Kessel. Stuttgart.

Meyer, Ernst (ed.) (1927). *'Spartakus im Kriege'. Die illegalen Flugblätter des Spartakusbundes im Kriege.* Berlin.

Mihaly, Jo (1986 [1982]). *. . . da gibt's ein Wiedersehn. Kriegstagebuch eines Mädchens.* Munich.

Mistinguett (1954). *Mein ganzes Leben.* Zurich.

Morgenthau, Henry (1918). *Ambassador Morgenthau's Story.* Garden City and New York.

Mostert, Johanna (1918). 'An den Gestaden des Friedens', *Töchter-Album* 64: 93–134.

Moule, Handley C.G. (1917). 'Open letter to the women of the nation', *Girls Own Annual* 38: 40–1.

Naumann, Friedrich (1913 [1899]). *Asia.* Berlin.

Naumann, Friedrich (1915). *Mitteleuropa.* Berlin.

Nicolai, Walter (1920). *Nachrichtendienst, Presse und Volksstimmung im Weltkrieg.* Berlin.

Oberzensurstelle (1973 [1917]). 'Kommunikationsüberwachende Vorschriften des Jahres 1917', in: H.-D. Fischer 1973: 194–275.

Oldenburg-Januschau, Elard von (1936). *Erinnerungen.* Leipzig.

Olszewski, Karl E. (1915). *Der Kriegs-Struwwelpeter.* Munich.

Pankhurst, Sylvia (1932). *The Home Front. A Mirror to Life in England during the World War.* London.

Parliamentary Debates of the House of Commons, Parliamentary Session 1917–18, 5th series.

Redlich, Joseph (1929). *Austrian War Government.* New Haven and London.

Redlich, Joseph (2011). *Schicksalsjahre Österreichs. Die Erinnerungen und Tagebücher Joseph Redlichs, vol. 1 and 2.* Vienna et al.

Reichsbank, Nachrichtenbüro für die Kriegsanleihen (ed.) [1916]. *Zur VI. Kriegsanleihe. Leitfaden und Nachschlageblätter zur Werbearbeit.* [Berlin]

Reichstagsprotokolle: *Stenographische Berichte der Verhandlungen des Deutschen Reichstags, 13. Legislaturperiode.* http://www.reichstagsprotokolle.de/rtbiiaufauf_k13.html.

Richert, Dominik (1989). *Beste Gelegenheit zum Sterben. Meine Erlebnisse im Krieg 1914–1918,* ed. by Angelika Tramitz and Bernd Ulrich. Munich.

Rickards, Maurice (1968). *Posters of the First World War.* London.

Rip (1915). *1915. Revue de guerre en 2 actes (22 avril 1915).* Paris. http://gallica.bnf.fr/ark:/12148/bpt6k65196365/f7.image.

Rivas, C. (=Yvonne Pouvreau) (1918). *La Lituanie sous le joug allemand 1915–1918. Le plan annexioniste allemand en Lituanie.* Lausanne.

Rolland, Romain (1983 [1952]). *Das Gewissen Europas. Tagebuch der Kriegsjahre 1914–1919.* 3 vols. Berlin.

Rühlmann, Paul (1918). *Die französische Schule und der Weltkrieg.* Leipzig.

Sassoon, Siegfried (1931 [1930]). *Memoirs of an Infantry Officer.* Leipzig.

Scheler, Max (1917). *Der Genius des Krieges und der deutsche Krieg.* Leipzig.

Schneider, Gerhard (2013). *In eiserner Zeit. Kriegswahrzeichen im Ersten Weltkrieg. Ein Katalog*. Schwalbach/Taunus.

Schulz-Besser, Ernst (1915). *Die Karikatur im Weltkriege*. Leipzig.

Schumacher, Tony (1915). *Wenn Vater im Krieg ist*. 3rd edition. Stuttgart.

Scott, James B. (ed.) (1921). *Official Statements of War Aims and Peace Proposals, December 1916 to November 1918*. Washington. https://babel.hathitrust.org/cgi/pt?id= uc1.32106015174201;view=1up;seq=7.

Seymour, Charles (ed.) (1926). *The Intimate Papers of Colonel House*. 4 vols. London.

Silber, Jules C. (1932). *The Invisible Weapons*. London.

Sombart, Werner (1915). *Händler und Helden*. Berlin.

Sonderausstellung (1915). *Sonderausstellung Schule und Krieg*, ed. by Zentralinstitut für Erziehung und Unterricht. Berlin.

Sowerwine, Aude and Sowerwine, Charles (eds) (1985). *Le mouvement ouvrier français contre la guerre 1914–1918. vol. II : L'opposition des femmes*. Paris.

Sowerwine, Aude and Sowerwine, Charles (1985 II, 2). 'Un devoir urgent pour les femmes'. (December 1915).

Sowerwine, Aude and Sowerwine, Charles (1985 II, 3). 'Circulaire. Fédération national d'institutrices et d'instituteurs'. (1 September 1915).

Sowerwine, Aude and Sowerwine, Charles (1985 II, 4). 'Les instituteurs syndicalistes et la guerre'. (25 May 1917).

Sowerwine, Aude and Sowerwine, Charles (1985 II, 5). Madeleine Vernet: 'Hélène Brion, une belle conscience et une sombre affaire'. (November 1917).

Sowerwine, Aude and Sowerwine, Charles (1985 II, 7). Marie et François Mayoux: 'La propagande pacifiste pendant la guerre. Notre affaire'. (1918).

Sowerwine, Aude and Sowerwine, Charles (eds) (1985). *Le mouvement ouvrier français contre la guerre 1914–1918. vol. III : L'opposition syndicaliste*. Paris.

Sowerwine, Aude and Sowerwine, Charles (1985 III, 1). Alfred Rosmer: 'I. La Conférence de Zimmerwald. Lettres aux Abonnés de la *Vie ouvrière*'. (1 November 1915).

Sowerwine, Aude and Sowerwine, Charles (eds) (1985). *Le mouvement ouvrier français contre la guerre 1914–1918. vol. IV : L'opposition anarchiste*. Paris.

Sowerwine, Aude and Sowerwine, Charles (1985 IV, 1). Pierre Chardon: 'Les anarchistes et la guerre. Deux attitudes'. Geneva (1915).

Sowerwine, Aude and Sowerwine, Charles (1985 IV, 3). '2eme lettre [aux abonnés des *Temps nouveaux*]. Un désaccord. Nos explications'. Patronnée et diffusée par le CRRI (May 1916).

Sowerwine, Aude and Sowerwine, Charles (1985 IV, 5). 'Réponse de Errico Malatesta au "manifeste des Seize". Anarchistes de gouvernement'. (March 1917).

Sowerwine, Aude and Sowerwine, Charles (1985 IV, 6). 'A propos du manifeste des Seize. Déclaration et protestation. Par le Groupe d'études anarchistes-communistes'. (May 1916).

Sowerwine, Aude and Sowerwine, Charles (1985 IV, 7). Maurice Charron: 'La guerre'. Geneva (August 1916).

Sowerwine, Aude and Sowerwine, Charles (1985 IV, 8). 'La guerre'. Anonymous. (November 1917).

Sowerwine, Aude and Sowerwine, Charles (eds) (1985). *Le mouvement ouvrier français contre la guerre 1914–1918. vol. V : Le comité pour la reprise des relations internationales*. Paris.

Sowerwine, Aude and Sowerwine, Charles (1985 V, 6). CRRI: 'Le parti socialiste italien et la guerre européenne'. (End of 1916).

Sowerwine, Aude and Sowerwine, Charles (eds) (1985). *Le mouvement ouvrier français contre la guerre 1914–1918. vol. VI : La minorité du Parti Socialiste.* Paris.

Sowerwine, Aude and Sowerwine, Charles (1985 VI, 1). Parti Socialiste, Fédération de la Haute Vienne: 'Rapport. Limoges'. (15 May 1915).

Sowerwine, Aude and Sowerwine, Charles (1985 VI, 2). 'Circulaire de la Minorité du Parti Socialiste aux Fédérations'. (November 1916).

Sowerwine, Aude and Sowerwine, Charles (1985 VI, 3). '2eme Circulaire de la Minorité du Parti Socialiste aux Fédérations'. (6 May 1917).

Sowerwine, Aude and Sowerwine, Charles (eds) (1985). *Le mouvement ouvrier français contre la guerre 1914–1918. vol. VII : Tracts et documents divers.* Paris.

Sowerwine, Aude and Sowerwine, Charles (1985 VII, 1). 'Femmes du Prolétariat. Où sont vos maris ? Où sont vos fils ?' (March 1915).

Sowerwine, Aude and Sowerwine, Charles (1985 VII, 3). 'Aux femmes du Prolétariat'. By Louise Saumoneau. (No date [1915?]).

Sowerwine, Aude and Sowerwine, Charles (1985 VII, 4). 'Aux Femmes du Prolétariat'. By Louise Saumoneau. (June 1915)

Spears, Edward (1968 [1930]). *En Liaison 1914. A Narrative of the Great Retreat.* London.

Steinlen, Théophile A. (1978). *Théophile Alexandre Steinlen 1859–1923. Staatliche Kunsthalle Berlin.* Berlin.

Stopford, F. (1916). *Raemaekers Cartoons.* New York.

Stuart, Campbell (1920). *Secrets of Crewe House. The Story of a Famous Campaign.* London. https://archive.org/details/secretsofcreweho00stua

Times History (1914–20). *The Times History of the War.* Vol. I–XX. London.

Troeltsch, Ernst (1915). 'Der Kulturkrieg', in: Deutsche Reden 1915. Vol. 3: 209–49.

Verhandlungen (1918). *Verhandlungen der Ersten Kammer der Stände-Versammlung des Großherzogtums Baden vom 48. Landtag (1917–18).* Protokollheft, Heft 163. Karlsruhe: 8–12.

Vogeler, Heinrich (1989). *Werden. Erinnerungen.* Fischerhude.

Waltz, Johann Jakob (Hansi) and Tonnelat, Ernest (1922). *A travers les lignes ennemies. 3 années d'offensive contre le moral allemand.* Paris. https://archive.org/stream/traversleslign00hans#page/n9/mode/2up.

Weber, Alfred (1999a). *Politische Theorie und Tagespolitik (1903–1933). Alfred Weber-Gesamtausgabe, vol. 7,* ed. by Eberhard Demm. Marburg.

Weber, Alfred (1999b [1915]). 'Gedanken zur deutschen Sendung', in: Weber 1999a: 116–77.

Weber, Alfred (1999c [1917]). 'Kontinentale Verständigung', in: Weber 1999a: 182–6.

Weber, Alfred (1999d [1915]). 'Bemerkungen über die auswärtige Politik und die Kriegsziele', in: Weber 1999a: 109–15.

Weber, Alfred (1999e [1920]). '[Eingabe an General Ludendorff]', in: Weber 1999a: 109–15.

Weber, Max (1989 [1916–17]). *Die Wirtschaftsethik der Weltreligionen. Konfuzianismus und Taoismus.* Max Weber Gesamtausgabe I, 19, Tübingen.

Wells, Herbert G. (1914). *The War That Will End War.* London.

Wilson, Trevor (ed.) (1970). *The Political Diaries of C. P. Scott, 1911–1928.* London.

Witkop, Philipp (ed.) (1933 [1918]). *Kriegsbriefe gefallener Studenten.* Munich.

Witzenmann, Walter (1998). *Der Krieg. Geographische, politische und zoologische Gedanken eines sechsjährigen am Anfang des Ersten Weltkrieges.* 2nd edition. Konstanz.

Yalman, Ahmed Emin (1930). *Turkey in the World War.* New Haven and London.

Yalman, Ahmed Emin (1957). *Turkey in my time.* 2nd edition. Oklahoma.

Zeman, Zbyněk (ed.) (1958). *Germany and the Revolution in Russia 1915–1918. Documents from the Archives of the German Foreign Ministry*. London.

Zislin, Henri (1916). *Album*. Vol. 1. Paris. http://www.kaskapointe.fr/images/zislin3.jpg (retrieved 27 August 2017).

Zuckmayer, Carl (1966). *Als wär's ein Stück von mir. Horen der Freundschaft*. Frankfurt/Main.

Zweig, Stefan (1984). *Tagebücher*, ed. by Knut Beck. Frankfurt/Main.

Zweig, Stefan (1998). *Briefe 1914–1919*, ed. by Knut Beck et al. Frankfurt/Main.

Zweig, Stefan (2001 [1942]). *Die Welt von gestern. Erinnerungen eines Europäers*. Frankfurt/Main.

Secondary literature

Acemoglu, Daron and Robinson, James A. (2013). *Why Nations Fail. The Origins of Power, Prosperity and Poverty*. London.

Achs, Oskar (2013). 'Von der Feder zum Säbel. Das Wiener Schulwesen im Ersten Weltkrieg', in: Pfoser and Weigl 2013: 420–9.

Afflerbach, Holger (2015a). 'War aims and the chances for a compromise peace during the First World War', in: Afflerbach 2015b: 237–54.

Afflerbach, Holger (ed.) (2015b). *The Purpose of the First World War. War Aims and Military Strategies*. Berlin and Boston.

Aksakal, Mustafa (2008). *The Ottoman Road to War in 1914. The Ottoman Empire and the First World War*. Cambridge.

Aksakal, Mustafa (2011). '"Holy War made in Germany"? Ottoman origins of the 1914 jihad', *War in History* 18: 184–99.

Albes, Jens (1996). *Worte wie Waffen. Die deutsche Propaganda in Spanien während des Ersten Weltkrieges*. Essen.

Allain, Jean Claude (1981). *Joseph Caillaux. L'Oracle 1914–1944*. Paris.

Altenhöner, Florian (2008). *Kommunikation und Kontrolle. Gerüchte und städtische Öffentlichkeit in Berlin und London 1914/1918*. Munich.

Altrichter, Friedrich (1933). *Die seelischen Kräfte des Deutschen Heeres im Frieden und im Weltkriege*. Berlin.

Amalvi, Christian (1998). 'L'apprentissage de la revanche en France dans la littérature de vulgarisation historique de 1871 à 1914', in: Giuntella and Nardi 1998: 53–65.

Artinger, Kai (2000). *Agonie und Aufklärung. Krieg und Kunst in Großbritannien und Deutschland im 1. Weltkrieg*. Weimar.

Ashworth, Tony (1980). *Trench Warfare 1914–1918. The Live and Let Live System*. London.

Audoin-Rouzeau, Stéphane (1990). '"Bourrage de crâne" et information en France de 1914 à 1918', in: Audoin-Rouzeau and Becker 1990: 163–73.

Audoin-Rouzeau, Stéphane (1992). *Men at War 1914–1918. National Sentiment and Trench Journalism in France during the first World War*. Oxford. [French original: 1986]

Audoin-Rouzeau, Stéphane (1993a). *La guerre des enfants 1914–1918. Essai d'histoire culturelle*. Paris.

Audoin-Rouzeau, Stéphane (1993b). 'Die mobilisierten Kinder: Die Erziehung zum Krieg in französischen Schulen', in: Hirschfeld et al. 1993: 151–74.

Audoin-Rouzeau, Stéphane (1994). 'L'enfant héroïque en 1914–1918', in: Becker et al. 1994: 173–82.

Audoin-Rouzeau, Stéphane (1997). 'Children and the primary school of France 1914–1918', in: Horne 1997b: 39–52.

Audoin-Rouzeau, Stéphane and Becker, Annette (2000). *14–18, Retrouver la Guerre*. Paris.

Audoin-Rouzeau, Stéphane and Becker, Jean-Jacques (eds) (1990). *Les sociétés européennes et la guerre*. Paris.

Axelrod, Alan (2009). *Selling the Great War. The Making of American Propaganda*. New York.

Badem, Candan (2014). 'Kars, Ardahan and Batum during World War I', Paper read at the conference titled 'Not All Quiet on the Ottoman Fronts, Neglected Perspectives on a Global War, 1914–1918', Istanbul, April 2014, www.hsozkult.de/conferencereport/id/tagungsberichte-5410.

Ballhausen, Thomas and Kren, Günter (2003). 'Musen in Uniform. Filmische Kriegsberichterstattung Österreich-Ungarns während des ersten Weltkrieges', in: Džambo 2003b: 83–97.

Bauerkämper, Arnd and Julien, Elise (2010a). 'Einleitung: Durchhalten! Kriegskulturen und Handlungspraktiken im Ersten Weltkrieg', in: Bauerkämper and Julien 2010b: 7–28.

Bauerkämper, Arnd and Julien, Elise (ed.) (2010b). *Durchhalten! Krieg und Gesellschaft im Vergleich 1914–1918*. Göttingen.

Baumeister, Martin (2005). *Kriegstheater. Großstadt, Front und Massenkultur 1914–1918*. Essen.

Bavendamm, Gundula (2004). *Spionage und Verrat. Konspirative Kriegserzählungen und französische Innenpolitik 1914–1917*. Essen.

Bazzanella, Angelo (1980). 'Die Stimme der Illiteraten. Volk und Krieg in Italien 1915–1918', in: Vondung 1980b: 334–51.

Beaupré, Nicolas (2006). *Ecrire en guerre, écrire la guerre. France, Allemagne 1914–1920*. Paris.

Beaupré, Nicolas (2014). 'Soldier-writers and poets', in: Winter et al. 2014, vol. 3: 445–74.

Becker, Annette (2014). 'Arts', in: Winter et al. 2014, vol. 3: 504–27.

Becker, Jean-Jacques (1977). *1914. Comment les Français sont entrés dans la guerre*. Paris.

Becker, Jean-Jacques (1986). *The Great War and the French People*. New York [French original: 1983]

Becker, Jean-Jacques, Winter, Jay and Krumeich, Gerd (eds.) (1994). *Guerre et Cultures 1914–1918*. Paris.

Beckett, Jan (1990). 'The real unknown army. British conscripts 1916–1919', in: Audoin-Rouzeau and Becker 1990: 339–55.

Beil, Christine (2004). *Der ausgestellte Krieg. Präsentationen des Ersten Weltkriegs 1915–1939. Tübinger Vereinigung für Volkskunde*. Tübingen.

Beitin, Andreas F. (2000). 'Geprägte Propaganda. Karl Goetz und seine "Lusitania-Medaille"', in: Zühlke 2000: 277–92.

Benda, Julien (1927). *La trahison des clercs*. Paris.

Bendick, Rainer (1999). *Kriegserwartung und Kriegserfahrung. Der Erste Weltkrieg in deutschen und französischen Schulgeschichtsbüchern (1900–1939/45)*. Pfaffenweiler.

Berg, Jan (2015). 'Alles verfügbare Geld gehört dem Vaterland! Kriegsanleihen als Finanzquellen des ersten Weltkriegs am Beispiel des Regierungsbezirks Stralsund', *Pommern. Zeitschrift für Kultur und Geschichte* 53, 4: 8–15.

Bernard, Georg (1993). 'Zu Weihnachten gab es Kanonen als Kriegsspielzeug', in: Hämmerle 1993: 242–7.

Besier, Gerhard (ed.) (1984). *Die protestantischen Kirchen Europas im Ersten Weltkrieg.* Göttingen.

Bessel, Richard (1997). 'Mobilization and demobilization in Germany, 1916–1919', in: Horne 1997b: 212–22.

Beurier, Joelle (2008). 'Information, censorship or propaganda? The illustrated French press in the First World War', in: Jones et al. 2008: 293–324.

Beyrau, Dietrich and Shcherbinin, Pawel P. (2010). 'Alles für die Front: Russland im Krieg 1914–1922', in: Bauerkämper and Julien 2010b: 151–77.

Bianchi, Bruna (2005). 'Exécutions sommaires et condamnations à mort au sein de l'armée italienne durant la grande guerre', in: Cazals 2005: 237–46.

Bianchi, Bruna (2008). 'Donne e uomini di pace in tempi di guerra', in: Isenghi and Ceschin 2008: 129–38.

Bianchi, Roberto (2016). 'Social conflict and control, protest and repression (Italy)', in: https://encyclopedia.1914-1918-online.net/article/social_conflict_and_control_protest_and_repression_italy?version=1.0.

Bihl, Wolf Dieter (1975). *Die Kaukasus-Politik der Mittelmächte. Vol. 1: Ihre Basis in der Orient-Politik und ihre Aktion 1914–1917.* Vienna et al.

Bihl, Wolf Dieter (1992). *Die Kaukasus-Politik der Mittelmächte. Vol. 2: Die Zeit der versuchten kaukasischen Staatlichkeit (1917–1918).* Vienna et al.

Bir, Christoph et al. (2000). 'Bewegte Bilder. Der Film – ein neues Medium propagiert den Krieg', in: Zühlke 2000: 327–96.

Bliembach, Eva (1992). '"Kriegslieferanten" aus dem Simplicissimus: deutsche Satire-Zeitschriften im unfreiwilligen Dienst der französischen Kriegspropaganda', in Kirchner 1992: 468–533.

Bonadeo, Alfredo (1995). *D'Annunzio and the great War.* Madison and London.

Boniface, Xavier (2008). 'Les aumôniers militaires', in: Robert Vandenbussche (ed.). *De Georges Clemenceau à Jacques Chirac: l'état et la pratique de la Loi de Séparation.* Lille: 131–47.

Bonzon, Thierry (1997). 'The labor market and the industrial mobilization 1915–1917', in: Winter and Robert 1997: 164–95.

Boulanger, Philippe (1998). 'Les embusqués de la Première Guerre mondiale'. *GMCC* 192: 87–100.

Bouloc, François (2008). '"War profiteers" and "war profiters": Representing economic gain in France during the First World War', in: Jones et al. 2008: 325–53.

Bourne, John M. (1989). *Britain and the Great War 1914–1918.* London et al.

Bragulla, Mareen (2007). *Die Nachrichtenstelle für den Orient. Fallstudien einer Propagandainstitution im Ersten Weltkrieg.* Saarbrücken.

Brandt, Susanne (1993). 'Kriegssammlungen im Ersten Weltkrieg: Denkmäler oder Laboratoires d'histoire?' In: Hirschfeld et al. 1993: 241–58.

Brenner, Andrea (2013). 'Das Maisgespenst im Stacheldraht. Improvisation und Ersatz in der Wiener Lebensmittelversorgung des Ersten Weltkriegs', in: Pfoser and Weigl 2013: 140–9.

Brocks, Christine (2008). *Die bunte Welt des Krieges. Bildpostkarten des Ersten Weltkriegs 1914–1918.* Essen.

Brocks, Christine and Ziemann, Benjamin (1994). '"Vom Soldatenleben hätte ich grade genug". Der Erste Weltkrieg in der Feldpost von Soldaten', in: Rother 1994b: 109–20.

Bruendel, Steffen (2003). *Volksgemeinschaft oder Volksstaat. Die 'Ideen von 1914' und die Neuordnung Deutschlands im Ersten Weltkrieg*. Berlin.

Bruendel, Steffen (2010). 'Vor-Bilder des Durchhaltens. Die deutsche Kriegsanleihe-Werbung, 1917/1918', in: Bauerkämper and Julien 2010b: 81–108.

Bruendel, Steffen (2014). 'Between acceptance and refusal – soldiers' attitudes towards war (Germany)' in: www.encyclopedia.1914-1918-online.net.

Bruntz, George G. (1938). *Allied Propaganda and the Collapse of the German Empire in 1918*. Stanford.

Bub, Gertraude (1938). *Der deutsche Film im Weltkrieg und sein publizistischer Einsatz.*. Doctoral Dissertation. Berlin.

Buschmann, Nikolaus (1997). 'Der verschwiegene Krieg: Kommunikation zwischen Front und Heimatfront', in: Hirschfeld et al. 1997: 208–24.

Bush, Julia (1984). *Behind the Lines. East London Labour 1914–1919*. London.

Cabanes, Bruno (2004). 'Ce que dit le contrôle postal'. in: Prochasson and Rasmussen 2004: 55–75.

Candeloro, Giorgio (1978). *Storia dell'Italia moderna, vol. VIII: La prima guerra mondiale, il dopoguerra, l'avvento del fascismo*. Milan.

Capozzola, Christopher (2008). *Uncle Sam Wants You: World War I and the Making of the Modern American Citizen*. Oxford.

Carsten, Francis L. (1982). *War against War. British and German Radical Movements in the First World War*. London.

Cazals, Rémy (ed.) (2005). *La Grande Guerre. Pratique et expérience*. Toulouse.

Ceadel, Martin (2014). 'Pacifism', in: Winter et al. 2014, vol. 2: 576–605.

Cecil, Hugh and Liddle, Peter H. (eds) (1996). *Facing Armageddon. A First World War Experienced*. London.

Ceschin, Daniele (2008). 'Confino di guerra. Gli internati civili tra disfattismo, persecuzione e repressione', in: Isnenghi and Ceschin 2008: 216–28.

Chickering, Roger (2002 [1998]). *Das Deutsche Reich und der Erste Weltkrieg*. Munich.

Chickering, Roger (2015). 'Strategy, politics, and the quest for a negotiated peace. The German case, 1914–18', in: Afflerbach 2015b: 97–115.

Christadler, Marieluise (1978). *Kriegserziehung im Jugendbuch. Literarische Mobilmachung in Deutschland und Frankreich vor 1914*. Doctoral Dissertation. Frankfurt/Main.

Cochet, Annick (1986). *L'opinion et le moral des soldats en 1916 d'après les Archives du Contrôle Postal*. Unpublished Doctoral Dissertation. Nanterre.

Cochet, Annick (1990). 'Les soldats français', in: Audoin-Rouzeau and Becker 1990: 357–66.

Cohen, Aaron J. (2002). 'Flowers of evil. Mass media, child psychology, and the struggle for Russia's future during the First World War', in: James A. Marten (ed.). *Children at War: A Historical Anthology*. New York and London: 38–49.

Coignard, Sophie and Wickham, Alexandre (1999). *L'omerta française*. Paris.

Collins, Larry J. (2004). *Theatre at War, 1914–18*. Oldham.

Collins, Ross F. (2008). 'Justifying war: American children's publications and the First World War', www.ndsu.edu/pubweb/~rcollins/491americanpower/ childrenspubsinwwI.pdf.

Collins, Ross F. (2011). *Children, War and Propaganda*. New York et al.

Collins, Ross F. (2012). 'This is your propaganda, kids. Building a war myth for World War I children', *Journalism History* 38: 13–22.

Collonges, Julien and Picaud, Carine (2008). 'Erlebebnisberichte und Propaganda: die Frontzeitungen des Ersten Weltkriegs', in: Thomas 2008: 104–32.

Corner, Paul and Procacci, Giovana (1997). 'The Italian experience of "total" mobilization, 1915–1920', in: Horne 1997b: 223–40.

Cornwall, Mark (1997). 'Morale and patriotism in the Austro-Hungarian army 1914–1918', in: Horne 1997b: 173–91.

Cornwall, Mark (2000). *The Undermining of Austria-Hungary. The Battle for Hearts and Minds.* Basingstoke, Hampshire.

Cornwall, Mark (2016). 'Das Ringen um die Moral des Hinterlandes', in: Rumpler 2016: 393–435.

Cornwell, Graham A. (2014). 'The Great War on the Moroccan front', in: Helmut Bley and Anorthe Kremers (eds). *The World during the First World War.* Essen.

Courmont, Juliette (2010). *L'odeur de l'ennemi 1914–1918.* Paris.

Cramer, Alan (1997). '*Wackes* at War. Alsace-Lorraine and the failure of German national mobilization 1914–1918', in: Horne 1997b: 105–21.

Creutz, Martin (1996). *Die Pressepolitik der kaiserlichen Regierung während des Ersten Weltkrieges.* Frankfurt/Main.

Cronier, Emmanuelle (2013). *Permissionnaires dans la Grande Guerre.* Paris.

Darmon, Pierre (2002). *Vivre à Paris pendant la Grande Guerre.* Paris.

DeBauche, Leslie M. (1999). 'The United States' Film Industry and World War One', in: Paris 1999: 138–61.

DeGroot, Gerard J. (1996). *Blighty. British Society in the Era of the Great War.* London and New York.

Deist, Wilhelm (1990). 'Censorship and propaganda in Germany during the First World War', in: Audoin-Rouzeau and Becker 1990: 199–211.

Deist, Wilhelm (1991). 'Aufgaben und Kompetenzen der Militärbefehlshaber', in: Wilhelm Deist, *Militär, Staat und Gesellschaft. Studien zur preußisch-deutschen Militärgeschichte.* Munich: 126–38.

Deist, Wilhelm (1996). 'The military collapse of the German Empire: the reality behind the stab-in-the-back-myth', *War in History* 3: 186–207.

Demm, Eberhard (1986). 'Alfred Weber im Ersten Weltkrieg', in: Eberhard Demm (ed.). *Alfred Weber als Politiker und Gelehrter. Die Referate des ersten Alfred Weber-Kongresses in Heidelberg.* Stuttgart: 22–39.

Demm, Eberhard (1990). *Ein Liberaler in Kaiserreich und Republik. Der politische Weg Alfred Webers bis 1920.* Boppard.

Demm, Eberhard (2000a). 'Barbusse et son Feu – La dernière cartouche de la propagande de guerre française', *GMCC* 197: 43–63.

Demm, Eberhard (2000b [1982]). 'Thomas Mann und Alfred Weber im Ersten Weltkrieg', in: Demm 2000d: 205–17.

Demm, Eberhard (2000c [1999]). 'Philosemitism and Antisemitism: Nietzsche, Sombart, Alfred Weber', in: Demm 2000d: 111–28.

Demm, Eberhard (2000d). *Geist und Politik im 20. Jahrhundert. Gesammelte Aufsätze zu Alfred Weber.* Frankfurt/Main.

Demm, Eberhard (2002a [1984]). 'Friedrich von der Ropp und die litauische Frage 1916–1919', in: Demm 2002k: 259–97.

Demm, Eberhard (2002b [1986]). 'Die Deutsch-Litauische Gesellschaft (1917–1918)', in: Demm 2002k: 299–313.

Demm, Eberhard (2002c [1988]). 'Les thèmes de la propagande allemande en 1914', in: Demm 2002k: 11–25.

Demm, Eberhard (2002d [1990]). 'Une initiative de paix avortée. Lord Lansdowne et le Prince Max de Bade', in: Demm 2002k: 365–79.

Demm, Eberhard (2002e [1993]). 'Propaganda and caricature in the First World War', in: Demm 2002k: 27–52.

Demm, Eberhard (2002f [1994]). 'Anschluß, Autonomie oder Unabhängigkeit? Die deutsche Litauenpolitik im Ersten Weltkrieg und das Selbstbestimmungsrecht der Völker', in: Demm 2002k: 133–8.

Demm, Eberhard (2002g [1996]). 'German teachers at war', in: Demm 2002k: 61–70.

Demm, Eberhard (2002h [2001]). 'Deutschlands Kinder im Ersten Weltkrieg. Zwischen Propaganda und Sozialfürsorge', in: Demm 2002k: 71–132.

Demm, Eberhard (2002i [2001]). 'Nationalistische Propaganda und Protodiplomatie als ethnisches Geschäft: Juozas Gabrys, die "Union des Nationalités" und die Befreiung Litauens (1911–1919)', in: Demm 2002k: 139–258.

Demm, Eberhard (2002j [2001]). 'World War I: Germany and France', in: Demm 2002k: 53–9.

Demm, Eberhard (2002k). *Ostpolitik und Propaganda im Ersten Weltkrieg*. Frankfurt/Main.

Demm, Eberhard (2009). 'Edgar Jaffé', in: Jarosław Suchoples and Katy Turton (eds). *Forgotten by History. New Research on Twentieth Century Europe and America*. Berlin and Münster: 86–101.

Demm, Eberhard (2014). *Else Jaffé-von Richthofen. Erfülltes Leben zwischen Max und Alfred Weber*. Schriften des Bundesarchivs Vol. 74. Dusseldorf.

Demm, Eberhard (2015). 'Alfred Weber, "Mitteleuropa" und die litauische Frage im Ersten Weltkrieg', *Annaberger Annalen* 23: 231–44.

Demm, Eberhard (2016). 'Censorship and propaganda in World War I and their impact on mass indoctrination in the 20th century', in: Suchoples and James 2016: 439–75.

Demm, Eberhard (2018a [2003–4]). 'La chanson française de la Première Guerre mondiale', in: Demm 2018h: 359–76.

Demm, Eberhard (2018b [2005]). '"Maikäfer flieg', dein Vater ist im Krieg". Wie Berliner Familien den Ersten Weltkrieg erlebten', in: Demm 2018h: 273–82.

Demm, Eberhard (2018c [2005]). 'Zwischen Kulturkonflikt und Akkulturation: Deutsche Offiziere im Osmanischen Reich', in: Demm 2018h: 213–48.

Demm, Eberhard (2018d [2007]). 'L'image de l'ennemi dans la propagande allemande et alliée pendant la Première Guerre mondiale', in: Demm 2018h: 345–58.

Demm, Eberhard (2018e [2011]). 'Friedrich Naumann, *Die Hilfe* und die orientalische Frage', in: Demm 2018h: 249–71.

Demm, Eberhard (2018f [2014]). 'Propaganda through cartoons', in: Demm 2018h: 321–44.

Demm, Eberhard (2018g [2016]). 'Kinder und Propaganda im Ersten Weltkrieg', in: Demm 2018h: 377–404.

Demm, Eberhard (2018h). *Von Wilhelm II. zu Wilhelm dem Letzten. Streiflichter zur Wilhelminischen Zeit*, ed. by Nathalie Chamba. Nordhausen.

Demm, Eberhard and Sterling, Christopher (2005). 'Propaganda', in: Spencer Tucker (ed.). *World War I Encyclopaedia: A Political, Social, and Military History*. Santa Barbara. Vol. 3: 941–5.

Denscher, Bernhard (2013). 'Überall vor den Plakaten bildeten sich Ansammlungen', in: Pfoser and Weigl 2013: 494–501.

Deutschland (1968). vol. 1, ed. by Fritz Klein. Berlin.

Deutschland (1969). vol. 3, ed. by Joachim Petzold. Berlin.

Deutschland (1970). vol. 2, ed. by Willibald Gutsche. Berlin.

Dewitz, Bodo von (1994). 'Zur Geschichte der Kriegsfotografie des Ersten Weltkrieges', in: Rother 1994b: 163–76.

Dikötter, Frank (2014). *Maos großer Hunger. Massenmord und Menschenexperiment in China (1958–1962)*. Stuttgart.

Dolderer, Winfried (1989). *Deutscher Imperialismus und belgischer Nationalitätenkonflit. Die Rezeption der Flamenfrage in der deutschen Öffentlichkeit und deutsch-flämische Kontakte 1890–1920*. Melsungen.

Domonkos, Margarete (1993). 'Wir strickten fleißig Schals und Socken . . ', in: Hämmerle 1993: 78–84.

Donson, Andrew (2010). *Youth in the Fatherless Land. War Pedagogy, Nationalism, and Authority in Germany, 1914–1918*. Cambridge, Mass., and London.

Donson, Andrew (2014). 'Children and Youth', in: www.encyclopedia.1914-1918-online.net.

Douglas, Allen (2002). *War, Memory and the Politics of Humor. Le Canard Enchaîné and World War I*. Berkeley et al.

Dreyer, Michael and Lemcke, Oliver (1993). *Die deutsche Diskussion um die Kriegsschuldfrage 1918/19*. Berlin.

Ducatel, Paul (1978). *Histoire de la IIIe république vue à travers l'imagerie populaire et la presse satirique, vol. IV, La Grande Guerre (1911–1923)*. Paris.

Düding, Dieter (1986). 'Die Kriegervereine im wilhelminischen Reich und ihr Beitrag zur Militarisierung der deutschen Gesellschaft', in: Jost Dülffer and Karl Holl (eds). *Bereit zum Krieg. Kriegsmentalität im wilhelminischen Deutschland 1890–1914*. Göttingen: 99–121.

Džambo, Jozo (2003a). 'Armis ad literis – Kriegsberichterstattung, Kriegspropaganda und Kriegsdokumentation in der k.u.k. Armee 1914–1918', in: Džambo 2003b: 10–37.

Džambo, Jozo (ed.) (2003b). *Musen an die Front! Schriftsteller und Künstler im Dienst der k.u.k. Kriegspropaganda 1914–1918*. Munich.

Eilers, Silke (2000). 'Propaganda in der Hosentasche. Politisches aus der Zündholzschachtel', in: Zühlke 2000: 179–212.

Eisermann, Thilo (2000). *Pressephotographie und Informationskontrolle im Ersten Weltkrieg*. Hamburg.

Elizalde, Maria-Dolores (2007). 'Les relations entre la Grande-Bretagne et l'Espagne pendant la Première Guerre mondiale par le biais des services des renseignements: organisation et objectifs britanniques en Espagne', GMCC 226: 23–36.

Englander, David (1987). 'Military intelligence and the defence of the realm: the surveillance of soldiers and civilians in Britain during the First World War', *Bulletin – Society for the Study of Labour History* 52, 1: 24–32.

Englander, David (1997). 'Discipline and morale in the British Army, 1916–1918', in: Horne 1997b: 125–43.

Ernst, Wilhelm (1933). *Die antideutsche Propaganda durch das Schweizergebiet im Weltkrieg, speziell die Propaganda in Bayern*. Munich.

Faccioli, Alessando (2008). 'Rulli di guerra nel cinema muto', in: Isnenghi and Ceschin 2008: 870–7.

Fava, Andrea (1993). 'All'origine di nuove immagini del'infanzia: Gli anni della Grande Guerra', in: Maria C. Giuntella and Isabella Nardi (eds). *Il Bambino nella Storia*. Naples: 145–200.

Fava, Andrea (1997). 'War, "national education" and the Italian primary school 1915–1918', in: Horne 1997b: 53–69.

Ferguson, Niall (1998). *Pity of War*. London.

Fiori, Antonio (2001). *Il filtro deformante. La censura della stampa durante la Prima Guerra mondiale.* Rome.

Fisch, Jörg (2010). *Das Selbstbestimmungsrecht der Völker. Die Domestizierung einer Illusion.* Munich.

Fischer, Christopher (2014). 'Of occupied territories and lost provinces: German and Entente propaganda in the West during WWI', in: Paddock 2014: 199–221.

Fischer, Doris (1973). *Die Münchner Zensurstelle während des Ersten Weltkrieges. Alfons Falkner von Sonnenburg als Pressereferent im Bayerischen Kriegsministerium in den Jahren 1914–1918/19.* Diss. Phil. Munich.

Fischer, Fritz (1984 [1967]). *Griff nach der Weltmacht. Die Kriegszielpolitik des kaiserlichen Deutschland 1914/18.* Düsseldorf.

Fischer, Heinz-Dietrich (ed.) (1973). *Pressekonzentration und Zensurpraxis im Ersten Weltkrieg.* Berlin.

Flemming, Thomas (2007). 'Zwischen Propaganda und Dokumentation des Schreckens. Feldpostkarten im Ersten Weltkrieg', in: Matthias Karmasin (ed.). *Krieg – Medien – Kultur. Neue Forschungsansätze.* Paderborn: 67–88.

Flemming, Thomas and Ulrich, Bernd (2014). *Heimatfront. Zwischen Kriegsbegeisterung und Hungersnot – wie die Deutschen den Ersten Weltkrieg erlebten.* Munich.

Fontana, Jacques (1997). 'Le prêtre dans les tranchées 1914–1918', *GMCC* 187: 25–39.

Forcade, Olivier (1998). *La censure politique en France pendant la Grande Guerre.* Doctoral Dissertation. University of Paris X.

Forcade, Olivier (2004a). 'Dans l'œil de la censure : voir ou ne pas voir la guerre', in: Prochasson and Rasmussen 2004: 35–54.

Forcade, Olivier (2004b). 'Information, censure et propagande', in: Stéphane Audoin-Rouzeau and Jean-Jacques Becker (eds). *Encyclopédie de la Grande Guerre.* Paris: 451–65.

Forcade, Olivier (2011). 'Zensur und öffentliche Meinung in Frankreich zwischen 1914 und 1918', in: Wolfram Pyta and Carsten Kretschmann (eds). *Burgfrieden und Union Sacrée. Literarische Deutungen und politische Ordnungsvorstellungen in Deutschland und Frankreich 1914–1933.* Munich: 71–84.

Fox, James. (2015). *British Art and the First World War, 1914–1924.* Cambridge.

Fraenkel, Ernst (1941). *The Dual State.* New York.

Freud, Sigmund (1905). *Der Witz und seine Beziehung zum Unbewussten.* Leipzig and Vienna. http://gutenberg.spiegel.de/buch/der-witz-und-seine-beziehung-zum-unbewussten-933/1.

Frevert, Ute and Schmidt, Anne (2011). 'Geschichte, Emotionen und die Macht der Bilder', *Geschichte und Gesellschaft* 37, 1: 5–25.

Frey, Stefan (2003). *'Unter Tränen lachen' – Emmerich Kálman. Eine Operettenbiographie.* Berlin.

Fuchs, Stephan (2004). *'Vom Segen des Krieges'. Katholische Gebildete im Ersten Weltkrieg. Eine Studie zur Kriegsdeutung im akademischen Katholizismus.* Stuttgart.

Führen, Franz (1936). *Lehrer im Krieg: Ein Ehrenbuch deutscher Volksschullehrer.* Leipzig.

Fuller, John. G. (1990). *Troop Morale and Popular Culture in the British and Dominion Armies 1914–1918.* Oxford.

Fulwider, Chad R. (2016). *German Propaganda and U.S. Neutrality in World War I.* Columbia, Miss.

Gankin, Olga H. and Fisher, Harold H. (1960 [1940]). *The Bolsheviks and the World War. The Origin of the Third International.* Stanford.

Gatrell, Peter (2005). *Russia's First World War. A Social and Economic History.* London et al.

Gatti, Gian Luigi (2000). *Dopo Caporetto. Gli ufficiali P nella Grande guerra: propaganda, assistenza, vigilanza.* Gorizia.

Gatti, Gian Luigi (2008a). 'Jusqu'au bout! Il fronte interno', in: Isenghi and Ceschin 2008: 280–8.

Gatti, Gian Luigi (2008b). 'Il morale, la morale', in: Isenghi and Ceschin 2008: 296–304.

Gatzke, Hans Wilhelm (1950). *Germany's Drive to the West. A Study of Germany's Western War Aims During the First World War.* Baltimore.

Geinitz, Christian and Hinz, Uta (1997). 'Das Augusterlebnis in Südbaden: Ambivalente Reaktionen der deutschen Öffentlichkeit auf den Kriegsbeginn 1914', in: Hirschfeld et al. 1997: 20–35.

Gencer, Mustafa (2002). *Bildungspolitik, Modernisierung und kulturelle Interaktion. Deutsch-türkische Beziehungen (1908–1918).* Münster.

Gerard, Alice (1998). 'La guerre et la paix dans le discours pédagogique français (1870–1914)', in: Giuntella and Nardi 1998: 39–51.

Gibelli, Antonio (1999). *La grande Guerra degli Italiani.* Milan.

Gibelli, Antonio (2014). 'Children and war (Italy)', in: www.encyclopedia.1914-1918-online.net.

Giuntella, Maria C. and Nardi, Isabella (ed.) (1998). *Le Guerre dei bambini. Da Sarajevo a Sarajevo.* Naples.

Goebel, Stefan (2014). 'Cities', in: Winter et al. 2014, vol. 2: 358–81.

Goebel, Stefan, Repp, Kevin and Winter, Jay (2012a). 'Exhibitions', in: Winter and Robert 2012b: 143–87.

Goebel, Stefan, Demm, Eberhard, Julien, Elise and Coppelmann, Dina (2012b). 'Schools', in: Winter and Robert 2012b: 188–234.

Goltz, Anna von der (2010). *Die Macht des Hindenburg-Mythos. Politik, Propaganda und Popularität im Ersten Weltkrieg.* Bielefeld.

Gooch, John (1996). 'Morale and discipline in the Italian army, 1915–1918', in: Cecil and Liddle 1996: 434–47.

Grandner, Margarete (2013). 'Hungerstreiks, Rebellion, Revolutionsbereitschaft', in: Pfoser and Weigl 2013: 558–65.

Grandt, Michael (2018). *GEZ.* Rottenburg.

Greenhill, Sam (2008). 'Secret of the Lusitania'. *Daily Mail*, 20 September 2008, online: http://www.dailymail.co.uk/news/article-1098904/Secret-Lusitania-Arms-challenges-Allied-claims-solely-passenger-ship.html (retrieved 25 November 2016).

Gregory, Adrian (2004). 'A clash of cultures. The British press and the opening of the Great War', in: Paddock 2004b: 15–49.

Gregory, Adrian (2008). *The Last Great War. British Society and the First World War.* Cambridge et al.

Grote, Hans Henning (1937). *Vorsicht! Feind hört mit. Eine Geschichte der Weltkriegs- und Nachkriegsspionage.* Dresden.

Guerrini, Irene (2008). 'Obbligare e punire: la giustizia militare', in: Isenghi and Ceschin 2008: 229–35.

Gullace, Nicoletta (1997). 'Sexual violence and family honour: British propaganda and international law during the First World War', *American Historical Review* 102: 714–47.

Gutsche, Willibald (1973). *Aufstieg und Fall eines kaiserlichen Reichskanzlers. Theobald von Bethmann Hollweg (1856–1921). Ein politisches Lebensbild.* Berlin.

Haddad, Galit (2014). 'Labour movements and strikes, social conflict and control, protest and repression (France)', in: www.encyclopedia.1914-1918-online.net.

Haimson, Leopold and Sapelli, Giulio (eds) (1992). *Strikes, Social Conflicts and the First World War*. Milan.

Hammer, Karl (1971). *Deutsche Kriegstheologie (1817–1918)*. Munich.

Hämmerle, Christa (ed.) (1993). *Kindheit im Ersten Weltkrieg*. Vienna et al.

Hanisch, Mark (2014a). 'Kein "Mastermind" – Max von Oppenheim und die Revolutionierung der islamischen Welt', in: Veltzke 2014: 102–13.

Hanisch, Mark (2014b). 'Max Freiherr von Oppenheim und die Revolutionierung der islamischen Welt als anti-imperiale Befreiung von oben', in: Wilfried Loth and Marc Hanisch (eds). *Erster Weltkrieg und Dschihad*. Munich: 13–38.

Hanna, Martha (2014). 'The couple', in: Winter et al. 2014, vol. 3: 6–28.

Hardach, Gerd (1973). *Der Erste Weltkrieg*. Munich.

Hartwagner, Siegfried (1942). *Der Kampf der deutschen Karikatur gegen England im Weltkriege 1914–18*. Doctoral Dissertation. Berlin.

Haste, Cate (1977). *Keep the Home Fires Burning. Propaganda in the First World War*. London.

Healy, Maureen (2004). *Vienna and the Fall of the Habsburg Empire. Total War and Everyday Life in World War I*. Cambridge.

Healy, Maureen (2013a). 'Vom Ende des Durchhaltens', in: Pfoser and Weigl 2013: 132–9.

Healy, Maureen (2013b). 'Eine Stadt, in der sich täglich Hunderttausende anstellen', in: Pfoser and Weigl 2013: 150–61.

Healy, Maureen et al. (2016). 'Social conflict and control, protest and repression (Austria-Hungary)', in: www.encyclopedia.1914-1918-online.net.

Hearnshaw, Fossey J.C. (1979). *The Centenary of King's College, 1828–1928*. London.

Heath, Robert L. and Bryant, Jennings (2008 [2000]). *Human Communication. Theory and Research. Concepts, Contexts, and Challenges*. New York and London.

Heise, Joachim S. (1999). '"Ein inniges Band zwischen Heimat und Front!" Kriegserlebnis und Sinnstiftung im Spiegel Betrieblicher Kriegszeitschriften: Das *Continental Kriegs-Echo*', in: Schneider 1999: 189–214.

Herf, Jeffrey (1984). *Reactionary Modernism. Technology, Culture, and Politics in Weimar and the Third Reich*. Cambridge et al.

Hewitson, Mark (2012). 'Black Humour: caricature in war time', *Oxford German Studies* 41: 213–35.

Higonnet, Margareth R. (2014). 'At the front', in: Winter et al. 2014, vol. 3: 121–52.

Hiley, Nicholas (1990). 'The news media and British propaganda, 1914–1918', in: Audoin-Rouzeau and Becker 1990: 175–81.

Hiley, Nicholas (1994). 'Der Erste Weltkrieg im britischen Film', in: Rother 1994b: 215–26.

Hiley, Nicholas (1997). 'The myth of British recruiting posters', *Imperial War Museum Review* 11: 40–57.

Hiley, Nicholas (2007). '"A new and vital moral factor": Cartoon book publishing in Britain during the First World War', in: Mary Hammond and Shafquat Towheed (eds). *Publishing in the First World War. Essays in Book History*. London: 148–77.

Hirschfeld, Gerhard et al. (eds) (1993). *Keiner fühlt sich hier als Mensch. . . Erlebnis und Wirkung des Ersten Weltkriegs*. Essen.

Hirschfeld, Gerhard et al. (eds) (1997). *Kriegserfahrungen. Studien zur Sozial- und Mentalitätsgeschichte des Ersten Weltkriegs*. Essen.

Hirschfeld, Magnus and Gaspar, Andreas (1982 [1929]). *Sittengeschichte des Ersten Weltkrieges*. Hanau.

Hobohm, Martin (1995 [1929]). 'Soziale Heeresmissstände im Ersten Weltkrieg', in: Wette 1995b: 136–45.

Hochschild, Adam (2011). *To End All Wars. How the First World War Divided Britain*. London.

Hoegen, Jesko von (2007). *Der Held von Tannenberg. Genese und Funktion des Hindenburg-Mythos*. Köln.

Höffler, Felix (1997). 'Kriegserfahrungen in der Heimat: Kriegsverlauf, Kriegsschuld und Kriegsende in württembergischen Stimmungsbildern des Ersten Weltkriegs', in: Hirschfeld et al. 1997: 68–82.

Hoffmann, Heike (1997). '"Schwarzer Peter im Weltkrieg": Die deutsche Spielwarenindustrie 1914–1918', in: Hirschfeld et al. 1997: 323–35.

Holl, Karl (1988). *Pazifismus in Deutschland*. Frankfurt/Main.

Holl, Karl (2007). *Ludwig Quidde (1858–1941). Eine Biographie*. Düsseldorf.

Holzer, Anton (2007). *Die andere Front. Fotografie und Propaganda im Ersten Weltkrieg*. Darmstadt.

Holzer, Anton (2008). *Das Lächeln der Henker. Der unbekannte Krieg gegen die Zivilbevölkerung 1914–1918*. Darmstadt.

Holzer, Anton (2013). 'Der illustrierte Krieg. Fotografie und Bildberichterstattung 1914–1918', in: Pfoser and Weigl 2013: 486–93.

Horne, John (1989). '"L'impôt du sang". Republican Rhetoric and Industrial Warfare in France 1914–1918', *Social History* 14: 201–23.

Horne, John (1994). 'Les mains coupées: "Atrocités allemandes" et opinion française en 1914', in: Becker et al. 1994: 133–46.

Horne, John (1997a). 'Re-mobilizing for "Total War": France and Britain, 1917–1918', in: Horne 1997b: 195–211.

Horne, John (ed.) (1997b). *State, Society and Mobilization in Europe during the 1st WW*. Cambridge.

Horne, John (2014). 'Atrocities and war crimes', in: Winter et al. 2014, vol. 1: 561–84.

Horne, John and Kramer, Alan (2001). *German Atrocities, 1914. A History of Denial*. New Haven.

Houlihan, Patrick J. (2012). 'Imperial frameworks of religion: Catholic military chaplains of Germany and Austria-Hungary during the First World War', *First World War Studies* 3: 165–82.

Hovland, Carl I. et al. (1974 [1963]). *Communication and Persuasion.Psychological Studies of Opinion Change*. New Haven and London.

Huber, Georg (1928). *Die französische Propaganda im Weltkrieg gegen Deutschland 1914–1918*. Munich.

Hull, Isabel V. (2014). *A Scrap of Paper. Breaking and Making International Law during the Great War*. Ithaca and London.

Ingram, Norman (2005). 'Le pacifisme de guerre: Refus de l'Union sacrée et de la synthèse républicaine', in: Cazals 2005: 77–85.

Irwin, Will (1919). 'An age of lies. How the propagandist attacks the foundation of public opinion', *Sunset* 43: 23–56.

Isnenghi, Mario (1977). *Giornali di trincea (1915–1918)*. Torino.

Isnenghi, Mario and Ceschin, Daniele (ed.) (2008). *La Grande Guerra: dall' Intervento alla 'vittoria mutilata'*. Vol. III of: *Gli Italiani in guerra*. Turin.

Jahn, Hubertus F. (1995). *Patriotic Culture in Russia during World War I*. Ithaca and London.

Jahr, Christoph (1998). *Gewöhnliche Soldaten. Desertion und Deserteure im deutschen und britischen Heer. 1914–1918.* Göttingen.

Jalonen, Jussi (2014). 'Jäger Movement', in: www.encyclopedia.1914-1918-online.net.

Janz, Oliver (2010). 'Zwischen Konsens und Dissens. Zur Historiographie des 1. Weltkriegs in Italien', in: Bauerkämper and Julien 2010b: 195–213.

Jeancolas, Jean Pierre (1994). 'Der französische Film 1914–1918'. in: Rother 1994b: 227–34.

Jeanneney, Jean Noel (1968). 'Les Archives de la commission du contrôle postal aux armées (1916–1918). Une source précieuse pour l'histoire contemporaine de l'opinion et des mentalités', *Revue d'histoire moderne et contemporaine* 15: 209–33.

Jeismann, Michael (1992). *Das Vaterland der Feinde. Studien zum nationalen Feindbegriff und Selbstverständnis in Deutschland und Frankreich 1792–1918.* Stuttgart.

Jelavich, Peter (1999). 'German culture in the Great War', in: Roshwald and Stites 1999a: 32–57.

Johann, Ernst (1973). *Innenansicht eines Krieges. Deutsche Dokumente 1914–1918.* Munich.

Jones, Derek (ed.) (2001). *Censorship: A World Encyclopedia.* Chicago and London.

Jones, Heather (2014). 'Prisoners of war', in: Winter et al. 2014, vol. 2: 266–90.

Jones, Heather et al. (ed.) (2008). *Untold War. New Perspectives in First World War Studies.* Leiden and Boston.

Jorio, Irène Di, Oosterlink, Kim and Pouillard, Véronique (2008). 'Advertising, propaganda and war finance. France and the US during WWI', http://www.ebha.org/ebha2008/papers/diJorio-Oosterlink-Pouillard_ebha_2008.pdf.

Joseph, Mathilde (2000). 'Le poilu du music-hall. L'image du poilu dans les music-halls parisiens pendant la Grande Guerre', *GMCC* 50, 197: 21–41.

Julien, Elise (2014). *Der Erste Weltkrieg.* Darmstadt.

Jüllig, Carola (1994). '"Ja, Frankreichs Geist, Du bist verbannt für ewig . . ." die erste Kriegspielzeit der Berliner Theater', in: Rother 1994b: 121–36.

Kahleyss, Margot (2000 [1998]). *Muslime in Brandenburg – Kriegsgefangene im 1. Weltkrieg: Ansichten und Absichten.* Berlin.

Kampen, Wilhelm van (1968). *Studien zur deutschen Türkeipolitik in der Zeit Wilhelms II.* Kiel.

Kaplan, Ines (2000). '"Die abgehackte Hand". Ein Beitrag zur Ikonographie der französischen Hetzkarikatur als Teil der antideutschen Propaganda während des Ersten Weltkrieges', in: Zühlke 2000: 93–122.

Karlsch, Rainer (1994). 'Die wirtschaftliche Entwicklung der Messter-Firmen', in: Loiperdinger 1994: 149–65.

Karner, Stephan and Lesiak, Philipp (eds) (2014). *Erster Weltkrieg. Globaler Konflikt – lokale Folgen – Neue Perspektiven.* Innsbruck et al.

Kayalı, Hasan (1997). *Arabs and Young Turks. Ottomanism, Arabism and Islamism in the Ottoman Empire, 1908–1918.* Berkeley et al.

Keene, Jennifer D. (2014). 'North America', in: Winter et al. 2014, vol. 1: 511–32.

Kennan, George F. (1964). 'The price we paid for war', *The Atlantic Monthly* 214, 4: 52–3.

Kennedy, Rosie (2014). *The Children's War. Britain, 1914–1918.* New York.

Kessel, Martina (2008). 'Laughing about death? German humor in the two world wars', in: Alon Confino et al. (eds). *Between Mass Death and Individual Loss. The Place of the Dead in Twentieth Century Germany.* New York and Oxford: 197–218.

Kessel, Martina (2012). 'Talking war, debating unity: order, conflict, and exclusion in "german humour" in the First World War', in: Martina Kessel and Patrick Merziger (eds). *The Politics of Humour. Laughter, Inclusion, and Exclusion in the Twentieth Century.* Toronto et al.: 82–107.

Kestler, Stefan (1994). *Die deutsche Auslandsaufklärung und das Bild der Entente-Mächte im Spiegel zeitgenössischer Propagandaveröffentlichungen während des Ersten Weltkrieges.* Frankfurt/Main.

Kiefer, Klaus A. (1999). 'Die Beschießung der Kathedrale von Reims. Bilddokumente und Legendenbildung – eine Semiotik der Zerstörung', in: Schneider 1999: 115–52.

Kilian, Jette (2008). 'Propaganda für die deutsche Kriegsanleihe im 1. Weltkrieg', in: Jürgen Wilke (ed.). *Massenmedien und Spendenkampagnen. Vom 17. Jahrhundert bis in die Gegenwart.* Cologne: 73–160.

King, David (1997). *Stalins Retuschen. Foto- und Kunstmanipulationen in der Sowjetunion.* Hamburg.

King, Erika G. (1989). 'Exposing the "age of lies". The propaganda menace as portrayed by magazines in the aftermath of World War I', *Journal of American Culture* 12: 35–40.

Kingsbury, Celia M. (2010). *For Home and Country. World War I Propaganda on the Home Front.* Lincoln.

Kluger, Josefine (1993). 'Jeden Tag wurde vor dem Unterricht die Kriegslage besprochen', in: Hämmerle 1993: 105–18.

Knežević, Jovana (2018). 'Reclaiming their city: Belgrade and the combat against Habsburg propaganda through rumours', in: Stefan Goebel and Derek Keene (eds) (2018). *Cities into Battlefields. Metropolitan Scenarios, Experiences and Commemoration of Total War.* Farnham and Burlington: 101–18.

Knieper, Thomas (2002). *Die politische Karikatur: eine journalistische Darstellungsform und deren Produzenten.* Cologne.

Knightley, Philippe (2002) [1975]. *The First Casualty. The War Correspondent as Hero and Myth-Maker from the Crimea to Kosovo.* Baltimore and London.

Koerber, Martin (1994). 'Oskar Messter – Stationen einer Karriere', in: Loiperdinger 1994: 27–91.

Komarnicki, Titus (1957). *Rebirth of the Polish Republic. A Study in the Diplomatic History of Europe, 1914–1920.* Melbourne et al.

Koch, Christian (2015). *Giftpfeile über der Front. Flugschriftpropaganda im und nach dem Ersten Weltkrieg.* Essen.

Köroglu, Erol (2007). *Ottoman Propaganda and Turkish identity. Literature in Turkey during World War I.* London and New York.

Kössler, Armin (1981). *Aktionsfeld osmanisches Reich. Die Wirtschaftsinteressen des deutschen Kaiserreichs in der Türkei 1871–1908.* New York.

Koszyk, Kurt (1968). *Deutsche Pressepolitik im Ersten Weltkrieg.* Düsseldorf.

Koszyk, Kurt (1973). 'Entwicklung der Kommunikationskontrolle zwischen 1914 und 1918' in: H.-D. Fischer 1973: 152–93.

Krakovitch, Odile (1991). 'La censure des théâtres durant la grande guerre', in: *Théâtres et spectacles hier et aujourd'hui. Epoque moderne et contemporaine. Actes du 115ᵉ congrès national des sociétés savantes.* Paris: 331–53.

Kramer, Alan (1994). 'Les "atrocités allemandes": mythologie populaire, propagande et manipulation dans l'armée allemande', in: Becker et al. 1994: 147–64.

Kriegel, Annie (1964). *Aux origines du communisme français 1914–1920, vol. 1.* Paris and The Hague.

Krivanec, Eva (2012). *Kriegsbühnen. Theater im Ersten Weltkrieg. Berlin, Lissabon, Paris und Wien.* Bielefeld.

Kröger, Martin (1994). 'Revolution als Programm. Ziele und Realität deutscher Orientpolitik im ersten Weltkrieg', in: Wolfgang Michalka (ed.) (1994). *Der erste Weltkrieg*. Munich: 366–99.

Kröger, Martin (2014). 'Traumreisen und Weltpolitik – Wilhelm II. und sein Orient', in: Veltzke 2014: 89–101.

Krollpfeiffer, Gert (1935). *Die 'Lustigen Blätter' im Weltkrieg 1914/1918. Der publizistische Kampf eines deutschen Witzblattes*. Munich.

Kruse, Wolfgang (1991). 'Die Kriegsbegeisterung im Deutschen Reich 1914. Entstehungszusammenhänge, Grenzen und ideologische Strukturen', in: Linden and Mergner 1991: 73–87.

Kruse, Wolfgang (1996). 'Krieg und Klassenheer. Zur Revolutionierung der deutschen Armee im Ersten Weltkrieg', *Geschichte und Gesellschaft* 22, 1: 530–61.

Kruse, Wolfgang (ed.) (1997). *Eine Welt von Feinden. Der große Krieg 1914–1918*. Frankfurt/Main.

Kuprian, Hermann J.W. and Mazohl-Wallnig, Brigitte (1998). 'Bambini e guerra – bambini alla frontiera: un esempio dalla monarchia austro-ungarica durante la prima guerra mondiale', in: Giuntella and Nardi 1998: 101–24.

Kurth, Karl (1937). *Die deutschen Feld- und Schützengrabenzeitungen des Weltkriegs*. Leipzig.

Laloux, Ludovic (2005). 'Aux origines de la croisade eucharistique: un soutien aux poilus lors de la Grande Guerre', *GMCC* 219: 45–51.

Lange, Britta (2003). *Einen Krieg ausstellen. Die 'Deutsche Kriegsausstellung' 1916 in Berlin*. Berlin.

Lasswell, Harold D. (1971 [1927]). *Propaganda Technique in the World War*. New York.

Leab, Daniel J. (2007). 'Total war on screen. The Huns in US-film 1914–1920', in: Thomas F. Schneider and Hans Wagener (eds). *'Huns' versus 'Corned Beef'. Representation of the other in American and German Literature and Film on World War I*. Osnabrück: 153–84.

Leed, Eric J. (1979). *No Man's Land. Combat and Identity in World War I*. Cambridge et al.

Lehmann, Joachim (1996). 'Der baltische Vertrauensrat und die Unabhängigkeit der baltischen Staaten ausgangs des Ersten Weltkrieges', in: Eberhard Demm et al. (eds). *The Independence of the Baltic States. Origins, Causes, and Consequences. A Comparison of the Crucial Years 1918–1919 and 1990–91*. Chicago: 157–65.

Lehmann-Russbüldt, Otto (1927). *Der Kampf der deutschen Liga für Menschenrechte vormals Bund Neues Vaterland für den Weltfrieden 1914–1927*. Berlin.

Leidinger, Hannes (2014a). '"Die vaterländische Pflicht an der visuellen Front". Bildberichterstattung und Bildpropaganda in Österreich-Ungarn unter besonderer Berücksichtigung der "östlichen Kampfschauplätze" 1914–1918', in: Karner and Lesiak 2014: 321–32.

Leidinger, Hannes (2014b). 'Ordnung schaffen', in: Hannes Leidinger et al. (eds). *Habsburgs schmutziger Krieg. Ermittlungen zur österreichisch-ungarischen Kriegsführung 1914–1918*. Vienna: 145–70.

Lein, Richard (2011). *Pflichterfüllung oder Hochverrat. Die tschechischen Soldaten Österreich-Ungarns im Ersten Weltkrieg*. Berlin and Vienna.

Lein, Richard (2014). 'Between acceptance and refusal – soldiers' attitudes towards war (Austria-Hungary)', in: www.encyclopedia.1914-1918-online.net.

Lemmermann, Heinz (1984). *Kriegserziehung im Kaiserreich. Studien zur politischen Funktion von Schule und Schulmusik 1890–1918*. Lilienthal and Bremen.

Le Naour, Jean-Yves (2001). 'Laughter and tears in the Great War: the need for laughter/ the guilt of humour', *Journal of European Studies* 21: 265–75.

Lerouge, Marcelle (2004). *Journal d'une adolescente dans la guerre 1914–1918*. Paris.

Linden, Marcel van der and Mergner, Gottfried (eds) (1991). *Kriegsbegeisterung und mentale Kriegsvorbereitung. Interdisziplinäre Studien*. Berlin.

Lindner-Wirsching, Almut (2006). 'Patrioten im Pool. Deutsche und französische Kriegsberichterstatter im Ersten Weltkrieg', in: Ute Daniel (ed.). *Augenzeugen. Kriegsberichterstattung vom 18. zum 21. Jahrhundert*. Göttingen: 113–32.

Lipp, Anne (1996). 'Friedenssehnsucht und Durchhaltebereitschaft', *Archiv für Sozialgeschichte* 36: 279–92.

Lipp, Anne (2003). *Meinungslenkung im Krieg*. Göttingen.

Liulevicius, Vejas G. (2000). *War Land on the Eastern Front*. Cambridge.

Loez, André (2014). 'Between acceptance and refusal – soldiers' attitudes towards war', in: www.encyclopedia.1914-1918-online.net.

Lohr, Erik (2003). *Nationalizing the Russian Empire. The Campaign against Enemy Aliens during WWI*. Cambridge and London.

Lohr, Erik (2004). 'The Russian press and the "internal peace" at the beginning of World War One', in: Paddock 2004b: 91–113.

Loiperdinger, Martin (ed.) (1994). *Oskar Messter. Filmpionier der Kaiserzeit*. Basel.

Loparco, Fabiana (2011). *I bambini e la Guerra*. Florence.

Loubat, Emmanuelle (2016). 'Theatre at the front', in: www.encyclopedia.1914-1918-online.net.

Lowe, Cedric J (2014 [1967]). *The Reluctant Imperialists. British Foreign Policy 1878–1902*. London.

Luban, Ottokar (2008). 'Die Massenstreiks für Frieden und Demokratie im Ersten Weltkrieg', in: Chaja Boebel and Lothar Wentzel (eds). *Streiken gegen den Krieg. Die Bedeutung der Massenstreiks in der Metallindustrie vom Januar 1918*. Hamburg: 11–26.

Lübbe, Herman (1969). *Politische Philosophie in Deutschland*. Basel.

Lüdke, Tilman (2005). *Jihad made in Germany. Ottoman and German Propaganda and Intelligence Operations in the First World War*. Münster.

Lunzer, Heinz (1981). *Hofmannsthals Politische Tätigkeit in den Jahren 1914–1917*. Frankfurt/Main.

Lunzer, Renate (2016). 'Making sense of the war (Italy)', in: www.encyclopedia.1914-1918-online.net.

Machtan, Lothar (2018 [2013]). *Der Endzeitkanzler. Prinz Max von Baden und der Untergang des Kaiserreichs*. Darmstadt.

Madigan, Edward (2008). 'Hidden courage: postwar literature and Anglican army chaplains on the Western Front, 1914–18', in: Jones et al. 2008: 63–94.

Magri, Susanna (1997). 'Housing', in: Winter and Robert 1997: 374–418.

Mai, Günther (1977). '"Aufklärung der Bevölkerung" und "Vaterländischer Unterricht" in Württemberg 1914–1918. Durchführung und Inhalte der deutschen Inlandspropaganda im Ersten Weltkrieg', *Zeitschrift für Württembergische Landesgeschichte* 36: 199–235.

Maier, Lothar (1983). 'Die Lloyd George-Koalition und die Frage eines Kompromissfriedens 1917/1918', *Historische Zeitschrift* Beiheft 8 NF: 47–87.

Malvern, Sue (2004). *Modern Art, Britain and the Great War. Witnessing, Testimony and Remembrance*. New Haven and London.

Marc, Michel (1990). 'Mythe et réalité du concours colonial: soldats et travailleurs d'outre-mer dans la guerre française', in: Audoin-Rouzeau and Becker 1990: 393–410.

Mariot, Nicolas (2013). *Tous unis dans la tranchée? 1914–1918, les intellectuels rencontrent le peuple*. Paris.

Marquis, Alice G. (1978). '"Words as weapons". Propaganda in Britain and Germany during the First World War', *Journal of Contemporary History* 13, 3: 467–98.

Marwick, Arthur (1991 [1965]). *The Deluge. British Society and the First World War*. London.

Maß, Sandra (2001). 'Der Traum des weißen Mannes. Afrikanische Kolonialsoldaten in propagandistischen Texten', *L'Homme* 12: 11–33.

Maurer, Trude (2013). 'Der Krieg der Professoren. Russische Antworten auf den deutschen Aufruf *An die Kulturwelt!*', in: Ungern-Sternberg and Ungern-Sternberg 2013: 163–201.

Maurer, Trude (2015). '. . . *und wir gehören auch dazu'. Universität und 'Volksgemeinschaft' im Ersten Weltkrieg*. 2 vols. Göttingen.

McKale, Donald M. (1998). *War by Revolution. Germany and Great Britain in the Middle-East in the Era of World War I*. Kent, Ohio and London.

McKeene, Sean (2017). *The Russian Revolution: A New History*. New York.

McKernan, Luke (2017). 'Topical budget: war and propaganda', in: www.screenonline.org.uk/film/id/583331/ (retrieved 30 October 2017).

McKeene, Sean (2017). *The Russian Revolution: A New History*. New York.

Medyakov, Alexander (2014). 'Propaganda at home. Russia', in: www.encyclopedia.1914-1918-online.net.

Melancon, Michael (1990). *The Socialist Revolutionaries and the Russian Anti-War Movement, 1914–1917*. Columbus.

Mensching, Gustav (1968 [1947]). *Soziologie der Religion*. Bonn.

Messinger, Gerry S. (1992). *British Propaganda and the State in the First World War*. Manchester and New York.

Metken, Sigrid (1994). '"Ich hab' diese Karte im Schützengraben geschrieben . . ." Bildpostkarten im Ersten Weltkrieg', in: Rother 1994b: 137–48.

Michael, Holger (2010). *Marschall Józef Piłsudski 1867–1935. Schöpfer des modernen Polens*. Bonn.

Miller, Suzanne (1974). *Burgfrieden und Klassenkampf. Die deutsche Sozialdemokratie im Ersten Weltkrieg*. Düsseldorf.

Millman, Brock (2000). *Managing Domestic Dissent in First World War Britain*. London and Portland.

Mionskowski, Alexander (2016). 'Authorities at war. The public opinion in Germany as a major concern of Austrian poets between 1914 and 1916', in: Suchoples and James 2016: 271–93.

Mock, James R. (1972 [1941]). *Censorship 1917*. New York.

Mock, James R. and Larson, Cedric (1968 [1939]). *Words That Won the War. The Story of the Committee on Public Information 1917–1919*. New York.

Mombauer, Anika (2014). *Die Julikrise. Europas Weg in den Ersten Weltkrieg*. Munich [English edition 2002]

Mommsen, Wolfgang J. (2004). *Der Erste Weltkrieg. Anfang vom Ende des bürgerlichen Zeitalters*. Frankfurt/Main.

Monballyu, Jos (2012). *Deserteurs voor de Vlaamse zaak. Over de Vlaamsgezinde militairen die naar de vijand overliepen*. Bruges.

Mondini, Marco (2014). *La guerra italiana. Partire, raccontare, tornare 1914–18*. Bologna.

Monger, David (2011). 'Soldiers, propaganda and ideas of home and community in First World War Britain', *Cultural and Social History* 8: 331–54.

Monger, David (2012). *Patriotism and Propaganda in First World War Britain : The National War Aims Committee and Civilian Morale*. Liverpool.

Monger, David (2015). 'Familiarity breeds consent? Patriotic rituals in British First World War propaganda', *Twentieth Century British History* 26 (4): 501–28.

Montant, Jean Claude (1968). *La propagande allemande en France 1915–1917*. Unpublished master dissertation Paris I.

Montant, Jean Claude (1980). 'La tentative française d'infiltration dans la presse allemande : l'affaire de la Kölnische Volkszeitung (février–décembre 1918)', *Revue d'histoire moderne et contemporaine* 27: 658–85.

Montant, Jean Claude (1989). *La propagande extérieure de la France pendant la Première Guerre mondiale. L'Exemple de quelques neutres européens*. Unpublished Habilitation Thesis. University of Paris I. Lille.

Montant, Jean Claude (1990). 'L'organisation centrale des services d'information et de propagande du Quai d'Orsay pendant la Grande Guerre', in: Audoin-Rouzeau and Becker 1990: 135–43.

Moreau, Odile (2016). *La Turquie dans la Grande Guerre. De L'Empire Ottoman à la République de Turquie*. Saint-Cloud.

Morgan, David W. (1975). *The Socialist Left and the German Revolution. A History of the German Independent Social Democratic Party, 1917–1922*. Ithaca and London.

Mueggenberg, Brent (2014). *The Czecho-Slovak Struggle for Independence, 1914–1920*. Jefferson.

Müller, Klaus-Peter (1983). *Politik und Gesellschaft im Krieg. Der Legitimitätsverlust des badischen Staats 1914–1918*. Stuttgart.

Müller, Klaus-Peter (1986). 'Organisation, Themen und Probleme der Volksaufklärung in Baden 1914–1918', *Zeitschrift für die Geschichte des Oberrheins* 134: 329–58.

Müller, Olaf (2005). 'Le Feu de Barbusse: la "vraie bible" des Poilus. Histoire de sa réception avant et après 1918', in: Cazals 2005: 131–40.

Müller, Olaf (2016). 'Le Feu (novel)', in: www.encyclopedia.1914-1918-online.net.

Müller, Sonja (2008). 'Toys, games, and juvenile literature in Germany and Britain during the First World War. A comparison', in: Jones et al. 2008: 233–57.

Murmann, Geerte (1992). *Komödianten für den Krieg. Deutsches und alliiertes Fronttheater*. Düsseldorf.

Museum für Kunst und Gewerbe Hamburg (ed.) (2014). *Krieg und Propaganda 14/18*. Munich.

Musner, Lutz (2013). 'Dem Krieg eine gefällige Form geben. Alice Schalek an der Isonzofront', in: Pfoser and Weigl 2013: 522–31.

Nachtigal, Reinhard (2006). 'Privilegiensystem und Zwangsrekrutierung. Russische Nationalitätenpolitik gegenüber Kriegsgefangenen aus Österreich-Ungarn', in: Jochen Oltmer (ed.). *Kriegsgefangene im Europa des Ersten Weltkriegs*. Paderborn: 167–93.

Nation, R. Craig (1989). *War on War. Lenin, the Zimmerwald Left, and the Origins of Communist Internationalism*. Durham and London.

Navet, Françoise (1994). 'Des journaux sanctionnés pour des dessins non échoppés (1914–1919)', *GMCC* 173: 35–51.

Navet, Françoise (2000). 'Censure et dessin de presse en France pendant la Grande Guerre', *GMCC* 197: 7–19.

Neitzel, Sönke and Horath, Daniel (eds) (2008). *Kriegsgräuel. Die Entgrenzung der Gewalt in kriegerischen Konflikten vom Mittelalter bis ins XX. Jahrhundert*. Paderborn et al.

Nelson, Robert L. (2011). *German Soldier Newspapers of the First World War*. Cambridge.

Nelson, Robert L. (2014). 'Soldier newspapers', in: www.encyclopedia.1914-1918-online. net.

Nettl, Peter (1967). *Rosa Luxemburg*. Köln and Berlin. [English original: 1965]

Neulen, Hans Werner (1994). *Adler und Halbmond. Das deutsch-türkische Bündnis 1914–1918*. Frankfurt/Main.

Newton, Douglas (2002). 'The Lansdowne "Peace letter" of 1917 and the prospect of peace by negotiation with Germany', *Australian Journal of Politics and History* 48: 16–39.

Nipperdey, Thomas (1986). *Wie modern war das Kaiserreich? Das Beispiel der Schule*. Opladen.

Nolan, Michael (2004). 'The Eagle soars over the nightingale. Press and propaganda in France in the opening months of the Great War', in: Paddock 2004b: 52–90.

Noll, Thomas (1994). 'Sinnbild und Erzählung. Zur Ikonographie des Krieges in der Zeitschriftenillustration 1914–1918', in: Rother 1994b: 259–72.

Oberhaus, Salvador (2007). *'Zum wildem Aufstande entflammen'. Die deutsche Propagandastrategie für den Orient im Ersten Weltkrieg am Beispiel Ägypten*. Saarbrücken.

Offenstadt, Nicholas (2010). 'Der Erste Weltkrieg im Spiegel der Gegenwart', in: Bauerkämper and Julien 2010b: 54–77.

Opfer-Klinger, Björn (2008). 'Ein unaufgearbeitetes Kapitel südosteuropäischer Nationalgeschichte: bulgarische Kriegsgräuel 1912–1918', in: Neitzel and Horath 2008: 279–92.

Oppelt, Ulrike (2002). *Film und Propaganda im Ersten Weltkrieg*. Stuttgart.

Ory, Pascal and Sirinelli, Jean-Francois (1986). *Les intellectuels en France, de l'affaire Dreyfus à nos jours*. Paris.

Orzoff, Andrea (2004). 'The Empire without qualities: Austro-Hungarian newspapers and the outbreak of war in 1914', in: Paddock 2004b: 161–98.

Ostermann, Patrick (2000). *Duell der Diplomaten. Die Propaganda der Mittelmächte und ihrer Gegner in Italien während des Ersten Weltkrieges*. Weimar.

Paddock, Troy R.E. (2004a). 'German propaganda: the limits of Gerechtigkeit', in: Paddock 2004b: 115–60.

Paddock, Troy R.E. (ed.) (2004b). *A Call to Arms. Propaganda, Public Opinion and Newspapers in the Great War*. Westport, Conn., et al.

Paddock, Troy R.E. (ed.) (2014). *World War One and Propaganda*. Leiden and Boston.

Panayi, Panikos (1989). 'Anti-German riots in London during the First World War', *German History* 7: 184–203.

Panayi, Panikos (2014). 'Minorities', in: Winter et al. 2014, vol. 3: 216–41.

Papadia, Elena (2016). 'Governments, parliaments and parties (Italy)', in: www. encyclopedia.1914-1918-online.net.

Pappola, Fabrice and Lafon, Alexandre (2005). '"Bourrage de crâne" et expérience combattante', in: Cazals 2005: 311–20.

Paris, Michael (ed.) (1999). *The First World War and Popular Cinema. 1914 to the Present*. New Brunswick and New Jersey.

Paris, Michael (2004). *Over the Top: The Great War and Juvenile Literature in Britain*. Westport, Conn.

Paris, Michael (2014). 'Film/cinema (Great Britain)', in: www.encyclopedia.1914-1918-online.net.

Patterson, David S. (2014). 'Pacifism', in: www.encyclopedia.1914-1918-online.net.

Paveau, Marie-Anne (2005). 'Citations à l'ordre des croix de guerre. Fonction des sanctions positives dans la guerre de 1914–1918', in: Cazals 2005: 247–57.

Perdelwitz, Richard (1939). *Die Polen im Weltkriege und die internationale Politik*. Leipzig.
Perloff, Richard M. (2010 [1993]). *The Dynamics of Persuasion. Communication and Attitudes in the 21st Century*. New York and London.
Perreux, Gabriel (1966). *La vie quotidienne des civils en France pendant la Grande Guerre*. Paris.
Peterson, Horace C. (1968 [1939]). *Propaganda for War. The Campaign against American Neutrality, 1914–1917*. Port Washington.
Petrone, Karen (1998). 'Family, masculinity, and heroism in Russian War Posters of the First World War', in: Billie Melman (ed.). *Borderlines. Genders and Identities in War and Peace, 1870–1930*. New York and London: 95–119.
Peureux, Christian (1972). *La propagande à l'école 1914–1918*. Unpublished Master Thesis, University of Paris I.
Pfoser, Alfred and Weigl, Andreas (ed.) (2013). *Im Epizentrum des Zusammenbruchs. Wien im Ersten Weltkrieg*. Wien.
Pietri, Nicole (1990). 'L'évolution des populations d'Autriche-allemande pendant la Grande Guerre', in: Audoin-Rouzeau and Becker 1990: 311–22.
Pignot, Manon (2012). *Allons enfants de la patrie. Génération Grande Guerre*, Paris.
Pignot, Manon (2014). 'Children and childhood (France)', in: www.encyclopedia.1914-1918-online.net.
Pipes, Richard (1990). *The Russian Revolution 1899–1919*. London.
Pisa, Beatrice (2015). 'Propaganda at home (Italy)', in: www.encyclopedia.1914-1918-online.net.
Pluviano, Marco (2008). 'Tempo libero in divisa: le Case del soldato', in: Isnenghi and Ceschin 2008: 704–10.
Pöppinghege, Rainer (2006). *Im Lager unbesiegt. Deutsche, englische und französische Kriegsgefangenen-Zeitungen im Ersten Weltkrieg*. Essen.
Polsakiewicz, Marta (2015). *Warschau im Ersten Weltkrieg. Deutsche Besatzungspolitik zwischen kultureller Autonomie und wirtschaftlicher Ausbeutung*. Marburg.
Ponce, Javier (2014). 'Propaganda and politics: Germany and Spanish opinion in WWI', in: Paddock 2014: 292–321.
Ponsonby, Arthur (1928). *Falsehood in War Time*. London.
Pöppinghege, Rainer (2006). *Im Lager unbesiegt. Deutsche, englische und französische Kriegsgefangenen-Zeitungen im Ersten Weltkrieg*. Essen.
Pourcher, Yves (1994). *Les jours de guerre. La vie des Français au jour le jour entre 1914 et 1918*. Paris.
Pressel, Wilhelm (1967). *Die Kriegspredigt 1914–1918 in der evangelischen Kirche Deutschlands*. Göttingen.
Procacci, Giovanna (1989). 'Popular protest and labour conflict in Italy, 1915–1918', *Social History* 14, 1: 31–58.
Procacci, Giovanna (1992). 'State coercion and worker solidarity in Italy (1915/1918): the morale and political content of social unrest', in: Haimson and Sapelli 1992: 145–77.
Prochasson Christophe and Rasmussen, Anne (ed.) (2004). *Vrai et faux dans la Grande Guerre*. Paris.
Proctor, Tammy M. (2010). *Civilians in a World at War, 1914–1918*. New York and London.
Purseigle, Pierre (2008). 'A very French debate: the 1914–1918 war culture, *Journal of War and Culture Studies* 1, 1: 9–14.
Pust, Hans Christian (2008a). 'Postkarten des Ersten Weltkriegs', in: Thomas 2008: 152–79.
Pust, Hans Christian (2008b). 'Vivatbänder', in: Thomas 2008: 204–9.

Pust, Hans Christian (2014). 'Kriegsnagelungen in Österreich-Ungarn, dem Deutschen Reich und darüber hinaus', in: Karner and Lesiak 2014: 211–24.

Pyta, Wolfram (2007). *Hindenburg. Herrschaft zwischen Hohenzollern und Hitler*. Munich.

Raithel, Thomas (1996). *Das 'Wunder' der inneren Einheit. Studien zur deutschen und französischen Öffentlichkeit bei Beginn des Ersten Weltkriegs*. Bonn.

Rajch, Marek (2007). 'Polnische Presse unter preussischer Militärzensur (1914–1916)', in: Claudia Glunz et al. (eds). *Information Warfare. The Role of the Media (Literature, Arts, Photography, Film, TV, Theatre, Press, Correspondence) in the Representation and Interpretation of War*. Göttingen: 105–12.

Rajsfus, Maurice (1999). *La censure militaire et policière 1914–1918*. Paris.

Ranitz, Ariane de (2014). *Louis Raemaekers. 'Armed with pen and pencil'. How a Dutch Cartoonist became world famous during the First World War*. Roermond.

Rasmussen, Anne (2014). 'Mobilizing mind', in: Winter et al. 2014, vol. 3: 390–417.

Rauchensteiner, Manfried (2013). 'Krieg als Chiffre des Friedens. Österreich-Ungarns letzter Krieg', in: Pfoser and Weigl 2013: 32–45.

Rauchensteiner, Manfried (2014). *The First World War and the End of the Habsburg Monarchy, 1914–1918*. Vienna et al.

Read, James M. (1941). *Atrocity Propaganda 1914–1919*. New Haven.

Rebentisch, Jost (2000). *Die vielen Gesichter des Kaisers. Wilhelm II. in der deutschen und britischen Karikatur (1888–1918)*. Berlin.

Reeves, Nicholas (1999a). *The Power of Film Propaganda. Myth or Reality?* London and New York.

Reeves, Nicholas (1999b). 'Official British film propaganda', in: Paris 1999: 27–50.

Reimann, Aribert (1997). 'Die heile Welt im Stahlgewitter: Deutsche und englische Feldpost aus dem Ersten Weltkrieg', in: Hirschfeld et al. 1997: 129–45.

Renz, Irina and Sauvage, Anne-Marie (2008). 'Der Krieg der Plakate', in: Thomas 2008: 62–77.

Ridel, Charles (2007). *Les embusqués*. Paris.

Ridel, Charles (2014). 'Propaganda at home (France)', in: www.encyclopedia.1914-1918-online.net.

Robb, George (2002). *British Culture and the First World War*. New York.

Robbins, Keith (1976). *The Abolition of War. The 'Peace Movement' in Britain, 1914–1919*. Cardiff.

Robert, Jean-Louis (1992). 'The Parisian strikes (August 1914–July 1919)', in: Haimson and Sapelli 1992: 29–44.

Robert, Jean-Louis (1997). 'The image of the profiteers', in: Winter and Robert 1997: 104–32.

Robichon, François (1994). 'Ästhetik der Sublimierung. Französische Kriegsmalerei', in: Rother 1994b: 284–300.

Roccucci, Adriano (2007). 'Mito della guerra e strategie politiche. La propaganda dei nazionalisti italiani durante la grande guerra', in: Rossini 2007b: 115–37.

Röhl, John C.G. (2008). *Wilhelm II. Vol. 3: Weg in den Abgrund 1900–1941*. Munich.

Rollet, Catherine, Cronier, Emmanuelle, Demm, Eberhard and Gregory, Adrian (2007). 'The home and family life'. in: Winter and Robert 2012b: 315–53.

Rose, Tania (1995). *Aspects of Political Censorship 1914–1918*. Hull.

Rose, Tania (2001). 'World War I: Britain', in: Jones 2001, vol. 4: 2647–9.

Roshwald, Aviel and Stites, Richard (ed.) (1999a). *European Culture in the Great War. The Arts, Entertainment, and Propaganda, 1914–1918*. Cambridge.

Roshwald, Aviel and Stites, Richard (1999b). 'Conclusion', in: Roshwald and Stites 1999a: 349–59.

Rosmer, Alfred (1936). *Le mouvement ouvrier pendant la guerre. Vol. 1: de l'Union sacrée à Zimmerwald.* Paris.

Rosmer, Alfred (1959). *Le mouvement ouvrier pendant la guerre. Vol. 2: de Zimmerwald à la Révolution russe.* Paris.

Rossini, Daniela (2007a). 'L'Internazionalismo Wilsoniano e la propaganda di guerra in Italia', in Rossini 2007b: 41–61.

Rossini, Daniela (ed.) (2007b). *La propaganda nelle grande guerre tra nazionalismi e internazionalismi.* Milan.

Rossini, Daniela (2008). *Woodrow Wilson and the American Myth in Italy. Culture, Diplomacy, and War Propaganda.* Cambridge, Mass., and London.

Rother, Rainer (1994a). 'Vom "Kriegssofa" zum "Flug an die Front". Anmerkungen zum deutschen Film im Ersten Weltkrieg', in: Rother 1994b: 197–206.

Rother, Rainer (ed.) (1994b). *Die letzten Tage der Menschheit. Bilder des Ersten Weltkrieges.* Berlin.

Roukes, Nicholas (1997). *Humor in Art. A Celebration of Visual Wit.* Worcester, Mass.

Row, Thomas (2002). 'Mobilizing the nation: Italian propaganda in the Great War', *The Journal of Decorative and Propaganda Arts* 24: 141–69.

Rudolph, Harriet (1997). 'Kultureller Wandel und Krieg: Die Reaktion der Werbesprache auf die Erfahrung des Ersten Weltkriegs am Beispiel von Zeitungsanzeigen', in: Hirschfeld et al. 1997: 283–301.

Rüger, Jan, Baumeister, Martin, Cronier, Emmanuelle (2012). 'Entertainments', in: Winter and Robert 2012b: 105–40.

Ruggenberg, Rob (1994). 'They died young. Kid soldiers of the Great War', www.greatwar. nl/frames/default-children.html (retrieved 9 October 2015).

Rumpler, Helmut (ed.) (2016). *Die Habsburger Monarchie 1848–1918, vol. XI: Die Habsburger Monarchie und der Erste Weltkrieg. Vol 1, part 1, Vom Balkankonflite zum Weltkrieg.* Vienna.

Ryan, Alan (1988). *Bertrand Russell. A Political Life.* London.

Sanborn, Joshua A. (2014). *Imperial Apocalypse. The Great War and the Destruction of the Russian Empire.* Oxford.

Sanders, Michael L. and Taylor, Philip M. (1982). *British Propaganda during the First World War 1914–1918.* London.

Saul, Klaus (1983). 'Jugend im Schatten des Krieges', *Militärgeschichtliche Mitteilungen* 34: 91–185.

Sbordone, Giovanni (2008). 'Tra classe e nazione. Socialisti al confine (1914–15)', in: Isnenghi and Ceschin 2008: 148–56.

Schaepdrijver, Sophie de (2014 [1997]). *De Groote Oorlog. Het Koninkrijk België tijdens de Eerste Wereldoorlog.* Amsterdam.

Scheer, Tamara (2010). *Die Ringstrassenfront. Österreich-Ungarn, das Kriegsüberwachungsamt und der Ausnahmezustand während des ersten Weltkrieges.* Vienna.

Scheer, Tamara (2016). 'Die Kriegswirtschaft am Übergang von der liberal-privaten zur staatlich-regulierten Arbeitswelt', in: Rumpler 2016: 437–84.

Schmidl, Erwin A. (2016). 'Die Totalisierung des Krieges', in: Rumpler 2016: 331–91.

Schmidt, Anne (2006). *Belehrung – Propaganda – Vertrauensarbeit. Zum Wandel amtlicher Kommunikationspolitik in Deutschland 1914–1918.* Essen.

Schneider, Franz (1988). *Die politische Karikatur.* Munich.

Schneider, Thomas F. (ed.) (1999). *Kriegserlebnis und Legendenbildung. Das Bild des modernen Kriegs in Literatur, Theater, Photographie und Film. Vol. 1.* Osnabrück.

Schöllgen, Gregor (1981). "'Dann müssen wir uns aber Mesopotamien sichern!" Motive deutscher Türkenpolitik zur Zeit Wilhelms II. in zeitgenössischen Darstellungen', *Saeculum* 32: 130–45.

Schramm, Martin (2007). *Das Deutschlandbild in der britischen Presse 1912–1919.* Berlin.

Schubert-Weller, Christoph (1998). *'Kein schönrer Tod'. Die Militarisierung der männlichen Jugend und ihr Einsatz im Ersten Weltkrieg 1890–1918.* Weinheim.

Schulte Strathaus, Ludwig (1938). *Das Bild als Waffe. Die Französische Bildpropaganda im Ersten Weltkrieg.* Würzburg.

Schumann, Andreas (1996). "'Der Künstler an die Krieger". Zur Kriegsliteratur kanonisierten Autoren', in: Wolfgang J. Mommsen (ed.). *Die Rolle der Intellektuellen, Künstler und Schriftsteller im ersten Weltkrieg.* Munich: 221–33.

Schwabe, Klaus (1969). *Wissenschaft und Kriegsmoral. Die deutschen Hochschullehrer und die politischen Grandfragen des Ersten Weltkriegs.* Göttingen et al.

Schwalbe, Hans-Hermann (1937). *Die Grundlagen für die publizistische Bedeutung der Karikatur in Deutschland.* Diss. Phil. Berlin.

Schwarz, Werner M. (2013). 'Der Krieg ist wirklich. Kino im Ersten Weltkrieg', in: Pfoser and Weigl 2013: 514–21.

Schweitzer, Richard (2003). *The Cross and the Trenches. Religious Faith and Doubt among British and American Great War Soldiers.* Westport, Conn. et al.

Scianna, Bastian M. (2017). 'German Atrocities 1914 – Revisited'. www.hsozkult. geschichte.hu-berlin.de/tagungsberichte/id=7409.

Seeber, Otto (1991). 'Kriegstheologie und Kriegspredigten in der evangelischen Kirche Deutschlands im Ersten und Zweiten Weltkrieg', in: Linden and Mergner 1991: 233–58.

Senin, Aleksandr (1993). 'Russian army chaplains during World War I', *Russian Studies in History* 32, 2: 43–52.

Shackelford, Michael (1998). 'Medals of Italy'. http://www.gwpda.org/medals/italmedl/ italy.html

Shand, James D. (1975). 'Doves among the eagles: German pacifists and their government during World War I', *Journal of Contemporary History* 10: 95–108.

Smith, Angela (2008). 'The girl behind the man behind the gun: women as carers in recruitment posters of the First World War', *Journal of War & Culture Studies* 1, 3: 223–41.

Smith, John T. (2001). 'Russian military censorship during the First World War', *Revolutionary Russia* 14: 71–95.

Sobolew, P.N. et al. (1972 [russ. 1967]). *Illustrierte Geschichte der Großen Sozialistischen Oktoberrevolution.* Berlin.

Sommer, Monika (2013). 'Zur Kriegsausstellung 1916 im Wiener Prater "als mächtige Antwort der Monarchie an das feindliche Ausland"', in: Pfoser and Weigl 2013: 502–13.

Sorlin, Pierre (1994). 'Der italienische Film in der Zeit des Ersten Weltkriegs', in: Rother 1994b: 235–40.

Sorlin, Pierre (1999). 'France. The silent memories', in: Paris 1999: 115–37.

Sorrie, Charles (2014). *Censorship of the Press in France 1917–1918.* Thesis. http://etheses. lse.ac.uk/3110/1/Sorrie_Censorship_of_the_Press_in_France.pdf.

Sorrie, Charles (2018). 'Industrial unrest in France 1917–1918, Three departments compared'. Typescript.

Soutou, Georges-Henri (2017). 'War aims and war discussions', in:
www.encyclopedia.1914-1918-online.net.

Spraul, Gunter (2016). *Der Franktireurkrieg 1914. Untersuchungen zum Verfall einer Wissenschaft und zum Umgang mit nationalen Mythen.* Berlin.

Squire, James D. (1935). *British Propaganda at Home and in the USA from 1914 to 1917.* Cambridge, Mass.

Stark, Garry D. (2009). *Banned in Berlin. Literary Censorship in Imperial Germany 1871–1918.* New York and Oxford.

Stegmann, Dirk (1972). 'Die deutsche Inlandspropaganda 1917/18. Zum innenpolitischen Machtkampf zwischen OHL und ziviler Reichsleitung in der Endphase des Kaiserreiches', *Militärgeschichtliche Mitteilungen* 2: 75–116.

Steuer, Kenneth (2014). 'German propaganda and prisoners of war during World War One', in: Paddock 2014: 155–80.

Stiaccini, Carlo (2015). 'War letters (Italy)', in: www.encyclopedia.1914-1918-online.net.

Stibbe, Mathew (2001). *German Anglophobia and the Great War, 1914–1918.* Cambridge.

Stites, Richard (1999). 'Days and nights in wartime Russia: cultural life 1914–1916', in: Roshwald and Stites 1999a: 8–31.

Stockdale, Melissa K. (2004). '"My death for the motherland is happiness": Women, patriotism, and soldiering in Russia's great war, 1914–1917', *American Historical Review* 109: 78–116.

Stoff, Laurie (2006). *They Fought for the Motherland. Russian Women Soldiers in World War I and the Revolution.* Lawrence, Kan.

Strachan, Hew (1996). 'The morale of the German army 1917–1918', in: Cecil and Liddle 1996: 383–98.

Strachan, Hew (2001). *The First World War. Vol. 1: To Arms.* Oxford.

Strachan, Hew (2004). *Financing the First World War.* Oxford.

Suchoples, Jarosław and James, Stephanie (eds) (2016). *Revisiting World War I. Interpretation and Perspectives of the Great Conflict.* Frankfurt/Main et al.

Swartz, Marvin (1971). *The Union of Democratic Control in British Politics during the First World War.* Oxford.

Swinton, Ernest D. (1940). *Augenzeuge. Hinter den Kulissen der britischen Weltkriegsführung.* Berlin.

Szlanta, Piotr (2014). 'Poland', in: www.encyclopedia.1914-1918-online.net.

Szymczak, Damian (2015). '1914–1920: comment les Polonais retrouveront-ils leur indépendance?', *GMCC* 260: 35–57.

Taylor, Alan J.P. (1972). *Beaverbrook.* London.

Taylor Allen, Anne (1984). *Satire and Society in Wilhelmine Germany. Kladderadatsch and Simplicissimus 1890–1914.* Lexington.

Therstappen, Aude (2008). 'Flugblätter und Propaganda', in: Thomas 2008: 78–95.

Thimme, Hans (1932). *Weltkrieg ohne Waffen. Die Propaganda der Westmächte gegen Deutschland. Ihre Wirkung, ihre Abwehr.* Stuttgart and Berlin.

Thomas, Marie (ed.) (2008). *In Papiergewittern. 1914–1918. Die Kriegssammlungen der Bibliotheken.* Paris.

Thompson, J. Lee (1999). *Politicians, the Press, and the Great War, 1914–1919 Propaganda.* Kent, Ohio and London.

Thorau, Peter (2014). 'Lawrence von Arabien – playing "Klein" on the other side', in: Veltzke 2014: 181–9.

Toeplitz, Jerzy (1979). *Geschichte des Films, vol. 1, 1895–1928.* Berlin.

Topitsch, Klaus (2000). 'Die Greuelpropaganda in der Karikatur', in: Zühlke 2000: 49–92.

Tortato, Alessandro (2008). 'Prigionieri degli italiani', in: Isnenghi and Ceschin 2008: 253–9.

Tosi, Luciano (1977). *La propaganda italiana all'estero nella prima guerra mondiale. Rivendicazioni territoriali e politica delle nazionalità*. Pordenone.

Trumpener, Ulrich (1968). *Germany and the Ottoman Empire 1914–1918*. Princeton, NJ.

Tumanova, Anastasiya (2014). 'Voluntary associations in Moscow and Petrograd and their role in patriotic campaigns during World War I (1914–February 1917)', *Jahrbücher für Geschichte Osteuropas*. 62, 3: 345–70.

Überegger, Oswald (2008). '"Verbrannte Erde" und "baumelnde Gehängte". Zur europäischen Dimension militärischer Normenübertretungen im Ersten Weltkrieg', in: Neitzel and Horath 2008: 241–78.

Überegger, Oswald (2015). 'Kulturelle Mobilisierung. Die österreichisch-ungarische Kriegspropaganda gegen Italien', in: Nicola Labanca and Oswald Überegger(eds). *Krieg in den Alpen. Österreich-Ungarn und Italien im Ersten Weltkrieg (1914–1918)*. Vienna et al.: 259–79.

Ullmann, Hans-Peter (2014). 'Finance', in: Winter et al. 2014, vol. 2: 408–33.

Ulrich, Bernd (1995 [1992]). 'Die Desillusionierung der Kriegsfreiwilligen von 1914', in: Wette 1995b: 110–26.

Ulrich, Bernd (1997). *Die Augenzeugen. Deutsche Feldpostbriefe in Kriegs- und Nachkriegszeit. 1914–33*. Essen.

Ulrich, Bernd and Ziemann, Benjamin (1997). 'Der soldatische Kriegserlebnis', in: Kruse 1997: 127–58.

Ulrich, Bernd and Ziemann, Benjamin (ed.) (2010). *German Soldiers in the Great War. Letters and Eyewitness Accounts*. Barnsley. [German edition: 1994]

Ullrich, Volker (1982). *Kriegsalltag. Hamburg im ersten Weltkrieg*. Cologne.

Ungern-Sternberg, Jürgen von (2016). 'Making sense of the war (Germany)', in: www.encyclopedia.1914-1918-online.net.

Ungern-Sternberg, Jürgen von and Ungern-Sternberg, Wolfgang von (2013 [1996]). *Der Aufruf 'An die Kulturwelt!' Das Manifest der 93 und die Anfänge der Kriegspropaganda im Ersten Weltkrieg*. Frankfurt/Main.

Uyar, Mesut (2013). 'Ottoman Arab officers between nationalism and loyalty during the First World War', *War in History* 20, 4: 526–44.

Vavro, Geoffrey (1996). 'Morale in the Austro-Hungarian army: the evidence of Habsburg army campaign reports and allied intelligence officer', in: Cecil and Liddle 1996: 399–412.

Veltzke, Veit (ed.) (2014). *Playing Lawrence on the Other Side. Die Expedition Klein und das deutsch-osmanischer Bündnis im ersten Weltkrieg*. Berlin.

Véray, Laurent (1994). 'Montrer la Guerre: La photographie et le cinématographe', in: Becker et al. 1994: 229–38.

Véray, Laurent (2014). 'Cinema', in: Winter et al. 2014, vol. 3: 475–503.

Verhey, Jeffrey (2000). *Der 'Geist von 1914' und die Erfindung der Volksgemeinschaft*. Hamburg.

Vescovo, Piermario (2008). 'Il teatro al fronte', in: Isnenghi and Ceschin 2008: 820–9.

Vitelleschi, Giovanni N. (1999). 'The representation of the Great War in Italian cinema', in: Paris 1999: 162–71.

Vogel-Walter, Bettina (2004). *D'Annunzio – Abenteurer und charismatischer Führer. Propaganda und religiöser Nationalismus in Italien von 1914 bis 1921*. Frankfurt/Main.

Vondung, Klaus (1980a). 'Propaganda oder Sinndeutung', in: Vondung 1980b: 11–39.

Vondung, Klaus (ed.) (1980b). *Kriegserlebnis. Der Erste Weltkrieg in der literarischen Gestaltung symbolischen Deutung der Nationen.* Göttingen.

Vorsteher, Dieter (1994). 'Bilder für den Sieg. Das Plakat im Ersten Weltkrieg', in: Rother 1994b: 149–62.

Waites, Bernhard (1987). *A Class Society at War. England 1914–1918.* New York et al.

Walker, Colin (2007). 'The Scouts Defence Corps and "The Red Feather"', www.scoutguidehistoricalsociety.com/redfeather.htm (retrieved 15 October 2015).

Wanderscheck, Hermann (1935). *Die britische Propaganda im Weltkrieg gegen Deutschland: 1914–1918.* Berlin.

Wanderscheck, Hermann (1936). *Weltkrieg und Propaganda.* Berlin. https://archive.org/details/Wanderscheck-Hermann-Weltkrieg-und-Propaganda.

Wanderscheck, Hermann (1940). *Die britische Lügenpropaganda im Weltkrieg und heute.* Berlin. https://archive.org/details/Wanderscheck-Hermann-Die-Englische-Luegenpropaganda/page/n35.

Ward, Larry W. (1981). *The Motion Picture Goes to War. The U.S. Government Film Effort during WWI.* Ann Harbour.

Watson, Alexander (2008). *Enduring the Great War: Combat, Morale and Collapse in the German and British Armies, 1914–1918.* Cambridge.

Watson, Alexander (2010). 'Fighting for another fatherland: the Polish minority in the German Army, 1914–1918', *English Historical Review* 126, 522: 1137–66.

Watson, Alexander (2014a). 'Morale', in: Winter et al. 2014, vol. 2: 174–95.

Watson, Alexander(2014b). '"Unheard of brutality": Russian atrocities against civilians in East Prussia 1914–1915', *Journal of Modern History* 86: 780–825.

Watson, Alexander and Porter, Patrick (2010). 'Bereaved and and aggrieved: combat motivation and the ideology of sacrifice in the First World War', *Historical Research* 83, 219: 146–64.

Weber, Frank (1970). *Eagles on the Crescent. Germany, Austria, and the Diplomacy of the Turkish Alliance 1914–1918.* London.

Weber, Hellmuth (1981). 'Die politische Karikatur im Dienst der imperialistischen Kriegsführung 1914–1918', *Wissenschaftliche Zeitschrift der Universität Halle* 30: 73–82.

Weber, Thomas (2011). *Hitlers erster Krieg.* Berlin [English edition 2010]

Weight, Angela (1994). 'Süße Täuschungen: Kriegsgenre Kunst in der Royal Academy 1915–1919', in: Rother 1994b: 273–84.

Weinrich, Arndt (2014). 'Visual essay: war and the State', in: Winter et al. 2014, vol. 2: 663–71.

Weintraub, Stanley (2001). *Silent Night. The Story of the World War I Christmas Truce.* New York et al.

Weise, Niels (2004). *Der 'lustige' Krieg. Propaganda in deutschen Witzblättern 1914–1918.* Rahden, Westf.

Welch, David (2014 [2000]). *Germany and Propaganda in World War I. Pacifism, Mobilization and Total War.* London.

Wells, Robert A. (2014). 'Propaganda at home (USA)', in: www.encyclopedia.1914-1918-online.net.

Wette, Wolfgang (1995a [1992]). 'Die unheroischen Kriegserinnerungen des Elsässer Bauern Dominik Richert aus den Jahren 1914–1918', in: Wette 1995b: 127–35.

Wette, Wolfgang (ed.) (1995b [1992]). *Der Krieg des kleinen Mannes. Eine Militärgeschichte von unten.* Munich and Zurich.

Wilke, Jürgen (1997). 'Deutsche Auslandspropaganda im Ersten Weltkrieg: Die Zentrale für Auslandsdienst', in: Jürgen Wilke (ed.). *Pressepolitik und Propaganda. Historische Studien vom Vormärz zum Kalten Krieg.* Cologne et al.: 79–125.

Wilkin, Bernard (2016). 'Isolation, communication and propaganda in the occupied territories of France, 1914–1918', *First World War Studies*, 7, 3: 229–42, doi: 10.1080/19475020.2017.1315314.

Will, Alexander (2012). *Kein Griff nach der Weltmacht. Geheime Dienste und Propaganda im deutsch-österreichisch-türkischen Bündnis 1914–1918.* Cologne et al.

Williams, Gordon (2005 [2003]). *British Theatre in the Great War. A Revaluation.* London and New York.

Williams, John (1972). *The Home Fronts. Britain, France and Germany.* London.

Wils, Lode (2015). 'Het aandeel van de "Flamenpolitik" in de Vlaamse natievorming', *Revue belge d'histoire contemporaine* XLV, 2/3: 216–37.

Wilson, Trevor (1979). 'Lord Bryce's investigation into alleged German atrocities in Belgium, 1914–1915', *Journal of Contemporary History* 14: 369–83.

Wilson, Trevor (1988 [1986]). *The Myriad Faces of War. Britain and the Great War, 1914–1918.* Cambridge.

Wiltsher, Anne (1985). *Most Dangerous Women. Feminist Peace Campaigners of the Great War.* London.

Winter, Jay (1988 [1986]). *The Great War and the British People.* London.

Winter, Jay (1991). 'Kriegsbilder: Die bildende Kunst und der Mythos der Kriegsbegeisterung', in: Linden and Mergner 1991: 89–112.

Winter, Jay (1999). 'Popular culture in Wartime Britain', in: Roshwald and Stites 1999a: 330–48.

Winter, Jay (2014). 'Propaganda and the mobilization of consent', in: Hew Strachan (ed.). *The Oxford Illustrated History of the First World War.* Oxford: 216–25 [New Edition]

Winter, Jay and Robert, Jean Louis (eds) (1997). *Capital Cities at War. Paris, London, Berlin 1914–1919. Vol. 1: A Cultural History.* Cambridge.

Winter, Jay and Robert, Jean Louis (2012a). 'Conclusion', in: Winter and Robert 2012b: 468–81.

Winter, Jay and Robert, Jean Louis (eds) (2012b [2007]). *Capital Cities at War. Paris, London, Berlin 1914–1919. Vol. 2: A Cultural History.* Cambridge.

Winter, Jay et al. (ed.) (2014). *The Cambridge History of the First World War. Vol. 1–3.* Cambridge.

Wolf, Fritz (2015). *'Wir sind das Publikum'. Autoritätsverlust der Medien und Zwang zum Dialog.* Frankfurt/Main.

Wood, Richard (1990). *Film and Propaganda in America. A Documentary History.* Vol. 1. New York.

Wrigley, Chris (1976). *David Lloyd George and British Labour Movement. Peace and War.* Hassocks and New York.

Wüstenbecker, Katia (2010). 'Die Vereinigten Staaten von Amerika: widerwillige Teilnahme am Ersten Weltkrieg', in: Bauerkämper and Julien 2010b: 217–37.

Yammine, Bruno (2013). 'De "Flamenpolitik" als continuiteit van de Duitse geopolitiek voor and tijdens the Eerste Wereldoorlog', *Belgisch Tijschrift voor Nieuwste Geschiedenis* XLIII, 2/3: 12–45.

Zeman, Zbyněk and Klimek, Antonín (1997). *The Life of Edvard Beneš 1884–1948. Czechoslovakia in Peace and War.* Oxford.

Zetterberg, Seppo (1978). *Die Liga der Fremdvölker Rußlands 1916–1918.* Helsinki.

Zhdanova, Irina (2017). 'Press/Journalism (Russian Empire)', in: www.encyclopedia.1914-1918-online.net.

Ziemann, Benjamin (1995). 'Verweigerungsformen in der deutschen Armee 1914–1918', *Jahrbuch für Historische Friedensforschung* 4: 99–122.

Ziemann, Benjamin (1997a). *Front und Heimat. Ländliche Kriegserfahrungen im südlichen Bayern 1914–1923*. Essen.

Ziemann, Benjamin (1997b). 'Katholische Religiosität und die Bewältigung des Krieges. Soldaten- und Militärseelsorger in der deutschen Armee 1914–1918', in: Friedhelm Boll (ed.). *Volksreligiosität und Kriegserleben*. Münster: 116–36.

Ziemann, Benjamin (2015). *Gewalt im 1. Weltkrieg. Töten – überleben – verweigern*. Essen.

Zollinger, Manfred (2013) 'Krieg der Spiele', in: Pfoser and Weigl 2013: 430–9.

Zühlke, Raoul (ed.) (2000). *Bildpropaganda im ersten Weltkrieg*. Hamburg.

Zunino, Bérénice (2014). *La littérature illustrée pour enfants à l'époque de la Première Guerre mondiale. Origine et évolution de la culture de guerre enfantine allemande*. Unpublished Dissertation, University of Paris IV/Free University of Berlin.

INDEX

Censorship and propaganda, keywords of this book, cartoons / caricatures and the eight principal belligerent countries, mentioned throughout, are not included in the index. The innumerable national propaganda organizations, ministries, parliaments, political parties, army commands, films, newspapers and periodicals are not indicated alphabetically, but are presented in superior headings arranged according to their countries.

The index was prepared by Nathalie Chamba.